DERN SUDAN

Sudan's modern history has been consumed by revolution and civil
war. The country attracted international attention in the 1990s as a
breeding ground of Islamist terrorism, and recently tensions between
the prosperous center and the periphery, between the North and the
South, have exploded in Darfur. In his latest book, Robert Collins,
a frequent visitor to and veteran scholar of the region, traces Sudan's
history across 200 years to show how many of the tragedies of today
have been planted in its past. The story begins with the conquest
of Muhammad ʿAli in 1821 and moves through the Anglo-Egyptian
Condominium to independence in 1956. It then focuses on Sudanese
rule in the post-independence years, when the fragile democracy established by the British collapsed under sectarian strife. It is these religious
and ethnic divides, the author contends, in conjunction with failed
leadership, that have prolonged and sustained the conflict in Sudan.
The author is a forthright and engaging expositor and is not afraid
to tackle some difficult themes. The book will make a singular and
important contribution to the history of this ravaged country.

ROBERT O. COLLINS is Emeritus Professor of History at the University of California, Santa Barbara. His recent publications include
*Civil Wars and Revolution in the Sudan: Essays on the Sudan, Southern
Sudan and Darfur, 1962–2004* (2005), *Darfur: The Long Road to Disaster* (2006), and *A History of Sub-Saharan Africa* (with James M. Burns,
2007).

A HISTORY OF MODERN
SUDAN

ROBERT O. COLLINS

University of California, Santa Barbara

CAMBRIDGE
UNIVERSITY PRESS

CAMBRIDGE UNIVERSITY PRESS
Cambridge, New York, Melbourne, Madrid, Cape Town, Singapore, São Paulo, Delhi

Cambridge University Press
The Edinburgh Building, Cambridge CB2 8RU, UK

Published in the United States of America by Cambridge University Press, New York

www.cambridge.org
Information on this title: www.cambridge.org/9780521674959

First published 2008

Printed in the United Kingdom at the University Press, Cambridge

A catalogue record for this publication is available from the British Library

Library of Congress Cataloguing in Publication data
Collins, Robert O., 1933–
A history of modern Sudan / Robert O. Collins.
p.   cm.
Includes bibliographical references and index.
ISBN 978-0-521-85820-5 (hardback) – ISBN 978-0-521-67495-9 (pbk.)
1. Sudan–History–1956–   I. Title.

DT157.3.C65   2008
962.404–dc22   2008003211

ISBN 978-0-521-85820-5 hardback
ISBN 978-0-521-67495-9 paperback

In memory of Louise J. Collins, my beloved *Mither*,
who throughout her long life told me to seek out
remote places and write about their past,
which I have done for fifty years

Contents

Figures

Maps

Preface

My subsequent obsession with Sudan first began during the academic year 1953–54 at Dartmouth College while writing a history honors thesis about Emin Pasha (Eduard Schnizter) and his administration of the Turco-Egyptian Province of Equatoria in the upper Nile valley (1878–89). I did not arrive in Sudan to continue my research until several months after independence on 1 January 1956. During the next fifty years I returned regularly to live, travel widely in every part of Sudan, and conduct historical research in the archives and the field. During these early decades one was free to travel without restraint and to probe the voluminous archives in the National Record Office in Khartoum, "the House of Abu Salim," and to conduct extensive research in the provincial and district records in southern Sudan. During these same years I was present when many of the events in the following narrative took place; when I returned to Sudan others were the subject of long hours of discussion in the cool of the evening with scores of Sudanese friends. I personally knew some of the prominent political players; those I did not were the subject of vigorous gossip and candid opinions during my visits. Now in the twilight zone of my life I have sought to bring to fruition my search for the Sudanese past in a comprehensive and readable history for the general public in which my insights, interpretations, and anecdotes are the culmination of my many books, articles, and essays supported by a voluminous compendium of memories accumulated during a half-century of experience, inquiry, and intellectual challenge.

Spelling can be a curse that often results in chaos, particularly when the documentation for a book, like this one, comes in many languages. Motivated by familiarity, practice, or ethnic pride, Africans, Arabs, and Europeans have spelled the name of a person, place, or event in a transliteration that reflects their own parochialism, patriotism, and panache. The result is often confusion rather than clarity. The only legitimate principle is consistency in the text. Consistency, however, is not a universal virtue and does not always guarantee clarity, in the search for which I have consequently

Anglicized or given the English equivalent for people, place-names, and events recorded in different languages. Place-names are spelled for understanding rather than in the local patois. Personal names are more precisely retained because they are complex, for everyone spells their name to their own satisfaction and not according to standardized rules of transliteration. If spellings are a curse, abbreviations are a necessary evil. When the name of the organization is first presented, the abbreviation is placed in parentheses, e.g. Revolutionary Command Council (RCC). In a few instances where the abbreviation appears in a later chapter I refresh the reader's memory by repeating the full name of the organization.

I wish to convey my special thanks to Alan Goulty who, as in the past, has read much of the manuscript to offer encouragement, corrections, and his thoughtful commentary. Jan Hogan, the ever helpful Keeper of the Sudan Archive at Durham University and co-author of *Images of Empire*, has graciously selected the illustrations. Steve Brown has, once again, employed his cartographic skills to fashion superb maps.

ROBERT O. COLLINS
Santa Barbara, California

Abbreviations

£E	Egyptian pounds sterling
£S	Sudanese pounds sterling
AACC	All-African Council of Churches
ACROSS	African Committee for the Relief of the Southern Sudanese
AFESD	Arab Fund for Economic and Social Development
AGI	Arab Group International for Investment and Acquisitions Co. Ltd. (Saudi Arabia)
ALF	Azanian Liberation Front
AMIS	African Union Mission to Sudan
ANAF	Anya-Nya National Armed Forces
APG	Anyidi Provisional Government
AU	African Union
BBC	British Broadcasting Corporation
BOAC	British Overseas Airways Corporation
bopd	barrels of oil per day
CARE	Cooperative for American Relief Everywhere
CBC	Canadian Broadcasting Company
CCI	Compagnie de Constructions Internationales
CEO	chief executive officer
CIA	Central Intelligence Agency (United States)
CMS	Church Missionary Society
CNODC	China National Oil Development Corporation
CNPC	China National Petroleum Corporation
COC	Convention Organizing Committee
COPI	Chevron Overseas Petroleum Incorporated (United States)
CPA	Comprehensive Peace Agreement
CPMT	Civilian Protection Monitoring Team
CUSS	Council for the Unity of Southern Sudan

DC	district commissioner
DGSE	Direction Générale de la Sécurité Extérieure (France)
DLF	Darfur Liberation Front
DoP	Declaration of Principles
DPA	Darfur Peace Agreement
DUP	Democratic Unionist Party
ECCI	Equatoria Central Committee of Intellectuals
EPLF	Eritrean People's Liberation Front
EPRDF	Ethiopian People's Revolutionary Democratic Front
ERDP	Economic Recovery and Development Programme
EU	European Union
FAN	Forces Armées du Nord (Army of the North, Chad)
FANT	Forces Armées Nationales Tchadiennes (National Armed Forces of Chad)
FIS	Islamic Salvation Front (Algeria)
FOP	Front of the Opposition Parties
FROLINAT	Front de Libération Nationale du Tchad (National Liberation Front of Chad)
GDP	gross domestic product
GDR	(East) German Democratic Republic
GIA	Groupe Islamique Armé (Armed Islamic Group, Algeria)
GNOPC	Greater Nile Operating Petroleum Company (Sudan)
GOS	Government of Sudan
GoSS	Government of South Sudan
GPLF	Gambella People's Liberation Front
HEC	High Executive Council (southern Sudan)
IBRD	International Bank for Reconstruction and Development (World Bank)
ICF	Islamic Charter Front
ICG	International Crisis Group
ICP	Islamic Committee for Palestine
IDP	internally displaced person
IGAD	Intergovernmental Authority on Development
IGADD	Intergovernmental Authority on Drought and Development
IMF	International Monetary Fund
INEC	Interim National Executive Committee (SSIM/A)
INLC	Interim National Liberation Committee (SSIM/A)
ISI	Inter-Services Intelligence (Pakistan)

IS-SOR	Internal Security/Islamic Security Service, *al-amn al-dakhil* (Sudan)
ITCZ	Inter-Tropical Convergence Zone
JEM	Justice and Equality Movement (Sudan)
JEO	Jonglei Executive Organ (Sudan)
JIM	Joint Implementation Mechanism (UN)
JMC	Joint Military Commission (UN)
JMM	Joint Monitoring Mission (UN)
LRA	Lord's Resistance Army
MFC	Mechanized Farming Corporation (Sudan)
MP	Member of Parliament
MPS	Mouvement Patriotique du Salut (Patriotic Salvation Movement, Chad)
MSF	Médecins Sans Frontières
NAS	Alliance of Professional Organizations and Trade Unions (Sudan)
NASC	National Alliance for the Salvation of the Country (Sudan)
NATO	North Atlantic Treaty Organization
NC	National Convention (SPLM/A)
NCDJCA	National Council for the Development of the Jonglei Canal Area (Sudan)
NCO	non-commissioned officer
NCP	National Congress Party (Sudan)
NDA	National Democratic Alliance (Sudan)
NGO	non-governmental organization
NIF	National Islamic Front (Sudan)
NPG	Nile Provisional Government (Sudan)
NRF	National Redemption Front (Darfur)
NSRCC	National Salvation Revolutionary Command Council (Sudan)
NSS	National Security Service
NUP	National Unionist Party (Sudan)
OAU	Organization of African Unity
OIC	Organization of the Islamic Conference
OLF	Oromo Liberation Front (Ethiopia)
OLS	Operation Lifeline Sudan
ONGC	Oil and National Gas Corporation (India)
OPEC	Organization of Petroleum-Exporting Countries
OSO	Other Shades of Opinion (Sudan)

Oxfam	Oxford Famine Relief
PAIC	Popular Arab and Islamic Congress
PCM	Provisional Council of Ministers (Sudan)
PDF	People's Defense Force (Sudan)
PDP	People's Democratic Party (Sudan)
PJTC	Permanent Joint Technical Commission (Egypt and Sudan)
PLO	Palestine Liberation Organization
PMHC	Political–Military High Command (SPLM/A)
PNC	Popular National Congress (Sudan)
PVO	private voluntary organization
QC	Queen's Counsel
RCC	Revolutionary Command Council (Sudan)
SACDNU	Sudan African Closed Districts National Union (southern Sudan)
SAF	Sudanese Allied Forces
SALF	Sudan African Liberation Front
SAM	Sayyid 'Ali al-Mirghani
SANU	Sudan African National Union
SAR	Sayyid 'Abd al-Rahman
SCA	Sudan Christian Association
SCC	Sudan Council of Churches
SCP	Sudan Communist Party
SFDA	Sudan Federal Democratic Alliance
SLM/A	Sudan Liberation Movement/Army
SNP	Sudanese National Party
SNWA	Sudanese Nationals Working Abroad
SPAF	Sudan People's Armed Forces
SPAFF	Sudan Pan-African Freedom Fighters
SPCC	State Petroleum Corporation of Canada
SPDF	Sudan People's Democratic Front
SPLA-Nasir	Sudan People's Liberation Army-Nasir
SPLM/A	Sudan People's Liberation Movement/Army
SPLM/A-United	Sudan People's Liberation Movement/Army-United
SPS	Sudan Political Service
SRP	Socialist Republican Party (Sudan)
SRRA	Sudan Relief and Rehabilitation Association of the SPLM/A
SRWU	Sudan Railway Workers' Union
SSB	Sudan Security Bureau

SSDF	South Sudan Defense Force
SSIM/A	South Sudan Independence Movement/Army
SSLM	Southern Sudan Liberation Movement
SSPA	Southern Sudanese Political Association
SSPG	Southern Sudan Provisional Government
SSU	Sudan Socialist Union
SSUM/A	South Sudan Unity Movement/Army
Sudapet	Sudan National Petroleum Corporation
SUNA	Sudan News Agency
SWTUF	Sudan Workers' Trade Union Federation
TMC	Transitional Military Council (Sudan)
TNA	Transitional National Assembly (Sudan)
TNC	Transitional National Council
TPLF	Tigray People's Liberation Front
UN	United Nations
UNHCR	United Nations High Commissioner for Refugees
UNRA	United Nations Relief and Rehabilitation Administration
US	United States
USAID	United States Agency for International Development
USAP	Union of Sudan African Parties
VMT	Verification and Monitoring Team
WAA	Workers' Affairs Association (Sudan)
WCC	World Council of Churches
WNBF	West Nile Bank Front

Glossary

'abd (pl. *'abid*)   slave

ajawiid muatamarat al-suhl   the traditional conference in Darfur used by rival ethnic groups to settle disputes

amir   military commander

ansar (Ansar)   partisans of Islam

ashiqqa' (Ashiqqa)   brothers by the same father and mother

ashraf   kinsmen of Muhammad Ahmad al-Mahdi

awlad al-bahr   people of the river

awlad al-gharib   people of the west

baliila   boiled, tasteless grain

bayt al-mal   house of wealth, treasury

bay'a   Islamic oath of allegiance

bazinqir   armed slave troops of individual traders in southern Sudan in the latter half of the nineteenth century

bilad al-sudan   "Land of the Blacks," the term used by medieval Muslim geographers for the great Sudanic plain stretching from the Red Sea to the Atlantic

dahabiah   large sailing vessel with cabins, used on the Blue and White Niles

dar   homeland, territory

dar al-harb   country of war

dar al-islam   the Muslim community

dura   sorghum, traditional grain for bread

effendi   *Turkish* name given to an educated bureaucrat in the Turkiya and civil servant during the Condominium

feddan (*faddan*)   1 *feddan* = 1.038 acres

faki   holy man

falasha   Ethiopian Jews

fashir   a Fur royal encampment

fellahin   small farmer of agricultural laborer in the Middle East, specifically Egypt

habub   sandstorm common throughout northern Sudan

harab   banditry

harakat al-tahrir al-islami hiwar   the Islamic Liberation Movement debate

hizb   political party

hudud   Islamic punishment for crimes, usually amputation

hükümdar   *Turkish* governor-general

jah   Fur customary taxes

ijma'a   consensus of the community

ijtihad   independent interpretation

ikhwan   brethren in a religious or military brotherhood

ird   inherited property of women

itthadiyyin   those who support Union, i.e. *hizb al-itthadiyyin*, Unionist Party

jabal   hill, small mountain

jabal hadid   ironstone plateau in southwest Sudan

jakab   *Fur* struggle; a Fur fighter with an automatic weapon supplied by Chad

jallaba   northern Sudanese petty traders

janjawiid   ghostly rider; evil horsemen

jaysh al-salaam jiech mabor   army of peace (Fartit militia) the White Army (Nuer)

jihad   struggle in the cause of God

jihadiyya   government slave soldiers

kafirin   unbeliever, infidel

kariyat al-salaam   Peace Villages in southern Sudan

kasha   forced deportation

khalifa   "steward," commonly used title for the leader of the Islamic community (*umma*), often rendered in English as Caliph

khalifat   stewardship, commonly used for the leader of Islam (Caliph)

khalwa   Islamic primary school

khawadja   *Turkish* "sir," but in Sudan a colloquialism for pale people, i.e. Americans and Europeans

kisra   Sudanese bread made from *dura*

kokora   *Bari* to divide equally

kuttab   Sudanese secular primary school

kwer-kong   permanent grasslands east of the Sudd and the Ethiopian escarpment *lukiko*   chiefs' court

mahdi   an inspired holy man who will come at the End of Time to bring
  justice and revive the glory of Islam

majlis   council, legislative assembly

makk   powerful Sudanese chief

mamur   Egyptian or Sudanese administrative assistant

marahil   in Darfur, a demarcated migratory pathway between settled
  farming land

marissa   beer

mudir   governor of a province in Sudan

mufti   one who interprets Islamic law and can issue a *fatwa*

mujadid   a reformer of Islam, one who renews the Islamic faith

mujahidiin   warriors engaged in *jihad* for Islam

mulazimiyya   a corps of mercenary soldiers, bodyguards

murahiliin   Arab militiamen

musalaha   reconciliation specific to the National Reconciliation between
  Sadiq al-Mahdi and President Numayri on 7 July 1977

mutathaqqifia   urban intellectuals

nas   ordinary Sudanese folk

nazir   head of a tribe or large clan

nizam al-jadid   New Model Army

pasha   *Turkish* the highest title in the Ottoman and Egyptian courts

qadi   Islamic judge

qa'id al-'amm   commanding officer

qiyas   analogy

qoz   sand and scrub

Qur'an   recitation for the book of divine guidance to be the literal word
  of Allah revealed to the Prophet Muhammad

razzia   raid

Reth   King of the Shilluk (Chollo)

Sadana   Sudanese slang for the cabal of officials surrounding
  President Numayri

sadd   barrier, obstacle applied to the great swamps of the Nile, the Sudd

salafist   "predecesors," a generic term for the Sunni school of thought
  that takes the pious ancestors (*salaf*) of early Islam as a model for the
  contemporary revival and reformation of Islam

shari'a   Islamic Divine Law

shartai   a district chief in the sultanate of Darfur and during
  the Condominium

shaykh   lord, revered wise man, Islamic scholar

shura   consultation, council, consultative body

sirdar   commander-in-chief of the Anglo-Egyptian army

sufi (sufism)   Islamic mystic

suq   market

tahjir   name of forced migration of Baqqara by the Khalifa in 1889–90

taifiya   Sudanese sectarian political parties

talib   a student attached to an Islamic reformer

tariqa (pl. *turuq*)   religious brotherhood

tawali al-sayast   political alliances

tobe   traditional flowing robe of Sudanese women

toic   rich, green pastures of southern Sudan that emerge as the flood-waters of the Sudd recede after the rains

tukl   grass home, hut

'ulama'   community of legal scholars of Islam and *shari'a*

'umda   mayor of a town, head of a large village

waliya   *sufi* holy men

zakat   alms tax

zariba   stockade of thorn bushes or stakes

zawiya   lodge, usually of a *sufi* brotherhood

zuruq (pl. *zurqa*)   dark blue, darkness, a pejorative term in Darfur meaning "Black Africans"

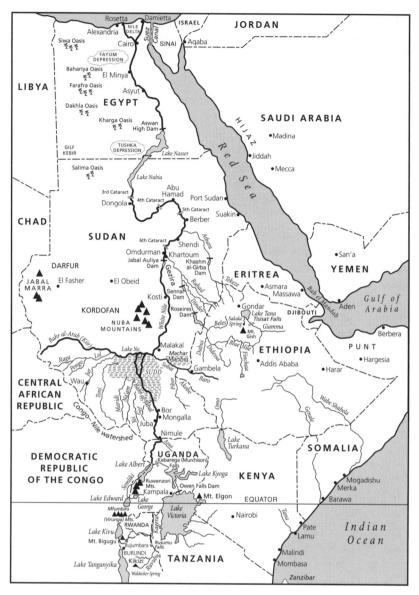

Map 1 The Nile Basin

Introduction

The historiography of Sudan is complex and long, spanning from the Kingdom of Kush (760 BCE–350 CE) to the present day, but the history of independent Sudan begins with the withdrawal of the British and Egyptian rulers on 1 January 1956. To be sure, the history of its ancient kingdoms – Kush, the Christian states, and the sultanates of Funj and Fur – have their own unique past that has captured the attention of archaeologist and historian alike, but any understanding of Sudan today is to be found in the events of the last 200 years. The coming of the Turks and the British before and after the Mahdist revolution (1881–98) not only added to the already dazzling diversity of the Sudanese peoples, but resulted in the creation of an artificial state controlled by new forms of governance. The Turks and Egyptians brought with them the civilizations and cultures from the Ottoman empire and the Arab world in the nineteenth century; the British introduced the imperialism, education, religion, and technology of the West in the twentieth. In their own way each of these invaders have left behind additional layers of alien institutions upon the deep indigenous themes that have been woven into the fabric of the Sudanese past.

The most enduring and compelling of these themes is the size and diversity of so vast a country as Sudan, which have been and remain a major ingredient in its history. Sudan is the largest country in Africa, nearly 1 million square miles spanning 18 degrees of latitude, the size of the United States east of the Mississippi, or nearly 2 percent of the total land mass of the world. The enormous size of the independent Democratic Republic of Sudan (*jumhuriyat al-sudan*), however, was only the eastern portion of the larger Sudanic plain, the *bilad al-sudan* of the medieval Arab geographers, that stretches from the Red Sea to the Atlantic Ocean, punctuated by plateaux and *jabals* and defined by the diverse highlands that surround it – the Congo–Nile watershed to the south, the Ethiopian escarpment and Red Sea Hills to the east, and the Sahara Desert to the north.

I

Stretching in every direction to the horizon, this plain appears to be a monotonous, homogeneous land mass, but that obscures its enormous diversity. In the far north this Sudanic plain becomes desert in Sudan. There are a few oases rich in salt but little water, isolated volcanic outcrops whose springs and caves have provided sustenance and shelter since Paleolithic times, and the *jizzu* (grazing in winter for camels from sporadic rains). Further south the *qoz* sand dunes and scrub become clay plains that support a mantle of savanna grasslands in the rains dominated in the east by the Nuba Mountains west of the White Nile that rise abruptly above the seemingly endless western Sudanic plain. Between the White and Blue Niles lie the fertile clay plains of the Gezira (*jazira*, island), whose natural slope from south to north has made possible vast irrigation schemes in the twentieth century. East of the Blue Nile below the Ethiopian escarpment the undulating grasslands of the Butana extend from the Ethiopian escarpment north to the Sahel on the borders of Nubia. Beyond are the arid, jumbled hills of the Red Sea that begin in Ethiopia and end in Egypt and whose rugged terrain overlooks a barren, narrow coastal plain of sand, rock, crystalline beaches, and thick coral reefs. These plains, east and west of the Nile, gradually rise southward and surround the shallow depression of the Sudd (*sadd*, barrier), the world's largest swamp.

One of the most formidable natural obstacles in the world, the Sudd is a labyrinth of 11,700 square miles of lakes, lagoons, and meandering channels. The lagoons and lakes rise and fall according to the amount of water from the equatorial lakes and seasonal rainfall to disgorge floating islands of aquatic plants, *sudd*, which coalesce into dams of aquatic vegetation that force the river to rise and cut a new channel around the obstruction, by which the process is repeated, forming new barriers in a never-ending cycle. Trapped in this vast expanse of swamp and lagoons enormous quantities of water are lost to evaporation and transpiration, so that whatever the volume flowing down from the great equatorial lakes or by rainfall the quantity of water that emerges from the Sudd remains approximately the same from one year to the next and is lost to both Sudan and Egypt. From the Sudd the land rises in the southwest to the ironstone plateau (*jabal hadid*) and the Congo–Nile watershed, whose many rivers flowing northeast across the ironstone cut deep ravines for the gallery forests and the beginning of the Congo tropical rainforest. Southeast of the Sudd the land rises to a series of mountains – Imatong, Didinga, and Dongotona, all 10,000 feet – and to the highest peak in Sudan, Mt. Kinyeti, 10,456 feet, on the Sudan–Uganda border.

The longest river in the world, the Nile and its tributaries flow south to north, a riverine spine throughout the entire length of Sudan that has defined the way of living for those Sudanese who have settled by its banks and that distinguishes them from the rural farmers and herdsmen on the Sudanic plains far beyond the river. Beginning on the Lake Plateau the Nile, called the Bahr al-Jabal (the Mountain River), plunges 80 miles down the gorge of the Bedden Rapids to meander through the Sudd to Lake No, from which flows the White Nile (*Bahr al-Abyad*) with those waters from tributaries that have survived massive loss in the Sudd and with the substantial Ethiopian contribution from the River Sobat, which provides 14 percent of the total Nile flow, so that the White Nile can run majestically northward to its great confluence with the Blue Nile at Khartoum. Rising in the highlands of Ethiopia the Blue Nile (*Bahr al-Azraq*) contributes 86 percent of the Nile waters for Sudan and Egypt, and, now as one, the Nile flows grandly to the north, gathering its last drop from the River Atbara, 1,800 miles from the Mediterranean, before making its great *S* curve to reach the historic southern frontier of Egypt at Aswan and the first cataract.

No other country in the world has such a varied and inhospitable climate as Sudan, a hot country where temperatures in Khartoum during May and June will average 106°F and 120°F or more in the heat of summer. When the winter winds blow from the north, these same temperatures average 60°F and as low as 43°F, this annual variation being created by two global air flows. In winter the cool, dry, northeast winds from arid Asia blow across Sudan, pushing the Inter-Tropical Convergence Zone (ITCZ) as far south as the Tropic of Capricorn. By April the ITCZ begins to move north, propelled by a massive body of moist air from which the exhausted northeasterly winds can no longer prevail. The variability of rainfall in Sudan ranges from almost nothing on the Egyptian border to more than 47 inches on the Congo–Nile watershed. The rain clouds from the South Atlantic that arrive in southern Sudan in April diminish in strength as they move northward, reaching Khartoum in July, often creating violent dust storms (*habubs*), and then retreating before the revived northeasterly Asian air mass.

This enormous variation in rainfall in turn results in the great diversity of plants and animals from which the Sudanese derive their livelihoods in five distinctive belts of vegetation from north to south. The desert, with less than 3 inches of annual sporadic rainfall, can only support permanent vegetation in the wadis, intermittent dry watercourses, while the Sahel beyond receives from 3 to 11 inches of rainfall that can sustain a mixture of grasses and acacia trees, one species of which, *Acacia senegal* (*hashab*), produces a major export, gum arabic. When the annual rainfall reaches 30 inches, the broad belt of savanna that spans Sudan from east to west is transformed into a mantle of succulent grasses broken by intermittent woodlands and reliable sources of water which rise to the ironstone plateau, the Congo–Nile watershed, and the mountains east of the Bahr al-Jabal.

If geography is one of the imperishable themes of the past 200 years of Sudanese history, Sudan's differing land mass and rainfall have sheltered an estimated 600 ethnic and linguistic groups, scores of which have consisted of only a few individuals. Historically, scholars have thus simply listed the various groups and their relationships, if any, of one to another. A more understandable method is to divide the Sudanese into two broad, encompassing categories – Muslims and non-Muslims. Muslims in Sudan can, in turn, be partitioned into those who claim an Arab identity and those who do not. Despite a common language and religion, Sudanese Arabs do not constitute a cohesive group but have been divided into two rather artificial congregations – the Arabized Nubians and Ja'ali (pl. Ja'aliyyin), those claiming descent from Ibrahim Ja'al, a descendant of al-'Abbas, uncle of the Prophet, who live in settled communities along the Nile, and the Juhayna nomads or semi-nomads of the plains.

The Arabized Nubians live today along the Nile in an area between the first and third cataracts known as Lower Nubia and retain a fierce loyalty to their pre-Arab Nubian architecture, culture, and language. Above the third cataract the Danaqla (sing. Dunqulawi), "men of Dongola," settled. They claim to be Ja'aliyyin but take great pride in their Nubian origins, and many of them still speak a Nubian dialect. They are separated from the rest of the Ja'aliyyin by the Shayqiyya confederacy living along the Nile from al-Dabba to the fourth cataract who do not claim descent from Ibrahim Ja'al and today remain very conscious of their own distinctiveness. The Nile from the fourth cataract to the Atbara confluence is Ja'ali country of the Rubatab and Manasir, and those living beyond the Atbara to the Sabaluqa Gorge who have specifically taken the name of Ja'aliyyin. There are also smaller groups scattered throughout Sudan who, for one reason or another, have been uprooted from their traditional societies and sought safety and identity by rallying around a Ja'ali leader or holy man, and thus make the dubious claim to be Ja'aliyyin.

With one exception, the Rufa'a, the remaining conglomerate of groups not of Ja'ali origin claiming Arab descent, are known collectively as the Juhayna. The Juhayna came from southern Arabia and thence into Upper

Egypt, from which they drifted southward into Nubia during the fourteenth century and from there south and west, absorbing indigenous non-Arab peoples comprising three dominant groups – Shukriyya, Kababish, and Baqqara. The Shukriyya are camel-owning nomads who in the eighteenth century established themselves in the pastures between the Nile, Atbara, and the Ethiopian foothills, known as the southern Butana, under the leadership of the Abu Sinn family. West of the Nile, Kababish roamed widely with their herds of camels, sheep, and goats across the Sahel of northern Kordofan. They were a loose confederacy of various Arab lineages who were forged together in the eighteenth century by a common way of life and amalgamated in the twentieth century under their famous Shaykh (Sir) ʿAli al-Tom (1874–1937). South of the Kababish on the savanna grasslands of Kordofan and Darfur the Baqqara arrived in the eighteenth century with their cattle from Bagirmi and Wadai in Chad. Despite many generations of taking slaves, concubinage, and intermarriage with the non-Muslim Africans in the neighboring Bahr al-Ghazal, which has changed their physiognomy, they have not abandoned Arabic or Arab culture and are, in fact, a collection of distinct sub-groups, among whom are the Rizayqat, Missariyya, Humr, Habbaniyya, and Taʿaisha.

On the plains of southern Kordofan rise the Nuba Mountains, a 90-mile range of well-watered squat mesas, rocky outcrops, and mountains rising 3–4,000 feet. Here in their mountain massif the Nuba have lived in isolation since the beginning of memory. They represent over fifty distinct ethnic groups speaking more than seventy different languages and practicing their traditional African religions, and came collectively to be called the Nuba in the twentieth century; they are not to be confused with the Nubians of the riverine Nile in northern Sudan, despite the fact that both groups speak languages of the same Nilo-Saharan linguistic family. Their isolation began to crumble in the nineteenth century under pressure from Baqqara Arabs from the plains. Arabic became the lingua franca, but English was frequently used by educated Nuba as their incredibly complex ethnic and linguistic societies continued to cultivate corn, millet, and *dura* (sorghum) on the hillsides, valleys, and plains below.

There were many Muslim Sudanese who did not claim an Arab heritage – the Beja, a Cushitic-speaking people in the Red Sea Hills. Among them were the Hadanduwa, originally camel-owning nomads, many of whom became farmers in the rich deltas of the Gash and Tokar spate rivers during the twentieth century. The northern branch of the Beja, the ʿAbabda, have for centuries controlled the vital route across the Nubian Desert from Korosko to Abu Hamad. Other non-Arab Muslims were Africans who had come in the distant past from the southwest on the fringe of the equatorial African rainforest to settle around the Jabal Marra massif in central Darfur (Land of the Fur). They were mostly farmers speaking Nilo-Saharan languages that related them linguistically to the Nubians and the Maasai of Tanzania. The Fur cultivated the fertile, well-watered valleys of Jabal Marra, as did the Dagu and Berti to the east and the Masalit to the west on the plains, with their spate wadis along the Chad frontier. North of Jabal Marra in the Sahel agriculture becomes marginal, and so the Zaghawa, of African origins, were camel nomads like their Arab neighbors, the Kababish, to the east.

If Muslims have dominated northern Sudan, non-Muslim Sudanese have prevailed in the South. Today they constitute one-third of the Sudanese and number some sixty distinct groups of Western and Eastern Nilotes, a generic and somewhat artificial term for those speaking Nilotic languages of the larger Nilo-Saharan family. The Western Nilotes constitute the Luo, Shilluk, Anuak, Acholi, Jur, and the two most powerful and dominant ethnic groups in southern Sudan, the Dinka and Nuer. These Western Nilotes command the grasslands that surround the Sudd, where the Dinka and Nuer are bound together by their cattle culture, while the Luo, Shilluk, and Anuak are primarily farmers with cattle. The Eastern Nilotes of Sudan, who also speak Eastern Sudanic languages, include a variety of modest-sized ethnic groups who number in the thousands rather than the hundreds of thousands – the Bari, Fajulu, Kakwa, settled farmers, and the Mandari, Taposa, and Turkana, cattle herdsmen.

The homeland of these African Nilotic Sudanese was at one time in central Sudan, specifically in the Gezira, and the last of them to leave, according to their traditions of migration, were the Dinka (in their own language the *jiang* or *moinjiang*) some time in the fifteenth century who pushed the Luo, who had gone before them, further into southern Sudan. Their migrations to the South had been made possible by the acquisition of Zebu humped-back cattle about 1000 CE from the Ethiopian borderlands that were more resistant to drought and accustomed to long-distance trans-humance. By the seventeenth century these Dinka had come into conflict with the Shilluk who, among the Nilotes, were the only people to establish a centralized state with a divine king (*reth*) who fiercely resisted all attempts by the Dinka to turn their agricultural lands into pasture. The history of Dinka–Shilluk relations during the next 200 years is one of interminable border wars punctuated by periods of fragile peace that did not come to an end until the reign of the Shilluk Reth Akwot (1825–35), who ended the Dinka threat to the integrity of his kingdom.

When Dinka living east of the Bahr al-Jabal migrated across the river into the Bahr al-Ghazal during the latter half of the sixteenth century they discovered rich soils inhabited by the indigenous Luo and Luel. By the twelfth century the Luo had occupied large portions of southern Sudan, until the great droughts and famine in the middle of the fifteenth and the first half of the seventeenth centuries precipitated their dissolution. Some Luo went north to found the Shilluk kingdom; others settled as the Anuak on the upper Sobat and Pibor rivers. Not all the Luo had participated in the great migration, and a few remained behind in settlements along the ironstone plateau, where relations between Luo farmers and the incoming Dinka herdsmen were largely amicable and cemented by intermarriage, in which the prestige symbolized by Dinka cattle attracted Luo farmers only too happy to be incorporated into pastoral Dinka society.

The Luel were the indigenous inhabitants who had settled some time about the eighth century in southern Sudan, where they are remembered for building mysterious mounds. They were a martial people who momentarily stalled the advance of the Dinka across the Bahr al-Ghazal in the seventeenth century. The Dinka ultimately forced the Luel to flee before them as far as the Bahr al-Arab, known to the Dinka as the Kiir, where the survivors were integrated into the multiplicity of non-Dinka societies living in the western Bahr al-Ghazal; those who remained behind were either absorbed by the Dinka or lived in tiny discrete enclaves until well into the twentieth century. Having completed their migrations, the Dinka settled into southern Sudan in three confederacies – Padang Dinka, Bor Dinka, and Bahr al-Ghazal Dinka – with twenty-six major sub-groups.

The other great Nilotic group that dominated the *toic* plains east and west of the Sudd were the Nuer (in their own language the *naath*). Although many Nuer today insist they were offshoots from the Dinka, the more convincing evidence indicates they were originally part of the Luo Diaspora who made their way into southern Kordofan long before the coming of the Dinka. Their oral traditions claim they left an arid, southern Kordofan around 1700 to settle in their present well-watered grassland (*kwer-kong*) east and west of the Sudd, where they have warred with the surrounding Dinka over cattle, pasture, and women for the past 300 years. After the Baqqara arrived in southern Darfur and Kordofan early in the eighteenth century their subsequent raids drove the Bul Nuer on the Baqqara border eastward around 1750, precipitating a domino effect by driving other Nuer groups before them. By the mid-nineteenth century the Nuer had hewn a 100-mile wide swath from the Sudd to the Ethiopian escarpment, absorbing and killing Dinka, capturing their cattle and women, and expanding

Nuerland fourfold, leaving the Dinka divided to the north and south to nurse painful memories that remain to this day.

The most recent Africans to make their home in southern Sudan were the Azande (sing. Zande, also called Niam-Niam). They speak a language of the Adamawa branch of the larger Niger-Congo linguistic family to which the Bantu languages belong. Under the leadership of their Avungara aristocracy the feared and successful Azande warriors first crossed the Congo–Nile watershed into Sudan from the Mbomu river valley in the first half of the nineteenth century only to come into conflict with the Arab slave traders until Gbudwe (Yambio) established his kingdom, whose expansion brought him into an indecisive war with the Dinka. When he was killed by a punitive government patrol in 1905, his kingdom was divided under British supervision among his sons.

The enormous ethnic and lingusitic diversity of Sudan has directly contributed to the third theme in modern Sudan – cultural racism. Racism is a complex and controversial subject, but its basic definition remains the belief that some ethnicities are superior or inferior to others. The deep-rooted racism in Sudan is more historical and cultural than based on color, and more individual and institutional than ideological. Throughout the millennia slavery in Sudan has been an historic and accepted institution justified by racial discrimination, which remains pervasive in contemporary Sudan through the use of the pejorative epithet *'abd* (pl. *'abid*), slave, for one having different cultural characteristics and either explicit or implied lower economic and social status.

Cultural racism has been less severe, the pretentious product of ethnic diversity in which the legitimacy of one group is defined at the expense of those with different cultural and linguistic characteristics. Thus, the people of the riverine Sudan, *awlad al-bahr* (people of the river), have long demonstrated their scorn for those ethnicities from the west, *awlad al-gharib* (people of the west), whom they regard as ill-bred, uncultured rustics. This has resulted in conspicuous political racism in which just three ethnic groups – Ja'aliyyin, Shayqiyya, and Danaqla (the *awlad al-bahr*) – have monopolized virtually all positions in government, from cabinet ministers to the most junior civil servants, during the past fifty years of independent Sudan, and which has become one of the major obstacles to the search for a national identity.

A definition of what constitutes identity is as elusive as any interpretation of racism, but defining who is a Sudanese constitutes yet another ingredient in cultural racism. At the time of the Turco-Egyptian conquest an Arab Islamic identity had been widely adopted by the inhabitants of northern Sudan whose ingredients were the Arabic language, claims to Arab ancestry, and Islam. In the half-century of the Condominium (1898–1956) British officials introduced English and the Western notion of nationalism among the sons of the notable Arab families they were educating who, in turn, began the search for the Sudanese. Although the term "Sudani" had a pejorative connotation, the emerging Western-educated elite gave it a new meaning, a label of national identity defined as Arab and Islamic that made it narrow and exclusive and holding little or no appeal to one-third of the inhabitants of Sudan who were non-Muslim, non-Arab Africans. Moreover, the rest of the Arab world did not always share the elite's belief that the Sudanese were authentic Arabs, while the elite themselves wrestled with the ambiguity that being Sudanese included Black Africans, with whom they did not wish to be confused, particularly when they were considered to be "Blacks" in Europe and North America. While most northern Sudanese would quietly acknowledge African ancestry, this fact paradoxically encouraged many of them to identify all the more fervently with their presumed Arab roots. Although this crisis of identity first emerged before the Second World War, after independence "Who are we Sudanese?" became a national debate among the intellectual elite that proved a principal motivation for the Islamist coup d'état of 30 June 1989 to establish a government committed to making all the Sudanese proper Arabs and fundamentalist (*salafist*) Muslims through a vigorous program of Arabization and Islamization.

CHAPTER I

The making of modern Sudan:
the nineteenth century

THE TURKIYA, 1821–1885

By 1820 Muhammad 'Ali, the Turkish Viceroy of the Ottoman sultan in Istanbul, had established his uncontested, personal, and autonomous control of Egypt and was now free to conquer Sudan to acquire slave recruits for his army and gold for his treasury. His invading army, under the command of Muhammad 'Ali's third son, Isma'il Kamil Pasha, consisted of a mixed bag of some 4,000 Albanians, Turks, Maghribis from North Africa, and Egyptian Bedouins, and a detachment of artillery under an American from Massachusetts. The invaders represented the very ambiguities of alien rule they imposed on the Sudanese. The invasion was launched from Egypt by the ruler of Egypt, but that is the extent of the "Egyptian connection." Since medieval times Egypt had been governed by a Turkish-speaking, multi-racial elite. They owed only theoretical allegiance to the Ottoman sultan – as did the Sudanese throughout the sixty-four years of *al-Turkiya* rule in Sudan – and were simply called *al-Turk* (Turks), whatever their ethnic origins. Egyptian Arabs played little role in political or military affairs, their presence represented by religious figures, artisans, and conscripts in the army. They occupied the lower rungs of the clerical and financial administration, occasionally rising to be subordinate officials. Thus the language of government was Turkish heavily charged with Persian and Arabic words, but after the death of Muhammad 'Ali Arabic gradually replaced Turkish in official correspondence. By the mid-nineteenth century most of the correspondence with Sudan was in Arabic, and during the reign of the Egyptian Khedive Isma'il (1863–79) Arabic became the language of government, Turkish being restricted to correspondence with Istanbul, but the senior military officers continued to speak Turkish and Isma'il himself did not speak Arabic. Hence, neither "Ottoman" nor "Egyptian" can adequately describe the Turkiya, and the best appellation that modern scholarship has devised is the awkward, almost whimsical, *Turco-Egyptian*.

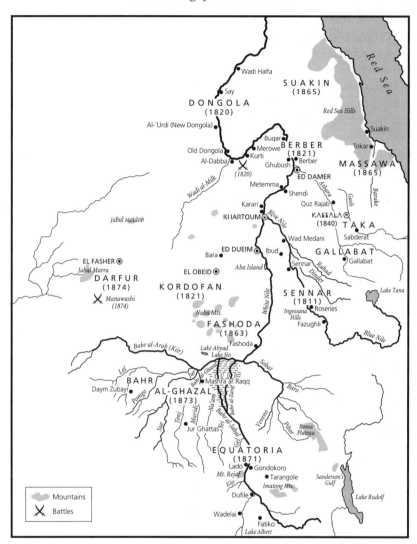

Map 2 The Turkiya

The invading Ottoman army met little resistance except from the Shayqiyya confederacy, whose long swords and lances were no match for the firepower of the Turks. Isma'il, however, was so impressed with their courage he enlisted them as irregular cavalry. In their loyal service to the Turks they were spread widely over the Sudan, which has enabled the Shayqiyya to play a pervasive role in the history of the whole of Sudan to the present day. All the Ja'aliyyin *makks* (Sudanese chiefs) from Berber to the confluence of the White and Blue Niles submitted without resistance and swore allegiance to the new regime, and on 12 June 1821 the last Funj Sultan, Badi IV, surrendered and was pensioned off into the limbo of history. Having occupied riverine Sudan Isma'il demanded heavy taxes from the Sudanese based on a census of slaves and animals. The traditional system of taxation in the Funj Kingdom had not been onerous – a tithe on irrigated and rain-grown crops, a sales tax on slaves and gold – but it was now to be replaced by one that extorted large numbers of slaves, cattle, and *dura*, plus a hut tax. The new assessment was unjust, exploitive, and a euphemism for confiscation. After he demanded a heavy tribute in cash and slaves from the Ja'aliyyin of Shendi, Isma'il and his retinue were burned to death in their quarters that night, and the Nile valley exploded in revolt.

Although the situation appeared desperate, the Turco-Egyptian regime had two advantages – superior firepower and the disunity of the Sudanese insurgents. The Shayqiyya remained loyal, and their irregular cavalry came to the assistance of beleaguered garrisons. In fury and remorse at the death of his son, Muhammad 'Ali ordered his army to spread "fire and sword" throughout fertile riverine Sudan, leaving behind a depopulated wasteland. It would be another sixty years before Sudan had sufficiently recovered for a Sudanese leader to mobilize the people in a single movement to challenge the Turks. The new Governor-General (*hükümdar*), 'Uthman Bey, an elderly Circassian Mamluk, founded Khartoum (*khartum*, elephant's trunk) on the spit of land at the confluence of the Blue and White Niles in 1825 and continued to harass the Sudanese farmers with the New Model Army (*nizam al-jadid*), consisting of slaves seized in the Nuba Mountains and Upper Blue Nile and trained by European drill instructors at Aswan into regular, disciplined troops, the *jihadiyya* under officers literate in Turkish, the language of command. From 1825 until the end of the Turkiya the *jihadiyya* and the loyal Shayqiyya irregular cavalry comprised most of the military strength of the Turco-Egyptian regime.

'Uthman Bey's successor, Mahu Bey, a Kurd, reduced taxes and curbed the excessive repression of the *jihadiyya*. In a remarkable gesture he assembled the remaining Sudanese notables in the Gezira for consultation on how best to restore order and convince the cultivators to return to their farms, and appointed a local *shaykh*, 'Abd al-Qadir wad al-Zayn, as his adviser for native affairs, who served a succession of Turkish Governors-General with wisdom and discretion until his death in 1857. Despite these beginnings of reform Muhammad 'Ali realized he needed an exceptional administrator to reverse the draconian methods that had passed for governance in Sudan. In June 1826 'Ali Khurshid Agha Pasha arrived in Khartoum to inaugurate a new era in the governance of the Sudanese. With the assistance of Shaykh 'Abd al-Qadir, Khurshid convinced those Sudanese who had fled to return and bring back into cultivation their abandoned lands, upon which the prosperity of the regime depended. He established a reasonable tax system that exempted every *faki* and *shaykh* from taxation, which instantly convinced a large and influential class to support the Turco-Egyptian administration. None of these developments, however, could quench the insatiable thirst for slaves. Khurshid organized an annual *razzia* to guarantee a regular supply of slaves, which hitherto had been haphazard and spontaneous. Between 1827 and 1833 he personally led annual slave-raiding expeditions up the White and Blue Niles and along the Ethiopian borderlands with mixed success, until he was recalled and heaped with honors by a grateful Viceroy in 1838. One of Khurshid's last activities was to prove the singular and most dramatic turning-point in the history of Sudan – his preparations for an expedition to open the White Nile and Africa beyond the Sudd.

Like most empire-builders Muhammad 'Ali had an infatuation with geography, which coincided with the growing interest of the African Association in Great Britain as well as of French learned societies as to the source of the White Nile. As early as 1836 he began to interrogate their consuls as to the source of the Nile in the expectation that its discovery would appease his obsession for gold. The French consul frequently reported that he found the Viceroy sitting on his divan surrounded by maps of the White Nile as far as El Eis, 150 miles south of Khartoum. He instructed Khurshid "to set out for the source of the Nile . . . even if you fail to discover the gold mines" but later gave command of his expedition to find the source of the Nile to a Turkish frigate captain, Salim *Kaptan*, commonly known as Salim *Qapudan* (captain).

Salim sailed in November 1839, accompanied by Joseph-Pons d'Arnaud, a French engineer, and Georges Thibaut, a trader. They met the *reth* of the Shilluk before proceeding past the Sobat confluence to Lake No and the mouth of the Bahr al-Jabal and the entrance to the Sudd. Tormented by hordes of mosquitoes, they meandered through the labyrinthine channels amid an awesome landscape of monotonous swamp, stale air, and stagnant water. Salim surrendered to the implacable Sudd near the modern town of Bor on 26 January 1840. The expedition returned to Khartoum and the fury of Muhammad 'Ali, who peremptorily ordered Salim to return to the White Nile on the north winter winds. Leaving again in November 1840, accompanied by Louis Sabatier, a French traveler, Ferdinand Werne, a German adventurer, and once again d'Arnaud, Salim broke out of the Sudd in January 1841 to discover beautiful wooded parklands densely populated with huge herds of cattle, flourishing cultivations, and an infinite number of elephants with precious ivory, until the end of navigation at the Bedden rapids forced them to return to Khartoum in August 1841. After the publication in 1848 of Werne's detailed description of his passage up the White Nile and through the Sudd with Salim, there were those prepared to exploit its ivory undisturbed by an indifferent government in Khartoum.

When Ahmad Pasha Abu Widan replaced Khurshid as Governor-General in 1838, he controlled only the riverine heartland north and south of Khartoum and "islands of authority" in Kordofan from which the *jihadiyya* sallied forth on patrols to "show the flag," capture slaves, and punish a recalcitrant *shaykh*, but he made no pretense at administration. In fact, in the vast interior of Sudan the Turco-Egyptian presence was little at best or non-existent at worst. The nomads remained elusive to foreign governance, and Abu Widan was more concerned with strong internal administration to curb corruption than expand the empire. Abu Widan was a rough soldier, a Circassian who did not hide his contempt for the Turks and Egyptian volunteers in the army, and his success as a strong and effective Governor-General may have been his undoing. He died mysteriously on 6 October 1843, rumored to have been poisoned by his wife, a daughter of Muhammad ʿAli.

The death of Ahmad Pasha Abu Widan inaugurated a new era, lasting twenty years from 1843 to 1863, in which Sudan, devoid of the strong leadership of Khurshid and Abu Widan, slipped into a stagnation that enabled the arrival of Christian Europeans to enhance their influence and wealth at the expense of the Muslim Turco-Egyptian government. Ironically, it was Muhammad ʿAli himself who precipitated the decline of his own creation by uncharacteristic vacillation, as the great Viceroy slipped into senility and paranoia until his death in 1849. His successor, ʿAbbas I (1849–54), was deeply conservative, secretive, and penurious. Unlike his grandfather he sought to keep the Europeans and their Western culture out of the Nile valley and spend as little money as possible to govern Sudan, which drifted toward becoming an economic backwater and a place to banish annoying officials to. Governors-General were non-entities who came and went every two years.

When ʿAbbas died in 1854 he was succeeded as Viceroy by Muhammad Saʿid Pasha, the very antithesis of Abbas. Saʿid had been educated by French tutors and was deeply influenced by Western culture, granting concessions to Europeans for the construction of the Suez Canal, the Eastern Telegraph Company, and the Bank of Egypt. He was profligate with money, and to ensure a steady supply began the imprudent floating of foreign loans through European banks. In the winter of 1856–57 he arrived in Khartoum. Appalled by what he found he seriously considered abandoning the country. He did not, but he divided Sudan into four provinces, each of which reported directly to distant Cairo. With no strong Governor-General and no central administration Sudan continued down the slippery slope of economic decay to foreshadow problems that were to dramatically shape the history of modern Sudan.

In December 1854 Saʿid ordered his powerless Governor-General to stop the slave trade. A post was established at Fashoda, the limit of Turco-Egyptian administration, to inspect the boats coming down the White Nile and to seize any contraband slaves, but this feeble attempt was, in fact, an attack on the institution of slavery itself that was to have disastrous results in the reign of Khedive Ismaʿil.

Slave dealing [in the Sudan] is considered by the natives as a legitimate and honourable source of profit, and all efforts at its suppression are viewed as an unjust and unreasonable interference with a custom sanctioned by the Koran, and with a time-honoured privilege.[1]

The Viceroy's second ominous act was the appointment in 1856 of a Christian Armenian, Arakil Bey al-Armani, Governor of Khartoum and Sennar, an act that deeply offended the simple Islamic piety of the Muslim Sudanese. Arakil Bey's sudden death in 1858 resolved this potentially explosive issue, but it established a precedent for the Khedive Ismaʿil to appoint a host of European Christians to high office in Sudan, with fateful consequences.

The third misadventure that determined the course of history in the Nile valley and over which the Viceroy had little control was the development of a substantial and very vocal European commercial community in Khartoum protected by their consuls and in alliance with the Vatican to introduce Christianity among the non-Muslim Africans in southern Sudan. In 1838 Muhammad ʿAli had been forced to abandon the government monopoly on trade with Sudan. In Cairo the terms of the free trade agreement were publicly acknowledged but in practice dutifully ignored in Khartoum by the Governor-General, who continued to enforce the commercial monopoly, particularly the government's control of the ivory trade. At the time the leading European merchant in Khartoum was Antoine Brun Rollet, who sought European allies in his struggle with the Governor-General and found them in the men of God. In 1846 Ignaz Knoblecher, a Slovene Jesuit, arrived in Khartoum, where he was befriended by Brun Rollet to forge an alliance between European commerce and Catholic Christianity. The missionaries needed the European merchants in Khartoum for transport and supplies; in return the merchants received the blessings of the Vatican and intervention by the influential Austrian consul in Khartoum, Konstantin Reitz, on orders from the Hapsburg Emperor Franz Josef, for Viceroy 'Abbas to give merchants and missionaries absolute freedom to navigate the White Nile.

By the mid-nineteenth century Victorian Britain had become obsessed with ivory. Between 1840 and 1870 the price and quantity of ivory had doubled on the London market. In 1851 twelve *dahabiahs* had sailed for Gondokoro to trade in ivory; ten years later there were eighty; and at the beginning of the reign of Isma'il Pasha in 1863 there were more than 120. At first the power of the traders and that of the Africans was roughly equal. On their boats the traders possessed the advantage of technological superiority, but once on land they were dependent on the Africans, who possessed the large hordes of accumulated ivory. When this source was exhausted the European traders themselves had to kill the elephants for their ivory, which required large numbers of armed Arab retainers and the construction of walled trading forts, *zaribas*, from the interior of which the hunters would sally forth to shoot elephants for their tusks and raid for slaves to carry them to the river and to cultivate the gardens that supplied the *zaribas*. The Arabs who settled around these forts obtained African wives and slaves to become a ruling caste by the power of their guns, a development that soon produced a "spiral of violence" of raid and counter-raid between Muslim Arabic-speaking northern Sudanese and the non-Muslim African-speaking peoples of southern Sudan that has characterized the history of the Upper Nile basin ever since.

By 1860 an estimated 12,000 to 15,000 slaves were sent north every year, which created its own dialectic – an insatiable demand for capital that in turn demanded more slaves, more raids, and more violence. By 1868 there were more than eighty *zaribas* scattered throughout the Bahr al-Ghazal, each with some 250 men and women accompanied by crowds of children. Those Africans living near a *zariba* were reduced to vassals who, along with captured slaves, cultivated the farms that fed the station. The financial success of the big traders from Khartoum, known as Khartoumers, soon attracted hundreds of *jallaba* who, pouring south from Darfur and Kordofan to settle within the security of a *zariba* with a donkey and a few cheap guns or goods to sell for a few slaves, made sufficient profit to repeat the process in an endless cycle. The Khartoumers loathed these *jallaba*, who obtained their slaves from the supply needed to support their slaving operations, but the Khartoumers were powerless to prevent them from buying slaves within the safety of their *zaribas*.

In 1863 Isma'il Pasha succeeded Sa'id as Viceroy of Egypt. He determined to end the reign of chaos in Sudan and restore its governance to the strong rule of his grandfather, Muhammad 'Ali. He was energetic, articulate, and utterly charming in a way that captivated foreigners and produced loyalty among those – European, Turk, and Arab – who served him. Despotism was the only form of government he understood, and he promptly abandoned the decentralization of Sa'id and substantially restored the powers of the Governor-General in Khartoum. As a Westernized Oriental potentate Isma'il sought with mixed success to drag Egypt and Sudan into the modern world by the introduction of Western technology – railroads, river steamers, telegraph networks, a modern army, government schools, a postal service – and those two symbols of Western imperialism, the abolition of the slave trade and the expansion of empire.

The Compagnie du Soudan launched in 1863 to build railways in Sudan collapsed in 1868. The development of wood-burning side-wheel steamers assembled in the Khartoum dockyard proved their worth by transporting up the White Nile the men and equipment to expand the Egyptian empire in the Upper Nile basin. Isma'il was most emphatic about the need to link Sudan with the Egyptian telegraph system, and the line had reached Wadi Halfa by 1866, Khartoum in 1874, and Suakin on the Red Sea in 1875. A postal service soon complemented the telegraph, and by 1880 there were post offices as far south as Fashoda and as far west as El Fasher in Darfur, from which the mail reached Khartoum in eleven days. Isma'il's favorite project, however, was rebuilding an army necessary to transform into reality his dreams of a vast empire in equatorial Africa. In 1866 he re-equipped the army with Krupp artillery and repeating Remington rifles from the United States to replace the standard muzzle-loaders, and recruited former Federal and Confederate American officers as military advisers led by Brigadier-General C. P. Stone, who was appointed chief of staff of the Egyptian army.

Islam in Sudan has traditionally been dominated by the rituals of popular mysticism, *sufism*, for which the legalistic structure of orthodox Islam in Egypt had no appeal. After the Turco-Egyptian conquest each of the Viceroys had sought to reform Sudanese Islam by appointing to the highest offices of Islamic law orthodox religious leaders from Egypt who firmly excluded the *sufi* mystics they contemptuously regarded as ignorant peddlers of superstition. This same mysticism of the popular *sufi* saints, however, became the dynamic appeal of Mahdism that would destroy the Turco-Egyptian regime in Sudan, and today *sufism* remains deeply rooted in the religious life of the rural Sudanese in opposition to the *salafist* Islam of the Islamists. The religious reformation of the Sudanese to accept formal Islam had been very gradual during the Turkiya, and it was not until the reign of Isma'il that the first Sudanese was appointed president of the Islamic teachers in Sudan, and the Sudanese began to emerge from their religious isolation through the relentless acceptance of Arabic, no longer Turkish, as the lingua franca of administration and the spread of literary Arabic through the growing number of *'ulama'*.

In 1866 Isma'il appointed Ja'far Pasha Mazhar Governor-General, who restored discipline in the army and established a corps of police from Shayqiyya irregulars, but he did little to disrupt the slave trade, whose merchants regularly eluded the river police on the White Nile or bribed them in order to pass down river to the slave markets. By the 1870s a new class of powerful merchant prince had transformed the slave trade by absorbing along with their *zaribas* rival traders with fewer resources and reorganizing their operations into sprawling corporate enterprises with complex systems of logistics and the procurement and transport of slaves. Two of the most visible and successful were Muhammad Ahmad al-'Aqqad east of the Bahr al-Jabal in Equatoria, and al-Zubayr Rahma Mansur in the Bahr al-Ghazal. Ahmad al-'Aqqad had held a monopoly on trade south of Gondokoro from the Khedive until his death in 1870, after which his son-in-law, Muhammad Abu Su'ud Bey al-'Aqqad, extended the firm's operations as far south as the Victoria Nile. Al-Zubayr Rahma Mansur was a Sudanese Ja'ali who had built up by 1873 an extensive empire in the western Bahr al-Ghazal, of which he was the sole master. Unable to challenge Zubayr's complete control, Isma'il symbolically annexed the Bahr al-Ghazal in 1873 by simply appointing Zubayr his Governor to do as he pleased.

The corruption and vested interests of his Turkish and Egyptian officers convinced Isma'il to recruit incorruptible Europeans morally committed to end the slave trade who had no objections to imperial expansion but happened to be Christians in a Muslim country. Having obtained the hereditary title of *khedive* from an impotent Ottoman sultan, at the opening of the Suez Canal in 1869 he engaged Sir Samuel Baker, the British explorer who had discovered the Albert Nyanza in 1864, to extend his empire south of Gondokoro, suppress the slave trade, and open the African kingdoms on the Lake Plateau to regular commerce. The Khedive assembled a massive expedition that left Khartoum on 8 February 1870 but did not break through the Sudd until thirteen months later in March 1871. Although Baker was possessed of boundless energy and great strength of character and physique, his domineering temperament contributed to his ineptitude as an administrator and his colossal insensitivity as an Englishman and Christian leading Turkish, Egyptian, and Sudanese Muslims on a mission to end the slave trade, an acceptable and established institution from which they had profited. He expanded the southern boundary of the khedivial equatorial empire to Fatiko north of the Victoria Nile. At the end of his contract Baker departed from Gondokoro in May 1873 and never returned to Sudan.

His successor as Governor of Equatoria was yet another Englishman, Charles George Gordon, a military mystic and, at 41, already famous for leading the Ever-Victorious Army in China that suppressed the Taiping Rebellion in 1864. During two and a half years he and his European staff restored discipline in the riverine garrisons in the Upper Nile and placed steamers and the Egyptian flag on Lake Albert as the western pincer movement to complement the eastern pincer of the Egyptian army advancing along the Red Sea and into Ethiopia in a futile attempt to realize Isma'il's grand and illusory scheme to envelop East Africa in his imperial embrace. In 1875 Isma'il launched three military expeditions into Ethiopia, all of which were forced to withdraw after two disastrous defeats by the Ethiopian host. This bizarre scheme, a geographical and political farce, soon collapsed when the British government protested; Isma'il abandoned his dream of a northeast African empire and recalled his troops. However, Isma'il's efforts to complete the plan of Muhammad 'Ali to conquer Darfur fared somewhat better than his abortive efforts in Ethiopia and East Africa. In 1873 al-Zubayr Rahma Mansur, now in his official capacity as Governor of the Bahr al-Ghazal, invaded Darfur, defeated the Fur army in January 1874, and entered the capital, El Fasher. He was rewarded with the title of *pasha* by an embarrassed Khedive, who was only able to exert his authority in Darfur after placing Zubayr under house arrest in Cairo, from which he was not released until 1899 after the Anglo-Egyptian conquest of Sudan.

Paradoxically, these years of frustrated Egyptian imperial expansion coincided with the drastic decline of Egyptian resources available to Isma'il that could no longer sustain the financial burden of empire. Faced with failure on the Ethiopian frontier, revolt in Darfur, and chaos in the Bahr al-Ghazal, the Khedive acquiesced in February 1877 to Gordon's demand that he be appointed Governor-General of the whole of Sudan to crush the slave

trade, and in August Isma'il duly signed the Anglo-Egyptian Slave Trade
Convention that required an end to the sale and purchase of slaves by 1880.
He hoped this humanitarian gesture would mollify the European powers
and financial creditors deeply concerned about his ability to pay even the
interest on the expanding Egyptian debt. Unfortunately, Gordon required
more than devotion to duty and dynamic energy to succeed at Khartoum.
His impulsive intuition, often guided by mystic religious convictions, failed
to understand the complexities of khedivial administration and was contemptuous of its officials, whom he impetuously appointed and dismissed.
Gordon was illiterate in Arabic and spoke little: an unorthodox but brilliant
soldier, a crusader, not a consummate administrator. Yet, he stabilized the
Ethiopian frontier, suppressed revolt in Darfur, and devoted all his energies to the abolition of the slave trade, not realizing that his crusade laid
the foundations for the cataclysm that was to follow. Frank, simple, and
energetic, Gordon was totally blind to Islamic definitions of slavery, and
he believed the only means to abolish the slave trade was the indiscriminate repression of the Khartoumers by Christian Europeans, some quite
inferior to his own Muslim Egyptian or Turkish officials, which further
compromised his leadership.

In 1879 Isma'il defied the European governments over the authority vested
in their British and French financial controllers, and they consequently used
their considerable influence at Istanbul to convince the Ottoman sultan to
depose the Khedive, who cleaned out the cash in the Abdin Palace and
sailed away to a gilded exile on the Bosphorus. When Gordon learned of
the abdication of Isma'il, whom he had admired and trusted, he promptly
resigned. The era of the Khedive Isma'il was over, and although the Turco-
Egyptian regime in Sudan stumbled along for almost another six years, the
Turkiya was drawing to a close, consumed by the revolt of Muhammad
Ahmad, al-Mahdi.

The legacy of the Turco-Egyptian regime has been overwhelmed but not
obliterated by the obsession with the Mahdist theocracy that succeeded it
and the Westernization that took place during the fifty years of the Anglo-
Egyptian Condominium. The geographical diversity and great distances of
Sudan, combined with the limited resources and capabilities of Turkish and
Egyptian officials, had confined their governance to the riverine heartland
and some administrative islands in the vast lands on the periphery, where
the authority of the central government was represented more by the *razzia*
than benevolent governance. Despite the introduction of formal Islam from
Egypt with the intention of eroding Sudanese *sufism*, Islam had made no
inroads among the non-Muslim Africans living on its southern frontier.

Despite the imposition of a central administration, which was often decentralized, the more unified administration had accomplished little to disturb the ethnic and linguistic diversity of Sudan despite the use of Turkish at first and then Arabic as the lingua franca of government. The bitter Sudanese memories of the sixty years of the Turkiya, which lingered long in Sudanese folklore, have faded, but the themes begun when Muhammad 'Ali dragged the reluctant Sudanese into the larger Islamic world to begin the process of modernization have remained to challenge the Sudanese at the beginning of the twenty-first century.

THE MAHDIYA, 1885–1898

In March 1881 on Aba Island, located in the White Nile 150 miles south of Khartoum, Muhammad Ahmad ibn 'Abdallah experienced several visions in which the Prophet appointed him the Expected Mahdi (*mahdi*, guided one). He first informed his confidant, 'Abdallahi ibn Muhammad Turshain, of this revelation and then his small circle of disciples before proceeding to El Obeid, the Turco-Egyptian capital of Kordofan. Here he publicly proclaimed his Mahdiship and emotionally appealed to the notables and the *nas* alike to abandon this world for the new age of righteousness and justice to follow. His message and charisma attracted a large following who secretly took an oath of allegiance (*bay'a*) to him. Upon his return to Aba Island he dispatched letters to the Sudanese leaders in northern Sudan passionately informing them he was, indeed, the Expected Mahdi.

Muhammad Ahmad ibn 'Abdallah was a 40-year-old Dunqulawi who from childhood had been deeply religious and well-educated in the Sammaniyya *sufi* order in a Sudan that he thought had become too worldly. He left the brotherhood and retired to Aba Island, where he led the life of a religious ascetic. He was a reformer, a *mujadid*, who claimed three Islamic titles – the Imam as head of the true Muslim community, the Successor of the Apostle of God to restore that community as the Prophet had done, and the Expected Mahdi who foreshadowed the end of a corrupt and unjust world, which coincided with the coming end of the thirteenth Muslim century. Indeed, his legitimacy as the Mahdi seemed confirmed to many when his followers on Aba Island overpowered a contingent of government troops sent to apprehend him, the survivors retreating in disarray to their steamers and Khartoum.

This initial success was sustained by two stunning victories by his growing number of supporters, called *ansar* (partisans of Islam, Ansar), over the *jihadiyya* of the hated Turks in December 1881 and May 1882 who, with spears and swords against rifles and artillery, convinced the mass of Sudanese to join the ranks of the Ansar who now besieged El Obeid. Those who flocked to take the *bay'a* were the pious men, slavers, and Baqqara Arabs. Clerics and *fakis*, who had a profound influence among the rural Sudanese, and members of the *sufi* brotherhoods in Sudan had long deplored the state of Islam, particularly the orthodox Islam introduced by the Turks which they regarded as heresy. These men now saw the opportunity to purify Islam in Sudan, for when the Mahdi spoke of misgovernment he meant theological, not political, corruption. The second group to support the Mahdi were those involved, one way or another, in the slave trade. Most of them were either Ja'aliyyin or, like the Mahdi himself, Danaqla. They had all lost profits, if not their livelihood, as a result of the curtailment of the slave trade by European Christian officials employed by the Khedive Isma'il. Now they could obscure their economic and political motives behind the reform of Islam which condoned slavery. The Baqqara nomads of Kordofan and Darfur were the third and most powerful supporters of the Mahdi. His confidant, 'Abdallahi, was the son of a Baqqara soothsayer who long before the revelations of Muhammad Ahmad had predicted the coming of a *mahdi*. His kinsmen did not necessarily share 'Abdallahi's religious enthusiasm, but they quickly perceived that a religious revolution would drive away the tax-collecting Turks. Their warrior tradition soon made them the shock troops, or *ansar*, of the Mahdist armies throughout the Mahdiya. After four months the besieged garrison in El Obeid surrendered, in January 1883, and the revolt swept eastward through the Gezira to the Red Sea Hills.

In a futile attempt to crush the Sudanese insurgency the British, who had occupied Egypt in 1882, reluctantly agreed that the Khedive could mobilize an Egyptian expeditionary force of 10,000 troops commanded by a British officer of the Indian Army, Colonel William Hicks. Hicks quarreled with his Egyptian staff; the Ansar harassed the column, filled in the wells, and littered their camps with propaganda among the despondent Muslim Egyptians to the effect that the Ansar were, indeed, the "Soldiers of God." On 5 November 1883 the expeditionary force was surrounded at Shaykan south of El Obeid and annihilated, with few survivors. The disaster at Shaykan was a staggering blow both in Sudan and Egypt. On the one hand the British steadfastly refused to intervene in Sudan on behalf of the Turco-Egyptians, but on the other they insisted the Egyptian residents should be evacuated, including civilians and their dependants. Not knowing what to do, the British Prime Minister, William Ewart Gladstone, agreed to send "Gordon for the Sudan," that heroic figure who had been the

Figure 1 General Charles Gordon Pasha, taken in 1884 just before his departure for Khartoum.

former Governor-General and suppressed its slave trade, and whose "name was worth an entire army." On 18 February 1884 Gordon, reappointed Governor-General, reached Khartoum and immediately discovered that both peace with the Mahdi and the evacuation of the Egyptians were quite impossible, leaving him with the only option of defending the city until it fell or a relief expedition came to the rescue. When the Mahdi himself arrived on 23 October to establish his headquarters on the west bank of the Nile opposite Khartoum in what became known as Omdurman, Khartoum was isolated and besieged. The following months were perhaps Gordon's finest as he rallied the demoralized population to defend the city while a British relief expedition made its lethargic advance into Sudan, creating a dilemma for the Mahdi as to how he should respond to this threat. He acted decisively. Ignoring the advice of his council to retire to Kordofan, he ordered the Ansar to storm the walls of Khartoum in the early hours of 26 January 1885, the time of year when the Nile is at low water, exposing solid ground by which the Ansar could reach the weakened defenses. The Egyptian garrison was destroyed, Gordon killed, and the city reduced to ruins. Two days later the steamers of the relief expedition arrived at the confluence of the two Niles. They were "Too Late" and ignominiously retired out of Sudan to face the fury of the British public.

Six months later, on 22 June, the Mahdi died after a short illness, leaving behind a skeletal administration controlled by his disciples, three of whom he had given the title of Companion of the Prophet. 'Abdallahi ibn Muhammad was the *Khalifat al-Siddiq*, the successor to the Caliph Abu Bakr; 'Ali ibn Muhammad Hilu became *Khalifat al-Faruq*, the successor to the Caliph 'Umar; and Muhammad Sharif was designated *Khalifat al-Karrar*, the successor to the Caliph 'Ali, cousin of the Prophet. As the prototype of Abu Bakr, the closest of the Prophet's Companions, the Khalifa 'Abdallahi, confidant of the Mahdi, was thus his likely successor. The Mahdi had also appointed two other powerful officials. Ahmad Sulayman, a Nubian and close friend, supervised the *bayt al-mal*, whose contents included those taxes sanctioned by *shari'a*, but throughout the Mahdiya the principal source of revenue during the early years was booty seized in battles. The chief judge, Ahmad 'Ali, was entitled *qadi al-Islam* (judge of Islam). He had been a judge in the Turco-Egyptian regime and was expected to apply *shari'a*, but the Mahdi himself, as did his *khalifas*, regularly heard cases and passed judgments.

Although the Khalifa 'Abdallahi possessed the best claim to succeed the Mahdi, and his Baqqara Black Flag division was garrisoned in Omdurman, his succession did not go uncontested. The death of the Mahdi had exposed the deep underlying tension between those Sudanese in the center, the riverine Ja'aliyyin and Danaqla, the *awlad al-bahr*, among whom were the Mahdi's kinsmen, the *ashraf*, and the *awlad al-gharib*, those vulgar rustic Baqqara. Both the *ashraf* and the *awlad al-bahr* were determined that the new ruler should be the Khalifa Muhammad al-Sharif, the son-in-law of the Mahdi, but the Baqqara supporters of 'Abdallahi in Omdurman prevailed, and the notables, including Muhammad Sharif, swore allegiance to him, after which he conferred on himself the exalted new title of *Khalifat al-Mahdi* (successor to the Mahdi). Although they had taken the oath of allegiance, neither the *ashraf* nor the *awlad al-bahr* were prepared to accept the rule of the Khalifa 'Abdallahi and immediately plotted to overthrow him by summoning the large Mahdist army of the west commanded by Muhammad Khalid, a riverine Dunqulawi and cousin of the Mahdi. The Khalifa reacted decisively. He isolated Khalid, secured the Gezira and its grain supplies for Omdurman, and in April 1886 ordered the two junior *khalifas* to disband their personal armed retinues and place them under the commander of the Black Flag division, his half-brother and closest adviser, Ya'qub Muhammad Turshain.

Having contained, for the moment, his internal enemies, the Khalifa now turned to the external challenges to his authority as he sought to pursue the Mahdi's goal to spread the puritanical Islam of the Mahdiya throughout the world by *jihad*. In the west his Baqqara Arabs in Darfur were confronted in 1888 by a rebellion of the African Fur and Masalit led by a *faki* among the Mahriyya nomads known as Abu Jummayza. A somewhat messianic figure, Abu Jummayza rallied the other Africans of Darfur – the Daju, Qimr, and Tama – to defeat two Arab Baqqara forces sent against them and swept eastward toward El Fasher, where he suddenly died of smallpox. Demoralized, his followers began to disperse and were easily defeated in February 1889 by the Baqqara before El Fasher. Darfur had been saved for the Khalifa, but his nephew and commander in Darfur, Mahmud Ahmad, spent much of the next five years quelling sporadic revolts and pacifying Darfur. Fur separatism has never died.

The Khalifa faced problems on his eastern frontier with Ethiopia similar to those in Darfur. At first the Ethiopians had severely defeated the Ansar in 1887, inflicting heavy losses. The Khalifa sent reinforcements, and his most able general, Hamdan Abu 'Anja, first had to suppress a mutiny in the Mahdist army led by another messianic figure not unlike Abu Jummayza in Darfur before he could make a successful raid in January 1888 on the ancient Ethiopian capital of Gondar, capturing much booty. Upon Abu 'Anja's death in January 1889 Zaki Tamal reorganized the army to meet the advance of a massive Ethiopian army under the personal command of Emperor John IV, who launched his assault on 9 March 1889. Just as the Mahdists were about to be overwhelmed a chance bullet killed the emperor, plunging the Ethiopian host into disarray and retreat. The head and crown of the emperor were sent to the Khalifa in Omdurman, and Ethiopia collapsed into anarchy. In the west and east the *jihad* of the Khalifa had been one of pacification, but the Holy War in the north was a legacy of the Mahdi's vision to conquer and purify all the lands of Islam. After numerous delays, a Mahdist army under the command of 'Abd al-Rahman al-Najumi marched in the heat of summer into Egypt where, on 3 August 1889 at the village of Tushki, the Ansar were totally destroyed by General

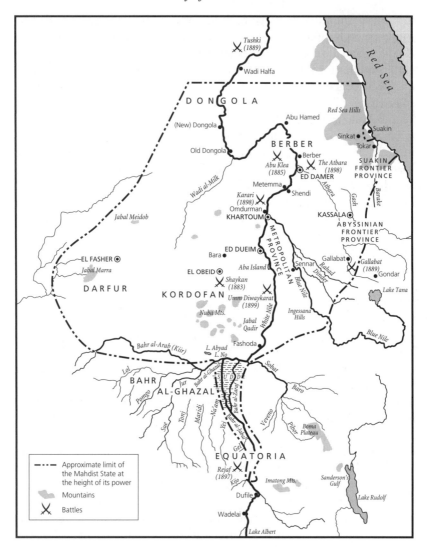

Map 3 The Mahdiya

Francis Grenfell, *Sirdar*, and the Egyptian army, killing al-Najumi and ending any threat to Egypt from the Mahdist State.

The failure of the center to control the periphery was nowhere more apparent than in the South. During 1883–84 the commander of the Ansar, Karam Allah Kurqusawi, had occupied most of the Bahr al-Ghazal until recalled by the Khalifa after the death of the Mahdi to suppress a dangerous insurrection by the Rizayqat Baqqara of southwest Darfur. The Mahdists never returned to the Bahr al-Ghazal, but in 1888 the Khalifa sent another Ta'a'isha Baqqara kinsman, 'Umar Salih, up the Nile to eliminate the last vestiges of Turco-Egyptian administration and its governor, Emin Pasha, in Equatoria. He arrived at Lado in October 1888 and captured Rejaf, but the following month he suffered a defeat by Emin's troops before Dufile on 28 November and three years later an even more severe loss at Wadelai in December 1891. 'Umar Salih retreated to Rejaf to confine his activities to raids into the countryside for supplies until 'Arabi Dafa'allah replaced him at Rejaf in 1893 to take command and confront the advancing forces of King Leopold of the Belgians' Congo Free State. He suffered a major defeat in March 1894 by the combined forces of the Congo Free State and the Azande led by their warrior king, Zemio. By 1897 the tide had once again turned against 'Arabi: he was decisively defeated by troops of the Congo Free State under the command of Captain L. N. Chaltin at the battles of Bedden and Rejaf in February 1897 and fled west near the present border with Chad, leaving no trace of the Mahdist State in southern Sudan.

Unable to consolidate his governance on the frontiers, his resources for expansion spent, and his best generals dead, the Khalifa was confronted by the tyrannies of nature, which he could of course not control. The consumption of limited foodstuffs by three large and voracious armies on the frontiers became a crisis in 1889 and 1890, when northern Sudan was subjected to successive droughts that resulted in meager harvests followed by famine, epidemics, and massive loss of life from each. The fate of the northern Sudanese was made ever more terrible by the Khalifa's decision in 1888 to order the Baqqara, and particularly his Ta'a'isha kinsmen, to leave their green pasturelands in Darfur and settle in and around Omdurman in order to turn these roving nomads into a loyal standing army to defend the regime against the machinations of the *awlad al-bahr*. The Baqqara were very reluctant to leave their homeland but during the early months of 1889 straggled into Omdurman, where they arrogantly demanded to be housed and fed from the dwindling supplies in the capital. The existing tension between the *awlad al-bahr* and *awlad al-gharib* was now transformed into implacable hostility exacerbated by the privileged position of the Khalifa's kinsmen, who held most of the great offices of state and the army. The Baqqara hated the city and longed for the wide-open spaces of Darfur, to which they began to return when they could escape the Khalifa's vigilance; those who were forced to remain by order of the Khalifa sulked as an overbearing and unproductive elite intolerant of discipline who could hardly be transformed into instruments by which to govern the Mahdist State.

The *ashraf* and the *awlad al-bahr* had never stopped plotting against the Khalifa, and the appearance of the Baqqara only spurred them on to conspiracy. On 23 November 1891 and led by the Mahdi's son-in-law, Muhammad Sharif, fully armed *ashraf* surrounded the Mahdi's tomb a few yards from the house of the Khalifa and prepared for a confrontation. Fearing that his Ta'a'isha guards, once fighting erupted, would likely sack the capital and flee with the booty to Darfur, the Khalifa negotiated a settlement with the *ashraf* in which he promised a general amnesty, the recognition due Muhammad Sharif, and a monthly pension for the sons and widows of the Mahdi. In return the *ashraf* laid down their arms. The Khalifa did not wait long to exact his revenge. Within a month seven notables of the *ashraf* were seized, sent to Fashoda, and beaten to death. In the Gezira, Danaqla were forcefully detained in January 1892 and one-third of their property confiscated, and in March Muhammad Sharif was himself arrested, tried by a summary court, and imprisoned for the duration of the Mahdiya. The *ashraf* and the *awlad al-bahr* had been finally broken; the Ta'a'isha autocracy was secure.

After seven tumultuous and debilitating years the Khalifa's authority was at last unchallenged, and the northern Sudanese, who had suffered greatly during those years, were now content to remain passive in their efforts to recover from the human and natural disasters that had overwhelmed them. In the five years 1892–98 the Sudanese experienced a modest return of prosperity and, to the relief of everyone in Omdurman, the Khalifa allowed the Baqqara to go home, replacing them with a corps of mercenaries, the *mulazimiyya*, consisting of 9,000 men loyal to the Khalifa alone who, at the time, withdrew from public view, appearing only on special festival days surrounded by his bodyguard. He had a great wall constructed around his residence behind which he adopted a more aloof and mysterious image in the tradition of an Oriental potentate. Internally, he sought to transform the theocratic state of the Mahdi into an Islamic monarchy in which the succession would pass to his eldest son, 'Uthman Shaykh al-Din.

Although the European scramble for and conquest of Africa was relentlessly proceeding elsewhere on the continent, Sudan appeared immune. Lord Cromer was not about to spend the money needed to rebuild Egypt on an expensive invasion of Sudan unless there was a European threat to the Nile waters. By 1896 the Khalifa had consolidated the support of the northern Sudanese, but his complacency was shaken when in March 1896 the British government authorized the Egyptian army to cross the frontier and occupy the province of Dongola in Nubian Sudan. The invasion was not another episode in the European conquest of Africa and had nothing to do with the Mahdist State. After the disastrous defeat on 1 March 1896 of the invading Italian army at the battle of Adua by the Ethiopian army of Emperor Menelik II, the Italian government requested a British diversion on the Nile to discourage any Mahdist attack on the weakened Italian garrison in Kassala. The British Prime Minister, Lord Salisbury, responded with alacrity to this splendid opportunity to seize Dongola at little cost as a prelude to the conquest of Sudan if any European power foolishly sought to control the waters of the upper Nile.

The origins of the conquest of Sudan actually had begun in 1889, that same critical year when the *awlad al-bahr* had first challenged the authority of the Khalifa. In June 1889 Lord Salisbury decided that Great Britain would oppose any attempt by a European power to interfere in the flow of the Nile waters that would threaten British authority in Egypt and their control of the Suez Canal. It was a momentous decision in the course of empire in Africa. Thereafter, his concerted Nile diplomacy neutralized the Italian and German designs on the Nile waters, but several years later he was faced with a more formidable threat when Captain Jean-Baptiste Marchand was ordered to lead a French expedition from Loango on the Atlantic to Fashoda on the upper Nile to secure its waters for France. During the next two years all of Salisbury's schemes to counter the French threat collapsed, leaving him with no alternative but to order General Horatio Herbert Kitchener, *Sirdar* of the Egyptian army, to go to Khartoum and the upper Nile to prevent the loss of its waters. In January 1897 Kitchener began his invasion by constructing a military railway to secure his communications, transport large numbers of troops, vast quantities of arms and supplies, and even gunboats in sections, to be assembled beyond the fifth cataract. The Khalifa was taken completely by surprise and responded by commanding Mahmud Ahmad to bring his large army of the west, which took months to reach his headquarters at Metemma, the capital of the Ja'aliyyin, north of Omdurman on the west bank of the Nile.

The Ja'aliyyin refused to obey the Khalifa's orders to relocate across the Nile on the east bank and prepared to resist any attempt by Mahmud and his army to seize their beloved town. On 1 July 1897 the Ansar launched a pre-emptive assault against the defiant Ja'aliyyin defending Metemma and savagely slaughtered them, sealing in blood the hatred of the a*wlad al-bahr* for the Ta'a'isha autocracy and immobilizing the army of the North sated with Ja'aliyyin loot. In January 1898 Mahmud led his army across the Nile, where he established a *zariba* in March on the north bank of the

Figure 2 Colonel H. H. Kitchener (seated) at Suakin 1888–89, with British officers of the 1st Brigade, Egyptian army.

Atbara river. Here on 8 April, Good Friday, Kitchener launched his British, Egyptian, and Sudanese brigades against the Ansar, killing and wounding several thousand; the Anglo-Egyptian casualties were a few hundred, and Mahmud was captured. The Anglo-Egyptian army went into camp to wait out the blistering heat of the Sudan summer. The Khalifa remained quietly in Omdurman waiting to fulfill the prophesy that the final victorious conflagration over the infidel would take place on the Karari plain north of the city.

On 1 September 1898 Kitchener established his crescent camp at 'Iqaya on the west bank of the Nile at the foot of the Karari plain. At dawn the following day some 60,000 Ansar hurled themselves with magnificent courage against the barbed wire, the withering fire of the repeating rifle, the deadly Maxim guns, and a fusillade from the gunboats. When the line of the charging Ansar began to waver, Kitchener ordered the advance, and the brigades of the Anglo-Egyptian army moved relentlessly forward. By late morning the battle was over. Over 11,000 Ansar lay dead, while another 16,000 were seriously wounded. Superior technology proved triumphant,

Figure 3 Egyptian army officers next to a decorated Sudan Military Railway engine before setting out for Atbara, en route to the Omdurman front, 1898.

for the British, Egyptian, and Sudanese brigades lost fewer than fifty killed and several hundred wounded. When he saw the day was lost, the Khalifa disappeared into the vast Sudan to the west. Kitchener and his entourage crossed the Nile to the ruined palace in Khartoum to hold a memorial service for the martyred Charles George Gordon that would have pleased his ghost. The Mahdist State was over.

The Khalifa had transformed the theocracy of the Mahdi into an Islamic state with a centralized administration under his personal rule supported by a bureaucracy. He had single-handedly prevented northern Sudan from crumbling into anarchy after the death of the Mahdi, but he was never able to divorce himself from the great themes that have determined the history of Sudan during the past 200 years. He did not have the technical means to mitigate the geographical power of so vast a land as Sudan, which was the principal reason he lost the South. Although his firm control in Omdurman consolidated the center, he never systematically exerted his authority on the periphery, east, west, north, or south, where he was constantly bedeviled by insurrections. He most certainly forged the deep hatred of the *awlad al-bahr* for the *awlad al-gharib*, but he never crushed those resilient river-ine Sudanese, as was demonstrated by the fruitless Ja'aliyyin resistance at

Metemma in 1897. Finally, the Khalifa never had to concern himself with non-Muslims, for the Mahdist State was not only firmly Islamic but its inhabitants all northern Muslim Sudanese.

Three days after his victory on the plains of Karari three Mahdist steamers arrived from the South riddled with French bullets. On 12 July 1898 Marchand had reached Fashoda, raised the French flag, and proclaimed the upper Nile French. Three weeks later Kitchener arrived with a mighty flotilla and his finest British troops fresh from their victory at Karari. Over brandy and cigars Kitchener and Marchand agreed, with considerable civility, to refer sovereignty over the Nile waters to their respective governments. When the news reached London and Paris, crowds surged through the streets demanding Fashoda or war. The British were prepared for war; the French were not. Marchand was recalled, and the Fashoda crisis was over. Britain controlled the Nile waters from the equatorial lakes of Africa to the Mediterranean Sea, and Egypt and the Suez Canal were now securely British. Even Emperor Menelik prudently promised in 1902 never to interfere with the flow of the Blue Nile and the Atbara tributary.

There are two poignant scenes that best symbolize the end of the Mahdist State and French imperial ambitions. On 24 November 1899 Colonel Sir Reginald Wingate, Director of Military Intelligence, cornered the Khalifa and 5,000 Ansar at Umm Diwaykarat, near the present town of Kosti. The Khalifa was found dead, prostrate on his sheepskin prayer rug, the Khalifa 'Ali wad Hilu on his right and his loyal Ta'a'isha relative, Ahmad Fadil, on his left. Today at Fashoda, under the penetrating African sun, are the iron crosses of the French officers who had marched across Africa to die there quietly from disease. With them died the Napoleonic imperial dream to bestride the mighty Nile.

CHAPTER 2

The Anglo-Egyptian Condominium

CONSOLIDATION AND REACTION: 1899–1936

The collapse of the Mahdist State presented the British government with a dilemma as to who should govern Sudan. The Anglo-Egyptian conquest had been undertaken not only to defend British imperial interests at Cairo and Suez by securing the upper Nile waters but also to recover the former Sudanese provinces belonging to the Khedive of Egypt. Kitchener's successful confrontation with Marchand at Fashoda had achieved the first objective, but achieving the second, British restoration of khedivial rule, would not be tolerated by a British public convinced that the Mahdist revolution was the result of Turco-Egyptian oppressive governance. Moreover, the British government could not simply annex Sudan as another colony, for its "reconquest" had been justified by restoring to the Khedive his former territories lost to the Mahdists. Lord Cromer cleverly proposed a "hybrid" solution, embodied in the Anglo-Egyptian "Condominium" Agreement of 1899, by which Britain and Egypt would share sovereignty. Sudan would be administered by a Governor-General appointed and recalled by the Khedive, but only on the advice of the British government. In effect, Cromer had created a new and separate sovereignty in Sudan whose administration would be controlled by a British Governor-General and those British officers whom he chose to appoint. All the Governors-General of Anglo-Egyptian Sudan were subsequently British, reporting through the British representative in Cairo to the Foreign rather than the Colonial Office in London. Thus Sudan was not a colony but a sovereign state in which the Governor-General had much greater independence than any colonial governor, for the Foreign Office regarded Sudan with indifference unless British imperial interests were specifically involved.

The termination of the Mahdist State did not end Mahdism or produce the pacification of the vast reaches of Sudan beyond the center whose inhabitants were ill-disposed to exchange the nominal authority of the

33

Source: Rosalind Caldecott, Sudan Archive, Durham University.

Map 4 Anglo-Egyptian Sudan

Khalifa for the *Turkiya al-thaniya* (the Second Turkiya), by which the Condominium government was known to the Sudanese. Mahdism re-emerged from time to time in the guise of several pretenders claiming to be the *al-Nabi Isa* (the Prophet Jesus) whose second coming was expected, according to Mahdist eschatology. These resurgences were easily contained, but they left a legacy of British distrust for Sudanese popular Islam throughout the Condominium. Although the government had little difficulty suppressing outbursts of religious fanaticism in the heartland of Sudan, the periphery remained for many years beyond its control. At the downfall of the Khalifa, 'Ali Dinar restored the old independent Fur sultanate, officially recognized by the Sudan government in 1900. Thereafter, he ruled with barbarous efficiency until the First World War, when he foolishly joined the Ottoman Turks in their *jihad* against Anglo-French infidels and renounced his allegiance to Khartoum. The Sudan government now had an excuse to launch a punitive expedition that defeated the Fur army before El Fasher in May 1916 and in November surprised and killed 'Ali Dinar, to incorporate Darfur into Sudan.

Southern Sudan, whose many different non-Arab, non-Muslim African ethnicities had been left alone during the Mahdiya, could not be occupied until the Sudd was made navigable in 1904 by *sudd*-clearing expeditions. Although the river now enabled military expeditions to reach the South, the conquest of southern Sudan was to take another thirty years, during which time administration was in the hands of British officers from the Egyptian army before a civil administration was firmly established in the 1930s. Seeking to build a bulwark against the spread of Islam, Lord Cromer in Egypt and Governor-General Sir Reginald Wingate in Sudan encouraged Christian missionaries to convert the southern Sudanese from their traditional religions to Christianity, teach them English, discourage the use of Arabic, and even prohibit the wearing of Arab clothing. The petty Arab merchants (*jallaba*) were promptly repatriated to the North, and in 1910 Wingate began the withdrawal of all Egyptian and northern Sudanese Muslim officers and troops from the South, replacing them with an Equatoria Corps, the "Equats", who consisted only of locally recruited southern Sudanese under British officers using English as the words of command, and who were strongly encouraged to adopt Christianity and Western dress.

Immediately after the end of the Mahdist State the administration of Sudan was carried out by British officers from the Egyptian army, but in 1905 Lord Cromer began the creation of a civilian Sudan Political Service (SPS) of able university graduates in good health and of good character, mostly from Oxford and Cambridge Universities, who were well compensated with pay, annual leave, and pensions. There were only some 400 members of the SPS throughout the fifty years of the Anglo-Egyptian Condominium, a ruling elite, most of whom were fluent in Arabic. The policy of leaving them to their own devices in remote outposts in northern Sudan fostered independent action and a paternalism bordering on condescension that often rendered them immune to criticism. The administrators in southern Sudan were a very different breed. They were contract military officers without pension known as the "Bog Barons," who ruled their satrapies by the power of panache, personality, persuasion, and prestige. They refused to learn Arabic, preferring to speak the local African languages of their subjects. In retrospect the sum of all these differences appeared to be a conscious "Southern Policy" promoting the separation of northern and southern Sudan, but in reality the British did not know what to do with southern Sudan, so that individual initiative, isolation, and ad hoc administrative decisions represented more a muddle than any coordinated and consistent policy.

The central government was controlled by the Governor-General; the only check on his independence came from the British Consul-General in Cairo or the Foreign Office in London, which happened rarely. The annual budget for Sudan had to be approved by the Egyptian Council of Ministers, but the subsidies paid by the Egyptian Treasury that had given the ministers an excuse to meddle in Sudanese affairs ended in 1913, when Wingate achieved a balanced budget. To supervise the administrative departments Wingate created three British secretaries – legal, financial, and civil – of which the civil secretary was the most powerful. He essentially acted as the Governor-General's chief of staff to whom each British *mudir* of the provinces reported, while they in turn supervised the British inspectors, called after 1922 district commissioners (DCs), usually assisted by Egyptian *mamurs*, who were gradually replaced by Sudanese after 1915. Education was promoted by the opening of the Gordon Memorial College in 1902 through public fund-raising in Britain to educate highly selected sons, mostly from the *awlad al-bahr*, to meet the clerical and accounting needs of the government.

Wingate, like the Turco-Egyptian Governors-General, strongly supported orthodox Islam for reasons of security and the containment of popular Islam. In 1910 he created a Board of Ulema with a hierarchy of orthodox officials who financed the construction of mosques and promoted the *khalwas* in which recitation of the Qur'an, not *sufi* rituals, was taught. In order to cultivate orthodox Muslims a parallel system to the Sudan Penal Code was implemented in the judiciary, whereby Muslims could settle personal and domestic disputes in the *sharia* courts supervised by the grand *qadi* at Khartoum. Agriculture was the foundation of Sudan's economy and the principal source of the government's revenue, but its development was retarded by an acute labor shortage. During the Mahdiya the population of

Figure 4 Students of the Gordon Memorial College gathered for an Armistice Day service as the head of the school reads the King's message, 1920–21.

northern Sudan had been reduced to only 2 million inhabitants. The dearth of labor clearly shaped the Sudan government's policy toward slavery. The slave trade was, of course, outlawed and its prohibition was enforced by the Slave Trade Repression Department, but the British were not about to precipitate a great social upheaval by sweeping decrees of emancipation. Any slave was granted manumission upon request, but slavery in a variety of forms was either ignored or tolerated.

As a consequence of the Egyptian revolution of 1919 British officials in Sudan had become deeply concerned about Egyptian subversion of the nascent class of Western-educated Sudanese who had rudimentary nationalist aspirations for Sudan, one of which was the unity of the Nile valley. When Lord Milner was sent to Cairo in 1919 to recommend the future constitutional relationship between Britain and Egypt, he firmly discouraged any recognition or expansion of this new educated class of Sudanese, who in the future would presumably inherit the administrative and judicial tasks of British officials. In their place Milner proposed a system of Indirect Rule, whereby the functions of governance would not descend to the educated Sudanese elite but be left to the traditional tribal authorities with a British resident to advise them. Indirect Rule had great appeal for many of the British officials in Sudan who had already established close relationships

Figure 5 Kordofan tribal court in session, c. 1930.

with the ruling chiefs, *shaykhs*, *nazirs*, and *'umdas*, the traditional leaders, and respected their judgments, which the rural Sudanese much preferred to the officious intrusion of an alien, educated Sudanese official, an *effendi*, or what some British officials disdainfully referred to as the "half-educated effendi."

As the official British colonial policy in Africa and particularly in Sudan, Indirect Rule "passed through three stages, the first as a useful administrative device, then that of a political doctrine, and finally that of a religious dogma."[1] The role of the local British district officers, presumably able to speak the vernacular language, would be as advisers only, interfering as little as possible in the conduct of tribal affairs and only introducing modern ideas, customs, and technology very gradually, so as not to upset the balance of traditional society, but preserve law and order, and ensure British rule. Moreover, Indirect Rule was government on the cheap, for it did not require costly Sudanese administrative officials, the *effendia*, and limited the very expensive British advisers to the small, affordable elite which the SPS had become. Some British officials even lyrically thought this attractive but regressive policy represented the *real* national feelings of the rural Sudanese in contrast to the rhetoric of post-war nationalism, and their view appeared corroborated when the Sudanese remained politically inert during the Egyptian revolution of 1919.

Figure 6 Leaders of the White Flag League posing in front of their banner, with the President of the League, 'Ali 'Abd al-Latif, sitting second from right.

Although the League of Sudan Union was founded in 1920 by the sons of prominent families and graduates of the Gordon Memorial College, its activities were confined to cultural events. Later it produced sporadic and anonymous anti-British circular letters but posed no serious challenge to British rule. During the war years and after the peace there ironically appeared a class of Muslim southerner Sudanese in the North who had severed their ethnic identity, acquired a smattering of education, and, having no northern traditional loyalties to constrain them, become actively hostile to British rule in Sudan. In May 1922 one such Muslim, 'Ali 'Abd al-Latif, a former Dinka army officer who had been cashiered for insubordination, published an article in *al-Hadara* demanding self-determination for Sudan but not unity with Egypt. He was imprisoned for "exciting disaffection," only to find himself a celebrity after his release from jail a year later. In 1923 he founded the White Flag League with financial and moral support from Egypt and Egyptians in Sudan, conveniently abandoned self-determination, and adopted the political slogan, Unity of the Nile Valley, which enabled the government to discredit him as a "half-educated" dupe of Egyptian politicians.

The League failed to attract a following, for it presupposed a sweeping reorganization of Sudanese society, but its activities convinced the growing class of educated Sudanese merchants, officials, and army officers with impeccable social pedigrees not to be pro-Egyptian but quietly to refuse any continuation of the Condominium. This class of *effendia* had been particularly disturbed in 1922 when the government, implementing Indirect Rule, ordered the promulgation of the Powers of Nomad Sheikhs Ordinance, and by 1923 the judicial powers of over 300 tribal *shaykhs* had been acknowledged, strengthened, and regularized. The ordinance visibly ignored the aspirations of those educated Sudanese in the government departments who were beginning to believe the illusion that they were the rightful heirs of their British rulers in Sudan.

In the early 1920s the introduction of Indirect Rule appeared to be the proper channel for Sudanese nationalism, for it conferred on the influential notables of the *sufi* orders and the Ansar greater authority to maintain the status quo against the new secular opposition. Sayyid 'Ali al-Mirghani of the Khatmiyya despised the White Flag League, as did Sayyid 'Abd al-Rahman, posthumous son of the Mahdi and spiritual leader of the Ansar. Both Sayyids personally detested 'Ali 'Abd al-Latif, but they skillfully manipulated his appeals for Unity of the Nile Valley to consolidate in the minds of their British masters that they were, in fact, the true representatives of the Sudanese who should receive the gratitude of the government, particularly when they had convinced their followers to support the British during the First World War. Ten years later, in 1924, they still preferred these same British officials to the new nationalists and employed all their considerable influence to prevent the Egyptians from attracting any mass following among the Sudanese.

During the spring and summer of 1924 anti-British demonstrations became more frequent and strident. 'Ali 'Abd al-Latif was imprisoned on 3 July, and on the 9th a revolt by the Railway Battalion of the Egyptian army had to be suppressed by British troops. More disturbing, however, was the mutiny in August of the Sudanese cadets from the Military School in Khartoum. They surrendered without a fight, their leaders were imprisoned, and the Military School promptly closed. All of these events gave greater credence for the "drastic action" demanded by Governor-General Sir Lee Stack, which became another excuse for his assassination on 19 November 1924 by an Egyptian nationalist, an act that enabled British officials to implement Plan E to evacuate the Egyptian army from Sudan. At the point of British machine-guns the Egyptian soldiers quietly boarded their trains without incident for repatriation to Egypt. The Sudanese officers of the Egyptian army were not so docile, however. Torn between their oath of allegiance to the king of Egypt and their British superior officers, units of the XIth Sudanese Battalion marched through the streets of Khartoum on 27 November, and when they refused to obey orders, British troops opened fire. The Sudanese hastily barricaded themselves in the military hospital and inflicted heavy casualties on the surrounding British troops, but were annihilated to the last man by artillery fire.

During the ten years following the crisis of 1924 Sudan experienced a dreary decade, characterized by the imposition of Indirect Rule within and the doleful impact of the Great Global Depression without. Firmly under British control, Sudan settled into a sonorous slumber. The farmers and herdsmen in their struggle for a subsistence living remained politically inert. The small group of radical proto-nationalists virtually vanished, while the more moderate members of the Western-educated elite sought to distance themselves from the radicals and, chastened by the recent display of British might, remained silently impotent. They quietly acquiesced in the relentless imposition of governance, known as Indirect Rule, that conferred legitimacy to rule upon the traditional tribal authorities who were the rivals, if not the opponents, of the Western-educated Sudanese for political power in Sudan. When Sir John Maffey was appointed Governor-General in 1926 he became the leading advocate for Indirect Rule and was ably abetted by Sir Harold MacMichael, who dominated the powerful civil secretariat from 1919 to 1934 in the expectation that the government's recognition of and support for the local, traditional authorities would guarantee the continuation of British overrule, hopefully thus neutralizing the growing influence of Sayyid 'Abd al-Rahman. In the vigorous pursuit of Indirect Rule the promulgation of the Powers of Sheikhs Ordinance in 1927 devolved the powers earlier bestowed on nomadic *shaykhs* in 1922 to the traditional *shaykhs* and chiefs of settled farming communities, dramatically transforming the administration of Sudan from geographically defined territorial units to the rulers of separate ethnic groups irrespective of administrative boundaries.

Unlike in the North the implementation of Indirect Rule in southern Sudan had farther-reaching goals, for the British were determined to assist the Christian missionaries to turn the tide against encroaching Islam. In 1922 the government promulgated the Passports and Permits Ordinance, which declared much of the South Closed Districts, thereby excluding the most effective proselytizers of Islam, the *jallaba* merchants. In the same year the British established chiefs' courts (*lukikos*) under the watchful eye of a British DC in an attempt to institutionalize the authority of southern chiefs. Gradually, the combination of all these ordinances and rudimentary

Figure 7 Group of Nuer chiefs at Meshra' Gwagol, captured in 1928 during a punitive
patrol against the Nuer, in retaliation for raids on the Dinka of Bor district.

institutions to exclude Muslims and Islam from the South, while isolating
southerners in what some critics contemptuously called an "anthropological
zoo," became known as Southern Policy. Unfortunately, in many southern societies the influential leaders, without which Indirect Rule could not
function, did not exist or were non-entities masquerading as chiefs, particularly among the populous Nilotic Dinka and the Nuer, whose numbers
were far in excess of the non-Nilotic farmers of Equatoria and their petty
chieftaincies. With their vast herds of cattle the Nilotes possessed no traditional rulers, no chiefs, only ritual specialists – leopard-skin chiefs of the
Dinka, the prophets among the Nuer. Their societies were organized by
"segmentary lineages" which settled disputes without the need or desire
for a single authority, a chief. With no single authority through which to
establish British control, let alone Indirect Rule, the Sudan government perceived no other option but force to convert the Nilotes to subjects, a process
which took over thirty years of punitive patrols. By the end of the 1920s the
Equatoria Corps had secured the subjugation of the Bahr al-Ghazal Dinka,
but the Nuer of the Upper Nile were quite another matter.

The Nuer were not only more elusive than the Dinka, disappearing into the great swamps of the Sudd or, when threatened, vanishing over the Ethiopian border, but they too had no chiefs, their prophets attracting large followings to raid the Dinka, now tax-paying subjects, for cattle and women and to defy the authority of the Sudan government. Consequently, British officers launched the conquest of Nuerland to eliminate the prophets, end raids against the Dinka, and enforce what came to be known as the "Nuer Settlement," "which is the building up of a native administration on the foundations of tribal customs and . . . even to the point of inventing an organization . . . when they have lost their own" – Indirect Rule.[2] Both in northern and southern Sudan eager British DCs began to seek out the traditional tribal rulers (an activity in which they often found themselves searching for lost tribes and vanished chiefs) in order to make Sudan safe for autocracy while limiting the growth of the Western-educated elite who, many British officials believed, would become a detribalized, discontented class contaminated by progressive ideas, like the Sudanese radicals of 1924, to threaten the British status quo.

Thus, in the North the government began to expand the number of primary schools of religious instruction, the *khalwas*, whose curriculum consisted of the rote memorization of the Qur'an, at the expense of government schools, *kuttabs*, teaching a secular curriculum. In southern Sudan education was provided by Christian missionaries who insisted as a crucial element in the government's Southern Policy that English be the lingua franca. Proficiency in English would be required for employment and promotion in government service in the South; Arabic and even colloquial Arabic slang were to be discouraged. By 1930 Indirect Rule, Closed Districts, and English as the language of education and government firmly set the course of Southern Policy and led to the relentless differentiation between northern and southern Sudan that, not surprisingly, has been widely interpreted by educated and politically conscious northern Sudanese as a deep, dark British plot to separate southern Sudan from the North. In fact, there never was any such conspiracy, for the British simply did not know what to do with southern Sudan, and until 1947 Southern Policy was characterized more by muddle, ad hoc decisions, and the failure of Indirect Rule than a conscious, agreed-upon policy rigorously applied.

If the years after 1924 were characterized by the assertion of complete British control and political retrenchment for the Sudanese, they were also years of unparalleled prosperity, much of which can be attributed to the Gezira Scheme launched in 1913 only to be stillborn until after the First World War, when it was resuscitated by additional guaranteed loans from

Figure 8 Construction of the Sennar Dam, which opened in 1926, showing the view
to the east.

London to construct an elaborate network of irrigation canals in the Gezira
and also the Sennar Dam to impound the Blue Nile waters for release by
gravity. The completion of the dam and the scheme by 1926 required a
new Nile waters agreement between Egypt and Sudan, namely the Anglo-
Egyptian Nile Waters Agreement of 1929, with its crucial clause permitting
the eventual expansion of the Gezira Scheme, which was managed by a
private company, the Sudan Plantations Syndicate, to organize the tenants
and market the cotton crop. The irrigated water was free of charge; 20
percent of the profits (from selling the cotton) went to the Syndicate, while
the government and tenants received 40 percent each, providing tenants
with a prosperity unknown to farmers in Sudan and a steady income for
the government. The enormous success of the scheme soon made it a
prototype for agricultural development in Africa and other growing projects
elsewhere.

Unfortunately, the years of prosperity did not last. The advent in 1929
of the Great Global Depression, which increased in severity during the
1930s, had serious repercussions in Sudan, whose economy was basically

dependent upon a single cash-crop, cotton, that was no longer in demand. Government revenue drastically collapsed by over 40 percent, which required severe retrenchment and economies in every government department, the principal burden of which fell upon the educated Sudanese. When the starting salary for graduates from the Gordon Memorial College, for whom the government was the principal employer, was slashed by 30 percent in 1931 the students went on strike. Although the government compromised and restored some of the cuts to end the strike, the settlement confirmed British suspicions about this rising educated class, on the one hand, and the fragile unity of the student strikers, on the other, which soon dissolved into two rival sectarian camps under the patronage of Sayyid 'Abd al-Rahman and Sayyid 'Ali al-Mirghani that were to haunt Sudan long after the British had departed in 1956.

Except for the student strike of 1931 the increasing numbers of politically active Sudanese remained quiescent despite the economic hardships of the Great Depression and the imposition of Indirect Rule, which left no political place for them in the administration of Sudan except as accountants and clerks. Political activism, radical causes, demonstrations, and strikes were replaced in these somnolent years by the appearance of study groups and literary societies which stressed the importance of education and cultivated greater political sophistication in their endless discussions and debates. Although carefully monitored by the British, these discussion clubs seemed perfectly harmless and were in fact a more positive outlet for the graduates' energies than demonstrating in the streets. Newspapers like *al-Nahda al-Sudaniyya*, *Mira't al-Sudan*, and *al-Sudan* flourished, but they were usually short-lived and their content was devoted more to poetry, short stories, and literary criticism than politics. The most popular and influential newspaper was *al-Fajr* (Dawn), with high standards of journalism and literary analysis that masked its editorials criticizing political developments. Unfortunately, *al-Fajr* failed to generate sufficient revenue and ended publication in 1937.

During these years British members of the SPS, many of whom had won the personal respect and confidence of their Sudanese subjects, genuinely supported the idea of Sudan for the Sudanese, a slogan that Sayyid 'Abd al-Rahman enthusiastically adopted but that many of his educated followers regarded as a subterfuge to ensure British hegemony, a view in which Egypt still appeared to be the only possible supporters of Sudanese nationalism. The result was a Sudanese ambivalence toward the Egyptians that vacillated between a visceral suspicion of Egypt and a belief that Egypt appeared to be their best hope to rid Sudan of its British masters. In 1935 this seeming contradiction was put to its first test.

In 1935 Benito Mussolini, the Fascist dictator of Italy commonly known as *Il Duce*, ordered the Italian army and air force to invade Ethiopia in revenge for their bitter defeat at the battle of Adua in 1896 and to fulfill Mussolini's grand design for a "New Rome" stretching from Tripoli, capital of the Italian colony of Libya, to Addis Ababa, soon to be the capital of the Ethiopian province of the new Italian empire. The one obstacle to the completion of the New Rome was the British presence in Sudan and Egyptian claims, which had never been renounced, of sovereignty over it. Both the British and Egyptians, in an unusual convergence of interests, agreed to cooperate to counter Italian aggression in northeast Africa. This was formalized by the Anglo-Egyptian Treaty of 1936, by which Britain secured its strategic interests at Suez and in the Nile valley, Egyptian claims to sovereignty in Sudan were respected, Egyptian troops would return to defend Sudan, and Egyptian immigration to Sudan would henceforth be unrestricted. No Sudanese had been consulted by either Britain or Egypt, and when the treaty was officially promulgated Sudanese moderate intellectuals regarded Article 11, that "the primary aim of their administration in the Sudan was the Welfare of the Sudanese," as yet another example of British arrogance and patronage. Those Sudanese who still looked to Egypt as the only possible ally in their nationalist cause were deeply embittered by the Egyptian sell-out to British interests.

The appointment of Sir George Stewart Symes as Governor-General of the Anglo-Egyptian Sudan in 1934 marked a watershed in British policy and administration in Sudan. He was aloof, opinionated, and pompous; many British officials in the SPS regarded him as little more than an opportunist, an advocate for reform who contemptuously dismissed criticism, which made him unpopular among the British partisans of Indirect Rule infatuated with tribal chiefs and *shaykhs*. He was quite prepared to forge a partnership with the Sudanese intellectual class, which presupposed a greater commitment to education and a thorough reform of administrative policy. All of this would cost money, but the worst of the Great Depression appeared over as the members of the SPS reluctantly and with severe misgivings began to gradually realize that they would have to come to terms with Sudanese nationalism.

NATIONALISM AND INDEPENDENCE, 1936–1956

In 1934 Governor-General Sir George Stewart Symes arrived in Khartoum with ambitious plans for reform that included the promotion of education, restructuring the administration, reconciliation with the moderate, educated Sudanese, and an end to Indirect Rule, all of which were only partially fulfilled when he departed in 1940, leaving behind in the peripheral regions of southern Sudan and Darfur little more than a barren legacy of neglect.

The powerful advocates of Indirect Rule in the SPS firmly believed that farmers and nomads did not require a literary education and that the need for a small, subordinate clerical class of Sudanese could be satisfied by teaching rudimentary English, more for communication than edification, and basic arithmetic to do sums for accountancy. There was, however, a core of British officials in Khartoum who realized that the introduction of a secular, Western curriculum could not be denied the Sudanese, and Symes gave them the authority for a thorough reform of education. In 1934 a new training college for elementary teachers was opened at Bakht al-Ruda, located on an isolated plain near Dueim. By 1936 schools of law, engineering, agriculture, and veterinary science had been approved and opened for students in a reformed Gordon Memorial College. A school of science followed in 1939, and one for the arts opened in January 1940.

Symes immodestly claimed credit for these reforms which were, in fact, very limited. In 1936 expenditure on education was still only 2.1 percent of the Sudan government's budget and lagged far behind that in other British colonies in Africa, which prompted the Foreign Office to request the De La Warr Educational Commission in East Africa to visit Sudan in 1937 and report. The Commission demanded a complete overhaul of education far beyond anything envisaged by Symes: teacher training colleges like Bakht al-Ruda should be established in every province and a new secondary school built, so that the Gordon Memorial College could be transformed from a secondary school into a college of higher learning. To implement the De La Warr report Christopher Cox from New College Oxford was installed as director of education. He drafted a comprehensive program to expand the number and proficiency of elementary school teachers, opened an intermediate school, and encouraged education for girls by establishing training centers to teach improved domestic skills. The *khalwas*, having failed miserably, were left to atrophy, while the *kuttabs* were to be transformed into intermediate schools. The year 1937 had indeed been a watershed in education in Sudan, but during the next twenty years before independence the reforms were implemented very slowly, and sometimes painfully. The technical schools were not integrated into a new Gordon Memorial College until 1945 and the Kitchener School of Medicine not until 1951, the same year that the Gordon Memorial College was renamed Khartoum University College as a sop to rising anti-colonial feelings.

Figure 9 Missionary sisters with some of their young pupils at a Roman Catholic mission
school in Wau in 1927.

Education in the South, like administration, presented unique problems
that were studiously ignored by the government during the 1930s and was
conveniently hidden behind the "grass curtain" of unsatisfactory missionary
education. Unlike in the North, Symes had no intention of spending any
money on the education of the southern Sudanese, whom he regarded with
contempt, and London saw no need to interfere in this wretched policy of
total neglect until 1936, when the Foreign Office suddenly discovered there
was not a single government school in the South and only two inspectors
of education to oversee missionary teachers, many of whom were more
interested in promoting Christianity than reading, writing, and arithmetic.
There had long been tensions between Catholic and Protestant missionaries
in the South, and in order to keep the peace the Sudan government had
arbitrarily imposed the "Sphere System," in which segregated Protestants
and Catholics could proselytize without fear of competition. Christopher
Cox was sent to report and strongly recommended that the time had come
for the government to support secular southern education, and in 1939 a
few inadequate grants-in-aid were made to the Church Missionary Society
(CMS) and the Verona Fathers, who readily agreed to open teacher training
centers run by professional educationalists, not missionaries.

If the British in Sudan could not prevent the commingling of education and politics, Symes and his civil secretary, Sir Angus Gillian, clearly perceived the end of Indirect Rule, also called "Native Administration," as the foundation for administration in Sudan. Except for a few remote nomads, supervision by tribal authorities, which was never defined by administrative boundaries, was quietly replaced by territorial units. In 1937 three far-reaching Local Government Ordinances were promulgated that reorganized the management of public affairs, not only in municipalities and towns, but in the rural areas as well. The downgrading of chiefs, *shaykhs*, and sultans could only be replaced by the expansion of the bureaucracy by educated Sudanese, who many members of the SPS had hitherto ignored or regarded with suspicion.

In February 1938 1,180 graduates from post-elementary schools throughout Sudan attended a gathering in Omdurman organized by Isma'il al-Azhari, a teacher of mathematics at the Gordon Memorial College and the president of the Omdurman Graduates' Club. With Azhari in the chair they set out to establish a Graduates' Congress to represent and promote the interests of educated Sudanese. The Congress elected a council of sixty which would decide policy; they in turn elected an executive committee of fifteen to manage the affairs of the Congress, which, unfortunately, represented the sectarian interests of those members who were followers of Sayyid 'Abd al-Rahman and Sayyid 'Ali al-Mirghani, who interjected into their deliberations a deep sectarian divide that ultimately doomed the organization. Acting on advice from British officials who favored the formation of such an association to represent the educated Sudanese, Isma'il al-Azhari, the first general secretary, composed an official letter to the government to explain that the concerns of the Congress were philanthropic, social, and those "matters of public interest involving the Government." He promised a "spirit of friendly co-operation and obedience to the requirements of law." The Congress has no "intention to embarrass the Government" and would refrain from any activities that could be construed as "incompatible" with the government's policy, but, he added, "we feel that the Government is aware of our peculiar position as the only educated element in this country and of the duties which we . . . feel to be ours." He specifically stated that the Congress did not claim to represent the Sudanese "in the fullest sense."[3]

This timid, if not obsequious, pledge that the members of the Congress would politically behave themselves was the price they perceived necessary to receive the blessing of the government, in which education became a safe and proper subject to find fault with the government. In July 1939 the

Graduates' Congress submitted a thoughtful report criticizing the government for the deplorable state of education in Sudan compared with that in its Arab and African neighbors, and demanding universal literacy, expansion at all levels of education, and the termination of "backward" mission education. The Congress was almost unanimous in its conviction that education was the keystone to promote the political process, a conviction that was widely held by members of the urban, literate Sudanese, many of whom were deeply involved in advancing their education themselves during their leisure hours as avid readers, and some of whom produced very sophisticated literary essays. British officials, whether liberal or reactionary, were very aware of the power of education but were helpless to keep politics and education separate, so that the classroom inevitably became political.

The fledgling Congress sorely needed the sanction of the government, and the civil secretary, Sir Angus Gillian, had realized that educated Sudanese needed a platform for their views, and so, in return for pledges "of friendly co-operation and obedience to the requirements of the law," he gave his assurance that the government would give the most careful consideration to the views of the Congress. During the next two years the moderate executive committee of fifteen, suspicious of the Egyptians, had increasingly alienated the younger progressives in the Congress, which came to a head when the Egyptian Prime Minister, 'Ali Mahir, visited Khartoum in February 1940. He hosted a tea party attended by over 100 graduates that provided an opportunity for the Congress president to proclaim the independence of the Congress from their British rulers and to express its hope of establishing close ties with Egypt and financial support for Congress social welfare projects. The Congress, now controlled by the followers of Sayyid 'Abd al-Rahman, began to fracture as the ranks of the Ansar themselves divided into the older, moderate members who remained loyal to the Sayyid and the younger, more radical members who resented his dominance and personal ambitions. The latter group, led by Isma'il al-Azhari and known as the Ashiqqa (*Ashiqqa'*, brothers by the same father and mother), sought to demonstrate their opposition to the Sayyid, challenge the British and Egyptian partners in the Condominium, and discredit the moderate members. They sent a respectful but provocative memorandum to the government on 3 April 1942 with twelve demands, most of which dealt with reasonable judicial and educational reforms, but they also insisted that at the first opportunity after the war "the British and Egyptian Governments [issue] a joint declaration, granting the Sudan . . . the right of self-determination . . . as well as guarantees assuring the Sudanese the right of determining their natural rights with Egypt in a special agreement between the Egyptian and Sudanese nations."4

The civil secretary, Sir Douglas Newbold, sent a crushing response on 29 July 1942 in which he not only dismissed the principal demands of the Congress but bluntly informed them that the wording and the effrontery to even submit their demands had "forfeited the confidence of the Government," a confidence that could only be restored if the Congress "confined itself to the internal and domestic affairs of the Sudan and renounce any claim, real or implied, to be the mouth piece of the whole country."5 Newbold's peremptory rebuff opened a window of opportunity for Azhari and his Ashiqqa to seize control of the Congress by amending its constitution to permit elementary school graduates, most of whom would support the radical Ashiqqa against the moderate followers of Sayyid 'Abd al-Rahman in a greatly expanded Congress. By 1943 Azhari had transformed the Ashiqqa into the first authentic Sudanese political party, whose platform was union with Egypt and whose slogan, the Unity of the Nile Valley, had great appeal for Sayyid 'Ali al-Mirghani, the taciturn leader of the Khatmiyya, which, historically, had been the principal supporter of Egypt in Sudan.

Sayyid 'Ali had grown increasingly apprehensive of the expanding power of his principal sectarian and religious rival, Sayyid 'Abd al-Rahman, and his Ansar, whom the British officials, in their whimsical passion for nicknames, dubbed SAR and SAM. Although personally conservative, he was now prepared to give his considerable influence and the support of his Khatmiyya to the more radical Ashiqqa in an alliance with Egypt in order to check the ambitions of Sayyid 'Abd al-Rahman to become king of an independent Mahdist Sudan, with (he presumed) the connivance of the British. For his part, Azhari desperately needed the Khatmiyya, for the Ashiqqa were relatively few in number and their radicalism was unattractive to many Sudanese, whereas the Khatmiyya were many, vociferous, and dominated the riverine *awlad al-bahr* and the nomads of northeast Sudan, and were particularly strong in the urban centers, while their Ansari rivals were relegated to the vast rural regions beyond the Nile. The Congress was now torn apart, exposing the chasm of sectarian interests between the historic secular and religious rivalries of Ansar and Khatmiyya and the ambition of the Sayyids that soon produced new political parties to fill the vacuum and protect sectarian interests.

In order to divert attention from the Congress and placate the growing concern felt by urban Sudanese for representation in governance the Advisory Council for northern Sudan Order of 1943 created a broader base than the narrow constituency which had constituted the Congress and included

Figure 10 Governor-General Sir Hubert Huddleston addressing the inaugural session of the Advisory Council for northern Sudan in May 1944. Sayyid ʿAli al-Mirghani and Sayyid ʿAbd al-Rahman al-Mahdi are seated at either end of the table.

twenty-eight ordinary members, eighteen of whom were selected from the newly created provincial councils, while the other ten were appointed by the Governor-General to reflect a variety of local social interest groups. The Advisory Council, in fact, was more symbolic than representative. True to its name, it was only advisory. Its agenda and the conduct of its discussions were fixed by the civil secretary. Its members chosen from the provincial councils were almost all tribal; the ten appointed by the Governor-General were all government civil servants. Politically minded Sudanese scoffed that its provincial members were ignorant rustics from the countryside turned into mere pawns of the government without any powers to make a difference. The Council was dismissed as a debating society by the growing number of alienated Sudanese who saw in its composition a conspiracy by the government to divide Sudan, for there was no member from the South. The Congress adamantly refused to participate in this charade and boycotted the Advisory Council, which lasted less than four years (1944–48) before being blown away by the winds of political change.

Sayyid ʿAbd al-Rahman was not one to remain idle in the face of the challenge from the Ashiqqa/Khatmiyya marriage of convenience. In 1945 his supporters founded the Umma Party (*umma*, nation, but the word also conveyed the idea of the community of Islam) under the patronage of the Sayyid and with a platform of complete independence for Sudan. Despite the appeal of an independent Sudan, the Umma had to confront two major disadvantages. It made no secret of its willingness to cooperate with the government to work together toward independence, which gave them the appearance of being tools of British imperialism, while the personal ambitions of Sayyid 'Abd al-Rahman compromised a large number of his moderate supporters who were not Ansari. By 1945 the sectarian rivalry between Sayyid 'Ali and Sayyid 'Abd al-Rahman had turned implacable, making any reconciliation impossible and escalating the hostility between Ansari and Khatmi. Nowhere did this sectarian rivalry become more manifest and bitter than in the deliberations of the Congress between the Ashiqqa/Khatmiyya unionists and the Umma/Ansar secessionists, which came to a head in April 1945. When the Congress executive committee sent its demands to the acting Governor-General for the British and Egyptian governments, the co-domini of the 1899 Condominium Agreement, to agree on a Sudanese government in union with Egypt and in alliance with Britain, its president, Isma'il al-Azhari, took the liberty in his covering letter of defining "union" as "union with Egypt under the Egyptian Crown."[6] In fury the Umma openly denounced Azhari and his Ashiqqa, boycotted the forthcoming Congress elections, and the Congress disintegrated. It had never represented the Sudanese, and nothing ever came of its plans for educational and economic development, leaving no program of reform or development for the emerging political parties other than "union" or "independence."

At the end of the Second World War Egypt and Great Britain embarked upon contentious negotiations to revise the Anglo-Egyptian Treaty of 1936 that were aborted over the future status of Sudan, euphemistically known as the Sudan Question. Egypt subsequently referred the matter in July 1947 to the United Nations, but it was ultimately withdrawn by the UN secretary-general and left unresolved. The bitter, long, and tortuous debate over the Sudan Question convinced the British in Sudan they must expedite and broaden their rudimentary proposals for Sudanese participation in the administration of the country in order to build a Sudanese bastion against Egyptian pretensions. On 17 April 1946 Governor-General Sir Hubert Huddleston had assured the Advisory Council that the "Sudanese will soon be governing their own country." Five days later the government announced the formation of an Administration Conference to recommend the "next steps in associating the Sudanese more closely with the administration of the country." After nearly a year of deliberation the first and seminal report of the conference was submitted on 31 March 1947, recommending the creation of a legislative assembly to represent the whole of Sudan, including the South, and to replace the Advisory Council, and an executive council in which half its members would be Sudanese. This produced a difficult dilemma for the Sudan government which, in the nearly fifty years of its existence, had never known what to do about southern Sudan. In 1946 nothing had changed, but the government could no longer procrastinate over defining the relationship between northern and southern Sudan.

By 1935 the administration of the South had been shaped by what was unofficially known and frequently misunderstood as Southern Policy, to protect the southern Sudanese from the external and alien influences of Arabic and Islam, which would undermine their traditional cultures, to prevent the expansion of Islam, and to promote the success of Indirect Rule. During the years of Southern Policy education had failed miserably. Many members of the SPS in the South, like their colleagues in the North, were deeply suspicious of the "half-educated" Sudanese as potential rivals to the traditional leaders they were committed to support so that Indirect Rule could function. The introduction of the "sphere system," by which the government had arbitrarily separated Catholic from Protestant missions to avoid religious friction, had transferred ancient European sectarian rivalries into southern schools and often generated unpleasant religious rivalry among the students.

In less than a year after his arrival in Khartoum Symes sought to define his policy in southern Sudan with particular reference to Southern Policy in a memorandum of 9 June 1935 that shortly proved to be a bundle of contradictions. As part of his progressive dismantling of Indirect Rule, Symes railed against the secrecy of Southern Policy, designed exclusively to isolate the South from Arab and Islamic influence by a "Chinese Wall" that should be replaced by free access for all to the lands beyond the rivers of southern Sudan, which would enable tribal institutions to evolve by economic development. Instead of pursuing these ideals, however, his ill-disguised disdain for what Sir Harold MacMichael, the powerful Civil Secretary, called the "Serbonian Bog" made them impossible to achieve. Symes was skeptical whether economic development alone could overcome the endemic backwardness of southern Sudan, and in order to reduce the perpetual annual southern deficit he slashed administrative costs by amalgamating provinces and eliminating "non-essential services", instituting a policy of "care and maintenance" which made a mockery of his pious pronouncements to abandon Southern Policy, open the South to outsiders, and give them free access to trade.

In the name of economy and efficiency, Symes first began to dismantle the small but effective administration in the South by amalgamating, with disastrous results, the two large provinces of Equatoria and the Bahr al-Ghazal in 1936 into one vast, sprawling administrative unit consisting of 160,000 square miles inhabited by 1 million people dispersed in a myriad tribes and languages with one DC for every 50,000 people. Virtually abandoned by Khartoum and isolated by geography, the Bog Barons devised ingenious and idiosyncratic innovations to meet the needs of their people that had little relevance to the doctrines of Indirect Rule. The introduction of the chiefs' courts in the South had been regarded as a major building-block of Indirect Rule, but in some courts the British DC often became the chief, while in others he restrained his judicial instincts, to become a bemused observer of a dysfunctional institution. Moreover, the search for a chief, particularly among the Dinka and the Nuer, had often proved to be a frustrating experience, for an appointed "government" chief was often ostracized by his fellow headmen, who regarded themselves as his equal. By the end of the decade Indirect Rule in the South had largely disappeared as an instrument of Native Administration, not by any fiat issued from Khartoum, but from the realities on the ground that relentlessly undermined it.

In 1940 Sir Stewart Symes was replaced by Sir Hubert Huddleston, and during the ensuing war years southern Sudan slipped into a quiescent period that could no longer be ignored after the submission in March 1947 by the Sudan Administrative Conference of its first report, which recommended a single elected legislative assembly for the whole of Sudan, forcing the government finally to declare its intentions for the forgotten South. By the summer of 1946 the Civil Secretary, Sir James "Willie" Robertson, had concluded in an official and secret memorandum of 16 December 1946 that the time had come for a southern policy "acceptable to, and eventually workable by, patriotic and reasonable Sudanese, Northern and Southern alike." Sudan would remain one, the South being "inextricably bound for future development to the Middle Eastern and Arabized Northern Sudan and therefore to assure that there should be educational and economic development and be equipped to stand up for themselves in the future socially, economically, as equal partners of the Northern Sudan and the Sudan of the future."[7]

Robertson's memorandum was widely distributed and was, at first, well received by British officials in the South, until they learned that the Sudan Administrative Conference meeting in January 1947 had proposed a legislative assembly to represent the whole of the country, which Robertson

Figure 11 Four Nuer local government officials, prior to a low-level flight
over the central Nuer district in 1947, and including on the left Buth Diu,
later one of the first southern members of the Legislative Assembly.

fully endorsed. They now vehemently argued that the southerners had not
been consulted and demanded specific safeguards for the South in any
ordinance establishing a legislative assembly. Robertson was taken aback,
and to mollify his own people in the Bog agreed to call a conference in
Juba to solicit southern Sudanese opinion. The Juba Conference was held
on 12–13 June 1947 in the Juba cinema. There were two crucial issues on

the agenda – southern participation in the proposed legislative assembly and the creation of safeguards against any legislation by a Sudanese legislative assembly that might hinder "the social and political advancement of the South." Seventeen southerners and three northern representatives were selected, including the ardent nationalist, Judge Muhammad Salih Shingeiti.

During the first day virtually all of the southern representatives argued that the South was not yet ready to participate in any legislative assembly, for "children must drink milk before they eat *kisra*," but during the long evening that followed Judge Shingeiti used his persuasive personality to intimidate and convince the educated southern representatives to change their minds, threatening that "if they did not do so they would have no say in the future Government of the Sudan."[8] The next day they were all emphatic that indeed the South must send representatives to the legislative assembly of a united Sudan, and the conference came to an end. In Sudanese mythology the Juba Conference is considered the critical event that forged the unity of Sudan by a conscious decision of the southern representatives, but in fact it simply provided a patina of legitimacy to the decisions for a united Sudan made by Robertson in December 1946 and reaffirmed in February 1947. The secretary to the conference, M. F. A. Keen, succinctly expressed the ill-disguised relief of the British officials from Khartoum: "If the Southerners had said they did not want to go with the North, we would not really have known what to do with the South."[9]

The educated southerners were obviously going to derive personal benefit from their support of Robertson's policy for a united Sudan, but the devil was in the details, the most contentious of which were safeguards "to ensure the healthy and steady development of the Southern peoples." Without them the southerners would be overwhelmed, to become the hewers of wood and the drawers of water for a supposedly superior northern aristocracy. The northern Sudanese and the Egyptians believed that under no circumstances should the South have any special treatment such as safeguards. Robertson believed that the inclusion of specific safeguards in the Legislative Assembly Ordinance would doom it to failure, the Governor-General's power of veto being quite sufficient to protect southern interests. By May 1948 safeguards had become a dead issue, however. The northern Sudanese were much too engrossed in promoting the Unity of the Nile Valley or independence to give any serious consideration as to how to make a unified Sudan a reality. The southern Sudanese continued to bask in their isolation, most of them remaining oblivious to the implications for them of the Juba Conference.

Having ostensibly secured the wish of the southerners to be included in the new legislative assembly, Robertson submitted the draft legislation to the British and Egyptian governments. After many months of delay caused by Egyptian intransigence and anxiety at the British Foreign Office, the Advisory Council in Khartoum unanimously approved the Executive Council and Legislative Assembly Ordinance on 3 March 1948. The first Legislative Assembly of Sudan met on 15 December 1948. It was composed of seventy-five members, ten of whom were nominated, the remainder being divided between fifty-two northerners, ten chosen by direct elections and forty-two indirectly by provincial electoral colleges; thirteen seats were specifically reserved for southerners. Since those advocating union with Egypt, the unionists, boycotted the elections and the number of Sudanese voting (particularly in the rural areas) was very small, sectarian interests were paramount to the outcome. Consequently, the well-organized Umma Party won an overwhelming number of seats, twenty-six, and could count on the support of four from the Independence Front, which enabled it to elect their party leader, 'Abdallah Khalil, Speaker of the Assembly. The remaining forty-four of the seventy-five consisted mostly of individuals whose election had been influenced more by Sudanese officials and tribal *shaykhs* than any party interests. Indeed, the assembly could hardly claim to be a representative body when all of its members were bound by close ties to religious or tribal notables, merchants, or government officials who were leaders of small, elite groups masquerading as political parties and dependent for the most part on the patronage of SAR or SAM, whose sectarian interests made a sham of any pretence at parliamentary democracy.

The unrepresentative composition of the Legislative Assembly, the dominance of the Umma, the absence of the Khatmiyya and its educated urban unionists, and the fact that it had spent an inordinate amount of time on petty procedural matters soon produced demands for its reconstitution. From their seemingly impregnable position in the assembly the Umma became increasingly insistent on their Sayyid's demands for immediate self-government, to which the government disingenuously responded that the assembly was too unrepresentative to render such a momentous decision. In March 1950 the Khatmiyya newspaper, *Saut al-Sudan*, published a series of articles proposing to reform the assembly by direct elections and to eliminate tribal *shaykhs*, whereupon the assembly would elect the executive council and remove its British members. Meanwhile, the disunited unionists, the Liberal Ashiqqa and the Ahrar Ittihadiyyin Party patched up their petty and personal differences to form a National Front that advocated self-government under the Egyptian crown instead of complete unification, a position which the inscrutable Sayyid 'Ali al-Mirghani could passively support.

On 16 November 1950 King Faruq opened the Egyptian parliament with a speech from the throne in which he intimated that Egypt would unilaterally abrogate not only the Condominium Agreement of 1899 but the Anglo-Egyptian Treaty of 1936. Sayyid 'Abd al-Rahman and the Umma intensified their vociferous demands for immediate self-government, and on 15 December 1950 the Umma majority forced through the assembly a resolution that passed by only one vote, 39–38, demanding that Britain and Egypt grant self-government by the end of 1951. The Egyptians were furious; the British were delighted, for it virtually isolated the unionists and provided them with the opportunity to support a previous motion recommending a commission to amend the Legislative Assembly Ordinance and restructure the assembly. A Constitutional Amendment Commission consisting of thirteen Sudanese and chaired by a British constitutional expert, Judge Stanley-Baker, duly began its deliberations on 22 April 1951. Six months later the Egyptian government retaliated by abrogating the Anglo-Egyptian treaties of 1899 and 1936, declaring a unified Egypt and Sudan under one king, and unilaterally unveiling a constitution for Sudan, all without consulting the Sudanese.

The Sudan government and all the Sudanese parties except the Ashiqqa peremptorily rejected this new Egyptian constitution, and the Legislative Assembly approved on 22 April 1952 a Self-Government Statute. The new government of Sudan was to consist of a council of Sudanese ministers, including a ministry for the South, responsible to a chamber of deputies of eighty-one members, most of whom were indirectly elected, and a senate of fifty, twenty appointed by the Governor-General and thirty chosen by electoral colleges in the provinces. The Governor-General became the Supreme Constitutional Authority, but his powers of veto were now limited to legislation affecting external affairs, public services, and the South. After three months of frustration, during which the British government had, under increasing pressure from the United States, sought a formula acceptable to the Egyptians concerning the sovereignty of Sudan, the Sudan Question suddenly became moot when, on 23 July, King Faruq was overthrown by the Revolutionary Command Council of young Egyptian officers led by General Muhammad Neguib, who was half-Sudanese and educated in Sudan, where he enjoyed considerable popularity.

Although the urban Sudanese, British, and Egyptians were obsessed after the war with political change and the accelerating march to self-government and ultimately independence, there were dynamic, if less evocative, transformations of the Sudanese economy that created new problems that the staid British officials in Sudan were personally and emotionally ill-equipped to manage. The insatiable post-war demand for cotton sent the price and consequently government revenue soaring, which produced large budget surpluses previously unknown to impecunious Sudan governments. A modest five-year development program was launched in 1946, to be followed by a much more ambitious plan for 1951–56 made possible by King Cotton. Sudan Railways were extended to Damazin and Nyala, new steamers were ordered, and Sudan Airways was established. Education and health received unprecedented funding, including the Gordon Memorial College and a new hospital in Khartoum. Considerable sums were spent on electrification, rural water supplies, and projects in the Gezira and the long-neglected southern Sudan.

In 1949 the Sudan Plantations Syndicate concession expired, to be replaced by an appointed Gezira Board to add another million feddans of irrigated cotton by 1953, plan for the mammoth Managil Extension, and Sudanize its staff from the overflowing cotton cornucopia. The enormous post-war success of the Gezira inspired the government to embrace a showpiece of development in the South which hopefully would deflect northern criticism of the government's neglect. "An Experiment in the Social Emergence of Indigenous Races in Remote Regions," a comprehensive scheme for development in isolated southwest Equatoria called the Zande Scheme, was to make the Azande self-sufficient by growing cotton and exporting manufactured cotton cloth, and was to be accompanied by improved roads, new schools, and an array of social services.

It remains unclear to this day if the Zande Scheme would have been a success if the government had not eviscerated much of the original comprehensive proposal, preferring to achieve projected profits rather than to make the Azande self-sufficient. In order to produce cotton economically 50,000 Azande were relocated from their beloved, sequestered *tukls* and resettled along the roads in large villages, where they were allocated plots and forced to grow cotton or labor on the roads. The Azande might have tolerated this dramatic upheaval in their way of life if they had been paid adequate wages, but they were so low that the distinction between free and forced labor was hopelessly blurred. By 1955 Zandeland was seething with open discontent, and on 25 July riots erupted in the textile mill town of Nzara. Less than a month later the mutiny of the Southern Corps in Torit ignited the conflagration that swept through the South and from which the Zande Scheme never recovered, adding yet another bitter case of injustice to the growing list of southern grievances on the eve of independence.

The substantial revenues generated by the demand for Sudanese food-stuffs during the Second World War had also produced a debilitating inflation to which the rural farmers were largely immune but which relentlessly eroded the standard of living of the relatively small but irreplaceable urban workers, whose wages were insufficient to compensate for rising costs. The price of staples like *dura* had doubled and continued to rise from the inflationary effect of the large amounts of government revenue from cotton injected into the economy. Low wages and high inflation spawned the birth of the Sudanese organized labor movement centered in Atbara, at the sprawling headquarters, machine shops, and rail yards of Sudan Railways, which employed some 20,000 workers. In June 1946 the skilled workers organized themselves into a Workers' Affairs Association (WAA), which had only won legal recognition from the government, however, after a strike on 13 July 1946 which was supported by over half the railway workforce and required ten days of mediation to be settled. A second three-day strike in January 1948 was followed by a third on 16 March, paralyzing the rail and steamer services until 18 April, when the government grudgingly approved only modest raises, which left a residue of hostility and suspicion between labor and government that came to characterize future labor relations in Sudan.

Seeking to recover from its dilatory and inept recognition that the labor movement was an economic and political force, the government passed a spate of labor legislation between 1948 and 1952, the most important of which was the Trade Union Ordinance of 1948, which gave legal recognition to registered unions. Within four years over 100 unions were registered, but most were small and soon disappeared. The survivors joined together in an umbrella Workers' Congress which in 1950 became the Sudan Workers' Trade Union Federation (SWTUF), dominated by the Sudan Railway Workers' Union (SRWU). By 1951 the SRWU had over 17,000 members, and by 1953 some 100,000 Sudanese belonged to unions within the SWTUF, which became increasingly more involved in its political goals – the end of British imperialism and self-determination for Sudan – than the terms of employment from which it had derived its legitimacy. In April 1952, however, the SWTUF overplayed its hand by calling a general strike which failed miserably and provided an excuse for the government in October to sever all contacts with the federation. Thereafter, the government negotiated the terms of employment with individual unions, no longer the SWTUF, which seriously undermined the federation as the representative of organized Sudanese labor. When the SWTUF denounced the Anglo-Egyptian Agreement of February 1953, which granted self-government and self-determination to the Sudanese, the federation isolated itself from the mass of Sudanese workers, who failed to respond to the SWTUF call for a general strike to protest the agreement. The SWTUF admitted its humiliating defeat, abandoned the strike, and never recovered from this rebuff. As the leaders of the SWTUF became increasingly involved in the Sudanese Movement for National Liberation, their original objectives to wrest better conditions for organized labor had become hopelessly compromised by political ambitions which dragged them into the sectarian rivalry of the Sayyids, losing all touch with the interests of the rank and file and hence their legitimacy and credibility to lead organized labor.

After becoming Egyptian prime minister on 7 September 1952 General Neguib and his fellow revolutionary officers adopted an entirely new course in Egyptian–Sudanese relations. They promptly discarded the slogan Unity of the Nile Valley and approached the Sudanese political parties, particularly Sayyid ʿAbd al-Rahman and the Umma, to call Britain's bluff by winning their support for the complete independence of Sudan. On 10 January 1953 Major Salah Salam signed the Political Parties Agreement with all the Sudanese parties by which Egypt agreed to self-determination and Sudanization within three years, an international commission to assume the powers of the Governor-General, and an electoral commission to supervise parliamentary elections. All foreign troops were to be withdrawn before self-determination. Safeguards for the South were studiously – and ominously – ignored. The game was over, pre-empted by the revolutionary Egyptian government with which neither Britain nor the Sudan government had cards to play at the negotiating table. On 12 February 1953 a new Anglo-Egyptian Agreement was signed in which most of the Egyptian proposals were retained. The Sudanese parties were jubilant; British officials were desolate. All, however, was not settled, for the February agreement had failed to resolve the crucial Sudan Question, the ultimate sovereignty of Sudan, union with Egypt or independence.

The international Electoral Commission, composed of a British, Egyptian, American, and three Sudanese commissioners to supervise the elections for the new assembly and senate, held its first meeting on 9 April 1953 and thereafter worked methodically to organize the parliamentary elections. If the February agreement had shaken the very foundations of British rule in Sudan, the November elections were an unmitigated catastrophe. While Sayyid ʿAli al-Mirghani quietly pledged the support of his Khatmiyya followers to the National Unionist Party (NUP) led by Ismaʿil al-Azhari, a

Figure 12 Policemen supervising voters at a polling station in Juba, during the first general election for self-government in 1953.

dysfunctional campaign for the Umma was run by Sayyid ʿAbd al-Rahman and his politically inept son, Sayyid Siddiq. They foolishly failed to forge an alliance for independence with the like-minded Socialist Republican Party (SRP), which isolated the Umma and converted a democratic election into a sectarian battle between the two Sayyids. No one, British or Sudanese, had predicted the NUP landslide when the results were announced on the morning of 30 November. The NUP swept fifty-one of the ninety-seven seats in the House of Representatives, a clear majority, the Umma trailing with only twenty-two and the SRP with a dismal three. The New Southern Party captured ten. In the Senate the NUP victory was even more pronounced, winning twenty-two of thirty-three elected seats; the Umma was left with only a humiliating seven seats, the other parties eleven. The pattern of voting was strictly along sectarian lines, with the exception of the South, where educated candidates were few. The NUP had promptly turned this vacuum to their advantage by running candidates, distributing cash, and winning three southern seats and the allegiance of other southern independents by bribery and worthless promises.

The sweeping victory by the NUP stunned the SPS, still in shock from the Anglo-Egyptian Agreement the previous February. They had failed to interpret the underlying motives of the Sudanese to whom they had devoted their careers and whom they believed with great pride they knew intimately. In fact, they were out of touch with their subjects. The massive Sudanese vote for the NUP was not an endorsement of unity with Egypt, as the British wrongly believed, but a repudiation of their stewardship. The unionists had never been able to articulate what form union should take, which had confused the voters, and when Sayyid 'Ali quietly threw his support behind the NUP, he had no intention of union with Egypt – only of ridding Sudan of the British. By 1953 the Sudanese had lost any enthusiasm for the Unity of the Nile Valley, and the vast majority who voted for the NUP sought to achieve two objectives: an end to the Anglo-Sudan government and any resurgence of its perceived ally, Sayyid 'Abd al-Rahman and Mahdism.

Isma'il al-Azhari swiftly formed a government in January, but the grand ceremonial opening of parliament was delayed until 1 March to allow the government to organize itself and prepare appropriate celebrations and a state visit by General Neguib to commemorate the event, which provided Sayyid 'Abd al-Rahman the opportunity to release his suppressed fury and frustration at his humiliating defeat and to demonstrate his hostility to union with Egypt and animosity toward the NUP and its patron. He sent word to his supporters in the countryside to march on Khartoum. Some 50,000 agitated Ansar appeared to welcome Neguib, but riots erupted when they tried to storm the Palace, killing ten policemen, including their British commandant who was hacked to death. Troops were rushed to the scene and opened fire to disperse the crowd, killing some twenty civilians. After intense pressure from British officials in the Palace Sayyid 'Abd al-Rahman ordered his followers to go home, the celebrations were cancelled, General Neguib hastily returned to Cairo, and order was restored.

The Khartoum riots soon became the catalyst that convinced Sudanese of every political persuasion that independence was the only viable option. When the popular General Neguib was overthrown by Gamal 'Abd al-Nasser, who was regarded with deep suspicion by younger Sudanese, disenchantment with Egypt deepened, symbolized by the rapid Sudanization that followed the installation of the Azhari government. The Anglo-Egyptian Agreement had stipulated a Sudanization Committee, which was quickly constituted in February 1954 with a majority of NUP members. It proceeded with the wholesale replacement of British officials, made less painful by generous compensation and pensions which, the Sudanese argued, were cheaper than an armed and costly insurrection to win freedom from British imperialism. On 17 December 1954 the last member of the SPS, Sir Gwain Bell, the civil secretary, boarded a steamer at Port Sudan to sail into the sunset.

The sweeping Sudanization by the NUP evoked criticism not only in Britain but also in Sudan as being reckless and spiteful, yet despite the extremely close and warm relationships between British officials and individual Sudanese, the former were no longer wanted as rulers, and if they had to go, the sooner the better for both – except for the southern Sudanese. Approximately 800 British and Egyptian posts were Sudanized, but only six southerners were appointed to junior administrative posts in the South, all the others being allotted to northern Sudanese, including the officers of the Equatorial Corps. The NUP members of the Sudanization Committee, ignoring the demands of their southern members, employed the same argument that the British had used for decades – there were no qualified southerners – which was a recipe for disaster. Gregoria Denk Kir, a southern merchant in Gogrial, summed up the bitter feelings that swept through the South: "Well, as it appears, it means our fellow Northerners want to colonize us for another hundred years."[10]

The tragedy of this decision assumes even greater magnitude, for despite all the historic cultural, ethnic, racial, and religious differences between the northern and southern Sudanese or the legacy of the slave trade, this ignorant and insensitive decision could have been avoided. No one in 1954 could undo the introduction of Christianity and English into the South. No one in 1954 could wave the magic wand of economic development to transform the South into a cornucopia of productivity. No one in 1954 could provide instant education; there is no such thing. But in 1954, by heeding the warnings from southern members of the NUP in parliament, by taking into account aspirations, not simply civil service exams, by demonstrating the unity of the nation and honoring lavish election promises, by including all of its participants, North and South, the government of Isma'il al-Azhari, by specific action visible to all southerners, could have taken a decisive step unimpeded by the weight of history, elevated by the optimism of a new beginning for Sudan, and within the abilities of men untrammeled by any cosmic forces beyond their control, to include the southern Sudanese in the administration of the new nation. They failed and within the year reaped the bitter seeds of insurgency they had sown.

On 18 August 1955, No. 2 Company of the Southern Corps, formerly the Equatorial Corps, stationed at its headquarters in Torit, broke ranks, rushed the arms depot, seized rifles and ammunition, and proceeded to run amok methodically killing all northerners – officers, merchants, women, and

Figure 13 Independence Day celebrations at the Kitchener statue in Khartoum,
1 January 1956.

children. Rumbles of southern discontent had begun soon after the results
of Sudanization were announced in October 1954 and became increasingly
bitter as inexperienced, alien northern Sudanese who knew literally nothing about the southern Sudanese – ethnicity, culture, language – assumed
administrative posts in the South. The Liberal Party, formerly the Southern
Party, sought to convene a conference in Juba to mobilize the widespread
discontent with Sudanization and demand a federal system for an independent Sudan which Azhari adroitly frustrated by a retroactive pay raise,
but by summer 1955 southern discontent had began to turn ugly, and when
the MP for Yambio in Zandeland was arbitrarily sentenced to twenty years
in prison on 25 July 1955, a huge demonstration was dispersed only after
the troops used tear gas. The following day Zandeland erupted with riots
at Nzara, the center of the Zande Scheme, and its textile mill, which were
dispersed when the police fired into the crowd, killing eight.

Rumors of further northern reprisals were rampant throughout the South
but particularly among the garrison at Torit, about to leave for Khartoum,
whose southern troops had become convinced that upon arrival in the
capital they would be enslaved or massacred, a rumor that seemed confirmed
by the hasty evacuation of the wives and families of their northern officers.
The mutiny of the Southern Corps at Torit on the 18 August spread like
wildfire before the rains. In all the major towns in Equatoria northern
officials and civilians were indiscriminately killed. Northern officials fled

Figure 14 Prime Minister Sayyid Isma'il al-Azhari (right) and Sayyid Muhammad Ahmad Mahjub, leader of the opposition, raising the Sudanese flag outside of the former Governor-General's palace, 1 January 1956.

from Wau, leaving control in the hands of the southern police, and in Malakal disturbances left six dead. When the British firmly refused to intervene it was not until 31 August that northern troops hastily flown into the South were able to restore order. Some 336 were known dead, 261 of whom were northerners. Most of the mutineers absconded into the bush; several surrendered, were tried, and executed. When the first northern troops cautiously entered Torit, it was completely empty, but the eerie silence hung in the air as a fateful omen for the beginning of a half-century of bloody, unrelenting civil war between northern and southern Sudanese in the valley of the upper Nile.

The departure of the British had removed all doubt from the minds of many members of the NUP, including Sayyid 'Ali al-Mirghani and perhaps even al-Azhari himself, that there was any further need for an Egyptian Connection. By the summer of 1955 few Sudanese were still supporters of union with Egypt, particularly after Salah Salam urged Egyptian military intervention during the "Southern Sudan Disturbances," as the debacle at

Torit was euphemistically called, and Azhari began to devise a means by which to circumvent the rather cumbersome procedures to achieve self-determination stipulated in the 1953 Anglo-Egyptian Agreement. By the end of November 1955 Azhari had outmaneuvered all his opponents, only to be favored by a stroke of good fortune. On 3 December 1955, for the first time in over a decade, the two Sayyids met in public to patch up their differences in order to achieve immediate independence, to be followed by a coalition government. Azhari had little choice but to agree, and on 19 December 1955 the House of Representatives unanimously voted to declare Sudan independent; the Senate followed with a similar motion on the 22nd. On 1 January 1956, at a hastily improvised ceremony, a proud Isma'il al-Azhari, "father of the new Sudan," lowered the flags of Egypt and the United Kingdom and gracefully raised the three horizontal stripes of red, white, and black of the flag of the new Republic of Sudan. The Condominium was over.

CHAPTER 3

Parliamentary and military experiments in government, 1956–1969

THE FIRST PARLIAMENTARY AND MILITARY GOVERNMENTS

The Sudanese reaction to Azhari raising the new Sudanese flag on 1 January 1956 was detached and subdued, an anti-climax to the intense sectarian politics of self-government. Ironically, Isma'il al-Azhari's declaration of independence rendered him expendable. Sayyid 'Ali al-Mirghani no longer required the marriage of convenience between his Khatmiyya and the Ashiqqa. In June 1956 twenty-one members of the coalition government, with the blessing of Sayyid 'Ali, who had never been comfortable with Azhari's political secularism, defected to form the People's Democratic Party (PDP) in another alliance of convenience with the Umma to defeat Azhari on 5 July 1956 by the decisive no-confidence vote of sixty to thirty-two and elect 'Abdallah Khalil, secretary-general of the Umma Party, prime minister. Unfortunately, the momentary reconciliation between the two Sayyids could not last, for the personal ambitions of Sayyid 'Abd al-Rahman, firmly supported by the Umma, on the one hand, and the orientation toward revolutionary Egypt by the PDP by Sayyid 'Ali, on the other, soon deteriorated into a raging altercation exacerbated by petty personal squabbles, deep mutual distrust, and the intransigence of sectarian rivalry that characterized the brief two-year rule of the Umma/PDP coalition, 1956–58.

The desultory state of parliamentary politics was accompanied by a dramatic downturn in the economy after the buoyant prosperity during the last years of the Condominium. Most of the members of the coalition government were economically conservative, quite content to follow the development policy of its predecessor based on a single crop, cotton, despite its vulnerability in world markets. In 1956 the excavation of canals for the Managil Extension of the Gezira Scheme was proceeding on schedule for completion in 1961–62 on the naïve assumption that the world demand for cotton could never be satisfied. In 1957 and 1958, however, a sudden depression in global commodity markets, combined with the government's

Figure 15 Sayyid 'Abd al-Rahman al-Mahdi presenting the sword of honor to 'Abd Allah Khalil, prime minister 1956–58.

stubborn and rigid policy of maintaining a high fixed minimum price, rendered Sudanese cotton uncompetitive, creating a huge accumulation of unsold cotton and a drastic depletion of Sudan's currency reserves from £S62 million in 1956 to a paltry £S8 million two years later, and plunging Sudan into an economic recession. Foreign exchange reserves plummeted.

Ironically, the 1956 census preserved the life of the fracturing coalition government, for it provided the basis on which to redraw the parliamentary constituencies for the elections, which greatly favored the rural sectarian vote at the expense of the urban secular electorate. In the first election for an independent Sudan in 1958 the Umma won sixty-three seats and the PDP twenty-six; despite having the largest percentage of the popular vote, the NUP captured only forty-four seats in the capital and the towns along the Nile. The old Umma/PDP coalition of convenience quickly formed a government, but it was soon rendered impotent by petty bickering and sectarian rivalry. The pro-Western Umma Party had strong feelings that in any new constitution the ailing Sayyid 'Abd al-Rahman should become head of state and president for life. This was not a new idea. In the past the

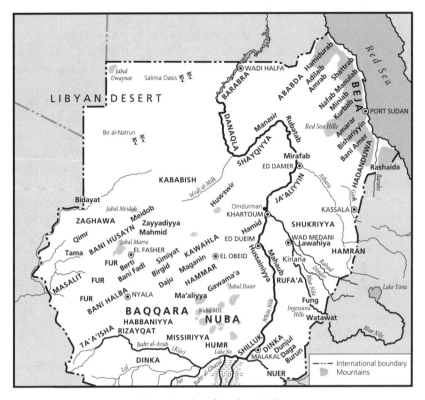

Map 5 Peoples of northern Sudan

Sayyid had envisaged himself "King" of an independent Sudan, which was anathema to Sayyid 'Ali and the pro-Egyptian Khatmiyya and its members in the PDP, but now his obsessive quest became entangled in the intricate web of bilateral relations with Egypt over the Nile waters and the offer of US aid.

The massive Managil Extension of 800,000 irrigated acres would require more Nile water, and the Egyptian High Dam (*Sadd al-'Aali*) at Aswan could not be constructed without adequate compensation for the resettlement of the Nubians of Wadi Halfa from the rising waters of its reservoir. This would require a revision of the 1929 Nile Waters Agreement (see pp. 74–5 below). The offer of US aid was much more contentious. In 1957 the United States had offered a tempting foreign aid package to ease the rapidly deteriorating Sudanese economy and provide financial assistance for ambitious development plans. 'Abdallah Khalil and the Umma were eager to accept

US financial assistance, but the PDP contemptuously refused, regarding US foreign aid as a transparent subterfuge to isolate Sudan from Egypt, which was now engrossed in serious discussions with the Soviet Union over the procurement of weapons from the Eastern Bloc and financial assistance for the High Dam.

Both of these issues served to lubricate the slippery slope of petty bickering, personal self-seeking, and cynical opportunism that plunged parliamentary government into disrepute. During the first two years of independence the southern Liberal Party MPs had been largely excluded from the political infighting between the Umma and the PDP. After the 1958 elections, however, personal and ethnic animosities soon split the party into rival factions whose MPs were easily seduced for their votes by cynical northern politicians in a highly competitive legislature. When southerners had demanded a federal constitution, the northern parties had disingenuously promised to "consider" federation in return for southern support for independence, only to scornfully reject and betray the southerners after independence had been achieved. Consequently, after the 1958 elections southern MPs readily switched loyalties for personal gain, so that the coalition government could not rely on their support against the opposition NUP, which forced 'Abdallah Khalil to adjourn the Constituent Assembly to avoid a vote of no confidence. Bizarre rumors of a coalition of the Umma and Azhari's NUP or a PDP/NUP alliance swept like a firestorm through Khartoum and the northern cities, igniting speculation in the press that a coup by the army was imminent.

On the morning of 17 November 1958, a few hours before the Constituent Assembly was to reconvene, the *Qa'id al-'Amm*, Major-General Ibrahim 'Abbud, ordered the army to secure the Three Towns (Khartoum, Khartoum North, and Omdurman, at the strategic confluence of the Blue and White Niles), declared a state of emergency, dissolved political parties, briefly detained ministers, and abolished trade unions. 'Abbud became prime minister and shortly thereafter president and minister of defense, a grandfatherly figure known kindly as "Pappa" 'Abbud with no political guile or ambitions, to rule through a Supreme Council of senior officers. Like hundreds of other Sudanese he was deeply distressed and easily persuaded that the time had come for the military to restore credibility and political stability to this new nation. The Sudanese reaction to this bloodless coup d'état was relief from the political exhaustion produced by three frantic years of cynical and unproductive party politics. After all, the Sudanese had already witnessed successful military coups d'état in Egypt, Iraq, and Pakistan. Sayyid 'Ali gave the coup his full support, particularly when most of its leaders were all Khatmiyya. Sayyid ʿAbd al-Rahman was more cautious, and his doubts foreshadowed the later Umma opposition to the military regime.

The ʿAbbud regime was more concerned about making the country governable than introducing any radical economic and social changes, but in their haste to seize control the officers had given little or no thought as to how the army was going to rule the country. Although the officer corps was predominately Khatmiyya and virtually all from the riverine *awlad al-bahr*, mostly Shayqiyya with some Danaqla and Jaʿaliyyin, the rank and file were almost exclusively from those marginalized peripheral Sudanese, the Nuba, Dinka, Fur, and Baqqara. Like the ephemeral unity of the politicians after independence, the solidarity of the professional officer corps began to unravel when two senior officers, who had been excluded from the Supreme Council, challenged the new regime. On 2 March 1959, in a fit of personal pique, Brigadier Muhay al-Din ʿAbdallah, commander of the Eastern Region, accompanied by Brigadier ʿAbd al-Rahim Shannan, marched on Khartoum. They surrounded ʿAbbud's residence and besieged the capital with their superior forces. Seeking to placate the mutineers, ʿAbbud appointed a new ten-member council which included al-Din and Shannan. Despite their presence on the Supreme Council, however, the dissidents remained dissatisfied and soon had a falling-out with the powerful Brigadier Hasan Bashir Nasr, the principal architect of the November coup. On 22 May the supporters of Shannan again marched on Khartoum, but Brigadier Bashir moved swiftly to arrest their leaders and ordered the troops to return to their barracks. Muhay al-Din and Shannan were summarily arrested in June, tried before a court martial, and sentenced to death for inciting mutiny. An uneasy stability returned to a regime still unsure of its support within the army when, in November 1959, Colonel ʿAli Hamid organized a mutiny of the more radical junior officers supported by a battalion at the infantry school in Omdurman that was brutally suppressed. The officers were tried and publicly hanged, which deeply shocked the Sudanese, unaccustomed to such harsh retributory punishments.

These desultory family squabbles within the armed forces were followed by the Sudanese public with titillated curiosity, if not amusement, that diverted its attention from the two major events of 1959 – the death of Sayyid ʿAbd al-Rahman on 22 March and the signing of the Nile Waters Agreement with Egypt on 8 November. The death of Sayyid ʿAbd al-Rahman marked the end of an era, for the great sectarian and nationalist leader had dominated Sudanese politics since the First World War and rescued the Ansar from the obscurity in which the British had sought to contain them after the collapse of the Mahdist State in 1898. His long life of some seventy-four years, business acumen, and political skill had made him rich, powerful, and perhaps wise. The modern Ansar sect and the Umma Party were his creations, but the culmination of his life's work and his greatest pride was the independence of Sudan. He was succeeded by his son, Sayyid Siddiq, who was but a shadow of his father and quietly passed away two years later, mourned by very few.

After the Revolutionary Command Council (RCC) in Cairo announced its intention in December 1952 to build the High Dam at Aswan, the Egyptians realized that the necessary negotiations for foreign financial and engineering assistance could not begin without a new agreement with Sudan over the allocation of the Nile waters. Moreover, the Egyptians could not begin construction without Sudan's consent, for the High Dam would flood much of Sudanese Nubia, driving thousands of Nubians from their homes and beloved date trees surrounding Wadi Halfa. For its part Sudan needed Egypt's concurrence for a greater share of the Nile waters to complete the Managil Extension and a dam at Roseires to store the water for Managil and electrify Khartoum. Acrimonious negotiations continued over the next four years until Egyptian–Sudanese relations reached their nadir in summer 1958. The coup d'état of November 1958 dramatically broke the hydrological morass. In March 1959 'Abbud formally requested that negotiations be reopened to resolve the dispute over the Nile waters. Having been virtually assured of Soviet financial and technical support, Egypt could now ignore the assistance offered by the United States and Great Britain and its humiliating conditions. Moreover, President Gamal 'Abd al-Nasser, who had finally forced his popular rival from the presidency in November 1954 on suspicion of collaboration with the Muslim Brotherhood, had spent years extolling the virtues of the High Dam, and he could not now risk a grievous blow to his personal prestige by failing to sign a piece of paper with the fatherly 'Abbud. Sudan had completed stage two of the Managil Extension and had begun the canalization for stage three, none of which would be operable without water from the Roseires dam, and in May 1959 Eugene Black, president of the World Bank, made it abundantly clear to the Sudanese that financial assistance for the dam was contingent upon a settlement of the Nile waters.

On 8 November 1959 Zakariya Mohie El Din for Egypt and Major General Talaat Farid for Sudan signed an agreement for the "full utilization of the Nile waters" amid handshakes, hugs, and kisses. The Nile Waters Agreement of 1959 not only cleared the way for dams at Aswan and Roseires, but it established the principle of equal sharing (50 percent) of any additional water obtained from conservancy schemes. Both Egypt and Sudan were able to substantially increase their established rights: Egypt received an increase to 55.5 bm³, a gain of 7.5 bm³; Sudan had a much more dramatic augmentation to 18.5 bm³, a substantial gain of 14.5 bm³, and much more than Egypt had previously offered. The agreement contained, however, several anomalies that would come back to haunt the signatories. Although the preamble referred to "full utilization" and "full control of the river" by Egypt and Sudan, the interests of the other upstream riparian African states, soon to be independent, were ignored. Bitter Ethiopian complaints officially and in the press were answered with stony silence. All of this appeared so practical and rational that there was a general feeling among the negotiators a settlement should have been concluded long before, until the talks nearly collapsed over the last item – compensation for the resettlement of thousands of Nubians to the alien environment of Khashm al-Qirba – which was resolved only by the personal intervention of President Nasser, whose disingenuous magnanimity melted Sudanese resistance; in his naïvety as one soldier to another, the honorable 'Abbud accepted Nasser's seemingly sensible compromise on the monetary compensation to Sudan for the inundation and displacement of the Wadi Halfans. It proved to be a disastrous mistake. By agreeing to accept barely half of what they had originally requested for compensation Sudan had to dig deep into its own meager treasury to find the funds to complete the resettlement of 50,000 Nubians to Khashm al-Qirba, which fifty years later had produced little more than an impoverished Nubian population and a dam half-filled with rich Ethiopian sediment and now quite useless. In 1960 the Egyptians began construction on the High Dam. A year later 'Abbud announced the construction of the Roseires and Khashm al-Qirba dams and the beginning of Nubian resettlement. Nubia exploded into violent demonstrations.

The Nubians had already expressed their unanimous opposition to any resettlement, but until it became a reality they had remained quiescent, if angry and bitter. Now they took to the streets in the towns along the Nile in violent demonstrations which soon spread to others inland with substantial Nubian communities. Their demonstrations became the magnet that pulled together the opposition to the military regime – schoolboys, university students, and the banished trade unionists who rallied around the leadership of the Sudan Communist Party (SCP) – whose various grievances had nothing to do with Nubian resettlement. Not only had the SCP been the only political party to oppose the military regime, but when the latter banned all political parties, the SCP, led by 'Abd al-Khaliq Mahjub, possessed the unique experience to operate underground learned from its

East European mentors, which enabled it to survive despite the relentless imprisonment of communists by 'Abbud. Moreover, the SCP was now able to exploit the Nubian demonstrations to grasp the leadership of the growing opposition and stage a week-long illegal strike of the railway workers in 1961, organize regular anti-government student demonstrations, mobilize the growing discontent in the Gezira Tenants' Association, and support the Front of the Opposition Parties (FOP) founded in November 1960 by all political party leaders except the Khatmiyya's. When the FOP sent a strong memorandum of protest in 1963 declaring 'Abbud and his officers would be held responsible for spreading terror in the country, twelve leaders from all the political parties, including the SCP, were arrested, which restored much-needed legitimacy to Sudanese communists and earned the implacable hostility of their ideological enemies, the Muslim Brothers.

The Society of the Muslim Brothers (MB) or simply the Brotherhood (*al-ikhwan al-musliman* or *al-ikhwan*) was founded in 1928 by Hasan al-Banna, who lived in the Egyptian delta. He was dedicated to cleansing Islam of its Western accretions and establishing a government based on Islamic principles by combining violence with humanitarian assistance to the marginalized poor of Egypt. By the end of the Second World War the Brotherhood had attracted a large following of loyal supporters. Sudanese living and studying in Egypt, who were themselves marginalized and discriminated against by Egyptians, found solace and support from the Muslim Brothers. Upon returning to Sudan they sought out Egyptian and Sudanese Brothers to found the Islamic Liberation Movement (*harakat al-tahrir al-islami*) in 1949. The Sudanese MB developed a small but dedicated following among secondary-school and university students, most of whom were *awlad al-gharib* from the rural, poverty-stricken west, appalled at the depravity of Sudanese political life that could only be extirpated by a return to the values of fundamental Islam and an Islamic form of government. They detested all military regimes, particularly that of General Ibrahim 'Abbud.

Ironically, the economic and financial prosperity of the Sudanese flourished during the military regime in direct proportion to their growing disgust with military rule. The generals may have been illiterate in economics, but they were practical men who had the good sense to abandon the coalition government's foolish determination to maintain the unrealistic price for cotton, and within two months they had disposed of the huge backlog of unsold cotton to fill the depleted treasury, produce a brief prosperity among the urban elite, and provide several years of domestic stability. Regular budget surpluses enabled the establishment of the Central Bank of

Sudan in February 1960, accompanied by large sums of bilateral financial assistance to Sudan from international lending institutions and bilateral trade arrangements with the Soviet Union and East European countries, on the one hand, and Britain and the United States, on the other. In June 1960 the International Bank for Reconstruction and Development (IBRD, the World Bank) provided a $15.5 million loan to complete the Managil Extension, and the following year the IBRD and West Germany agreed to finance the construction of the Khashm al-Qirba dam for Nubian resettlement and the Roseires dam to provide electricity for Khartoum. In March 1962 a beaming ʿAbbud snipped the ribbon to open the new rail line from Babanusa in southern Kordofan to Wau, the provincial capital of the Bahr al-Ghazal, to establish the only reliable overland link between northern and southern Sudan. In October 1962, however, an ambitious ten-year plan for development was launched that proved to be far beyond the limited capacity of the planners to achieve. Serious mistakes were compounded by creeping corruption, lack of fiscal accountability, and wasteful spending on pet projects for the military which soon absorbed the surplus revenue. The government's compromised credibility produced rumors of imminent economic collapse accompanied by growing disenchantment with the regime's attempt to institutionalize Sudanese participation in governance.

The military government had vainly sought to enlist popular Sudanese support through a pyramid of local, urban, and rural regional councils capped by a Central Council of seventy-two members designed by Chief Justice Abu Rannant and given legitimacy by the Province Administration Act of 1960 and the Local Government and Central Council Acts of 1962. Unfortunately, this pyramid was built from the top down, not the bottom up, and was dominated by military officers appointed by the government. The Central Council, which had no independent authority, was merely a bit of participatory window-dressing that fooled no one and guaranteed Sudan would continue to be run by the small clique, increasingly isolated from the mainstream of Sudanese life, of military men for their own personal gain and political interests which made them visible targets for the mistakes and creeping corruption in the government – an incendiary mixture which the Southern Problem ignited to consume the regime.

In 1959 the Southern Problem, as it came to be known, did not exist. To be sure, all the elements were in place – the northern Sudanization of southern administrative positions, the mutiny and subsequent disturbances, the broken promise of federalism for Sudan, and the deep-rooted ethnic, cultural, and religious differences that found their expression in the disdain for, disenchantment with, and discrimination against southern Sudanese by northerners. The harsh repression of the "Southern Sudan Disturbances" after the 1955 mutiny had stunned the southerners into momentary passivity, a brooding bitter silence awaiting a spark to ignite the conflagration that became known as the Southern Problem. The authoritarian 'Abbud and his lieutenants struck that spark. Since the army was the only national institution in a multi-ethnic and sectarian Sudan, it is not surprising that General 'Abbud and his officers naïvely assumed they could achieve national integration and unity by the application of proper military discipline to impose a rigid and insensitive policy of Arabization (*ta'rib*), which included the adoption of both an Arab identity and Arabic language, accompanied by Islamization of all non-Muslim, non-Arab African southerners.

In February 1957 the government of 'Abdallah Khalil had authorized the Ministry of Education to take charge of all mission schools and integrate them into the national educational system by a program of rapid Arabization in which, Arabic, not English, would be the language of instruction in southern schools. Islamization was to accompany and, indeed, was the logical sequel to Arabization, and both had 'Abbud's enthusiastic approval. Six intermediate Islamic Institutes (schools) were opened, mosques were constructed, and the sabbath was changed from Sunday to Friday. Thereafter, a rigorous military administrative policy was imposed on the South characterized by appalling ignorance, racial insensitivity, and shameless provocation, when no effort was made to sweeten the bitter pill of Arabization and Islamization with economic development. A scheme to grow and refine sugar at Mongalla was mysteriously transferred to an inferior location at Khashm al-Qirba for resettled Nubians. A projected paper factory at Malakal was conveniently forgotten, and its proposed fish-canning plant moved north to Jabal al-'Awliya. 'Abbud's educational policy was rigorously imposed, particularly at the Juba and Rumbek secondary schools from which the great majority of the southern educated elite had graduated. The students regarded the government's policy as a transparent continuation of northern "Arab" domination and went on strike. This gave the authorities an excuse to close the schools, which simply confirmed the students' suspicions.

All Christian missionaries were firmly forbidden to found new schools or practice their religion outside of their churches. Visas for those missionaries who went abroad on leave were not renewed, which was viewed by their former students as political as well as religious harassment. Now that the British rulers had departed, the Christian missionaries were the only ones left from the ancien régime for the government to blame for the growing southern hostility. In 1962 the Missionary Societies Act regulated the activities of

Christian missionary societies as a prelude to the expulsion of all foreign missionaries from the Sudan two years later. The vigorous imposition of Arabic and Islam, the harassment of the missionaries (many of whom had been their teachers), and the insensitivity of northern administrators wielding virtually unlimited powers convinced an increasing number of southern politicians – and fellow southerners like Father Saturnino Lohure, an ambitious Latuka Catholic priest, Joseph Oduho Aworu, a Latuka schoolteacher educated at Bakhat al-Ruda, and mission-educated Equatorians – to flee the country into Uganda. Here they founded the Sudan Christian Association (SCA) in 1961, but Saturnino and Oduho soon relocated to the much freer atmosphere of Kinshasa, capital of Zaire, where they were joined by William Deng Nhial, a young Dinka administrator from the Bahr al-Ghazal.

Here they founded the Sudan African Closed Districts National Union (SACDNU) but returned to Kampala in Uganda in 1963 as the Sudan African National Union (SANU). From Kampala they sought support for some 60,000 refugees who had fled to camps in Uganda and Zaire hastily organized by the United Nations Relief and Rehabilitation Administration (UNRA) in 1964. SANU soon absorbed the SCA and published the *Voice of the Southern Sudan* in London but was plagued by ethnic, factional, and personality differences over policy. SANU's most visible failure, however, was its inability to establish a viable SANU organization inside Sudan. Nevertheless, subterranean southern cells began to develop without SANU, one of which came to establish a rival southern political organization inside Khartoum called the Southern Front. A more dangerous manifestation of southern hostility than the impotent SANU was the gradual emergence of organized armed resistance within southern Sudan. In early 1963 some 400 volunteers, mostly Latuka, had formed the nucleus of a guerilla force at Agu Camp in eastern Equatoria under the nominal command of Lieutenant Emedio Tafeng Odongi, a Latuka and former lieutenant in the Equatorial Corps.

Several months later, on 19 August 1963, Joseph Oduho held a meeting at his house in Kampala with a half-dozen southerners, including Father Saturnino and Lieutenant Joseph Lagu Yakobo, a Madi, to whom Oduho had personally written urging him to defect and join the movement. They had gathered to organize the muddled guerilla movement in Equatoria. Father Saturnino proposed the movement be called the Sudan Pan-African Freedom Fighters (SPAFF), which would appeal to Pan-African leaders like Kwame Nkruma of Ghana whose support was needed, but others wanted a more legitimately indigenous name that would appeal to African southerners, as Mau Mau had done in Kenya, and settled on Anya-Nya, a combination of the Madi word *inyanya*, a fatal poison extracted from a river snake and greatly feared by the people of eastern Equatoria, and the Moru name, *manyanya*, for the army ant. At first the Anya-Nya in Equatoria raided isolated police posts in Equatoria, but the insurgents in the Bahr al-Ghazal under William Deng were quiescent until January 1964, when a well-armed Anya-Nya force under the command of Bernadino Mou Mou attacked Wau, capital of the Bahr al-Ghazal, killing more than a dozen soldiers, inflicting considerable damage, and capturing automatic weapons before being forced to withdraw after Bernardino was wounded and captured. This was the first substantive attack by the Anya-Nya against a fortified provincial capital and marked the beginning of sporadic but ill-coordinated attacks throughout the South. In 1964 the Anya-Nya probably numbered some 5,000 insurgents scattered in fragmented units under no single command. They studiously ignored the politicians of SANU, who held their first "National Convention" in the Silver Spring Hotel in Kampala from 7 to 14 October 1964 to elect Aggrey Jaden president and Phillip Pedak Leith vice-president, to the shock and dismay of Joseph Oduho who, having lost by one vote, stormed out of the hotel to form his own faction, the Azanian Liberation Front (ALF). Aggrey Jaden appointed Lagu commander-in-chief of the Anya-Nya with the rank of colonel.

Although the Anya-Nya was not a dangerous insurgency in 1964, its activities soon made the Southern Problem very visible to the urban northern Sudanese. The inability of the military to crush the rebels, those *'abid*, forced the 'Abbud government to placate its critics and improve its image by announcing in mid-October that it would permit public discussion of the Southern Problem by students at Khartoum University, which opened the floodgates of suppressed hostility against the regime. On the evening of 21 October the university students' union, a traditional center of opposition to all authority, held a meeting to discuss the Southern Problem during which its members contemptuously concluded that it would never be resolved so long as the military regime remained in power. Startled by the growing ferocity of student criticism, the regime quickly reversed its decision and banned all further meetings. The following evening, 22 October 1964, in open defiance of the ban, the students held another meeting on campus, a public challenge that the military regime could not ignore and that led to an inevitable confrontation between students and police. During the ensuing mêlée of tear gas and baton-wielding police several students were wounded, among them Ahmad Qurashi, who died in hospital that night.

During the night hundreds of students gathered at the hospital, and on the following day the funeral cortège numbered over 30,000 marchers, led by the university faculty in their formal gowns and chanting anti-government slogans. Demonstrations and riots erupted throughout Khartoum, cars were burnt, but neither the police nor the army could restore order. On Saturday 25 October 1964 the High Court, using its "supreme authority," issued a permit for a large demonstration led by a spontaneously organized group of teachers, engineers, lawyers, and even doctors calling themselves the National Front for Professionals, who were soon joined by trade unionists and radical members from the Gezira Tenants' Association. The Front's executive council, led by a galvanized SCP, called a general strike in which even the civil servants participated to paralyze Khartoum and the provincial towns. Meanwhile, the leaders of the prorogued political parties hastily met but sat helpless on the sidelines during the people's revolution, in which another twenty demonstrators were killed by troops trying to stem the flow of protest. The officer corps was deeply divided between junior officers sympathetic to the demonstrators and senior officers demanding their suppression by unrestrained force, if necessary. "Pappa" 'Abbud, who stood on the balcony of the Palace watching the demonstrators chanting anti-government slogans, was not about to have the blood of defenseless civilians on his hands.

On 26 October, one week after the death of the student Ahmad Qurashi, General 'Abbud announced the dissolution of the Supreme Council, and the usually reserved Sudanese poured into the streets, men dancing and women ululating to gather in huge crowds charged with delirious joy. An enormous celebratory wave swept through the capital, and the legend of a bloodless revolution soon became deeply embedded in Sudanese folklore. "Remember the October Revolution" became the rallying cry during the bloodless fall of Numayri's military regime in 1985 and has remained so in Sudanese anti-government demonstrations ever since. Four days of intense but more sober negotiations between the army and the United Front led to an agreement on 30 October 1964 to form a Transitional Government with, as its prime minister, Sirr al-Khatim al-Khalifa, the impeccable and respected head of the Khartoum Technical Institute and popular former deputy under-secretary for education in the South, with a cabinet including members from the Professionals' Front, three communists, two southerners, and one representative from each of the five political parties – the Umma, NUP, PDP, SCP, and the Muslim Brothers. President 'Abbud quietly departed on 14 November 1964; the day after leaving the Palace he was cheered by shoppers in the *suq* while purchasing oranges.

THE SHORT, UNHAPPY LIVES OF THE TRANSITIONAL AND
SECOND PARLIAMENTARY GOVERNMENTS

When Ibrahim 'Abbud banned all political parties, the Umma, NUP, and PDP virtually disintegrated, leaving the cohesive, underground SCP to take charge of the leftist leadership of the United Front and a "window of opportunity" to pursue its radical agenda before the conservative, traditional parties could recover and reorganize. The established parties had been acutely embarrassed by their failure to play any significant role in the collapse of the military regime. Outnumbered in the cabinet, they spread provocative gossip to "save the country from communism" by demanding immediate elections in which the traditional parties, which still commanded the overwhelming support of the Sudanese people, had a tactical advantage. In February 1965 Sayyid Sadiq al-Mahdi, son of and successor to Sayyid Siddiq al-Mahdi, unleashed tens of thousands of Ansar, who poured into Khartoum to roam the streets at night chanting Mahdist war songs as a demonstration of conservative strength that terrified the citizenry. Thoroughly intimidated by the Ansar, the United Front, whose professional rank and file, particularly the engineers and doctors, had become thoroughly alienated by the endless radical rhetoric from members of its executive committee more concerned with the interests of the SCP than the implementation of a progressive agenda, collapsed. Its cabinet resigned on 18 February 1965, and by 25 February Prime Minister Sirr al-Khatim al-Khalifa had organized a new cabinet now dominated by the Umma, NUP, and the recently formed Islamic Charter Front (ICF) as the political party of the Muslim Brotherhood.

Although the intense political ferment after the October Revolution consumed the attention of the northern Sudanese, the deteriorating situation in southern Sudan could no longer be ignored after "Black Sunday." On Sunday 6 December 1964 the large southern community in Khartoum had gathered to welcome the return of Clement Mboro, minister of the interior and the first southerner to hold an important cabinet post, from a tour of the South. When his plane was delayed, ugly rumors quickly spread that "Uncle" Clement had been murdered, and in their fury the southerners rampaged through the streets of Khartoum assaulting every and any *mudukuru* (those who rise early in the morning before the dew dries to seize slaves) – a nineteenth-century Bari term widely popularized among the southerners after independence as a derisive epithet for any northern Sudanese Arab – in what became a "race riot" that left nearly a hundred dead. When the army restored order that evening, the citizens of Khartoum had been given a visual and visceral demonstration of the Southern Problem. "Black Sunday" convinced many of the urban intellectuals (*mutathaqqifa*) that the differences between northern and southern Sudanese were irreconcilable and that the North would be better off without the South; others were equally convinced that the time had come to seek an expeditious political settlement. Four days after "Black Sunday" Sirr al-Khatim al-Khalifa, in response to a proposal by the leaders of SANU, granted an amnesty to all Sudanese who had left the country after January 1955 and agreed to organize a Round Table Conference to resolve the Southern Problem.

Three months of fitful and confused negotiations followed, characterized by deep suspicions, factional disputes, and personal differences among the southerners on the one hand and political maneuvering and manipulation by the northern parties on the other. The Round Table Conference was finally convened in Khartoum on 16 March 1965. SANU was represented by two rival delegations, one inside the Sudan, the other in exile outside. SANU-Inside was led by William Deng, a Dinka, who advocated a federal solution and unity; SANU-Outside was led by Elia Lupe, a Kakwa, and was composed of the leaders of the ALF, Father Saturnino and Joseph Oduho, and Aggrey Jaden, who had split from SANU to form the rival Sudan African Liberation Front (SALF) advocating complete independence for the South. The Southern Front of educated southerners living in Khartoum was led by Darius Bashir and Clement Mboro. There was also a fourth group of disparate southerners simply known as the "Other Shades of Opinion" (OSO) and represented by the Dinka Santino Deng, a token southern minister and reliable sycophant in every government from 1954 to 1964. The northerners were elated by this plethora of rival southern representatives which effectively eliminated any pretense at southern solidarity, a situation that they eagerly sought to exploit in order to dominate the proceedings.

The conference secretariat, supervised by the able Mohamed Omer Beshir, had prepared impeccable position papers on the fundamental differences between North and South. In the chair was the vice-chancellor of the University of Khartoum, Professor al-Nazir Dafa'allah. All the principal political parties were represented, and there were observers from Uganda, Kenya, Nigeria, Tanzania, Algeria, Egypt, and Ghana. When all of the northern party representatives firmly rejected separation and independence for the South, Aggrey Jaden petulantly decamped for Kampala after delivering his opening address, virtually abdicating SANU-Outside's role as the principal representative of southern interests to the growing influence of the Southern Front. After ten days of fruitless negotiations the exhausted participants could not reach a unanimous resolution on the constitutional status of the South, and the conference was abruptly terminated on 25 March 1965. To assuage their failure a twelve-man committee, six each from North and South, was organized as a working group to draft proposals for constitutional and administrative reform. The committee met regularly for another six months, during which its deliberations were methodically sabotaged by Hasan al-Turabi, the representative of the ICF, whose articulate charm and incisive legal skills could not be matched by any southerner and whose single vote could derail any decisions, all of which it was agreed must be unanimous.

There were seven main points of disagreement, three of which were critical. The southerners were adamant that the South be treated as one solid Southern Region, which was anathema to the northern representatives, who regarded a unified South as the first stage toward secession, which could best be frustrated by the Balkanization of the South into numerous administrative units. In a petulant outburst Turabi preferred the South to go its separate way rather than remain one region. Security was an equally divisive issue. The southern representatives insisted upon a southern security force, a local militia, that would defend the South and be responsible to the government of the South. This was indignantly rejected by the northern members. The third issue left unsettled was the power of the national legislature to override regional legislation by a majority or a two-thirds vote. Since a simple majority could be obtained without southern votes, the central government would be able to suspend southern autonomy and impose an Islamic constitution and laws on the South, a prophecy that came to pass seventeen years later. By December 1968 the frustration of the southern representatives, led by Abel Alier, reached breaking-point, and they stalked out of the committee, never to return. When the committee rendered its report in 1966, it was politely ignored by everyone. At the time, the failure of the Round Table Conference was a disappointment; in retrospect, it was a disaster. Its failure to resolve the Southern Problem strengthened the conviction on the part of an increasing number of southerners that their grievances could only be satisfied down the barrel of a gun. It deepened the pit of southern distrust of all northerners, and, like the Juba Conference of 1947, became another historic legend in the evolving saga of southern nationalism.

After the Round Table Conference had come to its dismal conclusion, the Transitional Government turned to electoral reform for the crucial parliamentary spring elections in 1965. The ineffectual Senate, represented mostly by traditional *shaykhs* and chiefs, was abolished, women were given the vote and the voting age was lowered to 18, and the five-man Supreme Council, which had the ultimate authority, ruled that the continuing State of Emergency in the South precluded elections in the southern constituencies. The lone southerner and representative of the Southern Front, Luigi Adwok Bong, a Shilluk graduate of Bakht al-Ruda, cast the deciding vote, for which he was summarily dismissed from the Southern Front and generously rewarded by his northern colleagues. Although some fifteen parties contested the elections of 1965, most of them consisted only of a few exuberant followers anxious to promote the ambitions of a local candidate. The rural areas controlled by the Ansar were solidly Umma, but unlike in 1958 the Umma had now organized an efficient and effective electoral machine rumored to have been financed by supporters in the Western world to win seventy-six seats. The NUP, also unlike in 1958, now suffered from a lack of discipline and unity disguised by a shroud of overconfidence, but it continued to control the riverine towns along the Nile with fifty-four seats. Most of the Khatmiyya constituencies in eastern Sudan outside of NUP control, however, were now won by ten Beja Congress members. Founded in 1957 by Beja intellectuals to mobilize the educated Beja in eastern Sudan, the Beja Congress advocated a federal system for Sudan and, as a maverick party, successfully contested hitherto safe seats for the DUP in the 1965 elections. The same phenomenon occurred in the Nuba Mountains, where independents, supported by the General Union of the Nuba Mountains, captured seven constituencies. Like their Beja counterparts, they had complained bitterly of the neglect that marked the first public expression of the growing disenchantment among the distinctive peoples of the marginalized periphery with the old politics of indifference conducted by the politicians in the central government in Khartoum. Victory for the conservatives was assured when the PDP, in a foolish fit of pique, decided to boycott the election, to pay a heavy price by gaining only three seats won by PDP members who had defied their party to participate. The ICF, dominated by the Muslim Brothers, managed to win five and the communists eight, all from the fifteen-member special graduates' constituencies. The most bizarre returns came from the South, where twenty southern constituencies were now represented by northern merchants who had fulfilled residence requirements, nominated themselves, and, facing no opposition, were duly elected by a handful of *jallaba* in southern towns.

The massive majority that the Umma and NUP could now muster enticed them into a marriage of convenience to form a coalition government which, after some distasteful bargaining, selected Muhammad Ahmad Mahjub prime minister. He made no secret of his intellectual prowess as the reason for his successful and profitable legal practice and later his skillful diplomacy as foreign minister. Unfortunately, his literary and legal talents were marred by his overweening ambition, pomposity, and vanity, which made him vulnerable to shameless flattery. Mahjub's handling of the Southern Problem dramatically demonstrated that northern politicians had learned nothing from the failures of the military regime in the South. He advocated a firm policy towards the southerners and accelerated 'Abbud's policy of Arabic and Islamization. In June 1965 he ordered the army specifically to harass and intimidate educated southerners, which culminated in two highly provocative incidents. When a soldier was killed by a southerner in an altercation over a prostitute on 8 July 1965 troops from the Juba garrison rampaged through the streets with the acquiescence of their officers, leaving some 1,400 southerners dead and most of the town in ruins. Four days later on 12 July at a jubilant wedding troops from the Wau garrison surrounded the ceremonies, opened fire, and methodically slaughtered seventy-six males of the southern elite.

The southerners responded with their feet, fleeing by the thousands into refugee camps in Uganda and the Congo, but scores of armed police, prison warders, game keepers, and even southern defectors from the army refused to join the wave of southern civilians fleeing into the refugee camps across the border to disappear into the bush to join the nearest Anya-Nya unit. As the ranks of the Anya-Nya swelled in dozens of scattered and independent camps these new recruits were, ironically, armed by defeated Congolese Simbas seeking food and sanctuary in 1965 in return for some 6,000 automatic arms and ammunition. As security throughout southern Sudan continued to deteriorate in proportion to the increase in Anya-Nya activity, the government inaugurated a policy of "collectivization," whereby the rural population of Equatoria was herded into thirty-three "Peace Villages" (*kariyat al-salaam*) surrounding the towns to deprive the Anya-Nya of food, shelter, and support from their country kinsmen. Although each household was given £S4 to build a house, a plot, and seeds, these Internally Displaced Persons (IDPs) were literally held hostage in return for information as to the whereabouts of the Anya-Nya. Disease was rampant in these confined camps, and hundreds died from malnutrition and cholera, epidemics the government vehemently denied. In the Bahr al-Ghazal and the Upper Nile which were contiguous with the northern provinces of Kordofan and the Blue Nile the government began to organize local militias in order to exploit historical ethnic rivalries to weaken the Anya-Nya, a strategy that became one of the government's most effective weapons during the next half-century of civil war.

Next to their inability to cooperate, the greatest weakness of the Anya-Nya was their failure to develop a political consciousness among the southern Sudanese, and they frequently alienated southerners by their arbitrary plundering of their cattle and crops. Many of the Anya-Nya military commanders developed a fierce disdain for the educated southern politicians who talked while they fought and died, and in some instances Anya-Nya captains even forbad the use of English to demonstrate their contempt for the intellectuals who would be the first to profit from any autonomy or independence they had won by war. Unfortunately, the southern politicians had only themselves to blame for the distrust and suspicion of the Anya-Nya commanders on account of their failure to forge viable political organizations in the South. The rival southern politicians were men of limited abilities, conceited personalities, and narrow vision unable to define, let alone articulate, a future that would unify the South against the North and were bewitched by a kaleidoscope of internal rifts, ethnic loyalties, and ideological confusion. In Kampala Joseph Oduho and Aggrey Jaden had momentarily set aside their differences to reconstitute the AFL, but their mutual distrust prevented the formulation of any concerted policy, which confirmed the Anya-Nya in their distrust of politicians. In March Vice-President Aggrey Jaden was forced to leave the AFL, but he worked assiduously to build a rival political party he called the "Home Front," renamed the Southern Sudan Provisional Government (SSPG) at its convention in August 1967 at Angurdiri. The convention, surprisingly, attracted a large number of southerners, Anya-Nya soldiers, and political officers, not just a handful of haggling politicians. This was the first large meeting held inside the South whose participants condemned the petty and personal quarrels of the politicians and resolved to forge a united front.

At first the provisional government was very active and seemed to many southerners its first effective political party after years of disunity. The "capital" of the government was established in southern Sudan at Angundri, the code name for the well-known Bungu Post, 30 miles southwest of Juba on the road to Yei and the Congo border, and a *Southern Sudan Gazette* appeared to disseminate information about and the policies of the SSPG. The *National Field Day*, a mimeographed review of the SSPG's activities, appeared irregularly to attest to the vitality of the provisional government, define its objectives, and formulate its policies. By the summer of 1968, however, the SSPG could only claim to control central Equatoria, and when its president, Aggrey Jaden, suddenly decamped without explanation to Nairobi, the SSPG collapsed. Ancient ethnic hostilities and the conditions of guerilla war obviously contributed to its demise, but the principal reason was the failure of its leadership.

The experiences encountered by those southerners who remained in Khartoum following the Round Table Conference appeared as frustrating as the futile political bickering by southern politicians in Kampala and southern Sudan. Although the old Liberal Party and the Sudan Unity Party continued to hang around the capital after the Round Table Conference, the Southern Front and SANU-Inside of William Deng were the only southern political organizations of any importance in Khartoum. The Southern Front was registered as a political party in June 1965 under the leadership of Clement Mboro. It published an informative and well-written newsletter, *The Vigilant*, which became an effective voice for the southern movement in general and a platform for the Southern Front in particular, despite the fact it was banned for six months after reporting the Juba and Wau massacres. William Deng's SANU-Inside had been launched several months earlier at a rally in Omdurman on 11 April 1965 which attracted some 2,000 southerners, and until 1967, when an internal split developed, SANU-Inside operated as the personal fief of William Deng. During the ensuing years, however, the southerners-inside became increasingly aware that self-determination or federation were completely unacceptable to all the northern political parties, and both the Southern Front and SANU probably would have accepted some sort of compromise, which indeed they ultimately did, (at Addis Ababa in 1972).

If Mahjub was obtuse about the South, he was equally inept in the North in his harsh treatment of the PDP and vendetta against the SCP. This behaviour at least did not threaten the political stability of the state; his personal antagonism toward Sadiq al-Mahdi, however, certainly did. Sayyid Sadiq al-Mahdi possessed impeccable credentials. He was the great-grandson of the Mahdi, which identified him with an historic religious tradition, but he also possessed a secular education acquired at Camboni College and at Khartoum and Oxford Universities. Returning from Oxford, he personified the very model of a modern Sudanese. He was young (22 years old) and worked for a year in the Ministry of Finance to emerge a strong critic of the 'Abbud regime, and his active role in the October Revolution won him immense popularity among the young urban intellectual elite. He demonstrated none of the indecisiveness and lack of vision of his latter years when he became president of the Umma Party in 1964. On 25 December 1965 Sadiq turned 30, making him eligible to run for parliament. He promptly won a by-election in the Blue Nile Province and the parliamentary leadership of the Umma Party. From the moment Sadiq took his seat in parliament his criticism of Mahjub became increasingly outspoken, which infuriated the vain and sensitive Mahjub, who lived under the illusion he was indispensable, despite the fact that as prime minister he was not head of the Umma Party. When Mahjub stubbornly refused to step down, a formal vote of no confidence on 25 July 1966 was carried 126 to 30, with 15 abstentions. Two days later Sadiq al-Mahdi became prime minister and formed a new cabinet.

Although his tenure as prime minister was brief, ten months from July 1966 to May 1967, he was the first Sudanese politician to construct an effective political machine. He appointed young, competent men to ministerial posts. He was the first politician with a national agenda that transcended sectarian traditions and the first to eschew the narrow personal and ethnic interests that had come to characterize Sudanese politicians, which won him respect and even admiration among non-Umma groups, as well as some southern politicians. He also sought to replace the lingering Transitional Constitution with a permanent one, and duly appointed a Constitutional Draft Committee which, after prolonged discussions, rejected both an Islamic and secular constitution, preferring a hybrid of the two, a constitution with an "Islamic orientation" proposed by the NUP, in which the members of the Committee found relief and comfort in a middle, non-controversial course, promptly sending it to the Constituent Assembly on 15 January 1968, where it was tabled but soon overtaken by events.

In May 1967 Isma'il al-Azhari withdrew the support of the NUP from Sadiq's coalition government, forcing a vote of no confidence on 15 May 1967. Sadiq was replaced as prime minister by Mahjub, who now presided over a ragtag coalition of the NUP, PDP, three southern parties, and the Imam's Umma. Having further debased parliamentary government its leaders had scorn and derision heaped upon them by the press and public amid a great deal of discussion that perhaps the time had come to let the military once again cleanse the fouled stables of incompetent politicians. Fearful that sectarian loyalty might prevail to reunite the Umma Party, Azhari, ever the consummate manipulator, launched the Democratic Unionist Party (DUP) on 12 December 1967, made up of disgruntled members of the NUP and PDP, and hastily scheduled elections in the spring of 1968 in anticipation of a DUP landslide against a divided Umma.

Voting commenced on 18 April 1968, and the results were announced in early May. Azhari's gamble was richly rewarded by the DUP winning 101 seats. The internal split of the Umma proved an unmitigated calamity. Sadiq's wing won only thirty-six seats, and he himself suffered a humiliating defeat by a strong Imam supporter, Muhammad Da'ud Khalifa, a distant relative of the Mahdi's successor, the Khalifa 'Abdullahi. The Imam al-Hadi wing equally divided the Umma Party, with thirty seats. The southern parties did not do well. The insecurity in the southern countryside favored the northern parties, whose supporters were located in those southern towns shielded by the army, which guaranteed a sizeable vote in their favor. The big losers were William Deng's SANU-Inside with only fifteen seats and the Southern Front with ten, which seemed to belie their vociferous claims that they could count on the southern vote. Since the graduates' constituencies had once again been abolished, the ICF had a dismal showing with only three seats representing Khartoum.

Despite its overwhelming majority, the unruly coalition of the DUP and the Imam al-Hadi's Umma faction, in which neither trusted the other, was led once again by the ineffectual Muhammad Ahmad Mahjub, who regarded himself above petty parliamentary politics, over which he had little influence, preferring to immerse himself in foreign affairs, particularly regarding the Arab states, in which he had demonstrated considerable skill when Umma foreign minister in the first parliamentary government. He could not, however, resist the temptation to meddle in African affairs, including border disputes with Chad and Ethiopia exacerbated by the substantial shipments of arms and supplies to the Anya-Nya by Mengistu Haile Mariam and his Ethiopian communist goverment, the Derg, and support for a host of radical African secessionist movements – Muslim secessionists in Eritrea, the anti-Bokassa movement in the Central African Republic, and the Simbas in the Democratic Republic of Congo who had received large arms shipments from Sudan. The contradiction between the conservative government of Sudan eagerly supporting a radical pan-African agenda, on the one hand, while killing African southern Sudanese, on the other, embarrassed and seriously eroded Sudan's credibility among the states of equatorial Africa, which even Mahjub's diplomatic dexterity could not reconcile.

Like foreign affairs, the economy was also largely ignored by the dysfunctional governments of Sudan, which enabled local notables, merchants, and Khartoum politicians to lease over 1.2 million acres by 1968 in the eastern region around Gedaref, in the Blue Nile, and in Kordofan for mechanized cultivation. These large farms generated considerable wealth and created a new class of affluent "absentee landlords" residing in the large towns whose participation in farming was limited to expeditious visits to ensure that the management of hired overseers was generating substantial profits. Other additions to the growing middle class were the new owners who took advantage of the rapid expansion of pump schemes to purchase large plots and grow irrigated cotton along the White and Blue Niles. Pump schemes differed from mechanical agriculture in that the tracts were sold at the market price, which limited the buyers to local administrative officials and merchants with sufficient capital to invest, who harvested a very substantial profit from their tenants who actually planted, weeded, and picked the cotton. Other buyers were local peasants who invested their meager savings accumulated by dabbling in trade and transport in small farms of 100 acres, some of which were watered by pump schemes, although most depended upon rainfall. They became a middle-class peasantry, which constituted about one-third of the rural population, while over half of the country folk remained as they had for centuries – poor peasants with small farms of 5, perhaps 10 acres.

As rural Sudanese society gradually became increasingly money- and market-oriented, a commercial elite emerged in the cities and towns to play a crucial role in the Sudanization of commerce. They were led by the *jallaba*, the historic community of traders from the Danaqla and Ja'aliyyin of the riverine Nile. After independence the *jallaba* were strategically located in the principal towns and the capital, where their historic trading networks enabled them to use their ethnic connections in the Ministries of Finance and Commerce, whose personnel were mostly Dunqulawi and Ja'ali, to obtain profitable licenses to expand their trading networks into substantial commercial ventures by financing regional middlemen, who in turn provided small sums to start up shops for local villagers. Family, ethnicity, and intermarriage characterized almost all of these new Sudanese commercial ventures. Intermarriage between the daughters of important local leaders and the new entrepreneurs was used to extend ethnic ties, which became the distinctive feature of Sudanese capitalism. Instead of an identifiable commercial class, Sudanese business became a collective of private family firms all engaged in carving out an ever larger slice of the market pie. The family firms were, by and large, very secretive, competitive, and quite prepared to use corruption in order to outmaneuver their rivals, which, when combined with political instability, inhibited the flow of Sudanese investment into big, expensive, long-term projects.

Despite the political turmoil, the government actively sought to promote economic development. An Industrial Development Corporation was founded in 1965 to manage government investments, followed in 1967 by the Organization and Promotion of Industrial Investment Act designed to invest in local industries, and in 1968 the Agricultural Reform Corporation was established as the first step in the nationalization of private cotton schemes. All of this economic activity by the government was more symbolic than substantive, for it operated an antiquated system of taxation, which relied almost solely on indirect taxes such as customs duties vulnerable to fluctuations in the global markets, and accounted for only 4.4 percent of government revenue, rather than a more stable system of direct taxation on personal and commercial income. The growing gap between revenue and expenditure was cheerfully resolved by an expedient spate of borrowing from international financial institutions that raised the national debt from £S3.9 million in 1965 to £S46 million four years later in 1969, a pattern of cavalier borrowing that soon became synonymous with Sudanese public finance.

When the Constituent Assembly gathered for its first meeting on 27 May 1968 Isma'il al-Azhari was rewarded for leading the DUP to a landslide victory by being re-elected president of the Supreme Council. Colleagues personally loyal to him were also elected to the same body, which completed the transformation of the post of the legally constituted head of state from a non-political institution with broad representation into a partisan instrument of the ruling coalition. After the election the work of the Constituent Assembly soon dissolved into a morass of intrigue and counter-intrigue complete with shoddy manipulation behind the scenes and accompanied by wild rumors and speculation in the press and among the public in which not a single member of the Assembly displayed any interest in the pressing problems of the nation. On 7 May 1969 the Umma Party and the DUP simultaneously announced their agreement on policies and the principles for the long-delayed constitution. Eighteen days later, on 25 May 1969, Colonel Ja'afar Numayri and his Free Officers seized the major installations in the Three Towns and peacefully took control of the Sudan government. Numayri's Free Officers were modelled on the Egyptian Committee of the Free Officers, led by Gamal 'Abd al-Nasser, who had overthrown the Egyptian monarchy in their coup of 23 July 1952 and were committed to secular, Arab socialism in Egypt. There were few who mourned the passing of Sudan's second parliamentary government. Little did they realize that during these twelve years of failed parliamentary and military government the two great issues that were to dominate Sudan at the end of the century – the Southern Problem and the marginalization of the periphery – had been born.

Sadly, no Sudanese had emerged after independence as a competent and effective national leader, one who could overcome his sectarian, ethnic, or regional loyalties to convince the complex diversity of the Sudanese to support a national agenda. The most intellectual, cosmopolitan, and politically sophisticated Sudanese appeared to have a perverse capacity to produce leaders of limited abilities, arrogance without restraint, and avarice without shame. Obsessed with their own personal pride and power, these petty men were prisoners of their own narrow, ethnic, and regional interests whose concept of leadership was debased by cynical party manipulation greased by nepotism, privilege, and often hard, cold cash that made a mockery of parliamentary government. The Sudanese, universally admired for their charm, warmth, hospitality, and humane virtues despite the paradox of appalling atrocities, deserved much better.

CHAPTER 4

The government of Ja'afar Numayri: the heroic years, 1969–1976

THE MAY REVOLUTION

Just after midnight on 25 May 1969 some 200 cadets from the Armored School were joined by two companies of paratroopers stationed in the relative seclusion of Khor Umar at the foot of the Karari Hills north of Omdurman for training exercises under the command of their Free Officers. Under cover of darkness they slipped silently into Khartoum in small units at carefully spaced intervals throughout the early hours of the morning. By 4:00 am the first group had disconnected the telephone system, seized the radio and television center, and secured the bridges straddling the Blue and White Niles. A second group had occupied army headquarters, arrested the senior commanders, and taken into custody sixty-four prominent politicians, among them Isma'il al-Azhari and Muhammad Ahmad Mahjub. As dawn was breaking at 6:30 am Radio Omdurman broadcast recorded speeches by Colonel Ja'afar Muhammad Numayri and Chief Justice Babikr 'Awadallah announcing the coup d'état and the founding of the Democratic Republic of Sudan, followed at 11:00 am by the names of the new members of the Council of Ministers under Premier Babikr 'Awadallah. This tiny force of fewer than 500 soldiers led by 6 officers had, astonishingly, staged a bloodless coup, the success of which now depended on immediately securing widespread support among the army and the Sudanese people.

When the communists assumed the leadership of the Professional Front that overthrew the 'Abbud regime in 1964, the SCP had discovered natural allies among junior army officers opposed to those senior officers determined to crush the popular will in November of that year. Thereafter, the SCP sought to establish a communist presence within the army; its secretary-general, 'Abd al-Khaliq Mahjub, actively recruited a group of officers who were either committed communists or fellow-travelers with whom a large number of "progressive" officers shared their views that Sudan required a restructuring of its social and economic systems in order to become secular, non-sectarian, and socialist. As early as 1961 the Free Officers' underground newsletter had expressed their intention to work with the popular movements to overthrow the 'Abbud regime. Of the fourteen members that comprised the inner circle of the Free Officers who met in late autumn 1968 to plan a coup and the structure of the revolutionary government, half were associated one way or another with the SCP. The conspirators agreed that power would be vested in a Revolutionary Command Council (RCC) on the Egyptian model led by Colonel Ja'afar Numayri, but that a prominent civilian, the respected former Chief Justice Babikr 'Awadallah, should be included in the RCC to win popular support for the coup.

By March 1969 plans for a coup in May had been drafted, but at a meeting in mid-April seven of the thirteen members present voted to postpone the coup until assured of support from the popular forces. Disgusted by the timidity of the majority, the minority "gang of six," who held the principal commands in the Armored School and the paratroopers, secretly conspired to stage the coup six weeks later on 25 May 1969 under the leadership of Colonel Ja'afar Muhammad Numayri. In 1969 Numayri was 39 years old, having been born in the Wad Nubawi section in Omdurman on 1 January 1930, the son of a postman. He graduated from the highly regarded Hantoub Secondary School, where his talents on the football field were more conspicuous than his performance in the classroom, which was barely sufficient to obtain an appointment to the Sudan Military College. While learning to be a military officer he also became thoroughly political, a great admirer of Gamal 'Abd al-Nasser and his pan-Arab socialist revolution. Soon after graduation in 1952 he readily gravitated into the orbit of the nascent Free Officers' Movement. In 1957 he was implicated in a failed plot to overthrow the government and summarily dismissed from the army, but was reinstated in the spring of 1959 for reasons that remain unclear. Thereafter he devoted as much time to recruiting young cadets into the Free Officers as to advancing his military career and by 1964 was the unacknowledged leader of the movement. After successfully completing a course at the US Army Command College at Fort Leavenworth, Kansas, he was appointed to command the Gebeit Training School for two years, 1967–69, which proved the ideal location to recruit young cadets for the Free Officers' Movement and plan for a successful coup d'état.

Throughout 25 May the ten members of the RCC met and secured the support of the crucial army units and security organizations, while Ja'afar Numayri himself offered seats in the RCC to Lieutenant-Colonel

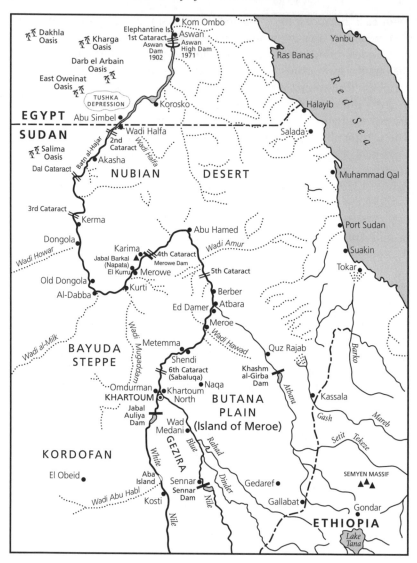

Map 6 The riverine heartland of Sudan

Babikr al-Nur Sawar al-Dahab, who was associated with the SCP, Faruq 'Uthman Hamdallah, a confirmed fellow-traveler, and another communist Free Officer, Hashim Muhammad al-'Ata', which convinced a reluctant SCP to support the non-communist members of the RCC in order to mobilize the popular forces to defend the new regime. The SCP disdainfully regarded the coup as petit-bourgeois, but the party leadership was convinced it could manipulate the RCC into the true path of revolution and defend the communists against their principal enemy, the Ansar. A week after the coup the SCP organized massive demonstrations in defense of the RCC, culminating in a huge political rally by the Federation of Workers Union in Abdel Moneim Square on 2 June. Leading Sudanese composers – Muhammad al-Amin, Muhammad al-Wardi, and 'Abd al-Karim al-Kabli – vied with one another to write songs of praise for the new regime, which had little to fear from the discredited political parties. Sadiq was arrested on 6 June, which enabled the Imam al-Hadi to lead the conservative Ansar/Umma opposition. The imam made no effort to hide his contempt for Numayri and the RCC, disdainfully turning his back on Khartoum and Omdurman to retire with his lieutenants to sulk on Aba Island, the fortified cradle of Mahdism. A month later Muhammad Ahmad Mahjub, himself, was incapacitated by another heart attack. And on 25 August 1969 that old political warhorse, Isma'il al-Azhari, died at the age of 69, which nullified any immediate threat to the regime from the NUP.

Although the SCP had seemingly committed its full support for the new regime, the first crack in its façade soon appeared. Like all the other Sudanese parties the SCP was divided by personality and ideology. To the dismay of the hard-liners advocating direct action, 'Abd al-Khaliq Mahjub had always argued that popular support must be achieved through patient political persuasion. The party was also divided as to the role of the army. A minority in opposition led by Mu'awiyah Ibrahim believed success depended upon an alliance with progressive junior officers; the majority argued that only action by the masses could overthrow the *petite bourgeoisie*, a division that was exacerbated when 'Abd al-Khaliq Mahjub at first demurred and then with great reluctance embraced the May Revolution.

Ja'afar Numayri deliberately sought to exploit these internal disputes within the SCP by appointing communists who he thought were closet nationalists to cabinet positions without consulting the SCP leadership. This was made all the more intolerable when Numayri sought the approval of the anti-Mahjub faction of Mu'awiyah Ibrahim for his various proposals. Relationships were further strained in October 1969 when Babikr 'Awadallah precipitated a furor in Khartoum with a statement that the Sudanese revolution could not progress without the active support of Sudanese communists. Anti-communist demonstrations erupted in Khartoum, and communist ministers were reshuffled in the government. Numayri assumed the premiership but kept Babikr 'Awadallah as his deputy, and the minister of justice, a leading member of the Mu'awiyah faction, was installed at the key Ministry of Economics and Foreign Commerce. To further consolidate the military in government the non-communist and anti-Mahdist Major Khalid Hasan 'Abbas was named Minister of Defense. Four of the five ministers who left the government were members of the SCP.

Having momentarily checked the communists, Numayri was confronted with a more formidable but predictable confrontation with the Ansar. During winter 1969 Imam al-Hadi had been actively inciting the Ansar to take violent action against the government, and in March 1970 he openly challenged Ja'afar Numayri and the RCC by unleashing the Ansar into Omdurman to stage a mass protest that was only suppressed by the army after great destruction of property and heavy loss of life. Numayri reacted swiftly, prodded by the fiercely anti-Mahdist Babikr 'Awadallah and Minister of Defense Khalid Hasan 'Abbas. He mobilized a large flotilla, steamed up the White Nile to Aba Island, and on 27 March launched his elite forces against the Ansar, who valiantly resisted behind their fortifications until overwhelmed by superior firepower. Trying to escape, the Imam al-Hadi was trapped and killed near the Ethiopian border on 30 March, leaving behind over 12,000 dead Ansar on Aba Island. The extensive holdings of the Mahdi's family were confiscated, and on 3 April Sadiq al-Mahdi slipped out of Sudan and into exile.

There was much more to the May Revolution than personal and political intrigue or violent repression against enemies on the left and right. The Free Officers were genuinely committed to economic and social reform in Sudan, which the RCC entrusted to the communists and socialists who dominated the Council of Ministers. In May 1969 Babikr 'Awadallah had outlined the steps necessary to replace foreign investment by imposing state monopolies on all imported and exported commodities, restrict private business, and establish close economic ties with socialist and Arab countries. The first government monopolies to control imports were established on 16 October 1969, followed on 9 May 1970 by the Sequestration Act, by which seventeen of the most profitable Sudanese companies were confiscated. In his speech to commemorate the first anniversary of the May Revolution President Ja'afar Numayri announced sweeping nationalization of all banks and insurance companies, including the Commercial Bank and Al-Nilein Bank owned by Sudanese. By the end of June 1970 the state had also nationalized virtually all companies large and small, offering compensation described by the *Times* of London as "neither fair, prompt, nor effective." In August the remaining estates and assets of the Mahdi and Mirghani families were seized.

This sweeping sequestration and nationalization were undertaken with a great deal of ideological enthusiasm but little understanding of how to administer complex private and international companies. Those appointed to manage these state corporations were politically correct but incompetent to master the details of their organizations, and what were once successful and profitable enterprises had now to be heavily subsidized, producing an additional financial burden the state could ill afford. State control of the Sudanese economy was accompanied by an ambitious Five-Year Industrial Development Plan that was badly flawed, poorly executed, and failed to achieve its objectives. Equally dramatic changes in Sudan's social policies accompanied the state seizure of the economy. Sweeping legislation in November 1970 gave greater powers to workers, generous debt and rent relief to Gezira tenants, and substantial increases in the number of students in intermediate and secondary schools.

Radical socialism also dominated the foreign policy of the RCC. Sudan established diplomatic relations with the East German Democratic Republic (GDR), which was followed by a spate of Sudanese delegations to most of the capitals of Eastern Europe, visits that were quickly rewarded by their emissaries bearing substantial soft loans – Bulgaria £6 million, the Czechs $10 million, the GDR £4 million, the Soviets £4 million, and the Hungarians $10 million. On 29 September 1969 the RCC announced that henceforth virtually all imported goods would come from those countries which had negotiated trade agreements, including most of the East European socialist countries, which dramatically shifted Sudanese trade from West to East. In 1970 Numayri embarked upon personal tours of Eastern Europe, China, and North Korea and began to take an active interest in Arab affairs, which was the direct result of his well-known commitment to Arab socialism. Relations with the West continued to deteriorate in direct proportion to American support for Israel.

Having crushed the Ansar, Numayri now turned to the communists, whose disagreements had become increasingly hostile during the winter and spring of 1969–70. The Mahjub faction of the SCP vociferously criticized Numayri for joining Egypt and Libya in the Federation of Arab Republics, known as the Tripoli Charter, on 27 December 1969, for both Nasser and Qadhafi had brutally smashed their communist parties. In March 1970, when Mahjub finally realized that Numayri was determined to crush the Ansar, he had grudgingly given his support, but the damage between them was irreparable. On 16 November 1970 Numayri abruptly dismissed three prominent pro-communists from the RCC – Lieutenant-Colonel Babikr al-Nur Sawar al-Dahab, Major Hashim Muhammad al-'Ata', and Faruq 'Uthman Hamdallah – accusing them of being indoctrinated by 'Abd al-Khaliq Mahjub to act independently as "selfish and unpatriotic agents of alien interests." Communist demonstrations became a common occurrence at the University of Khartoum, and the Beirut communist newspaper, *al-Kifrah*, published scathing attacks against Numayri, who struck back. On 12 February 1971 he delivered a caustic attack over Radio Omdurman in which he appealed to the intuitive Sudanese hostility toward communism and vowed to destroy the SCP, plunging Sudan into a cold war between Numayri and the communists throughout the spring of 1971. In his struggle with the Sudanese communists Ja'afar Numayri was quite prepared to go it alone, defying the support of virtually every Sudanese political organization – communists, Muslim Brothers, the NUP, the Umma, and SANU. His popularity plummeted; to the Sudanese he had become an autocrat, aloof, issuing a spate of decrees without consultation with his cabinet. His unpopularity can best be measured by the nine separate plots to overthrow him that were uncovered by his security forces since he came to power in 1969, and by July 1971 his future looked extremely bleak until, paradoxically, he was saved by his most implacable enemy, the communists.

When Ja'afar Numayri declared war on them in February 1971, the SCP had been actively plotting against him. On 29 June 'Abd al-Khaliq Mahjub escaped from a prison camp to find a safe haven in the Bulgarian Embassy, precipitating a spate of rumors in the capital that the "progressive elements" in the army were now planning to overthrow the regime. Nevertheless, on 18 July 1971 Numayri was openly boasting that he had secured Sudan from the communist threat, but the very next day, 19 July, Hashim Muhammad al-'Ata', forewarned he was about to be arrested, hastily and unilaterally launched the coup in broad daylight at 3:30 pm from barracks in the capital. Numayri, napping during the siesta at his guest house in Kafouri in Khartoum North, was seized and locked in a vault in the People's Palace, which had been captured by the rebels. 'Ata' had acted alone, without the approval of his two co-conspirators, Babikr al-Nur Sawar al-Dahab and Faruq 'Uthman Hamdallah, who were in London, or the approval of the SCP political bureau, which was taken completely by surprise. 'Ata' had made several fatal mistakes. He foolishly permitted demonstrators in support of the coup, including many of the communists he had immediately freed from prison, to march through the streets of Khartoum during the morning of 22 July waving red flags and shouting communist slogans that provoked the latent Sudanese hostility toward the communists felt by the citizens of the Three Towns. When 'Ata' announced over Radio Omdurman the same day an agricultural and industrial revolution to replace capitalist development, the Sudanese reaction in the countryside ranged from sullen alienation to open hostility. The Khartoum garrison remained loyal to 'Ata', but he had made no effort to solicit support from the Northern Defense Corps at Shendi, which remained loyal to Numayri and was preparing to march on the capital. Ja'afar Numayri himself had been rescued after a fierce firefight on 21 July by loyal troops from the Shagara Tank Command who stormed the People's Palace.

Moreover, the conspirators had seriously misjudged the reaction to the coup by President Muhammad Anwar al-Sadat (who had succeeded Nasser upon his death in October 1970) in Cairo and Mu'ammar Qadhafi in Tripoli. Sadat judiciously sent representatives to negotiate with 'Ata', but he ordered Egyptian troops guarding the Jabal Awliya Dam to march on Khartoum and the Egyptian air force to fly in elite Sudanese troops from the Suez Canal to the Wadi Saidna air base north of the capital. Late in the evening of 21 July Numayri broadcast on radio and television that he had returned with the help of the people and Allah. When Qadhafi ordered Libyan jets to force the BOAC plane carrying Babikr al-Nur and Faruq Hamdallah to land at Tripoli, they were arrested, handed over to Numayri, and executed. By the afternoon of 22 July, Hashim Muhammad al-'Ata' was completely isolated, and the seventy-two-hour coup came to a melancholy conclusion. Three principal leaders of the SCP, 'Abd al-Khaliq Mahjub, al-Shafi Ahmad al-Shaykh, and Joseph Garang, were immediately and secretly tried and promptly hanged. Other known communists were arrested; some were gunned down in the streets. The security forces rounded up another 3,000 leftists for questioning and detention.

The Sudanese were taken aback by the hasty secret trials and summary executions, not because of any sympathy for the communist leaders, but because they had been proud of the bloodless coups of the past, and political violence had been generally frowned upon in Sudanese political life after Numayri slaughtered the Ansar. Many Sudanese were stunned by the power of the communist movement, toward which they had a visceral revulsion. The communists had always sought to disguise their search for power by organizing alliances with other non-communist leftists, but they deluded themselves by frequently overestimating their own strength, mis-interpreting the hostility of their allies toward sectarianism and corrupt parliamentary politics as enthusiasm for the Marxist cause. When the time came to stand up and be counted, many fellow-travelers disappeared, leaving only an emasculated and much diminished hard core. The dramatic recovery of Numayri's popularity was as much derived from his determination to crush the communists as his flamboyant escape, which had great appeal to the Sudanese penchant for panache. The SCP, however, managed to survive the counter-coup. Two weeks after Mahjub's execution Muhammad Ibrahim Nuqud was elected secretary-general, but his leadership was ineffectual. The SCP never recovered its former strength, as many of its fellow-travelers and intelligentsia drifted over to the new Sudan Socialist Union (SSU), leaving the rump to churn out bombastic denunciations of Numayri and his policies.

Ja'afar Numayri was badly shaken by the events of 19–22 July 1971. They caused this opportunistic pragmatist to swing to the right and station himself more squarely in the center of Sudanese society in search of a broader base for his authoritarian rule. He correctly perceived that the sudden restoration of his popularity was not because of past policies, which the mass of Sudanese found distasteful, but because he was a more palatable alternative to the communists. In both the RCC and the Council of Ministers communists and their fellow-travelers were replaced by "neutral technocrats" – Dr. Ja'afar Muhammad 'Ali Bakhit, minister of local government and resident intellectual, Dr. Mansur Khalid, the cosmopolitan lawyer and minister for foreign affairs, and Ibrahim Mun'im, the pragmatic, market-oriented minister of finance – who enjoyed Numayri's confidence and support. Hoping to capitalize on his purge of the leftists Numayri sought greater popular participation and approval by holding a plebiscite. On 14 August 1971, before the largest mass demonstration ever witnessed in Khartoum, Numayri announced that the RCC had nominated him for the presidency of Sudan, to be decided by a popular plebiscite on 10 October by which the Sudanese people could vote yes or no as to whether President Numayri should remain in office for another six years. Radio Omdurman announced the results two days later: Ja'afar Numayri had won 98.6 percent of the vote. He followed this lop-sided approval of the electorate by proclaiming the SSU would henceforth control the Sudanese press, five subversive trade union leaders were to be expelled, and a fifteen-member Politburo organized to manage the SSU as the sole political organization permitted in Sudan to mobilize popular participation in government, an instrument but not an institution capable of dealing with the Southern Problem.

SOUTHERN POLITICIANS, ANYA-NYA, ADDIS ABABA, AND AUTONOMY

In their address to the nation on 25 May 1969 neither Ja'afar Numayri nor Babikr 'Awadallah had mentioned the Southern Problem, but it could not be ignored. All but two members of the RCC had served as army officers in the South, and their approach was simply to provide better arms for the army to crush the "Mutiny"; the communists, however, had long argued for southern autonomy. On 28 May 1969 Abel Alier had outlined a program for the South approved by the Steering Committee of the Southern Front and SANU-Inside that benignly declared that the Southern Problem was political, not military, and best resolved by negotiation, and that a cabinet office for southern affairs be established. The communist Joseph Garang had been duly appointed minister for southern affairs, but his authority was soon rendered impotent by the ill-disguised contempt for him and his ministry by northern officials in the South. When Abel Alier, now minister for supply and trade, prepared a memorandum in October 1970 arguing for dialogue with the Anya-Nya, he was scorned by the Council of Ministers and ignored by Numayri.

Meanwhile, in the South the president of the SSPG, Aggrey Jaden, had sought to centralize the Anya-Nya command and appointed Major-General Emedio Tafeng Odongi, an illiterate Latuka with limited military experience, commander-in-chief of the Anya-Nya, now grandiloquently entitled the Anya-Nya National Armed Forces (ANAF), with Joseph Lagu his chief of staff. Lagu deeply resented his demotion to chief of staff to Tafeng, whom he regarded as incompetent, and refused to take orders from him. The demotion sealed Lagu's contempt for southern politicians. Convinced that the military, not the politicians, should manage the affairs of the movement, he began in June 1967, after the crushing defeat of the Arabs in the Six-Day Arab–Israeli War, to secure sole command of the Anya-Nya by soliciting arms from Israel. The southerners had previously only a few furtive contacts with Israel in 1965 and 1966, but when Lagu had been chief of staff of the SSPG he wrote to Israeli Prime Minister Levi Eshkol offering his services and for the Anya-Nya to open a second front in southern Sudan against the Arabs in return for arms. His overtures were well received, and the Israelis arranged for him to visit Tel Aviv in December 1967 for intensive military training, including plans for Israeli air drops. Lagu returned to Kampala with funds for the politicians to travel, promote the movement, and purchase a car. During the winter and spring of

1967–68 the rift between Lagu and the leadership of the SSPG could no
longer be concealed from the Israelis, particularly after Lagu had established
his separate headquarters in eastern Equatoria at Owiny-ki-Bul (*Acholi*, listen to the sound of the drum), from where he informed the Israelis that he
had permanently disassociated himself from the SSPG. When Aggrey Jaden
suddenly abandoned the SSPG in August, the frustrated Israelis thereafter
ignored southern politicians and dealt solely with Lagu.

Joseph Lagu was born in the small hamlet of Monokwe in Moli,
Madiland, about 80 miles south of Juba. Son of the chief clerk of the
customs post and river port at the strategic Sudan–Uganda border town of
Nimule, Lagu was exposed in childhood to the constant flow of many peoples, and his flair for languages enabled him to acquire fluency in Acholi,
Dinka, and Juba (southern) Arabic in addition to Madi. Through his father's
efforts he began his education at the CMS Akot Elementary School, where
he was baptized into the Anglican faith before advancing to the CMS
Nugent Intermediate (Junior Secondary) School at Loka and finally gradu-
ating from "the Eton of the South," the Rumbek Senior Secondary School.
Having passed the university entrance examination, Lagu was one of two
southerners admitted in 1958 to the Sudan Military College in the entering
class of seventy cadets. Commissioned a lieutenant in 1960, he was posted
to the 10th Battalion of the Northern Command. Disgusted with the treatment of southerners and the flight for their lives of southern intellectuals
seeking safety in Uganda and Congo during the 'Abbud regime, he defected
in 1963 to join the SANU politicians in Kampala, where he was present
at the founding of the Anya-Nya on 19 August 1963. He became increasingly uncomfortable with the endless personal vendettas of the southern
politicians and soon distanced himself from political intrigue, confining his
activities to commanding, recruiting, and training the Anya-Nya in eastern
Equatoria. He successfully remained aloof from the squabbles of politicians in a succession of dysfunctional southern governments and avoided
the armed ethnic clashes in central Equatoria between Dinka and Bari. Now
firmly in control of the flow of Israeli weapons, Lagu easily consolidated
his sole command of the Anya-Nya.

The Israelis remained cautious throughout 1968 as they observed the
collapse of the SSPG and the increasing isolation of its successor, the Nile
Provisional Government. In January 1969 Lagu again visited Israel for intensive training and to arrange for the visit of an Israeli military assessment
team, which recommended two monthly air drops of arms and ammunition into eastern Equatoria. In June 1969 the Israelis were also instrumental
in obtaining the permission of Ethiopian Emperor Haile Selassie, who was

openly sympathetic to the southern liberation movement as a countermove to Sudanese and Arab support for the Eritrean insurrection, to open a training camp in Ethiopia to funnel arms and Anya-Nya into the Upper Nile. In late summer 1969 the Israelis were also able to obtain permission from a very reluctant President Milton Obote to use Ugandan air space to ferry weapons to Lagu in return for training Ugandan pilots to fly the Israeli Fouga jet fighters, but when this marriage of convenience collapsed under pressure from Numayri and Obote's own opposition in Uganda, the commander-in-chief of the Ugandan army, Idi Amin, a Nubi of Sudanese descent whose kinfolk were the Kakwa in northwest Uganda and southern Sudan, surreptitiously continued the flow of Israeli arms to Lagu's headquarters at Owiny-ki-Bul, where teams of four or five Israeli military advisers were rotated every six weeks. In January 1971 the first of many batches of Anya-Nya officers arrived in Israel for short courses in weapons and explosives, as well as radio transmission, military management, and primary medical care.

In order to fill the vacuum created by the departure of Aggrey Jaden in August 1968 his vice-president, Kamilo Dhol, a Dinka from Aweil, organized a second national convention to decide the fate of the SSPG which gathered on 19 March 1969 at Balgo-Bindi inside the Congo (Zaire) border. After several days of endless debates the convention renamed the SSPG the Nile Provisional Government (NPG), with a constitution and an elected president, Gordon Muortat Mayen, a Dinka. He filled his cabinet with younger, better-educated men than the aging generation of southern politicians in which the Dinka were now dominant and quite unacceptable to many ethnic Equatorians. Internal warfare soon erupted in summer 1969 between the Dinka retiring from Balgo-Bindi and the Bari Anya-Nya from nearby Angundri (Bungu). Joseph Lagu studiously refused to intervene in this debacle, devoting his energies to establishing his headquarters at Owiny-ki-Bul, consolidating his authority by training cadres of Anya-Nya personally loyal to him, and organizing the distribution of Israeli weapons and military equipment arriving by air and through Uganda and Ethiopia. A momentary challenge to Lagu occurred in November 1969 when Tafeng defected from the NPG and founded the Anyidi Provisional Government (APG), but despite the assistance of the Biafran German mercenary Rolf Steiner to train the Anyidi Anya-Nya, Tafeng could not compete with Lagu. He dissolved the APG and joined Lagu but, now an old man, played no further role in the southern liberation movement. Steiner had accompanied Tafeng to Owiny-ki-Bul where, however, he was not welcomed by the Israelis, who regarded him as a "Nazi" and who convinced Lagu to arrange for his transit across the border to Uganda. He was promptly arrested by the Ugandan authorities and handed over to Khartoum, where he was tried and imprisoned for life but later released after the signing of the Addis Ababa Agreement in 1972.

Gordon Muortat Mayen's failure to restore Israeli arms shipments to the NPG sealed his fate. Eighteen months had now passed since the initial trickle of weapons from the Israelis, now diverted to Lagu, had ceased, and his senior Dinka officers surrounded his residence at Balgo-Bindi and persuaded Muortat to dissolve the NPG and declare his loyalty to Joseph Lagu. The inglorious collapse of the NPG was the last political obstacle to Lagu asserting his undisputed authority, and in a symbolic gesture he renamed the ANAF the Southern Sudan Liberation Movement (SSLM) in January 1971. Since he and he alone controlled the flow of arms, Anya-Nya commanders from all over the South made their way to Owiny-ki-Bul to swear loyalty to their commander-in-chief in return for guns. Lagu also abandoned Aggrey Jaden's concept of an ethnically integrated national army and instead reorganized the Anya-Nya into separate ethnic units. Henceforth, Bari Anya-Nya would remain in central Equatoria, Dinka Anya-Nya in the Bahr al-Ghazal, and Nuer Anya-Nya in the Upper Nile. The Equatorians could easily be supplied from Owiny-ki-Bul, while the Anya-Nya in the Bahr al-Ghazal could still receive arms and ammunition from the armory in Angundri (Bungu) of Jaden's old SSPG now under Lagu's control. The Upper Nile, as always, proved fiercely independent, logistically difficult to reach, and a place where Lagu's authority remained more symbolic than real. In order to consolidate his control in the Upper Nile he created an Annual Command Council and, late in 1970, appointed Brigadier Joseph O. Akuon, a Nuer and Anya-Nya regional commander in the Upper Nile as his deputy commander-in-chief to organize the Israeli arms shipments from Ethiopia.

The symbolic unification of the Anya-Nya command structure combined with the arms from Israel rapidly intensified the guerilla war. The political chaos created by the incompetence of southern politicians and the rise and fall of southern governments during 1966 and 1967 had reduced the Anya-Nya to independent assaults on isolated posts, night raids on the edges of the well-fortified towns, and the more successful ambushes of army convoys on lonely roads. During 1968–69 these furtive attacks had become better coordinated by the installation of a communications network of power-generated radios that enabled Lagu to receive reports and to direct operations throughout much of the South. In 1970 the civil war entered a new phase made possible by Israeli weapons, training, and signals equipment in which the Anya-Nya mounted an aggressive offensive, heavily mined all the major roads in Equatoria, shelled Juba with artillery, and prepared a set-piece battle for the strategic town of Morta. Numayri responded to the increased Anya-Nya activity by sending Soviet advisers, weapons, and Soviet MIG 17s and helicopters to support the army. The battle for Morta raged during September and October 1970, during which the town changed hands in fierce fighting with heavy losses on both sides, including several Soviet helicopters, until 20 October, when Anya-Nya reinforcements recaptured the town, inflicting heavy losses. The following year, 1971, Numayri ordered a major offensive throughout Equatoria, but it met with mixed success, although during it Lagu's headquarters at Owiny-ki-Bul was overrun by Sudanese troops supported by two battalions of Egyptian commandoes. The Anya-Nya retaliated, destroying a major army base at Naupo in western Equatoria in May, where they used Israeli anti-tank guns to great effect against Soviet armor. By the end of the year the Anya-Nya had fought the Sudanese army to a stalemate.

Equatoria is a province of heavily forested mountains and valleys east of the Bahr al-Jabal. West of the Nile along the Congo–Nile watershed thick gallery forests tower above the hundreds of streams and a dozen major rivers which flow through woodlands interspersed with tall grasslands to the *sadd*, the perfect environment for guerilla warfare. The Upper Nile and the Bahr al-Ghazal, however, constitute the eastern section of the great plain of savanna, woodlands, and Sahel which stretches across Africa from Senegal to the Ethiopian highlands and the Red Sea. During the rains the *sadd* overflows to inundate much of the Upper Nile and the eastern Bahr al-Ghazal grasslands, bringing military operations to a standstill. During the dry season (from October to April) the water recedes into the *sadd*, leaving a vast sea of grass which, when burnt, becomes a flat, blackened surface, exposing the viscous cotton soil into which sink the wheels and treads of truck and tank. Consequently, insurgency becomes a question of furtive raiders retiring under cover of darkness, and the security forces are confined largely to excursions from fortified posts on the navigable rivers and the more deadly attacks from the air against Anya-Nya columns exposed on a vast open plain with no place to hide.

Until 1969 the ill-equipped Nuer Anya-Nya had confined their military operations to the provincial capital, Malakal, and to ambushing river traffic, punctuated by occasional firefights at Pochalla in 1963 and Nasir in 1964, but they suffered a severe defeat at Akobo in 1965. Despite the air force flying regular sorties and indiscriminately bombing villages from Malakal to the Ethiopian border, the Nuer Anya-Nya, now equipped with

Israeli weapons through Ethiopia, launched a better-coordinated offensive in 1970, ambushing army convoys and sinking a steamer on the Sobat river. After a month of heavy fighting the Nuer Anya-Nya scored their greatest victory in December 1970 and January 1971, capturing Pocahalla, where they killed over 150 Sudanese troops, and seizing a large quantity of arms, ammunition, and even 82mm cannons. During the same winter dry season the Bahr al-Ghazal Anya-Nya, led by officers trained in Israel, systematically mined the major roads to Wau, ambushed an armored column at Tead-Adhol, and ripped up the rails of the strategic railway line to Wau. This startling resurgence of the Anya-Nya, now numbering some 13,000 men throughout southern Sudan, was nonetheless insufficient to drive the northern Sudanese army from the heavily fortified towns in the South. They had, however, clearly demonstrated by 1971 that the Sudanese army was incapable of conquering southern Sudan, leaving President Numayri with no other option but to resolve the Southern Problem by a political solution.

As a condition of his appointment in July 1971 of Abel Alier as minister of southern affairs to replace the executed John Garang, Numayri agreed that Abel Alier should open a dialogue with the SSLM. He also appointed him Sudan's representative to tour western Europe raising funds for half a million southern refugees. During the tour Abel became closely acquainted with members of the World Council of Churches (WCC), the Lutheran World Federation, Norwegian Church Aid, and Oxfam in London, all of which had worked with southern refugees. Upon his return to Khartoum he met in June and August with a delegation of the WCC, the All-African Council of Churches (AACC), and the Sudan Council of Churches (SCC), which reported that the SSLM was indeed willing to negotiate on the basis of a united Sudan. On 9 January 1971 Abel Alier and General Muhammad al-Baghir Ahmad, a pragmatic army officer who had command of the security forces in each of the three southern provinces, met in the Ghion Hotel, Addis Ababa, with Dr. Lawrence Wol Wol, Mading de Garang, Elisapana K. Mulla, Job Adier, and the Rev. Paul Puoth from the SSLM. The Rev. Burgess Carr, secretary-general of the AACC, who had led the first church delegation in June, acted as chair, and Sir Dingle Foot QC, who had advised African independence movements in East Africa, was retained by the SSLM for legal advice, although he did not himself attend the meeting. The initial atmosphere of tension and distrust had mellowed by the second day, and before departing each group agreed to study the documentation exchanged and to meet again a year later in January 1972.

At first Numayri appeared disappointed that Abel Alier had not returned with an agreement, but he ordered a unilateral cease-fire. At the same time the SSLM made considerable efforts to impress upon the Anya-Nya commanders that the time had come for talks with the government. By January there appeared to be a general willingness to open negotiations that was greatly facilitated by two unrelated incidents. In August 1971 the sacred spear, Lierpiou, a principal deity of the Anya-Nya, had been returned from the National Ethnographic Museum in Khartoum to the Gwalla, bringing great joy to the Bor Dinka. By itself this was an insignificant gesture, but it was accompanied by the appointment of respected southerners as commissioners for each of the three southern provinces, which did much to improve the sullen hostility of the southern Sudanese. Then, on 6 December 1971, a Sudan Airways Fokker left Khartoum on a routine flight to Malakal and mysteriously disappeared. Seventeen days later, on 23 December, an Anya-Nya unit under Captain Sunday Gideon rescued the survivors, treated their injuries, fed them, and led them to the nearest government post. Widely publicized reports in the media of this dramatic rescue included glowing testimony by the survivors of their humane treatment, contradicting the northern media's distorted image of the Anya-Nya as "bandits" and "terrorists."

The historic negotiations opened on 16 February 1972 in the Addis Ababa Hilton Hotel with the blessing of Emperor Haile Selassie on the fundamental understanding that the talks were to produce a plan for regional autonomy within a united Sudan, not the separate state originally demanded by the SSLM. Many years later southern critics of the Addis Ababa Agreement denounced the southern negotiators for not insisting upon secession, but they forget the open hostility of African governments in the 1970s toward secessionist movements. Such movements had been ruthlessly suppressed in the Congo and Nigeria with the overwhelming approval of the Organization of African Unity (OAU), which had steadfastly opposed separatists. There was much sympathy in Africa for "the black peoples of southern Sudan," but few had any enthusiasm for their independence, including Haile Selassie, who was fighting his own secessionist movement in Eritrea. The leaders of the SSLM in London appeared to be oblivious to this consensus among African governments, as were the Anya-Nya in 1972, who believed they were fighting for independence, but not their commander-in-chief, Joseph Lagu. With the concurrence of the senior SSLM (Anya-Nya) commanders, he carefully selected an SSLM delegation to continue negotiations "until a solution was found" that precluded any discussion of secession.

The SSLM was led by Ezbon Mundiri, a blunt, obstinate, and tough negotiator, who had served as minister of communications in the Transitional Government. Although hard-line secessionists, Dr. Lawrence Wol Wol and Mading de Garang had been involved in the negotiations since November and could not be excluded. Albino Batali, Colonel Frederick Brian Maggot, Angleo Voga Morgan, Lagu's personal assistant, and Job Adier, SSLM emissary in Addis Ababa, and the Rev. Paul Puoth, who completed the delegation of eight, were all flexible on secession. The government's delegation was also selected with care. Abel Alier was the only southerner and was personally appointed by Numayri to lead the delegation. The selection of the remaining delegates was not so simple. Most northern Sudanese of any station were appallingly ignorant of the remote South and its inhabitants. Moreover, many of the senior northern politicians were firmly opposed to the talks, insisting on a military solution. Numayri chose Major-General Muhammad Ahmad al-Baghir, who had been with Abel at the November meeting with the SSLM. Dr. Ja'afar Bakhit, who was prepared to grant substantial powers to the South, favored a single southern region, but he had little use for the Anya-Nya. 'Abd al-Rahman 'Abdullah, who had been chairman of the Twelve-Man Committee on the South after the failure of the Round Table Conference in 1965, was the director of the Academy of Public Administration, which had trained northern administrators for posts in the South. Numayri completed the delegation with Dr. Mansur Khalid, appointed foreign minister in October 1971 and a suave, sophisticated attorney very sympathetic to the southerners, and two senior military officers. Brigadier Mirghani Sulayman Khalil and Colonel Kamal Abashir Yassin had little sympathy for the South, but they had been classmates at the Military College in the early 1950s of Colonel Frederick Maggot and Joseph Lagu respectively whose old acquaintance perhaps could foster a spirit of cooperation.

By mutual agreement the discussions began with specific issues that could be resolved more readily than contentious constitutional questions. English was to remain the principal language of the South and Arabic the official language of Sudan; southern regional languages would be left to develop. Six principal issues were soon resolved amid lengthy and often emotional discussions usually resulting in compromises. The South would remain one region as defined by the boundaries at independence, 1 January 1956; areas of southern concentration outside the South, like Abyei, would decide to remain outside or join the South by referendum. The southern region would be governed by a People's Regional Assembly and a High Executive Council (HEC) of ministers who would have authority over local government, education, public health, natural resources, and police. The national government would continue to control defense, foreign affairs, currency, inter-regional communications, and national economic, social, and educational planning. The president of the HEC would be appointed by the president of the Republic of Sudan in consultation with other members of the Council. Juba was declared the regional capital.

Indeed, the talks had progressed much more smoothly than either the SSLM or the government had thought possible, until they became hopelessly deadlocked on 19 February over the question of security, which starkly revealed the deep distrust between northern and southern Sudanese. The SSLM insisted upon a separate army commanded by southern officers; the government delegation absolutely opposed any such force, convinced that its formation would be the first step toward separation. This implacable impasse was referred to the emperor of Ethiopia, who emphasized the OAU's belief in the sovereign unity of African states that could only be achieved by one united army under a single command, but he allowed that the Sudanese army should be composed of equal numbers of northerners and southerners. After another four days of intense negotiations a compromise was reached based on the emperor's formula. The composition of the national army, the Sudan People's Armed Forces (SPAF), would be in proportion to the population, with a Southern Command of 12,000 officers and men, 6,000 of whom would be southerners. After this contentious issue was resolved agreement was easily reached on those remaining, and on the evening of 27 February 1972 the delegates initialed the Addis Ababa Agreement as well as a Cease-Fire Agreement and the protocols for the Interim Administrative Arrangements which concerned amnesty, reparations, relief, rehabilitation, and resettlement, as well as the temporary composition of units of the armed forces in the South.

The Addis Ababa Agreement was well received by Numayri, and on 3 March 1972 he endorsed the agreement at a political rally in Wad Nubawi in Omdurman, ordered a cease-fire, signed the Southern Provinces Self-Government Agreement, and declared that henceforth 3 March would be a holiday known as National Unity Day. Three days later he embarked upon a triumphal tour of the South, where massive gatherings of southerners vividly celebrated his bringing peace to their war-torn land. Suddenly the SSLM requested a delay. Caught between southern separatists and the joyous celebrations by the southern peoples and demands by the influential southern political leaders in Khartoum and London for him to sign the agreement, Joseph Lagu hesitated until assured that those southerners integrated into the Sudan army would be Anya-Nya. Thereafter, he had no other option but to sign. At 4:30 pm on 27 March 1972 Major-General Joseph Lagu and Dr. Mansur Khalid ratified the Addis Ababa Agreement at the imperial palace packed with Sudanese and presided over by His Imperial Majesty. It was an historic but flawed agreement, for many of its articles were dependent upon mutual trust when there was none.

For a few fleeting years President Ja'afar Numayri appeared to be a truly national leader, embracing all Sudanese irrespective of ethnicity, cultures, lineage loyalties, and religion. He basked in an outpouring of international acclaim as a peacemaker in a war-torn country when, in 1972, there were very few in Africa. He relished the adulation and the rumors of a nomination for the Nobel Peace Prize. When Lagu, after some hesitation, arrived in Khartoum with his SSLM entourage, Numayri rewarded him with the very senior rank of major-general in the SPAF and membership of the Politburo of the SSU, with the authority to integrate the Anya-Nya into the army, but not the vice-presidency he expected; the separatists in the bush contemptuously believed he had been bought. The more onerous task of organizing the southern regional government fell to the architect of the Addis Ababa Agreement and vice-president, Abel Alier, whom Numayri unilaterally nominated president of the Interim High Executive Council without consultation.

Within a few days Abel had selected his cabinet of eleven regional ministers, seven of whom were exiled politicians, "outsiders," and four political activists from within, "insiders," labels of identity that symbolized lingering animosities. They all flew to Juba on 24 April 1972 and began to govern. Appointments to the civil service that soon followed were skewed in favor of Equatorians, for mission-educated Equatorians in 1972 far outnumbered their contemporaries from the more populous Nilotes of the Bahr al-Ghazal and Upper Nile, which exacerbated historical ethnic passions. Tribal chiefs who were the stewards of traditional authority were conspicuously absent from the autonomous government, as were the few educated refugees returning to the South, who complained bitterly at their exclusion. The immediate issue facing this fragile government was the repatriation and resettlement of half a million southern Sudanese from refugee camps in neighboring states and another half million IDPs inside Sudan. The Repatriation and Relief Commission was established to receive returnees coming over the border and transport them to their homes with the help of the United Nations High Commissioner for Refugees (UNHCR), assisted by a host of humanitarian non-governmental organizations (NGOs), including among others the African Committee for the Relief of the Southern Sudanese (ACROSS), Norwegian Church Aid, Oxfam, World Service, the

Catholic Relief Organization, the Catholic Charity Caritas, and the Red Cross, who were not to know that they would all remain active in southern Sudan for the next twenty-five years. The IDPs slowly emerged from hiding deep in the bush or from the Peace Villages first constructed in 1965.

The most sensitive and emotive articles in the Addis Ababa Agreement concerned the integration of southerners into the police, prisons, and army. Although the army claimed to be the only "national" institution in Sudan, its composition could hardly claim to represent the "nation." An overwhelming majority of the rank and file and non-commissioned officers (NCOs) were westerners; the officer corps was predominantly from the riverine tribes, particularly the Shayqiyya. The integration of southerners implied a sweeping reorganization of the armed forces to make a genuinely "national" army, but that threatened the vested interests of the northern officers and rankers of the SPAF. Although many northerners were willing to accept autonomy for the South, there were few who favored integration of the armed forces. Those opposed took comfort in the language of the Agreement that integration was a "temporary arrangement" to be accomplished in five years. Some in the military and even some in civilian circles interpreted that to mean the Agreement would automatically dissolve after five years. Others interpreted the Agreement to mean that the integration of southerners into the army's Southern Command would end after five years, the units then being posted throughout the country, where their presence in the armed forces would disappear through dismissals, retirements, and resignations. They deeply resented special treatment for the South, and many officers were angry and bitter at the thought of accepting "terrorists" into their beloved army. There were numerous resignations in protest. The opposition reasoned, quite rightly, that this political settlement had greatly strengthened Numayri. Failure to implement the Agreement would be a major step toward overthrowing the regime, and his Achilles heel was the integration of the armed forces. Many of the Anya-Nya and returnees believed that those Anya-Nya integrated would be outnumbered and disposable. There were, finally, those southerners who regarded integration of the armed forces optimistically as the first step toward national integration of Sudan's diverse cultures, religions, and races. Nevertheless, they were also the first to insist that the new Southern Command be composed predominantly of southerners who, upon leaving the army, would be replaced by locally recruited southern replacements.

Some 3,000 northern police and prison wardens in the South were swiftly replaced by Anya-Nya selected by the Police and Prisons Commission, but the Joint Military Commission, having five years to complete the integration of the army, moved more slowly and with greater caution than police and prisons. By July 1973 the recruitment and training of 6,203 Anya-Nya, 2,067 from each province, had been completed and was approved on 31 July. The remaining 7,600 Anya-Nya were absorbed as laborers in such government departments as roads, forestry, and agriculture. Most of them were dismissed in 1974 when the Special Fund for transition was exhausted. Training in weapons, logistics, and tactics was necessary to close the gap between the rustic Anya-Nya and the regular soldiers of the army, including Major-General Lagu himself, as well as a young Captain John Garang de Mabior, the future commander of the Sudan People's Liberation Army (SPLA), who was sent off to the United States and Fort Benning, Georgia, on Lagu's recommendation, for advanced training. Other "absorbed" Anya-Nya officers and NCOs were stationed at the headquarters of Southern Command, which was reorganized into six infantry battalions of absorbed Anya-Nya and five of the old army. By November 1975 the battalions were now composed of mixed personnel, and by 1976 the reorganization of Southern Command into an integrated and self-contained unit was complete. This was an astonishing achievement, given the lack of enthusiasm for integration in both civilian and military circles in the North and suspicious Anya-Nya in the South. It was not accomplished, however, without numerous ugly incidents by absorbed Anya-Nya – mutinies in Juba in December 1974 and at Akobo in March 1975, and the desertion of a fully equipped company from Wau in an abortive attempt to restart the insurgency in the bush. These and other potentially violent incidents, which would have destroyed the political settlement at Addis Ababa, were sometimes defused by the personal intervention of Regional President Abel Alier, but especially by Major-General Lagu, the former by the diplomatic language of an accomplished jurist, the latter by his prestige as the former commander-in-chief of the Anya-Nya, discretion, and the overwhelming authority of a modern major-general.

During the first eighteen months the Regional Transitional Government worked quietly and with surprising success to organize the relevant agencies of the Regional Government and the more daunting task of the repatriation, relief, and rehabilitation of 1 million returnees. The passage of a new national constitution in May 1973 which included the Southern Sudan Self-Government Act enabled the elections in October 1973 of the Regional Assembly responsible for the governance of the South and to which the HEC was accountable. During its four-year term the Assembly was characterized by lively debates, feeble understanding of parliamentary procedure, and motions of censure frequently proposed for no other reason than personal vindictiveness. Nevertheless, the Assembly passed mundane legislation without which the Regional Government could not function, and resolved serious and potentially explosive issues over the safety of southerners sent north for training, and charges of corruption over a large purchase of educational materials which precipitated heated charges and counter-charges that nearly dissolved the Regional Government before the matter was peacefully defused. The contentious question of the language of instruction in schools was satisfactorily settled by instruction in the vernacular languages, English, and Arabic in an ascending level of the educational ladder.

Right from the start of their proceedings members of the Assembly had taken their constitutional supervisory powers over the HEC and the various government ministries very seriously. They had bitterly resented the fact that President Numayri had nominated Abel Alier, "a northern stooge," as the sole candidate for president of the HEC, which guaranteed his election, despite the terms of the Addis Ababa Agreement that the president of the HEC should be elected by the Assembly and appointed by the president of the Republic. Moreover, some members of the Assembly were very envious of the HEC, whose ministers enjoyed generous privileges, including better salaries, free housing, and cars, and a substantial gratuity upon resignation so that those who most aspired and conspired to become ministers did not hesitate to use specious accusations, personal vindictiveness, and ethnic hostility against those in office. The fledgling Southern Regional Government was not the first or the last to flounder in political inexperience and inadequacies during its first fragile efforts to govern. Many skeptics, both in the North and abroad, firmly believed that the southerners were quite incapable of effective governance, but when the Assembly's four-year term expired on 19 December 1977 its members could take pride that they had indeed been able to govern. Democracy was alive and well in southern Sudan.

THE SSU, THE CONSTITUTION, AND PROSPERITY

In 1969 Ja'afar Numayri rightly perceived that the Sudanese would welcome a pragmatic, trans-sectarian government so long as the May Revolution was not just another military coup, a return to the militarism of 'Abbud. As early as January 1970 he announced his intention to form a broad-based political organization, not a party. The SSU would replace all the old political parties and transcend tribal, sectarian, regional, and ideological boundaries. The SCP was ideologically opposed to the SSU and managed to delay its creation until its fall from grace on 19 July 1971 (see pp. 100–02 above). The newly constituted SSU was to replace the multi-party system, whose sectarian parties had made a mockery of parliamentary government, by a broad-based organization whose aim was to make policy and mobilize the popular will behind distinctive programs recommended by specialized committees of "technocrats" who would provide "scientific" solutions. The SSU consisted of a massive pyramid, at the bottom of which were 6,381 Basic Units Committees, each with its elected committee and above which were four levels – 1,892 Section Conferences, 325 District Conferences, 34 Sub-Province Conferences, and 10 Province Conferences – culminating at the tip of the pyramid in the National Congress. The diminishing number of representatives at each level would be elected by the conference below. The National Congress elected its president, who appointed the secretary-general and half the members of the Central Committee, the other half being elected by the Congress. The fundamental flaw in the SSU was the hopeless confusion in the minds of the Sudanese between the Basic Units of the SSU and those of local government. To them the SSU was merely duplicating, frequently in competition for resources, the self-help schemes for health clinics and schools of local government authorities. The confusion was further compounded when the same individuals who served on local government councils in one capacity also served on the basic units committees in another.

Consequently, at the local level the SSU failed to evolve into the instrument for change it was meant to be or the forum for popular representation for which it was designed. This ambivalence was even more apparent at the national level, where the distinction between the SSU as a distinct, separate forum for democratic dialogue and the operations of government became hopelessly blurred, so that to the Sudanese the SSU simply represented another agency of the government, not an independent, dynamic, political organization. The result was a climate of competition between the SSU, the only political institution, and the government, which enabled Numayri, the consummate manipulator, to play off one against the other, a strategy that led to the ultimate extinction of both.

The temporary resolution of the Southern Problem at Addis Ababa now made it possible for Numayri to resolve the long-unsettled question of a permanent constitution to replace the much-amended temporary constitution of 1956. He convened a committee of three chaired by Jaʿafar Bakhit which produced a draft constitution based on the revised temporary constitution tabled in the spring of 1968 as well as on the constitutions of France, India,

Algeria, Tunisia, and Egypt. This draft and later counter-drafts were the subject of vigorous debates in the Assembly and the media that soon polarized around the two central issues that had strangled all previous efforts – identity and religion. The secular constitution, a complex document with some 225 articles, passed by the Assembly and promulgated on 8 May 1973, appeared to have resolved these two contentious issues by describing Sudan as a "unitary, democratic, socialist and sovereign republic, and a part of both the Arab and African entities." The African identity was defined by incorporating the Southern Sudan Self-Government Act (Article 8) in the constitution. The more emotive issue of religion was presumably settled by Article 16, which provided for freedom of religion, to the fury of those led by Ja'afar Bakhit who demanded that the constitution should uphold the values of Islam and *shari'a* as the principal sources of legislation. At the time many Sudanese were rightly skeptical that these two great conundrums for Sudan had been permanently laid to rest.

The life of this permanent secular constitution proved to be very brief. In 1975 a constitutional amendment severely curtailed human rights, and by 1977 Numayri was rapidly eroding the powers of the Legislative Assembly by regularly employing Article 106, Provisional Republican Orders, to draft legislation that was then approved pro forma by the Assembly. Although the constitution had numerous checks (Articles 106, 107, 111, and 118) on presidential powers, including the dissolution of the Assembly and the declaration of a state of emergency, within a few years Numayri repeatedly ignored them. Since Sudan possessed no tradition of constitutional history, the president was able to interpret the constitution to his own satisfaction by twisting the meaning of the text. Without strong independent party leadership, a vigilant legislature, and an independent judiciary, a president like Numayri could easily amend the constitution to emasculate it, and during the next decade the Sudanese viewed with increasing alarm the degeneration of the constitutional presidential system into the autocracy of President Ja'afar Numayri.

The failed communist coup of 19 July 1971 and the Addis Ababa Agreement of 27 March 1972 not only changed the course of domestic policy but also produced a dramatic reorientation of the economy. State intervention in the economy was abandoned in favor of a more cooperative approach between the various commercial and financial agencies of the government and of foreign governments, companies, and international organizations like the International Monetary Fund (IMF). By 1973 thirty expropriated companies and banks had been returned to their owners, and a variety of new legislation was passed to protect private investment: two

Figure 16 President Numayri with Sharif al-Tuhami (left) and a group of military officers.

Development and Promotion of Industrial Investment Acts, in 1972 and 1974; the Development and Encouragement of Agricultural Investment Act 1976; and the Encouragement of Investment Act 1980. Economic policies were dutifully reoriented to satisfy the economic policies demanded by the IMF.

The reorganization of the Sudan economy coincided with the sudden accumulation of vast amounts of revenue by the Gulf petroleum-producing states created by the spiraling increase in the price of oil after the Organization of Petroleum-Exporting Countries' (OPEC) boycott of its dependent customers in the West who had supported Israel in the Arab–Israeli War (known as the Yom Kippur or Ramadan War) of 1973. Having vast sums to invest, the Arab petroleum-producing states sought to alleviate their dependence on food from Western sources by investing in agricultural production in Sudan. With an estimated 63 million acres of uncultivated land and another 200 million available for grazing, the Arabs envisaged Sudan as the "breadbasket" of the Middle East with its vast land, cheap labor, and water available from the Nile and rainfall, to be financed by the Arabs and its production boosted by the agricultural technology of the West. In 1973 the Arab Fund for Economic and Social Development

(AFESD) agreed to invest $6 billion in Sudan during the first ten years of a more ambitious twenty-five year Basic Programme for Agricultural Development in Sudan of some 4 million acres. The Five-Year Industrial Development Plan of 1970 was revised by two "Interim Programmes" (1973–74, 1976–77) which increased the amount of investment in agriculture by some 15 percent to achieve self-sufficiency and then generate a surplus for export. Unlike the original Five-Year Plan of state intervention these schemes were a combination of state-owned enterprises, cooperative ventures with private investment, and others undertaken exclusively by private enterprise.

By the mid-1970s all of these incentives had produced a dramatic increase in funds for development from £S278 million in 1972–73 to £S433 million in 1973–74, and £S666 million in 1974–75. In 1976, when the "heroic years" of Ja'afar Numayri's presidency were coming to an end, the financial resources for development had risen to over £S1,000 million. The £S180 million Rahad Scheme brought under cultivation 300,000 acres of cotton and groundnuts irrigated by a 50-mile canal linking the Blue Nile with the Rahad river. It was funded by AFESD and the governments of Kuwait, Saudi Arabia, and the United States. Moreover, Roland "Tiny" Rowland, the British entrepreneur, and his Lonrho Ltd. signed a joint venture in February 1975 with the Sudan government to invest $25 million in the Kenana Sugar Company to develop the world's largest sugar plantation near Kosti on the White Nile and make the insatiable Sudanese demand for sugar self-sufficient by its refinery producing annually 300,000 tons of refined sugar. Lonrho itself became the sole purchasing agent for the Sudan government in Great Britain at considerable profit. By the time the refinery had begun production in 1981 the cost had become astronomical: officially $750 million, unofficially $1 billion. Faced with rising costs and a recession in the sugar market by 1984, it could only continue to operate by means of a substantial government subsidy, for it cost more to grow Kenana sugar than import it.

By 1976 the Arabs, mostly Saudis with unlimited petro-dollars, had financed two other major sugar-growing schemes at West Nile and another at Hajar al-Salaya north of Rabat with a capacity of 110,000 tons a year. The addition of smaller industrial projects, most of which were intertwined with agriculture, increased the value of industrial assets from £S67 million to £S143 million by 1975. The Interim Programmes specifically included greater government expenditure for infrastructure – new rolling stock and the improvement of the operational efficiency of the railway system, which had badly deteriorated in the late 1960s, docks at Port Sudan, and all-weather tarmac roads from Khartoum to Port Sudan and from Wad Medani to Sennar and Kosti on the White Nile. One of the greatest problems with governing Sudan has always been the dearth of telecommunications over its vast area, which was partly solved by the completion of an extensive microwave network complete with satellites by 1974.

A more ambitious project not included in the Interim Programmes was the excavation of the Jonglei Canal. In 1901 Sir William Garstin, undersecretary of state for public works in Egypt, had proposed the excavation of a canal, the Garstin Cut, that would transmit fresh water from the equatorial lakes to the White Nile that otherwise would be lost by evaporation and transpiration in the Sudd. This proposal was revived in 1946, but it was not until December 1971 that a sub-committee of the Egyptian–Sudanese Permanent Joint Technical Commission (PJTC), responsible for the hydrological implementation of the 1959 Nile Waters Agreement, presented an entirely new scheme for a canal 174 miles from the village of Jonglei on the Bahr al-Jabal to the confluence of the Sobat and White Nile rivers that would not change the regimen of the Sudd. The amount of land that would be reclaimed by the diversion of swamp water into the canal would be negligible, and the first all-weather overland road to link northern and southern Sudan would be built along the canal embankment. The signing of the Addis Ababa Agreement in February 1972 and the subsequent Southern Provinces Self-Government Act in March had now made possible the Jonglei Canal, and the final contract was signed between the PJTC and the French company, Compagnie de Constructions Internationales (CCI), on 28 July 1974 to construct Jonglei at a cost of £S52 million. An additional £S18 million was allocated for local development projects in the canal zone.

Although it was self-evident that the Jonglei Canal would have an enormous impact on the Nilotes living in the canal zone, the announcement of the project at first aroused little interest in southern society except among those in the Assembly who conspired to use Jonglei to topple the government of Abel Alier. A clandestine document was widely circulated among southern students and junior officials in the river towns of Juba, Bor, and Malakal claiming that 2 million Egyptian *fellahin* would be settled in the canal zone under the protection of Egyptian soldiers. A second set of rumors, equally bizarre but believed, was circulated declaring that the canal would drain the Sudd and destabilize the normal meteorological processes: there would be no swamp, no evaporation, no clouds, no rainfall, only a desert for the Egyptian *fellahin* to plough. All these rumors found fertile soil in Juba, where the threat of "Dinkacracy" was deeply rooted among the local Bari. On 17 October 1974 students from the Juba Commercial

Secondary School held a protest demonstration, and the police, having no tear gas or riot gear, ignominiously retreated before a barrage of stones to the protective walls of their headquarters. Emboldened by their success, the next day the students, joined by junior government employees, rampaged through the streets, breaking into shops and setting cars afire. They were only dispersed when the police shot into the crowd, killing two students. A state of emergency was declared, a curfew imposed, and some 200 demonstrators arrested, except the few who escaped to East Africa to provide passionate but ignorant propaganda for a clique of environmentalist activists convinced the canal would result in the desertification of the Sudd.

Both the regional and central governments reacted swiftly to control the damage. Abel Alier delivered an informed and calming speech to the Assembly in which he emphasized that no Egyptian peasants or troops were being sent to the South and described the many benefits to be derived from the construction of the canal. He ended his peroration with a ringing challenge:

I wish to say that although this [Jonglei] canal is a Central Government project, the Regional Government supports it and stands for it. If we have to drive our people to paradise with sticks we will do so for their own good and the good of those who come after us.[1]

President Numayri promptly appointed the National Council for the Development of the Jonglei Canal Area (NCDJCA) charged with "formulating socio-economic development plans for the Jonglei area," a Jonglei Executive Organ (JEO) responsible for conducting studies of the effect of the canal, and development projects for the people of the canal zone. No sooner had the JEO begun its task in 1976 than the Jonglei Canal came under a withering assault from impassioned environmentalists. From its origins in the Nairobi headquarters of the United Nations Environmental Programme the hue and cry of environmentalists was picked up by the European press, particularly in Germany and France. A steady stream of sometimes thoughtful, often strident, and frequently ignorant articles poured forth from the media led by a coalition of environmental groups in Europe and the United States known as the Environmental Liaison Center, with headquarters in Nairobi, demanding an immediate moratorium on all work in the canal zone. In 1977 the United Nations Conference on Desertification, held in Nairobi, provided a global forum for those who denounced the canal, particularly Professor Richard Odingo of Nairobi University, who dramatically declared, "Here is a canal being built in an area that could easily be Africa's next desert," which was absolute nonsense.[2]

The heated international debates culminated in a packed meeting sponsored by the Royal Geographical Society in London on 5 October 1982
entitled "The Impact of the Jonglei Canal in the Sudan." Twenty-five years
before, the Jonglei Investigation Team had conclusively demonstrated that
the canal would have no significant impact on precipitation. The multi-
volume studies of the canal zone undertaken for the JEO by Mefit-Babtie
Srl. from 1979 to 1983 substantially confirmed that conclusion.

The economical and speedy construction of the longest navigable canal
in the world was to be made possible by the "Bucketwheel," an awesome
machine, five stories high, weighing 2,300 tons, and consuming 10,400
gallons/day (40,000 liters, 900 tons) of fuel. This behemoth had to be fully
automated in order to keep the great wheel and its twelve buckets simultaneously revolving and rotating 180° precisely on grade in a plain where the
slope is only 2¼ inches/mile. Guided by a laser beam, the wheel itself would
complete a revolution every minute while simultaneously rotating 180° to
dig a canal over 130 feet wide and 20 feet deep, the buckets depositing the
debris onto a conveyor belt to the east bank, thus creating the all-weather
road. No sooner had the Bucketwheel shifted into high gear than the align-
ment of the canal was significantly altered in 1981. The original canal was a
straight line from Jonglei to the mouth of the Sobat. When the JEO learned
that the beds of the Atem and Bahr al-Jabal rivers approaching Jonglei were
extremely unstable, the entrance to the canal was moved upstream to Bor,
adding 56 miles and £S10 million to the cost of the canal, an extraordinary
bargain at 1981 prices, as the Bucketwheel crawled relentlessly forward to
its rendezvous with the Bahr al-Jabal at Bor.

Another large development project also not part of the Interim Programmes was the beginning of petroleum exploration of 200,000 square
miles of southern Kordofan and the Upper Nile by Chevron Overseas
Petroleum Incorporated (COPI). Northern Sudanese politicians were less
than enthusiastic. Privately, until the discovery of oil many northern
Sudanese would have been delighted to have the South secede and end
its accursed drain on the national treasury. Publicly, northern politicians
and civil servants remained convinced that if there were oil deposits in
southern Sudan, a fundamental bond of unity would be removed, enabling
the South to separate. This conviction soon appeared immutable through
a series of unfortunate episodes marred by disagreements and mispercep-
tions over oil. When President Numayri visited the United States in 1978
with his new Minister for Energy, Dr. Sharif al-Tuhami, who had been
openly disparaging of any oil development in the South, the American
media disclosed that commercial quantities of oil had been discovered

"in the southern part of western Sudan," to be piped 900 miles to Port Sudan for the international markets. The report was widely broadcast over the Voice of America; the South exploded in protest.

Waves of prolonged demonstrations surged through the southern towns demanding that the pipeline should pass "southern oil" through southern Sudan and East Africa to Mombasa. Khartoum reacted to the demonstrations by peremptorily replacing the southern garrison at Bentiu under the command of Captain Salva Kiir Mayardit, who was to become president of the autonomous Government of Southern Sudan in 2005, with a battalion of 600 northern troops from the western command. Other provocative incidents soon followed. When Khartoum sought to redraw the boundary between North and South in July 1980 to include the oil fields and rich grazing land of the Upper Nile and the Bahr al-Ghazal in Kordofan, southern students took to the streets in protest at this flagrant violation of the Addis Ababa Agreement. With little grace Numayri rescinded his decree, but northern and southern views over oil exploration and exploitation became ever more divergent and acrimonious.

In November 1980 President Numayri addressed the National Assembly to present the petroleum policy of his government. The small refinery scheduled for construction at Bentiu would be replaced by a 400-mile pipeline to pump the Bentiu crude to a larger refinery at Kosti in the North. Southern students again took to the streets, and the HEC and Regional Assembly angrily denounced his decision, for the loss of the refinery would simply condemn the greater Bentiu area to perpetual underdevelopment. Although Numayri refused to reverse his decision, he did agree to a package of government and Chevron initiatives that included a development authority in Bentiu, while Chevron undertook to improve health, drinking water, and education in the Bentiu Area Council. The southern Sudanese sullenly simmered in humiliation at their impotence, which Numayri did not let them forget when he grandly announced that he had abandoned his refinery at Kosti for an 870-mile pipeline to pump Bentiu crude directly to Port Sudan for export to the international markets.

These were nonetheless ebullient and prosperous years in which the large infusion of Arab and international capital trickled down into the *suq* and the pockets of even the most impoverished Sudanese. Even the casual foreign visitor could not but be aware of the optimism and buoyant belief in a rosy future that pervaded the Sudanese, particularly in the Three Towns of the center, whose prosperity continued to widen the gap between the heartland and the periphery, which was presumably content to receive the scraps from the bountiful dinner table of development in Khartoum. The president had demonstrated a national leadership that the Sudanese deserved, the SSU had provided a structure for the political mobilization of the people, and the economy was booming. This stability and growth could not have been made possible without the apparent resolution of the Southern Problem which enabled many northerners to leave the southerners alone to get on with their own affairs. Numayri basked in the glow of his enhanced prestige and wide support for his regime throughout the country. On New Year's Day 1976 there were few Sudanese who would have predicted their bubble was about to burst, and that President Ja'afar Numayri's regime would relentlessly disintegrate without the slightest token of remorse from his subjects.

CHAPTER 5

The government of Ja'afar Numayri: the years of dismay and disintegration, 1976–1985

JULY 1976, NATIONAL RECONCILIATION, AND REGIONALISM

In 1976 Numayri was in complete control. He had resolved the Southern Problem, created the SSU, reorganized his cabinet, and encouraged large amounts of Arab and international capital to launch a host of badly needed and widely publicized development schemes. Unfortunately, at the height of his popularity and prestige he became intoxicated by the prospects of absolute authority and in the future began to lose his way. He increasingly believed that he could rule without the traditional institutions of governance, guided instead by superstition and religious spirituality and surrounding himself with a Palace cabal of servile "cheerleaders." During his youth and early life in the army Ja'afar Numayri had displayed little interest in Islam beyond the routine obligations of a Muslim. He smoked cigars, enjoyed his Scotch, and loved John Wayne westerns. He appears to have found his spiritual solace in superstition and divine inspiration. In 1974 he installed Sharif 'Abdalla, a dubious *faki* from El Obeid, as grand *mufti* in the People's Palace. Numayri abruptly abstained from drink, sending a circular, *Guided Leadership*, to his senior officials to take the pledge not to drink alcohol. It was largely ignored but foreshadowed a growing insistence that his followers become more devout Muslims. The more he received divine guidance, the less he needed to observe the constitution.

Led by Dr. Bahaa al-Din Muhammad Idris, the Palace cabal evolved in what first appeared to be innocuous circumstances. Idris had been a lecturer in zoology at the University of Khartoum until he was forced to resign for divulging examination questions to a girl student. He became the assistant to Dr. Yammani Yaqub, the secretary-general of the National Council for Scientific Research, of which President Numayri was chairman. Idris soon ingratiated himself to Numayri, who returned his servile obeisance by appointing him state minister for special affairs in October 1972 over the strong objections of his cabinet ministers. No one seemed to know what functions the minister for special affairs was supposed to perform, but in August 1973 Numayri granted Idris blanket authority to negotiate on behalf of the government all agreements concerning development projects, and by 1974 he was firmly entrenched in the Palace as his assistant. He brought in Muhammad Mahjub, an unknown contributor to the army journal, who became Numayri's speech writer. Idris also installed Salim Eisa, a dubious Lebanese journalist from Beirut who, in turn, introduced Adnan Khashoggi to Idris and Numayri.

Adnan Khashoggi, known as "AK," was a flamboyant Saudi business-man and arms-dealer of Turkish descent educated in Alexandria at Victoria College and in California at Chico State and Stanford Universities. In 1974 he arrived in Khartoum and quickly established a close friendship with Ja'afar Numayri cemented by flights in his private jet and cruises on his luxurious yacht, *Nabila*. Numayri was captivated by Khashoggi's charisma and impressed by his intimate connections with royalty in Saudi Arabia, Imelda Marcos, widow of the exiled president of the Philippines, and even President Nixon of the United States. Khashoggi soon wielded great influ-ence over the impressionable Numayri from his palatial presidential guest house staffed by servants hand-picked by Idris.

During the next two years Khashoggi, with charm and panache, negotiated on behalf of Sudan at least a half-dozen multi-million-dollar international loans, all of which circumvented the process and plans for development carefully prepared in the first Interim Programme (1973–74) of the 1970 Five-Year Development Plan by offering private international investors exorbitant rates of interest that Sudan could ill afford but that were immensely profitable for Khashoggi. Basking in the illusion of per-petual prosperity created by both the genuine and fraudulent infusion of large amounts of capital, Numayri appears to have never thought to ques-tion the feasibility of or the need for these glamorous projects. Against all advice from his financial advisers between 1973 and 1974 Khashoggi managed a $200-million loan guaranteed by Saudi Arabia and negotiated additional loans for an oil refinery that was never built, imported German Magrius trucks unfit for Sudan, and the construction of a textile factory that never turned a profit, all of which circumvented the institutional process by which financial and trade agreements were supposed to be concluded. All this contributed to the deteriorating relationship between Numayri and his ministers.

On 25 January 1975 Ibrahim Moniem Mansur, the able minister of finance known for his integrity, abruptly resigned over rather spurious accusations in the Assembly. Numayri was furious. Goaded by his "cheerleaders" to beware ministers seeking power, at noon the following day he abruptly sacked his most able ministers, those "technocrats" who had been appointed specifically to make the May Revolution a reality by scientific studies, sound planning, and solid institution of government. They were replaced by "cheerleaders," sycophants, and men of little talent. Two days later Numayri delivered a scathing denunciation of his former ministers written by Muhammad Mahjub, the favorite of Idris, which the National Assembly unanimously declared an historic turning-point in the May Revolution.

On the afternoon of Thursday 5 September 1975 Colonel Hasan Husayn led an attempted coup d'état by discontented paratroopers, mostly westerners, *awlad al-gharib*, who deeply resented the neglect of the west by Khartoum, which had been made all the more visible after the granting of autonomy to southern Sudan. They arrested their senior commanders, seized Radio Omdurman to broadcast victory, and deceitfully announced that President Numayri was under house arrest. In fact, Numayri had suddenly decided to spend Thursday night in his official residence inside the army barracks, but instead of taking command of the loyal troops, as he had done in 1971, he ignominiously fled from Khartoum to hide in the house of a close friend in Gereif. Numayri having abdicated leadership, his loyal generals, led by the indomitable Muhammad al-Baghir, first vice-president and chief of staff of the army, proceeded to crush the coup, and within two hours the rebels had surrendered. The coup was in itself a minor incident, but it had momentous consequences.

The mere chance coincidence that he had decided to deviate from his rigid routine and not sleep in his rest house that Thursday night reinforced Numayri's superstitious nature. Acting on these instincts, he emasculated the remaining constitutional restraints to autocratic rule. Article 82 of the permanent constitution of 1973 had bestowed upon the presidency sweeping powers that Numayri now interpreted as investing the president as a person with the ability to be the living, personal embodiment of the will of the people, which had never been the intention of the authors of the constitution. He promptly pushed through the subservient Assembly an amendment to Article 82 that allowed the president to "take such action and make such decisions as he deems fit and his decisions in this respect shall be binding and valid in accordance with these provisions." His critics were appalled and cynically sneered that his motto had become *le peuple, c'est moi* (I am the people). Others were less concerned, for personalities have always been at the center of Sudanese political life, whether those of a tribal chief, *shaykh*, *nazir*, or the head of a *sufi* brotherhood. Many Sudanese regarded the situation with equanimity or positively preferred a strong personality with consummate political skills to the unfamiliar and artificial institutions created by "technocrats." Thereafter, constitutional institutions were gradually replaced by presidential rule characterized more by political manipulation than constitutional correctness following the dramatic events of July 1976.

Well before dawn on Thursday 2 July 1976 the First Vice-President, General Baghir, cabinet ministers, and senior government officials were gathered at the airport to welcome the return of President Numayri from a visit to the United States and France. He was scheduled to arrive at exactly 5:00 am, but, unbeknown to the president, his entourage aboard the plane, or the spectators on the ground, the presidential jet unexpectedly touched down a half-hour early. After the customary greetings the welcoming party was beginning to disperse when the airport and the capital suddenly erupted in a fusillade of gunfire at precisely 5:00 am. Numayri was immediately whisked into hiding; General Baghir rushed to the People's Palace to organize the resistance, skeptical whether the few forces at his command in Khartoum could hold the capital if he proved unable to communicate with the army units at Wadi Seidna, Shendi, and as far away as Damazin. However, Bona Malwal, the Dinka minister of information, made communication possible through his ingenuity: he used the offices of the Sudan News Agency (SUNA) to relay messages from General Baghir to army units throughout the country and at Suez, and to the world beyond via the small radio station at Juba to Nairobi. When army units began to pour into Khartoum from the North and the Blue Nile on the Friday afternoon, the assault had stalled, and by the end of Saturday the army had mopped up the last pockets of resistance. Those insurgents who fled were pursued and shot in the desert. Many innocent civilians had been killed, damage to property was extensive, and Numayri emerged from hiding more than ever convinced of the power of divine guidance that had delivered him to the airport a half-hour early.

The attempted coup d'état of July 1976 had long been planned by Libya with the connivance of Ethiopia and the Soviet Union. Mu'ammar Qadhafi had never forgiven Numayri for having refused to participate in the Tripoli Charter and had visions of including Darfur in his dream of a Libyan Arab Sudanic empire, a dream that Numayri did not share. The Ethiopians were convinced that the Eritrean insurgency would collapse without support from Sudan, and the Soviet Union had turned against Numayri after the failure of the communist coup and the expulsion of all Soviet advisers. The actual planning was left to Sadiq al-Mahdi, who had fled to Tripoli after the defeat of the Ansar at Aba Island. Here he was joined by the Sharif al-Hindi, and the two leaders founded the National Front in exile, a coalition of the Umma Party, the NUP, the DUP, and the ICF, later renamed the National Islamic Front (*al-jabhah al-islamiyah al-qawmiya*) and known popularly as the NIF, all in opposition to the Numayri regime. Qadhafi had established twenty camps in southern Libya where Soviet advisers trained and armed recruits for the Islamic Legion. Two of these camps, Judda'im and Ma'Ra, were built specifically to train some 2,000 mercenaries to overthrow Numayri. Some of the recruits were from the Islamic Legion, but most of the insurgents were Sudanese Ansar from neglected Darfur, and loyal to Sadiq al-Mahdi. During the spring of 1976 they crossed the desert, buried their Soviet arms in the sand outside Omdurman, and infiltrated the city as seasonal workers. Two days before 2 July they returned into the desert, recovered their arms, reorganized, and then slipped back into Khartoum, poised to launch the attack at precisely 5:00 am with help from the Muslim Brothers. If Numayri's plane had not arrived early, it is almost certain he and most of the important officials of the Sudan government would have been instantly killed.

The defeat of the Ansar mercenaries in the streets of Khartoum had been a very near thing, and many Sudanese were deeply shocked by the extent of the violence, and by the sham trials and swift executions that followed. Sadiq and the Sharif al-Hindi were tried *in absentia* and sentenced to death. The failed coup, however, had revealed to Ja'afar Numayri his vulnerability, and also that the National Front opposition (the NIF), which hitherto had appeared from Khartoum to be quiescent, could no longer be ignored. By extending an olive branch of reconciliation he sought to divide the opposition between those persuaded to return to Sudan and those who chose to remain in exile. At the behest of Numayri two prominent Sudanese families in the United Arab Emirates initiated negotiations with Sadiq al-Mahdi that at first did not go well, but at a second meeting on 7 July 1977 in Port Sudan, National Reconciliation (*musalaha*) was announced and widely proclaimed in the Sudanese and international media.

The agreement did not require any sweeping changes to the regime. Sadiq accepted a single party, the SSU, which he agreed was more suitable to Sudan than the old dysfunctional multi-party system, but he insisted that the SSU become more open and representative of the Sudanese. Sadiq was appointed to the SSU Political Bureau, but he never took his seat or participated in its deliberations. Political prisoners were released, harassment of the Ansar by the security forces ceased, and many of Sadiq's supporters were rehabilitated into the civil service. A general amnesty was proclaimed, which included the Muslim Brothers, and even many of the communists returned from exile. Although Sadiq mouthed rhetorical statements about his willingness to reconcile, his real reasons remain obscure to this day. In fact, he had few options. Having failed in July, he could not risk another attempt from outside, and in exile he could do little to alleviate the discrimination against his followers. He returned in September 1978, but by the end of that year he began to have doubts whether Numayri would keep his promises made at Port Sudan to introduce institutional reforms, and once again departed into exile.

Sadiq's ambivalence was not shared by the Sharif al-Hindi, who had no intention of returning, or Hasan al-Turabi, who openly committed himself to the regime in order to rebuild the Muslim Brothers under its patronage. Despite opposition from the more militant *ikhwan* led by Sadiq Abdullah 'Abd al-Majid, Turabi convinced the majority to support his long-term program to expand the Brotherhood acting as a *shura*, not the old party structure dedicated to the "revival of Islamic activity" (*ihya al-nastat al-islami*) by proselytizing and teaching. He systematically began to build a broader organization based on Islamic principles, *shari'a*, as the foundation for an Islamic state. In order to demonstrate his commitment to reconciliation he eagerly participated in the SSU as a senior official. In return Numayri appointed Hasan al-Turabi attorney-general, which enabled him to revive the question of *shari'a* thought dead and buried by the Addis Ababa Agreement and the constitution of 1973.

National Reconciliation was clearly a triumph for Numayri. He had divided and neutralized the opposition of the NIF, cynically neglected to initiate the reforms promised in 1977, and regarded a pluralistic SSU more a matter of form than substance. The old guard in the SSU had been extremely hostile to National Reconciliation, both ideologically and personally, but in alliance with the returnees from the NIF, who were now dependent upon him, Numayri was able to dismiss their objections and remain in complete control. Preoccupied with National Reconciliation, Numayri could not ignore the growing discontent on the periphery, particularly in the west but also among the Nuba. During a speech at the annual meeting of the Central Committee of the SSU on 10 March 1979 he announced before some 500 assembled delegates a regional division of northern Sudan similar to the regional autonomy already established in the South that was enthusiastically received, particularly among alienated westerners, and in February 1980 the annual meeting of the SSU General Congress endorsed Numayri's plan for regionalization, and the docile Assembly duly passed the Regional Government Act 1980 which established five regions in northern Sudan – Northern, Eastern, Central, Kordofan, and Darfur. The authority currently wielded by the unmanageable bureaucracies of the central ministries would be devolved to each region, which would have an elected assembly and nominate three names from which the president would select one as regional governor who would appoint regional ministers to administer the powers transferred from Khartoum.

In the end the center of gravity in Khartoum proved too strong for meaningful devolution of governance to the regions except for education, which already had a long tradition of local control. There was stiff resistance from some ministries in Khartoum whose civil servants simply gave lip-service to devolution. Moreover, Numayri's increasing obsession with personal power convinced many Sudanese he was becoming an imperial president more like a British governor-general of Sudan than a president of the United States, an impression symbolized by his selection of loyal regional governors. To their dismay, however, the northern Sudanese soon discovered that instead of ruling regionally they were completely dependent upon central government to finance local projects for schools, health clinics, and even their more ambitious development schemes. The savings generated by a modest decline in central government personnel were more than offset by the rapid expansion of the regional administration by patronage, which coincided with an impending awareness that Sudan was on the brink of economic collapse.

Economically, regionalism appeared to contradict Numayri's passion for large-scale development projects. Since the early 1970s investment had been concentrated in the central regions known as the "golden triangle" – the Kenana Sugar Scheme on the White Nile, the Rahad Scheme on the Blue Nile, and mechanized farming in Kassala and Kordofan – with very little in the periphery. Development was now the responsibility of the regions, which soon led to the incongruous situation of some regional governments sending their own delegations abroad to seek funds from the Arab world just when the Ministry of Finance and the Central Bank of Sudan were desperately trying to forestall the impending financial crisis. The more Numayri proclaimed the importance of spreading democracy throughout Sudan to the local level, the more he exposed his own undemocratic and autocratic rule. The rapidly growing number of critics of the regime cynically dismissed his regionalism as "merely a way of enhancing the presidential system, ridding Khartoum of the scourge of party politics, and keeping the regions acquiescent and malleable."[1]

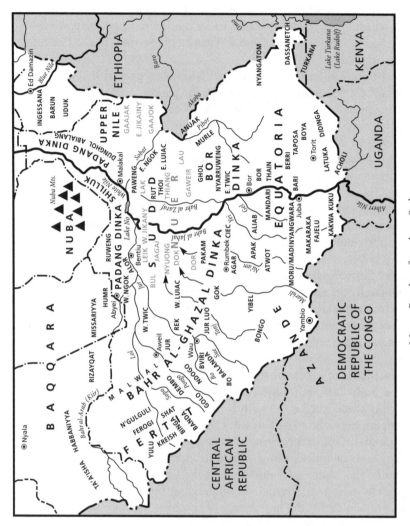

Map 7 Peoples of southern Sudan

THE RISE AND FALL OF THE SOUTHERN REGIONAL GOVERNMENT

In December 1977 the First Southern Regional Assembly, having completed its mandatory term, dissolved and prepared for elections which were to prove more contentious than those in 1973. The previous four years represented the first political experience of governance the southern Sudanese had ever known and, not surprisingly, the members of the Assembly and the HEC had soon formed disparate political groups of similar ethnic, ideological, regional, and personal likes and dislikes. The old-guard politicians who had not been included in the HEC or had lost in the previous election were embittered and sought revenge. The dismissal of four ministers in 1974 and the brief detention of Clement Mboro in 1975 by Abel Alier, president of the HEC, had further polarized political life in Juba. The following year, 1976, Abel Alier had ordered the arrest of two other prominent members of the old guard, Benjamin Bol and Joseph Oduho, for attempting to incite the Anya-Nya to seize Juba airport and resume fighting in the bush. They were later released in the general amnesty issued in December 1977 by President Numayri as a condition of National Reconciliation. They continued to carry a bitter grudge against Abel, however, as many Equatorians became increasingly alarmed by the "Dinka Cabal" surrounding the president of the HEC.

The opposition to Abel Alier quickly rallied around the commander of the First Division Southern Military Command, Major-General Joseph Lagu, who was bitter and jealous over Numayri's hitherto favoritism for Abel, perhaps because it was he who had won autonomy for southern Sudan on the field of battle and at Addis Ababa. Moreover, Lagu had received moral and financial support from Sadiq al-Mahdi, who still represented the opposition to Numayri despite the trappings of reconciliation. Disingenuously, Numayri was delighted to ostensibly support Lagu's political aspirations, for it provided the opportunity to remove him from the army and thus please his senior officers, who had been hoping to rid themselves of that "southerner" major-general. He sent First Vice-President, Abu al-Gasim Muhammad Ibrahim, to persuade Abel to quietly withdraw and to divide and rule the southerners. Having no other candidate, the Assembly unanimously elected Lagu president of the HEC. He now owed his position to Numayri, who in turn promptly dismissed him from the army.

Lagu had few of the qualities of Abel Alier to be the leader of the regional government. At times politically naïve and thin-skinned, he alienated those who had brought him to power, manipulated the Regional Assembly, and possessed neither the personality nor the political skills to establish a working relationship with Numayri or, for that matter, any influential northerners, if that were possible. Using his presidential powers he created a host of new regional directors complete with handsome salaries, all of whom were Equatorians, which contributed to the ethnic hostility between them and the Dinka. Moreover, the new politicians of the South appeared to have learned little from the old guard, for the vigorous debates in the Assembly were frequently characterized by vindictive personal attacks and unsubstantiated, vituperative charges. Lagu was accused of embezzlement, for there was little doubt in Juba that corruption had become conspicuous in direct proportion to his dispensation of patronage, particularly to the Dinka Samuel Aru Bol, vice-president of the HEC and speaker of the Assembly, a post Lagu had created. Samuel was soon implicated in mishandling some £S30,000 for the resettlement of refugees, which precipitated a storm of opposition led by Clement Mboro, Bona Malwal, Abel Alier, and the "Dinka Cabal" determined to depose Lagu. Twenty-four members of the Assembly charged Lagu with usurping its authority and acting unconstitutionally. Late in 1979 they petitioned President Numayri to dismiss Lagu, providing Numayri an excuse not only to be rid of him but to dissolve the Regional Assembly, which he did, in February 1980. Numayri had been infuriated when members of the Assembly had earlier organized angry demonstrations to protest the decision by the government and Chevron to export Bentiu crude via a pipeline to Port Sudan rather than through southern Sudan and East Africa to Mombasa. He never forgave Lagu for neither condemning nor stopping the demonstrations.

Elections to the Third Regional Assembly ended in May 1980, and Abel was overwhelmingly elected to a second presidential term. His new cabinet was a careful balance between Dinka and Equatorians, while he concentrated mostly on domestic issues and on expanding programs begun during his first term – training programs, agricultural extension services, education, and primary health care. The greatest disappointment for the South had been the failure of economic development, for it was totally dependent upon central government, which was more interested in large-scale projects within the "golden triangle" than schemes in the far-away swampy South. Many northern officials resented southern autonomy and were not about to divert scarce resources to development schemes in the South. By 1981, however, Numayri could no longer ignore the strident complaints of the southerners and so sent his Minister of Finance, Badr al-Din Sulayman, to the South, accompanied by senior officials from the Bank of Sudan and the Agricultural, Industrial, and Commercial Banks, which agreed to open

branches in Juba and provide $9 million from the Kuwaiti Fund to reha-
bilitate the Zande Cotton Scheme at Nzara. All of these rather mundane
issues, however, were soon overwhelmed by the controversial division of
the South.

During summer 1980 a small booklet was commissioned by the Solidarity
Group for the Unity of Southern Sudan chaired by Abel Alier. Published
by the Southern Regional Government, Nile Printing Press, Juba, it was
entitled *The Re-Division of the Southern Region: Why it Must Be Rejected*,
commonly known as *The Solidarity Book*. It savagely criticized Numayri
and northern officials. Numayri himself was accused in it of cowardice for
hiding during the three days of the July 1976 failed coup, leaving the reader
with the impression that he had been saved by the courage of southern
officers and troops in the army repelling the mercenaries. Worse, it made
reference to Arab–Israeli relations in which the Arabs were treated shabbily.
Numayri was apoplectic; senior members in the central government were
furious not only at the accusations but also at the fact they had been written
in literate English by southerners! In September Numayri abruptly revived
an earlier proposal submitted to him by the Equatoria Central Committee
of Intellectuals (ECCI) under the patronage of Eliaba James Surur using
the Bari word *kokora*, to divide equally, which has become a popular slogan
to this day, and advocating the division of the South into three separate
regions, but the Political Bureau of the SSU took no action. Ten days later,
on 4 October 1980, Numayri unilaterally and unconstitutionally dissolved
the Regional Assembly, dismissed the HEC, and appointed as president of
a "transitional regional government" General Gismallah 'Abdullah Rasas, a
southern Muslim and friend of Lagu, who recommended to Numayri that
he lead such a government.

The reaction of southerners was instantaneous and intense opposition.
Numayri was equally belligerent, for he knew that in any confrontation
with the South he could count on the NIF, the central government, the
bureaucracy, and Joseph Lagu, who had written a glossy booklet entitled
Decentralization: A Necessity for the Southern Provinces of the Sudan published by the Palace and arguing that "Dinka domination" justified the
division of the South. Philip Obang, an Anuak with no love for the Dinka,
secretary-general of the Friendship, Solidarity, and Peace Council of the
SSU, and former commissioner of the Upper Nile Province (1976–78),
circulated mimeograph tracts in Khartoum endorsing Lagu's proposal for
division. The dissolution of the Regional Assembly and the appointment
of Rasas, who had no southern experience and no instructions except to
do as he was told, had come as a complete surprise to the southerners

and precipitated student demonstrations against his appointment and the division of the South but, oddly, not against Numayri himself. Suddenly and again without warning, Numayri reversed himself. In February 1982 he dramatically postponed any decision on division and, in a disingenuous demonstration of democracy, called for new elections in the spring. In the past southern voters had been primarily concerned with local issues and personalities, but in the spring of 1982 the division of the South deeply divided the electorate, who rallied either to the redivisionists represented by the ECCI under the patronage of Joseph Lagu or to the Council for the Unity of Southern Sudan (CUSS) championed by Abel Alier. Many Equatorians believed that division would "liberate them from the Dinka." This slogan had great appeal to the large numbers of refugees – soldiers, elites, and businessmen – who had returned to Equatoria after the collapse of the Idi Amin regime in April 1979 without jobs, to blame most of their economic misfortunes on the Dinka. Their hostility spilled over into the countryside, where large herds of Dinka cattle had invaded Equatoria during the great floods of the 1960s, precipitating open conflict with the farmers of Equatoria for the use of their land either to graze or cultivate. The election returned Joseph James Tambura, *Wiri Gbia* of the Azande and a divisionist, president of the new HEC by 61 votes to 49 for Clement Mboro, a committed unionist, after receiving powerful support from the northern Sudanese Commandant of Southern Command, a delegation from Khartoum led by the speaker of the National Assembly, and members from Islamic fundamentalist organizations bearing considerable amounts of cash that made certain the defeat of the southern unionists and aroused latent fears of Arabization and Islamization. Joseph Lagu duly received his reward for championing redivision – Abel Alier's second vice-presidency, which he had long coveted.

Six months later President Ja'afar Numayri once again toured the Southern Region, in December 1982. In Rumbek, where he had been cheered as the savior of the South in 1972 and 1975, he was now met by a very hostile demonstration of jeering and stone-throwing students from the famous Rumbek Secondary School strongly opposed to division. He lost his temper, publicly cursed the students, closed the school, and arrested prominent unionists in the Regional Assembly. That evening in Juba, to the shock of a hastily assembled rump of the HEC, Numayri demanded they immediately submit recommendations for a division of the South into three provinces. Having no constitutional authority to amend unilaterally the Southern Regional Self-Government Act, the HEC adamantly refused. A month later, in January 1983, the Southern Regional Congress of the

SSU voted overwhelmingly to preserve the Addis Ababa Agreement and the unity of the South. Numayri deferred making a decision but had not forgotten nor forgiven his hostile reception by the students at Rumbek which festered to becloud his judgement out of all proportion to the incident.

On 5 June 1983 President Jaʿafar Numayri abruptly announced over prime-time national television his Republican Order Number One ostensibly to divide the Southern Region into three regions – Bahr al-Ghazal, Equatoria, and the Upper Nile, with separate capitals at Wau, Juba, and Malakal. In fact, the sweeping provisions of his decree abrogated the remains of the Addis Ababa Agreement of 1972, which had established the Southern Regional Autonomous Government, which was in turn enshrined in the constitution of 1973 by the Southern Provinces Self-Government Act. In a dramatic display, coldly calculated, Numayri had cavalierly consigned the Addis Ababa Agreement to the wastebasket of history. Perhaps this very visible symbol of his growing autocracy was not surprising, for his political belief in his absolute rule had now come full circle by embracing Arabic and fundamental Islam more fervently than the ʿAbbud regime and setting the government of Sudan on a course of Arabization and Islamization it has pursued ever since.

In the history of independent Sudan there has always been a persistent and pervasive assumption that Sudan was an Arab nation all of whose citizens would eventually adopt Arab culture, language, and religion. Tragically, this deep-seated conviction was completely divorced from reality. Less than half the Sudanese are of "Arab" extraction in a vast country with some 400 distinguishable ethnic groups speaking as many separate languages, and one-third of them are not Muslims. Although this kaleidoscopic cultural landscape pervades the whole of the country, it is most conspicuous in southern Sudan. Seeing it as remote and cursed by a history of slaving, the northern Sudanese were appallingly ignorant of the South, its people, their cultures, and their traditional religions. Although many northerners today regard the introduction of Christianity into southern Sudan in the twentieth century as the principal cause of the chasm between North and South, Christianity, like Islam, was at best a veneer that has never replaced local cultural and religious values that run very deep in traditional southern societies. Perhaps this is not surprising, for in the history of the African past scholars, often obsessed with the appearance of Christianity and Islam, have habitually discounted the role of traditional religions in shaping the history of the African peoples. The central issue of modern Sudan has been the Sudanese quest for identity whereby African indigenous cultures can peacefully co-exist with an imported Arab culture in a Sudan dominated by neither. For a few short years the Addis Ababa Agreement had resolved this dilemma. Ja'afar Numayri, in his quest for autocracy and Arab domination, destroyed that vision, leaving a disembodied legacy of cultural warfare and devastating violence that has cursed Sudan to this day.

Republican Order Number One abolished the Southern Regional Assembly, which was to be replaced by three emasculated provincial assemblies with very limited powers. They could no longer question or even debate national legislation, virtually eliminating the constitutional barrier that had hitherto checked any interference by the president and those seeking to revive a theocratic system of governance based on Islamic fundamentalism. Regional governors were now no longer elected but appointed by presidential decree. Southern officials were stripped of their fiscal authority to raise revenue, concentrating all financial and economic power in central government, which effectively terminated the financial independence granted at Addis Ababa. Arabic would henceforth be the only official language in Sudan, which reduced English to the status of the vernacular languages. The critical revision in the Republican Order, however, dismantled the carefully crafted arrangement for security devised at Addis Ababa and effectively eliminated the mandated proportion of southerners in the armed forces. Those armed forces in the South would henceforth be under the direct command of the local military commanders, the minister of defense, and ultimately the president, who decided to transfer the absorbed units of the army in the South to garrison duty in the North and west.

Republican Order Number One, in fact, was the culmination of National Reconciliation with Sadiq al-Mahdi and the leaders of the NIF at Port Sudan in July 1977 at which Numayri had promised to revise the Addis Ababa Agreement. By 1978 influential personalities from the NIF were now active in the SSU with a specific agenda for the South, part of which pre-dated the May Revolution. They were adamantly opposed to a single southern region, a secular constitution, autonomy, the English language, and the security arrangements which gave southerners an equal role in Southern Command. Moreover, elements from the NIF, particularly the Muslim Brothers, made it quite clear that their support for Numayri was contingent upon the emasculation of Addis Ababa and his imposition of an Islamic constitution. Numayri did not have long to discover the folly of his decision. The master of calculation was now convinced the South was powerless to oppose him. How wrong he was. Instead of a committee of southern politicians attempting to defend southern autonomy, he suddenly was shocked to discover in May 1983 that he now faced a sophisticated military insurrection, not just a rabble of Anya-Nya, led by young southern officers trained in his own army and determined to rid Sudan of Ja'afar Numayri.

In order to eliminate the presence of southern armed forces in the South, Numayri had ordered, late in 1982, the absorbed battalions of the First Division of Southern Command – 105th at Bor, 110th at Aweil, and 111th at Rumbek – to be transferred to garrison duty in the North and west. The Aweil garrison bitterly complained but left for Darfur in December 1982; in January 1983, the Bor garrison of the 105th refused to follow. Many of the former southern Anya-Nya had become dissatisfied when their integration into the SPAF had not met expectations; others had developed a sense of inferiority when they realized their education and training were not comparable to those of the rank-and-file regulars of the old army with whom they now served. Most damaging, however, was the blatant discrimination against those Anya-Nya seeking admission to the Military College. According to the Addis Ababa Agreement one-third of each new class at the college would consist of southerners, but between 1974 and 1982 the number of southern cadets was less than 5 percent. All of these grievances came to a head in the first week of May 1983. The Division Headquarters in Juba refused to pay the April salaries when Major Kerubino Kuanyin Bol, Dinka commandant of the 105th Battalion garrison at Pochalla, arrived to take command of the Bor garrison on the brink of mutiny. He immediately "borrowed" 250 sacks of *dura* to feed his hungry troops and fortified the town. A soldier, thought to be a spy from headquarters, was lynched. On 8 May Major Kerubino peremptorily forbad a steamer carrying a company of the Armored Division to dock at Bor, for he rightly suspected that the armored troops had arrived to disarm the garrison.

A week later the Armored Division returned and at dawn on 16 May 1983 launched an assault on the 105th Battalion garrisons at Bor and Pibor. At Bor fierce fighting continued throughout the day until dark, when the 105th, led by the wounded Major Kerubino, slipped away from their barracks and disappeared into the bush. Before dawn the next day, 17 May, the 105th at Pibor garrison had vanished; the Pochalla garrison crossed over the Akobo into Ethiopia with their arms. The attack and flight of the 105th Battalion at Bor on 17 May was followed less than three weeks later by Republican Order Number One on 5 June 1983 abrogating the Addis Ababa Agreement and dissolving the Southern Regional Government, and by the beginning of the second southern insurgency and civil war. By July over 2,500 soldiers from Southern Command had defected to the new guerilla base at Belpam in Ethiopia; another 500 were scattered throughout the bush in the Bahr al-Ghazal.

At first few southerners had paid much attention to the malcontents from the old Anya-Nya who had refused to be absorbed into the SPAF after Addis Ababa. During the latter years of the 1970s they were no longer regarded by southern civilians as guerillas fighting Arabs but simply bandits hiding in the Sudd and surrounding bush concerned more with local grievances and frequently fighting their former comrades-in-arms sent to disarm them in the name of the Addis Ababa Agreement. When Numayri unilaterally abrogated the agreement, the "bandits," collectively known as Anya-Nya II, who had opposed the Addis Ababa Agreement, determined to seek independence, and put aside their differences to search out southern chiefs, police, and soldiers to explain that their fight was not with them but with the Arabs. They behaved with great discipline and motivation, in contrast to the non-integrated northern troops in the rural areas who harassed and often shot southern civilians. By 1982 Akwot Atem, a Twic Dinka from Kongor, was actively raiding in the Upper Nile from Ethiopia and was soon in contact with three former Anya-Nya officers who had served together in the Upper Nile – Colonel John Garang, Lieutenant-Colonel Samuel Gai Tut, a Nuer from Akobo trained in Israel and sacked from the absorbed SPAF in 1974 for insubordination after threatening Major-General Lagu with his pistol, and Major William Abdullah Chuol, a Lak Nuer who had resigned from the army in sympathy with Gai Tut. In 1982 even Major Kerubino Kuanyin, who previously had hunted Anya-Nya II units near Jonglei, now made contact with Anya-Nya II. He had visited their camps in the bush before being transferred to command the Bor garrison. The task of welding together the disparate units of Anya-Nya II and the southern defectors from the Sudan army, police, and prison wardens into an effective guerilla army became the task of the senior southern commanding officer, Colonel John Garang de Mabior.

Colonel John Garang was no ordinary officer. A Twic Dinka, he was born on 23 June 1945 in the village of Wangkulei some 60 miles north of Bor in the Upper Nile Province. After his parents died when he was 10, an uncle paid his school fees to attend elementary and intermediate schools in Wau and Rumbek, but after being rejected by the Anya-Nya as too young in 1962, he was sent to Magamba Secondary School in Tanzania, where he excelled to win a scholarship at Grinnell College, an outstanding liberal arts college in Iowa from which he graduated with a BA in economics in 1969. He was quiet, bright, and studious, winning another scholarship to study economics at the University of California, Berkeley, but decided to return to East Africa specifically to study African agricultural economics as a Thomas J. Watson Fellow at the University of Dar es-Salaam. The 1960s was the exhilarating decade of African independence in which virtually every university student was irresistibly drawn to political action. John was no different and became active in the University Students' African Revolutionary Front, where he met Yoweri Museveni, later president of Uganda and a close ally during the second Sudanese civil war.

After two years at Dar es-Salaam he could no longer resist the temptation to enlist once again in the Anya-Nya which, in 1971, was now unified under Major-General Joseph Lagu and inflicting successive defeats on a demoralized Sudan army. As one of the best-educated Anya-Nya recruits he was given the rank of captain and served with Samuel Gai Tut and William Abdullah Chuol in the Upper Nile. Many at Owing-ki-Bul dismissed the effrontery of this overeducated newcomer, who had only been in the Anya-Nya six months, during which he had not participated in any active fighting or experienced harsh living in the bush. A year later he was readily absorbed into the Sudan army under the terms of the Addis Ababa Agreement and during the next eleven years rose steadily through the ranks from captain to colonel after having excelled in the US Army Infantry Officers' Advance Course at Fort Benning, Georgia, in 1974. In 1977 he was given leave from the army to return to Iowa to study for a PhD in agricultural economics at Iowa State University in Ames and awarded an MSc in agricultural economics in 1980 and a PhD the following year. He had written his doctoral dissertation on the Jonglei Canal, arguing that the Nilotic plain was the most suitable region in Sudan for rain-fed agriculture, but he was contemptuous of the current structure and incompetent management of the JEO. He felt it was quite incapable of developing any schemes in the canal zone and would "likely end up merely containing and managing poverty and misery in the area."[2] His experiences of a superb liberal arts education at Grinnell and later his rigorous graduate training at Iowa State in the heartland of America had left a profound impression upon John Garang. If the United States could fashion a free, secular, democratic, and united society from its own ethnically diverse and multi-cultural society practicing many religions and living in peace, why not Sudan? Upon returning to Sudan in 1982 he was appointed head of the prestigious Staff College in Omdurman.

In May 1983 Numayri had dismissed the discontent of the 105th Battalion at Bor, believing it could be easily resolved by sending Colonel John Garang to settle the matter among his fellow Dinka in his own home territory. After the flight of the 105th during the night of 16 May, the following day John Garang, ostensibly on leave to join his wife and two children at Wangkulei,

met Abel Alier, who expressed concern for his safety. Garang, calmly reply-
ing that he would be safe, left Abel never to see him again, and departed for
his rendezvous with the 105th at Bilpam. John Garang had indeed nothing
to fear, for he had been at the center of the conspiracy that had planned the
defection of the 105th as the beginning of an insurgency to overthrow Ja'afar
Numayri. Although the mutiny at Bor appeared, certainly to Numayri, a
spontaneous and isolated incident, it had been planned by Garang, Kerubino, and a handful of other conspirators throughout spring 1983. Garang
himself had formally founded the SPLM on 6 April 1983 and, in anticipation of the Bor mutiny six weeks later, drafted the *Manifesto, Sudan People's
Liberation Movement* which was released to the public on 31 July 1983, the
best proof that the Bor mutiny was hardly a spontaneous incident, for its
aims had been discussed months before the insurgency erupted in May 1983.
As the senior and best-educated southern military officer, John Garang was
the obvious choice to lead both the civil and military wings of the new
movement, the Sudan People's Liberation Movement/Army (SPLM/A),
but his claim to leadership of the movement did not go unchallenged by
more senior members within the SPLA high command. Motivated largely
by personal antipathy, jealousy, and delusions of self-importance, members
of the high command squandered much time and energy in the pursuit of
their own personal survival and enrichment while hatching conspiracies.
Garang skillfully sought to exploit these rivalries by posting those he distrusted to remote commands, and he convened the high command only to
give their perfunctory approval to his pre-determined agenda. After 1985
the high command did not meet for another six years.

The first and most pressing problem was to forge a new army from the
defectors of the 104th and 105th Battalions, deserters from Anya-Nya II,
the police, prison guards, and mutineers and from the massive defections
from the SPAF by southern soldiers in Waat, Rumbek, Malakal, Fangak,
Nazir, Benitu and as far away as Nzara in western Equatoria. There were
incessant wrangles over seniority, but the paramount difference – a united
Sudan or a separate southern state – had been momentarily smothered by
a patina of cooperation to overthrow Numayri that would require the support of Ethiopia, the price for which was unity for Sudan. Neither Emperor
Haile Selassie nor the communist Haile Miriam Mengestu could support a
separate southern Sudan in their long struggle with the separatist Eritreans,
and African lack of support for separatist movements had changed little
from the 1960s years of nation-building. Consequently, during his broadcasts over Radio SPLA, Garang dispensed with the pseudo-Marxist jargon
that had marred the *Manifesto* and confirmed many in the United States in

the belief that the SPLM/A were a bunch of Marxists and instead recited a list of legitimate grievances in practical language that could resonate with all Sudanese – the collapsing economy, dearth of basic foodstuffs, growing unemployment, inflation, devaluation of the currency. He emphasized that the revolution was not for a separate South, which would resolve nothing, but a revolution for all the Sudanese to build a "New Sudan," a federation with a central government committed to fight against racism and tribalism. An ever-growing number of northern Sudanese eagerly listened to these objectives on Radio SPLA, which were conspicuously absent from the government-controlled media. Many southerners were willing to accept unity as a step toward eventual independence. Others believed that the North and South could live together, but before committing themselves to unity they wanted sincere concessions from the northerners. Some, particularly Anya-Nya II, remained adamant, committed to fight for nothing less than complete independence.

The deep divide between unity or separation soon reappeared after the heady days of the founding of the SPLM/A by the challenge to Garang's leadership from the older Anya-Nya veterans, the Nuer officers Samuel Gai Tut and William Abdullah Chuol, and the Twic Dinka, Akwot Atem, all separatists to the core who had kept their own units separate from the SPLA. At first Garang left Anya-Nya II alone, but under increasing pressure from Ethiopia the SPLA and Ethiopians hunted down and killed Gai Tut in May 1984, while William Abdullah Chuol murdered the older, respected warrior Akwot Atem in August to take command of the remnants of his Anya-Nya forces. In late 1984 the Gaajak Nuer governor of Upper Nile, D. K. Matthews, acting upon instructions from Numayri, began to provide arms, ammunition, and uniforms to Chuol and his 300 men to establish a rearmed Anya-Nya II as a government militia in alliance with the Bul Nuer under the leadership of Paulino Matip to cut the SPLA supply lines from Ethiopia and intercept the steady stream of recruits coming from the northern Bahr al-Ghazal and Upper Nile to SPLA camps at Itang, Bonga, and Bilpam for arms and training. During these years the SPLA had little presence in Equatoria, being regarded by hostile Equatorians as a "Dinka Army." When two columns of 1,500 poorly trained and ill-disciplined SPLA each were sent into Equatoria in January 1985, the first was swiftly defeated by the army supported by armed Mundari Equatorians; the second was mauled near Torit in February by the army and armed Acholi and fled for safety in Uganda. Garang, however, persisted, and by the end of 1985 the SPLA was firmly entrenched on the Boma Plateau in eastern Equatoria near the Ethiopian border, which became its headquarters inside Sudan.

By November 1984 Garang had also decided that raids and skirmishes needed a more demonstrable incident to prove that the SPLA was a force with which to be reckoned. He ordered SPLA units to strike at the two successful development projects in southern Sudan in order to embarrass the government by terminating the operations of Chevron and CCI. On 3 February 1984 Anya-Nya II, evidently with the knowledge and approval of John Garang, struck at the new Chevron base camp under construction at Rub Kona across the Bahr al-Ghazal river from Bentiu. During the night the insurgents indiscriminately fired into the barges used by foreign employees, killing three and wounding several others reading or sleeping in their rooms, despite repeated declarations by the Minister of Energy, Dr. Shariff al-Tuhami, that the army was perfectly capable of defending the oil wells and protecting Chevron personnel. After a heated exchange between the chairman of the board, president of Chevron Overseas Petroleum, his staff, and Sharif al-Tuhami, who demanded to know how many employees Chevron was prepared to sacrifice before withdrawing from Sudan, the Chevron officials shut their briefcases, left the room, and never returned. Chevron retained the concession until 1991, when it was sold to a Sudanese consortium, Arakis Petroleum of Canada, Talisman Energy Inc. of Canada, and finally to the Greater Nile Petroleum Company (GNOPC), which included the China National Petroleum Company (CNPC), Petronas of Malaysia, and Sudapet Ltd. of Sudan.

Garang's decision to terminate the excavation of the Jonglei Canal had been made three months before the incident at Rub Kona and coincided with the Bor Conference of 10 November 1983 convened by the JEO and consisting of members from the PJTC, international aid agencies, the Mefit-Babtie research team, and local Dinka dignitaries; officers from the SPLM/A were particularly conspicuous. It was a tempestuous meeting in which all the grievances against the canal were vehemently expressed in true Nilotic fashion, followed by warnings from the SPLA to CCI to immediately cease operations in the canal zone. When CCI failed to heed this threat, the SPLA kidnapped seven French and two Pakistani workers, bringing the Bucketwheel to an ungainly halt. As a gesture of goodwill Garang released the hostages, but CCI resumed work on the canal in January 1984. On 10 February the Jamus Battalion of the SPLA struck. They easily dispersed the army guards at the sprawling Sobat base camp of CCI, seized six hostages, and quietly left after destroying the camp and telling the French camp director they would return after dark. Fortunately for the panic-stricken employees and their dependants, the CCI steamer *Biarritz* arrived to evacuate all CCI personnel to safety in Malakal. The Sobat Camp was deserted, leaving the Bucketwheel silent and forlorn, like a dead elephant, at mile 166 to rust in the heat and humidity of the Upper Nile.

THE CONVERSION OF JA'AFAR NUMAYRI, MUSLIM BROTHERS, AND ECONOMIC COLLAPSE

Whether the conversion of Ja'afar Numayri to fundamental Islam was an act of faith or manipulation, or a bit of both, remains unclear. After the failed communist coup of 19 July 1971, however, he began to make public gestures of piety and openly expressed his friendship with the *waliya*. Every Thursday the president's office would announce the town or village where he would perform the Friday prayers. Whether this was an act of piety or just good politics no one seemed to know. During Ramadan he sent special invitations to *sufi* leaders to the People's Palace, where he dispensed grants to subsidize their religious celebrations, build mosques, and support their *zawiyas*. In January 1974 in his report to the National Congress of the SSU he emphasized that religion was not just an individual matter of faith but "the cornerstone and basis of all social and political institutions in society as a whole." During the next two years and against the objections of the newly created Ministry of Religious Affairs, which represented the views of the orthodox *'ulama'*, he quietly infiltrated influential *sufis* into the SSU to cement their support for his regime.

During these same years Numayri appears to have defined for himself the relationship between religion and society which was later published in *The Islamic Way, Why?* (*al-nahj al-islami li-madh*, Cairo: al-maktab al-misri al-hadith, 1980). He attributed the backward condition of the Sudanese to the creeping decadence of Islamic societies and the introduction of Western governance, education, economics, and values under colonial rule that, after political independence, had disrupted the proper practice of Islam in Sudan. In order to reverse this regression the Sudanese must seek cultural independence by purging themselves of adopted Western values and reassert their conviction and commitment to Islam. In April 1977 Numayri took that ideal a step further by appointing a Committee for the Revision of Sudanese Laws on Islamic Principles that most certainly facilitated reconciliation with Sadiq al-Mahdi and the NIF in July.

During these years his conversion to the Islamic way of life was not only inspired by his belief in revelation but also, ironically, by his increasing obsession with superstition. He interpreted the miraculous way he had survived the attempted coups of July 1971 and 1976 as acts of spiritual deliverance in which he had been divinely guided by the Prophet to lead His people. During these same years Numayri became preoccupied with the prospect of death after American doctors at Walter Reed Hospital in Washington DC had diagnosed a serious cardio-vascular condition in 1979. Thereafter, he began to see signs and have premonitions of his passing, and at the cost of several million Sudanese pounds constructed his mausoleum – the opulent El Nilien mosque by the White Nile at the entrance to Omdurman. Having "miraculously" survived a second operation in 1982 he returned to Khartoum more determined than ever to complete his Islamic agenda. In September 1983 he surprised everyone, even the Muslim Brothers, by suddenly announcing the legislation, known as the September Laws, to implement *shari'a* throughout Sudan, including the South. He also declared himself Imam and demanded the *bay'a* from the senior members of his government, as had Muhammad Ahmad al-Mahdi and his Khalifa during the Mahdiya.

The implementation of *shari'a* was soon accompanied by the drastic *hudud* punishments of Islamic justice imposed by hastily created "courts of decisive justice" (*mahakim al-'adala al-najiza*) presided over by the Muslim Brothers. Amid full media coverage promoted by the government press thousands of gallons of alcohol, including Dewars Scotch whisky so beloved of the Sudanese elites, were poured into the Nile, while bulldozers crushed hundreds of bottles into the El Nilien corniche road between the Palace and the Blue Nile. Henceforth, the consumption of alcoholic beverages, including *marissa* beer, the staple drink of the ordinary Sudanese, the *nas*, was strictly forbidden, with severe punishments for its distillation or consumption. Over 150 men were condemned to public execution or amputation before large crowds purposely gathered to witness their punishments, which all government ministers were required to attend, including Attorney-General Hasan al-Turabi, who fainted while watching his first amputation. Those Sudanese unwilling to publicly witness these gruesome scenes could listen to descriptions on nightly radio or watch them on Omdurman television, followed by endless hours of Islamic rhetoric. On 30 September, an "historic day," Numayri released 13,000 prisoners from Kober Prison, many of them hardened criminals, declaring he had forgiven them as the Prophet had forgiven the people of Mecca who had persecuted Him.

At the time there was great speculation within and without Sudan as to Numayri's motives for the sudden introduction of *shari'a*. Some thought he had become unstable and irrational from his illness and many years in power. Many saw his behavior as the culmination of a long process of conversion to fundamental Islam. The cynics simply regarded his obsession with Islam as another political maneuver by the master manipulator to obscure the spreading unrest from a rapidly deteriorating economy. The popular response to *shari'a* varied from dismay in the towns, whose citizens enjoyed many of the pastimes prohibited by *shari'a* and increasing interaction with the international community, to fear of the inquisition that was certain to follow its imposition. To the southerners Numayri's declaration of *shari'a* was the last nail in the coffin of the Addis Ababa Agreement and the end of any support for him. Many of the rural folk in northern Sudan, however, were delighted that the imposition of *shari'a* would cleanse the fleshpots of the capital and end religious corruption, as Muhammad Ahmad al-Mahdi had done a century before.

During the next eighteen months Numayri delivered a steady stream of speeches invariably beginning with a verse from the Qur'an and describing his "mission" to establish Islam among the Sudanese, as had the Prophet. He lectured the people of Wad Medani about their sexual promiscuity. He informed the people of Kassala, who had just been inundated by a flash flood, they were to blame for having sinned against Allah and his *shari'a*. On 30 April 1984 in an apocalyptic speech he castigated those on strike for being "adverse to striving in the cause of Allah." Numayri's speeches became ever more strident. He refused to take any personal blame for the collapse of the economy, comparing himself to the Prophet Muhammad to the point of heresy, and condemning certain Sudanese individuals, which provided evening entertainment for astonished and disbelieving Sudanese unaccustomed to public displays of profanity from a foul-mouthed Imam. The headlines in the Khartoum daily *al-Sahafa* dripped with blood: "Emergency courts in one month only, 333 years of imprisonment, fines totaling £S557,141, and 19,351 lashes."[3]

The *hudud* punishments reached their climax with the execution of Mahmud Muhammad Taha. Since the 1950s Taha had advocated in public lectures, the press, and a dozen books the social, political, and religious reform of Islam. He opposed Nasser's Arab nationalism, preached peaceful co-existence between the Arab states and Israel, and praised the Addis Ababa Agreement. He even deplored the dissolution of the SCP, despite his opposition to Marxism, and advocated equal rights for women, many of whom in Omdurman and Khartoum eagerly joined his movement, the Republican Brothers. Banned from the national media Taha and his Brothers and Sisters became familiar figures on the street corners and parks of the Three Towns, peacefully passing out pamphlets and news-sheets to indulgent citizens who tolerated them with benign amusement as harmless people with principles. After the imposition of *shari'a* the Republicans declared their public opposition to the Numayri regime, and

Figure 17 Mahmud Muhammad Taha, leader of the Republican Movement, who was imprisoned under the government of President Numayri and hanged at Kobar prison, Khartoum, 18 January 1985.

on 25 December 1984 Taha wrote a mild leaflet, *Either This or the Flood* (*hatha aow al-tawafan*), demanding the repeal of *shari'a* and the return of civil liberties. Numayri resolved to make an example of Taha. On 5 January 1985 he and four Republicans were arrested, tried for apostasy, convicted, and, on Friday 18 January, at Kobar prison before several hundred people, Mahmud Muhammad Taha was hanged at dawn; his body was dumped somewhere in the desert west of Omdurman. To Numayri's astonishment Western governments and the international media reacted with vehement outrage. The Sudanese were no less appalled by Taha's execution. The residents of the Three Towns, particularly the influential professionals, merchants, and businessmen, were shaken. For many Sudanese this display of brutal, personal, and unnecessary vengeance was the beginning of the end of President Ja'afar Numayri.

Even some of the Muslim Brothers had cringed at the hanging of Taha, even though they had been the major beneficiaries of Numayri's conversion under the skillful leadership of Hasan al-Turabi. During these years Turabi had perceived that National Reconciliation could restore and expand the influence of the Brotherhood by infiltration into the SSU. Against the vehement opposition of the more militant Brothers Turabi had totally reorganized the movement to win a large bloc of seats in the elections for the new People's Assembly, which enabled him to purge the hard-line members. By 1980 he had developed a host of initiatives to enlist recruits for an Islamic Sudan from secondary schools and the University of Khartoum who would one day be secondary school teachers, university professors, lawyers, doctors, engineers, civil servants, and cadets in the Military School. None of these initiatives, however, would have any immediate effect on the fortunes of the Islamic movement, but with patience and perseverance Turabi would reap his reward at the end of the century.

Support for students and the expansion of the membership of the Muslim Brothers, however, could not have been undertaken without the resources to finance them. Turabi and his Brothers assiduously constructed an elaborate financial network to collect donations from the Gulf Arabs, Sudanese abroad, wealthy Sudanese businessmen who perceived that a successful commercial enterprise served Allah, and particularly the new Islamic banks, all of which were very sympathetic to Islamic education by an organization with a dedicated and effective leadership. Hasan al-Turabi was closely connected to the board of directors of the Faisal and Tadamon Islamic Banks, which enabled him to channel a steady stream of financial donations for the movement to build a new, large mosque near the University of Khartoum and found the Islamic University in Omdurman.

Sadiq al-Mahdi, his Ansar, and the *sufi* orders, particularly the Khatmiyya, soon became alarmed by the Muslim Brothers' infiltration into the SSU, the secondary schools, the universities, and the Islamic banks. Like the Brothers, Sadiq al-Mahdi believed that Islam should play a central role in Sudanese Muslim society and as a principal source of legislation, but he had strong opinions that Islamization did not require an interpretation of the Qur'an and the *shari'a* as they were at the time of the Prophet Muhammad. He argued that the *shari'a* revealed by the Prophet was sufficiently flexible to adapt to different events at different times and in different places, and that man was quite capable of such an adaptation in order for the schools of Islamic jurisprudence to realistically dispense justice within contemporary circumstances. Thus, Islam should be the guide to legislation but not be enshrined in any permanent Islamic constitution, as advocated by the Muslim Brothers. Like the Muslim Brothers and the Ansar, the *sufi* orders also believed the institutions of state and society should be Islamized, but that Islamization should incorporate the contribution of the *fakis* to Islamic jurisprudence, in which Islamic legislation should conform to *qiyas* and *ijtihad*, anathema to the Brotherhood.

The return of the religious notables during reconciliation coincided, ironically, with the rise of a "new class" of secular, prosperous, and international Sudanese businessmen with little social standing in traditional northern Sudanese society. They were small in number; in 1981 no more than twenty of them were millionaires, but they were very conspicuous. They flaunted their wealth in a manner repugnant to most Sudanese, who disapproved of the nouveaux riches. They were assertive and ostentatious, parvenus and opportunists without social standing. Many Sudanese believed, perhaps out of envy, that their wealth had been acquired by devious means without the "trust" that was the bedrock of Sudanese commercial life. Ironically, the "new class" did little to enhance Numayri's stature but much to embarrass him in the eyes of the urban Sudanese, for without social standing they preferred to become rich by exploiting Numayri's gullibility for grand schemes by flamboyant entrepreneurs and opportunistic sycophants.

Conspicuous consumption was not the monopoly of the nouveaux riches. The first to join the Sudanese bourgeoisie were the "grain barons" who had a spectacular rise by exploiting the search for the "Breadbasket of the Middle East" by mechanized agriculture. In 1968 the Mechanized Farming Corporation (MFC) had been established with generous funding from the World Bank. By 1977 over 8 million acres were being intensively cultivated for quick profits. First the woodlands were leveled, which increased the rate of erosion and destroyed the precious source of charcoal by which 90 percent of the rural *nas* cooked their food and the highly prized wood for the furniture of the urban Sudanese. Then the intensive mechanized cultivation by tractors and deep-furrowed plows soon impoverished the fragile topsoil, unless expensive fertilizers and erosion-prevention measures were implemented, which was rare. After several years of very profitable yields the exposed land became increasingly infertile, a dust bowl torn by the fierce north winds from Asia and the Sahara. Although the MFC had in place strict regulations for land management, they were simply ignored by the "gentlemen" farmers and corrupt officials. When the yield per acre no longer proved profitable, the "gentleman" farmer would simply move on to another leasehold of virginal land, practicing a mechanized "shifting cultivation," the traditional mode of agriculture used by Africans for centuries.

Organized labor, like the communists, had never recovered from the events of July 1971 and the absorption of the unions into the SSU. Moreover, unlike skilled urban workers, unskilled rural laborers had no tradition of unions and were mostly employed in the construction industry, which had none. As inflation spiraled upward and the price of basic foodstuffs, increasingly unsubsidized, rose faster than wages, the gap between rich and poor Sudanese produced envy, discontent, and urban unrest made all the more apparent by the austere restructuring of the economy demanded by the IMF. The influx of rural poor into the cities not only overwhelmed the public-service agencies but produced large numbers of unemployed and homeless, mostly from the South and west, on the streets, to the consternation of the middle-class urban dwellers, as Khartoum grew by 6.6 percent annually, with 1,343,000 inhabitants in 1983. Never very imaginative in the face of new challenges, the regime reacted with a heavy hand. Early in 1980 the migrants were first rounded up, put in trucks, and deported (*kasha*) back to the southern and western countryside, a practice since employed by every subsequent Sudanese government. By 1981 dissatisfaction had turned to violence. In June 1981, 8,000 members of the Sudan Railway Workers' Union at Atbara went on strike, bringing the country to a standstill. Numayri was furious. He deployed the army, abolished the union, dismissed all 45,000 members of the railway workers from the government payroll, and amended the labor laws to make strikes a treasonable act. No other union dared support the railwaymen, who went back to work alienated, sullen, and hostile. Numayri addressed the nation, urging the Sudanese to make sacrifices by eating cheap, boiled, tasteless grain (*baliila*) in place of *dura*; in December there were massive demonstrations and violent riots brutally quashed by the police, security forces, and the army.

The major threat to the regime from strikers, ironically, came not from organized labor but from middle-class professionals with the support of their fellow townsmen and -women. As their working conditions and pay deteriorated, judges, doctors, engineers, and university professors refused to work, led by the judiciary in that "summer of discontent," 1983. An angry Numayri retaliated, but it was one thing to crush the railway workers, quite another to intimidate the professionals. The judiciary struck en masse for three months and were soon joined by the influential Lawyers' Association. On 12 August 1983 with little grace Numayri reinstated some of the judges, accompanied by propitiatory offerings of a generous increase in salary and benefits which *al-Sahafa* tartly labeled as "bribes." The judges were followed by the doctors demanding more pay. Taking their cue from the judges, they resigned en masse. After threatening prosecution for high treason, Numayri again retreated, released the arrested doctors, denied that he ever issued his ultimatum, and met all their demands. To prevent any future strikes, however, he issued Presidential Decree Number 258 on 30 April 1984 declaring martial law, which remained in force until he was overthrown a year later.

The rise of the "new" middle class was accompanied by the steady deterioration of the economy and the failure of Numayri or his officials to prevent its disintegration. At the heart of the decline was Numayri's relentless concentration of the decision-making process into his own hands – the quintessential micro-manager. Unfortunately, his personal control of decision-making might have been checked and balanced by an adequate planning and implementation of the economy and its development schemes, but by 1981 the Ministry of Planning had been downgraded to a department with no authority to impose coordination among the relevant ministries. Even if there had been sound economic planning, problems within the civil service rendered its implementation most unlikely. After the May Revolution the civil service became increasing political, its officials reluctant to make even ordinary decisions, preferring to pass them on to ministers or the presidential office. By 1976 the government had become a bloated bureaucracy of 250,000 civil servants to administer some 15 million Sudanese and consisted largely of the unemployable and politically correct, both of whom were adept at make-work to fill time and space – 120,000 in central government, 130,000 in local government. Another 100,000 Sudanese had jobs in some 60 public corporations in which positions were created for those with few skills but with patronage, parents, or proper connections. The system was perfectly designed to foster corruption at every level from the Palace Cabal to the lowest official or *jallaba* in some remote province. The 60 public corporations were particularly susceptible to corrupt practices, and between 1975 and 1982 over 800 cases of embezzlement over £S1,000 were reported, resulting, however, in only 81 successful prosecutions.

Development schemes in Sudan were expensive and financed mostly by borrowed money. When they failed to produce a return on investment because of poor planning, mismanagement, and corruption the difference was usually reconciled by government subsidies from more borrowed money. In 1973 the value of Sudan's imports was roughly equivalent to its exports, inflation was low, and service on the debt easily managed. By 1983 foreign debt had reached over $7 billion, with an annual debt service of interest and repayments of nearly $1 billion and a trade deficit of $1.2 billion in a country of 17 million Sudanese, most of whom earned only a subsistence income. By 1978 the Sudan economy could no longer sustain its huge external debt, and thereafter the government routinely defaulted on its debt payments. The increasing size of the foreign debt precipitated soaring inflation and fewer financial resources to purchase imported staples – petroleum, sugar, cement, spare parts – compounded by a drastic decline in exports. In 1973–74 the cotton crop produced 1.74 million bales, with a yield per acre second only to Egypt. In 1983–84 only 550,000 bales of cotton were harvested, with a yield one-quarter that of Egypt's, for the exhausted soils of the Gezira were desperately in need of rehabilitation. Despite ambitious plans in the Interim Programme to rejuvenate Sudan Railways, the volume of tonnage fell dramatically from 2.8 million tons in 1971 to 1.5 million tons in 1983. Numayri seemed oblivious to the relentless disintegration of the Sudan economy – what Sudan cynics called "Numayrimetrics."

In 1974 Robert McNamara, then President of the World Bank, had refused to help Sudan's growing financial mess, citing the astronomical rate of interest charged by the banking syndicate organized by Adnan Khashoggi which implied either mismanagement or corruption. Four years later the World Bank agreed to provide regular support in return for a tough restructuring of government finance – devaluation of the Sudanese pound, drastic cuts in the generous subsidies of basic consumer commodities, a free market to replace the monopolies of state corporations, and the rehabilitation of the Gezira to restore cotton yields. Virtually every Sudanese loathed these humiliating restrictions. Devaluation accelerated the soaring inflation, imports upon which the Sudanese depended were now more costly, and the abolition of subsidies on basic commodities hurt the common folk, *al-nas*, to whom international fiscal management was a mystery. Rehabilitation and free markets did increase yields of cotton, *dura*, and wheat, but they had little impact on the availability of staple foodstuffs for the poor. By 1984 the World Bank had become the hated symbol of austerity that precipitated a series of demonstrations which increased in number and violence and ultimately led to the downfall of Ja'afar Numayri.

Tragically, economic austerity coincided with the great drought in the west that produced famine, refugees, and much suffering and death that could have been alleviated. In 1983–85 the recorded rainfall at El Fasher was only one-third the annual average, which accelerated the rate of desertification. Regional officials, particularly the able and respected Fur Governor, Ahmad Ibrahim al-Diraig, had circulated a comprehensive report warning of the impending disaster among all embassies and international organizations in Khartoum. Numayri at first ignored all of these warnings and then grandly announced there was no drought in Darfur, only scurrilous rumors, at a time when Sudanese were flocking to a film of starving Ethiopians accompanied by a commentary attacking the Ethiopian government for not feeding its people. In 1984 300,000 westerners in Darfur and Kordofan, the despised *awlad al-gharib*, descended upon the Nile towns of the *awlad al-bahr*, particularly Omdurman, seeking food and water like their forefathers had done during the Mahdiya. The army was ordered to round up these refugees, truck them back to Darfur, and dump them in the withered and waterless scrub, but by 1985 over 50,000 starving westerners had managed to remain in refugee camps west of Omdurman. Others spilled over to settle in Dar es-Salaam (through those personal connections that characterize Sudan commercial life) 30 miles southeast of Khartoum on the Medani road, the first squatters of what became known as the "Black Belt" of western and southern refugees that had surrounded the capital by the 1990s.

The ravages of the great drought in Ethiopia and Sudan could not be hidden from the international community, which responded with much-publicized efforts to provide food for starving Sudanese. In January 1984 the United States Agency for International Development (USAID) reported the desperate conditions in Darfur and was the first Western nation to respond by sending 82,000 tons of *dura*, the first shipments arriving in November 1984. Using a Sudanese-US private company, Arkell-Talab, convoys of trucks were organized to haul *dura* westward by subverting the powerful cartel of Sudanese truck-owners. The following year, 1984–85, the harvest was a disaster, for the drought had now spread into the mechanized rain-fed cultivations in Kordofan which normally supplied 80 percent of Sudan's cereal grains. Thereafter, no one could protect Numayri from the acerbic pens of the international press once its journalists learned he was absolutely unmoved by the tragedy. By March 1985 international private voluntary organizations (PVOs) such as the Cooperative for American Relief Everywhere (CARE) and Oxford Famine Relief (Oxfam) were at work in the west to report that 1 million Darfuris were starving despite the fact that Sudan's mechanized farms were still harvesting *dura*. By 1985 over 95,000 Darfuris had died of starvation, and over 60 percent of 14,163,000 Sudanese in northern Sudan had been affected by the drought, with 2,201,000 malnourished and susceptible to disease.

By the spring of 1985 the master of manipulation had few individuals, political groups, or sectarian brotherhoods left to divide and rule. For sixteen years, at that time the longest personal rule in the history of modern Sudan, Numayri had collaborated with communists, Anya-Nya, the NIF, *sufis*, Islamic fundamentalists, and traditional tribal chiefs and *shaykhs* in order to secure his personal power, only to betray them. The Muslim Brothers had been the last supporters of Numayri and the last to be discarded, having served their purpose. He had assumed the titles of Field Marshal, Supreme Commander, and Imam, the last of which many regarded as blasphemy. Titles did little to improve his image, for in his pursuit of autocratic rule the economy had been brought to the verge of collapse, drought and famine stalked the land, the second civil war had erupted in the South, and in his overbearing speeches to the nation, of which there were many, he could not hide his contempt for the "apathetic" and "cynical" Sudanese.

Finally, in March 1985 Numayri turned against his last political supporters, the Muslim Brothers, and made them scapegoats for all that had gone wrong in Sudan. In a broadcast on national radio on 10 March 1985 he accused a "religious sect" of plotting to overthrow the government and promptly arrested Hasan al-Turabi, the presidential adviser on foreign affairs, Ahmad 'Abdal-Rahman of the SSU and former minister of the interior, al-Mikashfi al-Kabashi, president of the Appeals Court, and, over the following weeks, another 1,000 Muslim Brothers. Two weeks later, on 26 March, students at the Omdurman Islamic University, a stronghold of the Muslim Brotherhood, staged a large anti-government demonstration in Omdurman. The following day, in response to another decrease in subsidies inflating the price of basic commodities, a large and spontaneous demonstration spread throughout Khartoum by students, the unemployed, and many disgruntled Sudanese. These demonstrations for the first time singled out Numayri personally and were ruthlessly suppressed. He declared a state of emergency to reinforce martial law declared the previous year and revived the kangaroo courts of "decisive justice." The presiding judge was usually a Muslim Brother who dispensed "Islamic Justice" for a long list of innovative offenses, the punishments for which were public floggings, amputations, and executions. The Sudanese watched with dismay and disgust; the international community reacted with universal condemnation as President Ja'afar Numayri boarded his presidential plane, enshrouded in his own fantasy world, for a private visit to Washington DC to consult with his American doctors and search for cash and yet more loans from the IMF and the United States.

On 3 April a peaceful anti-government demonstration led by the professionals – doctors, lawyers, airline employees, and engineers – attracted 20,000 angry Sudanese. It resulted in the formation of the Alliance of Professional Organizations and Trade Unions (NAS), led by Khalid Yagi and modeled on the Professionals' Front of 1964, flying the old Sudanese flag and calling for a general strike the following day, 4 April. Even in the army, the ultimate source of Numayri's authority, the more senior officers had begun to regard his tenure in the People's Palace as a disgrace to a once proud institution. Numayri in Washington remained unconcerned, but Sudanese patience had come to an end. The general strike on 4 April 1985 completely paralyzed the capital, but during the next two days the conservative senior officers, led by Major-General 'Abd al-Rahman Muhammad Siwar al-Dhahab, commander-in chief and minister of defense, resolved not to return meekly to barracks like their predecessors in 1964, but to take the initiative from the "Popular Forces."

On the evening of 6 April Siwar al-Dhahab appeared on national radio and television to announce that the army would "yield to the wishes of the people" but would retain control of the country. On 7 April Numayri cut short his visit to Washington and hastened to return to Sudan and restore order, but his plane was diverted to Cairo, where he was given sanctuary by his old friend President Husni Mubarak in an opulent villa in the suburb of Heliopolis, where he remained in exile for the next fourteen years. As in October 1964 the Sudanese in the towns took to the streets to rejoice. Few in Sudan mourned the passing of Ja'afar Numayri, for they were still in search of a national leader who could transcend the curse of sectarian, ethnic, and regional loyalties to forge the multi-cultural diversity of Sudan into a nation for all the Sudanese.

CHAPTER 6

The Transitional Military Council and third parliamentary government

THE TMC

On the day following his broadcast to the nation Major-General Siwar 'Abd al-Rahman Muhammad al-Dhahab entered into a flurry of negotiations with the leaders of the Alliance of Professional Organizations and Trade Unions, renamed to fit the occasion the National Alliance for the Salvation of the Country (NASC) and known simply as Tagamu'a. The NASC was not a political party but a coordinating council of over a dozen organizations, each with its own agenda, brought together by their hostility to Numayri and an ill-defined belief in democracy. They included many very able Sudanese but not a single one with the charisma, personality, and vision to lead them. After many long hours of debate and discussion at the staff club of the University of Khartoum their leaders, on 8 April 1985, finally forged the Charter of the Alliance for National Salvation, which was a summary of their common goals. The Charter called for a period of transition of no more than three years, during which the 1956 constitution, as amended in 1964, would be revised and ratified by a referendum, fundamental freedoms would be guaranteed, and regional autonomy restored in the South. There was little in this Charter to which one could take exception, but as in the past the heady days of intellectual discourse gave way to presumptuous deals, the pursuit of personal interests, and preposterous claims to authority among the old sectarian parties or the "Popular Forces" of 1964 now known in 1985 as the "Modern Forces."

A proud, conservative sympathizer of the Muslim Brothers and the new NIF of Hasan al-Turabi, who had refused to sign the Charter, Siwar al-Dhahab dismissed the document and, on 9 April 1985, announced the formation of a Transitional Military Council (TMC) of fifteen senior officers who commanded the elite units surrounding the capital, each of whom had their own ideological and personal differences. Some were silently loyal to Numayri, others were radicals sympathetic to the NASC, a few opposed

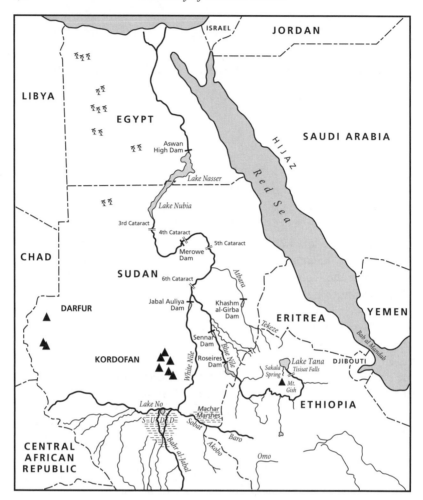

Map 8 The Sudanese Nile

civilian rule, and the remainder were sympathetic to the Muslim Brothers and the NIF. The TMC declared a state of emergency, suspended the constitution, dissolved the SSU, the National and Regional Assemblies, released political prisoners, and after a mass protest decided to disband the hated security forces. A few of Numayri's prominent officials, the Sadana, were arrested for show trials, especially First Vice-President 'Umar Muhammad al-Tayib, but most members of the ancien régime were left alone. The Tayib trial was a cause célèbre televised daily for six months that captivated the attention of the citizens of Khartoum and aroused the despair of officials in Washington. As the mastermind of Operation Moses, during which some 6,000 *falasha* were airlifted from Sudan to Israel in 1984 with the connivance of the CIA he was sentenced to 64 years in prison, fined £S4 million, and had all his properties confiscated. Washington was not pleased by the detailed disclosures during the trial of the role played by US embassy officials and CIA agents who allegedly paid Tayib $2 million for his services.

During the negotiations between the TMC and the NASC, Siwar al-Dhahab and his colleagues had agreed to appoint a civilian Provisional Council of Ministers (PCM), which entailed intricate negotiations within the NASC to select a prime minister. Dr. Ghizuli Dafallah, president of the Medical Association, who had been imprisoned by Numayri, was duly appointed on 22 April, and three days later the fifteen-member PCM held its first meeting. The TMC was represented on the PMC by the Minister of Defense, Major-General 'Uthman 'Abdullah Muhammad, whom some incorrectly regarded as the dominant member of the TMC, and Abbas Madani, a former police commissioner charged with dismantling the rumored 45,000 members of Numayri's State Security Organization. The radicals were represented by Dr. Amin Makki Madani and Muhammad Bashir Hamad, the minister of culture and information, and there were the requisite token three seats for southerners: Samuel Aru Bol, now leader of the Southern Front, the newly formed and predominantly Nilotic Southern Sudanese Political Association (SSPA), was appointed deputy prime minister; Oliver Batally Albino, who had been in Numayri's cabinet, was minister of public services (until dismissed for possession of drugs at Jidda airport); and a lone, empty seat awaited John Garang, who wisely demurred from joining the new northern military regime until its intentions became clear. None of the traditional parties were represented on the PCM.

Both the TMC and PCM were quite aware they would quietly disappear at the end of the transitional period, which did not encourage either body to devote their limited energies to controversial matters. Initiatives were discouraged, risks avoided, and difficult decisions postponed, their inactivity justified on the grounds that such decisions should be left to their elected successors. The government gradually slid into a limbo of lethargy. The TMC refrained from making policy, without which the departments for which the ministers were responsible could hardly recover from the internal vendettas and deterioration in personnel and morale suffered during the later Numayri years. The three major differences between the TMC and PCM that had haunted every previous government of independent

Sudan – the constitution, *shari'a*, and the South – could not be concealed. Both the TMC and the ministries argued that they should be the sole source of constitutional legislation during the transitional period. After much disputatious discussion and on one of the rare occasions when the two councils met together, they agreed that the PMC would initiate draft legislation, the TMC would then approve, and its chairman, Siwar al-Dhahab, would sign the draft into law. This compromise was followed by long and acrimonious constitutional debate that concluded with the promulgation of an interim constitution in October 1985. This, ironically, reverted to the provisional constitution of 1956 as amended in 1964 which had proved, despite its title, to be the most enduring document of independent Sudan. Autonomy for the South and the regionalism imposed by Numayri were preserved, along with special legislation for the transitional period. The most divisive issue between the TMC and PCM was *shari'a*. After much discussion the TMC convinced a reluctant PCM to leave decisions regarding *shari'a* to the new Constituent Assembly, effectively abdicating any responsibility for this contentious issue. This was most unfortunate, particularly in regard to *shari'a* and the September Laws of 1983, for the TMC possessed the authority to eliminate this great rock upon which the Sudanese ship of state could founder, but the conservative generals, led by Siwar al-Dhahab, viscerally could not abandon *shari'a* as the foundation of the Republic of Sudan.

While the TMC, the NASC, and the political parties maneuvered to establish an authoritative presence in Khartoum, the southerners had remained quiescent, circumspect, and suspicious. They had little faith in their northern brothers and were not about to rush into a repeat of the 1964 Round Table Conference that had failed so miserably. Most of the southerners, particularly the elites, were certain that the removal of Numayri was not about to change the attitudes, perceptions, and prejudices of the northern Sudanese. John Garang succinctly summed up southern feelings from his clandestine radio station in Ethiopia, saying that the TMC was "Nimeirism without Nimeiri." Numayri's minister of defense was now the head of state, his army chief of operations the minister of defense, and his commissioner of police the minister of the interior. Garang remained aloof and spurned his seat on the PCM, for the responsibilities shared between the TMC and PCM were unclear at best, opaque at worst. The NASC was a collectivity of interest groups incapable of governing, and the legitimacy of the sectarian political parties was still in question on account of their past support for Numayri. Garang clearly enunciated the position of the SPLM/A in his memorandum of 18 July 1985 to the OAU:

Figure 18 Followers surrounding Sayyid Sadiq al-Mahdi, imam of the Ansar and former prime minister of Sudan.

Figure 19 Sadiq al-Mahdi.

was created in response to Garang's demands at Koka Dam for a national constitutional conference. Sadiq al-Mahdi, now 50, had emerged after some years of infighting as the undisputed leader of the Umma Party and the spiritual leader or imam of the Ansar. Now both a political and religious leader, he had returned as prime minister in a much stronger political position than during his previous brief tenure as a young man in 1966–67 and was unsympathetic to the rising tide of Islamic fundamentalism led by his brother-in-law, Hasan al-Turabi, who had refused to join Sadiq's coalition as leader of the NIF. Sadiq was fondly remembered as the Oxford-educated, tolerant, young, modern man of the 1960s, and there were great expectations that he was that Sudanese who could lead and revive Sudan from the damage done during the Numayri years. He failed. To this day there is no adequate explanation for the collapse of his premiership. Having been twenty years in the political wilderness, either in exile or as a supplicant after National Reconciliation, the dynamism and idealism of the youthful heir to the Mahdist tradition seemed to have disappeared, leaving him a bundle of indecision over the great questions facing Sudan – *shari'a* and the South. He appeared cast adrift, feeling most at home in Saudi Arabia as the heir to his great-great-grandfather's fundamentalist Islam, or in England as the scion of the Western academic tradition of Oxford and British tolerance in government and society. Unable to abandon his sectarian role or ally with the Westernized secular professionals of the NASC, he abdicated this opportunity to embrace the national leadership he coveted.

In a series of speeches before the Constituent Assembly in June and July 1986 he unveiled an agenda worthy of a national leader. He was committed to abolish the *shari'a* 1983 September Laws, promote the Charter for the Defense of Democracy, which had been drafted by the NASC, and support his new Ministry of Peace and National Constitutional Affairs to thrash out the Southern Problem with John Garang. Sudan would be studiously non-aligned in foreign relations. Corruption, which had become endemic during the Numayri regime, would be vigorously investigated, particularly in the civil service, banks, and business community. He also promised reforms in the army, which had not been re-equipped since 1967. Despite the fact that Sadiq had few ideas about how to revive Sudan's failing economy his was a national agenda by a national leader and was received with relief and optimism by many Sudanese.

Then things fell apart. Sadiq was soon attacked from within and from without. By mid-summer the cabinet had become immobilized by petty squabbles and disagreements over policy. After the fall of Numayri, Sadiq al-Mahdi had repeatedly pledged to repeal the September Laws, but he floundered in a pit of compromise and irresolution as *shari'a* became the central issue in the prolonged negotiations with the SPLM/A. On 31 July 1986 the southern parties in the Constituent Assembly, known as the Southern Bloc, walked out, declaring that "Islam as the country's orientation is unacceptable." They were followed by Father Philip Abbas Ghabbush and his Sudanese National Party (SNP) representing the Nuba. By autumn 1986 Sadiq's resolution to repeal the September Laws had disappeared, and he refused to risk a vote of no confidence on *shari'a* in the Constituent Assembly that would have forced its members to show their true colors. His indecision and failure to produce acceptable Islamic laws to replace those of September 1983 prevented any agreement with the SPLM/A. The "Modern Forces" in the capital and NASC, who had supported Sadiq, expecting him to promote democracy, repeal *shari'a*, and then settle with the SPLM/A, felt betrayed.

By the beginning of 1987 politics in Sudan had reverted to the sectarian squabbles, personal bickering, and political manipulation that had characterized the second parliamentary governments from 1965 to 1969 – the inability of the DUP and Umma to work together in a coalition government, the failure of the Constituent Assembly to act as a national forum, a floating foreign policy, and the relentless continuation of a crippled economy. In May 1987 a more serious crisis erupted over Sadiq's reshuffling of the cabinet. The reason for the reshuffle was more personal than substantive: a slow-motion replay of the 1960s. The prime minister sacked the Minister of Commerce and Supply, Dr. Muhammad Yusuf Abu Harirah, a young and outspoken DUP critic of the government, for his ministry's failure to curb the black market and for visible corruption in granting commercial licenses, a perennial source of bribery. Sadiq then dismissed Sharif Zayn al-'Abidin al-Hindi, his DUP deputy prime minister and minister for foreign affairs, and dissolved the Council of Ministers, blaming all of them for the collapse of his government. The DUP was embarrassed and angry, regarding the dismissal of their ministers as crass manipulation to weaken the party by encouraging its internal division between al-Hindi and the Mirghani family. This appeared to be confirmed when Sadiq, during a BBC interview on 31 May 1987, cynically exploited politics and religion to favor and protect his extended family even after the TMC had restored their assets, estates, and lands.

In June 1987 Sadiq finally proposed to introduce a new set of laws as alternatives to *shari'a*, as well as new legislation concerning criminal law, banking, and *zakat*, the alms tax. Although there was vigorous dissent from southern politicians that alternatives to the September Laws would not bring peace, and complaints from northern secularists, the Bar Association, and even the Muslim Brothers that the prime minister had offered nothing new in relation to the Southern Problem, Sadiq's proposals were adopted by the Assembly by a vote of 138 to 52 on 21 June 1987 in which the opposition was a strange combination of the Southern Bloc, the communists, and the NIF, each voting for very different reasons. Invigorated by the approval of the Constituent Assembly for his agenda, Sadiq agreed to give the opening address at a conference in Khartoum to consider the establishment of an Islamic Sudan. During the address his pledge to end the September Laws for "better, more humane and more progressive Islamic laws" was nearly swamped by the NIF chanting "No replacement for God's legislation!" Among the southerners and secular northerners there was a growing fear that foreign Islamic zealots, who had begun to appear in Sudan during the mid-1980s, were now a perverse influence on the home-grown variety of Sudanese Islamic fundamentalism. The prominent southern journalist, former minister of information and culture, and then editor of the *Sudan Times*, Bona Malwal, perceptively reported: "The present debate over an Islamic constitution draws more from political thinking of feudalism than from democratic thought. Under the slogans of democracy the spirit of democracy is being crushed."[2]

No sooner had the new coalition Council of Ministers been formed than it was enveloped in another crisis, once again more petulant than persuasive, when the prime minister humiliated his DUP coalition partner. In August 1987 the Umma Party replaced one of the two DUP members of the Supreme Council of State with one of their own and then sacked the DUP Deputy Prime Minister and Minister of the Interior, Sayyid Ahmad al-Husayn, accusing him of receiving half a million Sudanese pounds from the Egyptian embassy in return for information. The continuing paralysis of the coalition government stimulated speculation about a national government that would include the NIF, which had been vociferous in its opposition. In order to capitalize on Umma vindictiveness the NIF launched an intense campaign of vilification against Sadiq, his coalition government, its policies, and its personalities. It was very ugly but extremely effective. Having been smeared for weeks, Sadiq denounced his opponents on the left for trying to impose a secular system "on the spears" of the SPLA and on the right for disrupting the economy and destroying the democratic process. Just as the coalition government had reached its political nadir in civility and effectiveness, it was ironically given a brief respite by the SPLA.

On 11 November 1987 the SPLA captured Kurmuk, a commercial cross-ing on the Sudan–Ethiopian border only 450 miles southeast of the capital and not far from Damazin and the Rosieres Dam which supplied 60 percent of Khartoum's electricity. Although its capture was yet another embarrass-ment for the government, the ruling parties sought to exploit the loss of Kurmuk in order to divert attention from their failure to govern and the appalling political mess in Khartoum. With unlimited funds from the NIF the local press transformed the capture of an insignificant market town into a massive invasion by aliens from outer space. War hysteria swept through the capital, whose citizens now had visions of black Africans of the SPLA strutting down the El Nilien corniche road past their palace. The govern-ment declared the mobilization of its citizens to defend the nation in its peril. After a month of frantic appeals to defend the homeland, the army recaptured Kurmuk on 22 December 1987, only to see the retiring SPLA disappear into the forests across the border. The *Sudan Times* aptly summed up this giddy experience: "Kurmuk has served to focus the attention of the nation on the war. Hopefully, it will also focus the attention of the nation on the need for peace."[3]

Kurmuk was, in fact, only a minor skirmish in a long civil war, but it had far-reaching consequences that were to become an increasing reality by the end of the century. There was much talk in Khartoum society in the evening that perhaps the time had come to divide Sudan into North and South, the opposite of John Garang's vision of a new united Sudan. More-over, Kurmuk had raised the consciousness of what constituted *Arab* and *African*, for their Arab neighbors – Libya, Iraq, Saudi Arabia, and Jordan – pledged military support for Sudan. Egypt remained silent as the Sphinx, but the whole issue of the dichotomy of the Sudanese "identity" became increasingly intense, with visions of Arabs and Islam being overwhelmed by African *kafirin* from the *dar al-harb*. After Kurmuk and the New Year, politics returned to its limbo of leaderless recrimination, wrangling, and manipulation for control of the security organizations, the redistribution of ministers, and the authority of the prime minister. This provoked Sadiq on 15 March 1988 to demand the Constituent Assembly give him unques-tioned powers or accept his resignation. Sadiq's bold challenge perplexed many members of the Assembly, but they were reluctant about forcing a vote of no confidence and so, astonished by his sudden display of decisive-ness, they overwhelmingly passed his controversial program. It was Sadiq's finest hour, but it was a pyrrhic victory, for there was massive dismay and disenchantment with the political process among the citizens of the Three Towns.

When Sadiq had challenged the Constituent Assembly to give him greater authority to implement his political program, he was only able to mobilize sufficient support by cobbling an alliance together with Hasan al-Turabi and the NIF. In return for his pledge to pass the "substitute *shari'a* laws" within two months, Turabi and the NIF would provide sufficient support in the Assembly to give him the power he was seeking. The country was languishing in a civil war, economic collapse, and a great deal of unnecessary misery, and most Sudanese were extremely skeptical whether the new unholy coalition of such disparate bed-fellows as the Umma, DUP, and NIF could provide effective government or last long when its members placed personal gain and political gratification before the more practical resolution of the nation's problems.

During the next two months the issue of the September Laws continued to smolder, the secularists and southerners insisting the prime minister fulfill his pledge to terminate them, while Sadiq dithered, which further undermined his credibility. Sadiq formed his cabinet on 15 May 1988 in which Hasan al-Turabi, the principal architect of the September Laws when Numayri's attorney-general in 1983, was once again appointed attorney-general to craft the substitute September Laws promised by Sadiq. Politics in Khartoum had come full circle. The opposition vehemently objected to the new *shari'a* code, but it could hardly prevail unless the coalition government began to unravel, which it duly did in July 1988. Muhammad 'Uthman al-Mirghani, president of the DUP and patron of the Khatmiyya, suddenly admonished the Assembly against any hasty passage of Turabi's new *shari'a* laws and instructed the sixty-two DUP MPs in the assembly to vote against them. The new *shari'a* laws were placed before the Constituent Assembly on 19 September 1988. The prime minister stood by his brother-in-law, but the Union of Sudan African Parties (USAP), the communists, and other leftist parties stormed out of the Assembly. Debate on the new laws proceeded until 4 October, when the exhausted lawmakers sent the substitute *shari'a* laws to committee for further study. Many members breathed a momentary sigh of relief, despite the fact that the September Laws were not about to die in committee.

Ever since Mirghani's cautious warning about the new laws in July, the DUP had been increasingly marginalized by the Umma and NIF, or more specifically by the prime minister now reconciled with his brother-in-law, Hasan al-Turabi. The DUP slide to the periphery was accompanied by the Umma–NIF axis becoming ever more uncompromising not only about the new substitute laws but also the war, which decided Muhammad 'Uthman al-Mirghani to open direct talks with the SPLM/A in Addis Ababa. On

16 November 1988 both parties agreed to a cease-fire, the abrogation of all military agreements with Egypt and Libya, an end to the state of emergency, and the postponement of the proposed *shari'a* laws until after the convening of the promised national constitutional conference by the end of 1988. Muhammad 'Uthman al-Mirghani returned to Khartoum a conquering hero, the "King of Peace," and was greeted at the airport by thousands of Sudanese who surged through the streets to rejoice at his bold action in breaking through the political stagnation that had characterized Sadiq's leadership. Finding himself between the uncompromising NIF and the euphoria of DUP popularity, Sadiq sought and received from the Assembly authorization to convene a national constitutional conference on 31 December 1988. The NIF voted solidly against the motion, for it did not endorse the DUP–SPLM/A agreement, its ministers resigned, and the party left the coalition government on 28 December 1988, a week after anti-government riots had surged through the streets of Khartoum in support of peace.

After a month of convoluted negotiations Sadiq managed to reconstruct his coalition government on 1 February 1989 with a new cabinet consisting of ten Umma Ministers, eight NIF, and four other token portfolios for the southerners. One final portfolio was given to a Nuba faction for the first time in history. No sooner had the new coalition government been formed, however, than the Umma suffered two severe set-backs. The popular and respected Minister of Defense, Major-General 'Abd al-Majid Hamid Khalil, suddenly resigned in mid-February to protest Sadiq's failure to support the DUP–SPLM/A agreement. Without his steadying influence and practical advice the government once again drifted with the political tide as the brooding influence of the NIF finally came to fruition with the appointment of Turabi as deputy prime minister and minister for foreign affairs; other NIF members received the strategic portfolios of the interior, justice, and social affairs. On 20 February 1989 the successor to Khalid as commander-in-chief of the army, Major-General Fathi Ahmad 'Ali, delivered an ultimatum to the prime minister signed by 150 senior officers demanding he form a national government, accept the DUP–SPLM/A agreement, and reverse the deteriorating economy. A torrent of negotiations swept through the capital, culminating on 6 March 1989 when forty-eight political parties and the trade unions signed a "National Declaration of Peace" which embraced the DUP–SPLM/A agreement. The NIF refused to sign. Unable to make a decision, Sadiq stalled for time, disingenuously demanding the Assembly debate the National Declaration.

During the following weeks the pressure on Sadiq to implement the army memorandum and the National Declaration of Peace demonstrably increased in the Assembly and the media until he publicly announced his full support for the DUP–SPLM/A agreement on 11 March 1989 and petulantly dissolved his government. A great sigh of relief and hope swept through the citizens of the Three Towns longing for peace. The more cynical citizens scoffed that Sadiq, faced with heavy losses in the war and a struggling economy, had exhausted all his options except that of forming a new government, "The National Unity Front," on 22 March 1989 that included all the major political parties bar the NIF. The formation of a government of National Unity, however, coincided with the suspension of debate on *shari'a* on 1 April 1989, effectively tabling its reintroduction, which precipitated violent demonstrations by NIF supporters in the streets for a week before they were quelled by riot police; one protestor died. The NIF newspaper, *al-Rayah*, denounced the vote as a "forgery," and an NIF mob tried to storm the British embassy in protest against the publication of novelist Salman Rushdie's *Satanic Verses*.

Unfortunately, the new national government did little to justify its name as it wallowed in political stalemate. Dissatisfaction with Sadiq and his government deepened. Throughout spring 1989 rumors even circulated in Khartoum that Egypt was plotting a coup to restore Ja'afar Numayri to power. Finally, in exasperation even the Constituent Assembly demanded the resignation of the prime minister and the total abrogation of the September Laws of 1983. This was indeed a decisive and dramatic act that appears to have finally persuaded the prime minister on 10 June 1989 to order a cease-fire with the SPLM/A, end the state of emergency, freeze the September Laws, and abrogate the military pacts with Egypt in anticipation of the postponed national constitutional convention, to take place in September 1989, which presumably would endow these acts with legitimacy. On 29 June Sadiq initialed the laws officially suspending the September Laws to be endorsed by the Council of Ministers the following day and the Constituent Assembly on 1 July. On the night of 30 June 1989 a coup d'état by the elite paratroop brigade and the army engineers, planned by the NIF and led by Brigadier 'Umar Hasan Ahmad al-Bashir, swiftly swept away like a gigantic *habub* all hope of a secular, democratic, and united Sudan. Once again Sudan had failed to produce a national leader. Indecisive, torn between East and West, and immobilized by *shari'a* and an unwinnable war, Sadiq had dithered during the past three years on the issues of peace and the Islamization of law and society; the NIF architects of the coup sought to fill that vacuum.

THE REALITIES OF CIVIL WAR

When Sadiq al-Mahdi formed his first government in May 1986, he appears to have been genuinely interested in peace for a unified Sudan: he established a new Ministry of Peace and the Constitution, and met with Garang on 31 July 1986 at the OAU summit in Addis Ababa. Their nine hours of discussion, however, did not go well. Sadiq gratuitously lectured Garang that time was "short" and that if he continued to wage war, he would unleash the full might of the army. Garang curtly responded that time was not "short" but on the side of the SPLA: the Sudan army simply could not win a war in southern Sudan. They departed each with his irreconcilable differences but in the spirit of Koka Dam agreed to continue the dialogue. In that same spirit a twenty-five-member delegation from the NASC met with a thirty-one-member delegation from the SPLM/A for five days from 5 to 11 August 1986. The meetings were candid but amicable and practical, and both delegations were optimistic that these meetings were a positive beginning to end their differences. Unfortunately, they were either captives of their own preconceptions or naïve optimists. Two weeks later on 26 August 1986 a Shilluk contingent of the SPLA shot down with a Soviet SAM-7 missile a Sudan Airways Fokker Friendship approaching Malakal, killing sixty passengers. When he learned of the tactless radio messages by gloating SPLA commanders, Sadiq denounced the SPLA as "a terrorist group," refused to continue any further talks with the SPLM/A, and used Anya-Nya II to destroy a wide swath of Shilluk villages from Papwojo in the South to Padiet in the North, which precipitated a mass migration of Shilluk IDPs to the North.

During his meeting with Sadiq, John Garang had every reason to believe that time was on his side. Although the SPLA campaigns of 1985–86 had been launched against southern tribal militias – Murle, Toposa, and Fartit – motivated by revenge to settle old scores, replace supplies lost to the Anya-Nya II, and discourage other dissident southerners from organizing their own militias, Garang decided in 1987 to change tactics and ordered the SPLA to win over their former militia adversaries, rather than beat them into submission, with some success. In Equatoria the SPLA established highly mobile units to contain the army in its fortified towns to alleviate demands for their food from nearby villagers. In the Bahr al-Ghazal and Upper Nile they imposed a one-off food tax, after which the civilians presumably would be left alone from arbitrary seizure. Gradually the popularity of the SPLA increased, helped by the army's harsh treatment of those southerners suspected of supporting them.

While the army had to contend with the SPLA insurgency, the Khartoum government remained the legitimate civil authority in southern Sudan but was plagued by a host of civilian problems – refugees, IDPs, shortages of food, and disease. To resolve these problems Sadiq installed on 23 March 1987 a new administration for the South led by a Council of Ministers represented by the governors of Equatoria, the Bahr al-Ghazal, and the Upper Nile, a Council for the South, and three regional administrations. Four of the six southern parties rejected the prime minister's new southern civil administration, a bizarre contraption composed of confusing and contradictory components that provided paychecks for meaningless work. During spring 1987 there followed a flurry of antagonistic and contradictory contacts between the government and the SPLM/A concerning the Koka Dam agreement that must have perplexed and discouraged Sadiq who, on 22 April 1987, declared in the Constituent Assembly that Koka Dam was a flawed document, and a few days later on 27 April he refused to recognize the legitimacy of the SPLM/A, derisively declaring that "The Garang movement is no more than an Ethiopian pawn." In February 1987 Garang had his ten-page memorandum widely distributed in Sudan in which he emphasized that the SPLM/A was a national, not a regional, movement seeking "legitimate" national aspirations, and not a pawn of Ethiopia, Libya, the Soviet Union, or Cuba, which had been a common theme in the government media. Many northerners who subsequently visited Addis Ababa – members of the Umma Party, the DUP, and the Southern Bloc – all returned to report that it was a grave error to believe that Garang was just an Ethiopian puppet. Compared with the muddled leadership in the government his policies were a laser beam of clarity – "the SPLA will continue to fight and win until serious talks begin on the basis of Koka Dam."

While Sadiq and Garang engaged in their futile and unproductive rhetorical duel, the SPLA had scored significant military success in 1987. During the previous four years the SPLA had rapidly expanded as thousands of southern farmers, herdsmen, and children rushed to join the movement seeking adventure, security, and food, but also motivated by a deep, ill-defined sense of what could best be described as "southern patriotism." There was little screening of volunteers, and virtually no one was turned away, including children, who became gun-toting child-soldiers, which later was an egregious embarrassment for the SPLM/A with its Western humanitarian supporters. Training in the camps was rigorous in harsh living conditions at Bonga and satellite camps at Bilpam, Dima, and Buma which produced a combat division every year – Jarad 1984, Mou Mour 1985,

Kazuk 1986, Zalal 1987, Intifadha 1988, and Intisar 1989. Those officers and men who were deployed from the training camps were highly motivated, and as they surged from one victory to another morale soared.

After heavy fighting and losses on both sides, the SPLA captured Pibor, Ayod, and Jokau. Successful assaults were launched against Bentiu, Fashoda, Kapoeta, and Maridi. The critical fuel depot at Malakal airport was destroyed. With the army in disarray and facing defeat, Sadiq made the fateful decision to unleash the Baqqara militia, the *murahiliin*, to contain the SPLA in the Bahr al-Ghazal and Upper Nile, which tragically coincided with the great famine from the drought that had reached southern Sudan. Moreover, the great drought of the 1980s was accompanied by Numayri's misguided dismantling of Native Administration by the traditional author-ities – *shaykh, nazir, 'umda*, and chief – in the 1970s. They were replaced by local councils, many of whose members had little or no knowledge of the indigenous, often unwritten, rules by which disputes had been settled in the past. The loss of their authority also contributed to their loss of respect among their young men. In virtually every society, youth have always chafed under the authority of their elders, but in traditional Baqqara society the erosion of traditional authority was facilitated by external causes over which the elders had little control.

Historically the Baqqara – Rizayqat, Missiriya, and Humr – and the Dinka of the northern Bahr al-Ghazal – the Malwal, Twic, Ngok, and Ruweng – have contested the rich pasturelands on either side of the Bahr al-Arab (Kiir) river with an "intimate enmity" that has ranged from close cooperation to ethnic slaughter, such as when 200 Ngok Dinka were mas-sacred at Muglad in 1965. No longer did the leaders of the Rizayqat Baqqara and the Malwal Dinka sit together in council to settle their interminable disputes over grazing, water, and peace on the frontier. By 1983 the local councils had utterly failed to settle complex Baqqara–Dinka cattle cases and other disputes. This coincided with the economic crisis of the Numayri regime, which had closed the usual opportunities for a livelihood for young Baqqara, now severely aggravated by the great drought that spread relent-lessly after 1983 into southeast Darfur, southern Kordofan in 1984, and the Bahr al-Ghazal in 1985. Herdsmen saw their livestock die, destroying the collected wealth of the middle-aged and the birthright of the young. Both these human and natural calamities created a mass of unemployed, discon-tented, and reckless youths who could now readily obtain cheap automatic weapons in the *suq* to recover their wealth by means of the *razzia*, which, to young, bored Baqqara youth, became a challenging adventure to loot and kill the Dinka in the warrior traditions of their Mahdist forefathers.

During the autumn of 1986 and winter of 1987 a steady stream of dispossessed Dinka fleeing from the *murahiliin* raids flowed into and through southern Darfur and Kordofan. Ever since the outbreak of the first Anya-Nya civil war in the 1960s large numbers of Dinka had crossed the Bahr al-Ghazal to settle among the Baqqara, where they were employed for token wages in menial tasks – field hands, herdsmen, housekeepers, construction laborers – and by May 1986 some 17,000 Dinka had congregated at Ed Daëin in southern Darfur. Agents from the NIF had been active in the town, inciting the Baqqara residents to destroy the Dinka church, which was not only their place of worship but also a thriving social center with mysterious panels for solar electricity that were wrongly supposed to be for communicating with the SPLA. On Friday 27 March 1987 Rizayqat attacked the church after a prayer service and drove the Dinka to seek safety in the police station. The following morning the police, fearing they could not control the mob, crammed every Dinka they could find into a freight train bound for Nyala and safety. The huge Baqqara mob barricaded the tracks, set fire to the wooden freight cars, and lighted fires under the metal ones; the fortunate Dinka suffocated, the unfortunate were roasted to death. While the train burned, the Baqqara ran amok through the town killing and mutilating any Dinka they found. Fifteen hundred Dinka perished, mostly women, children, and the elderly; the government firmly denied that any massacre had taken place.

During that same winter of 1986–87 in the northern Bahr al-Ghazal *murahiliin* had destroyed scores of Dinka villages and their crops, and rustled hundreds of thousands of cattle. Over 250,000 Dinka fled south of the Lol river seeking sanctuary and protection from the SPLA, who rushed to the rescue, drove the *murahiliin* across the Bahr al-Arab, and in January 1987 pursued them into southern Kordofan, where they trapped a large contingent supported by the army, killing over 150 and recovering 4,000 head of cattle. When the army failed to halt this SPLA winter offensive, General Fadlallah Burma Nasr, a Rizayqat Baqqara from Lagowa in southern Kordofan, was appointed state minister of defense by Sadiq in February 1987 with orders to reverse the advance of the SPLA. He proposed that the government arm the southern Baqqara youth – Rizayqat, Missiriya, and Humr – with automatic weapons, Soviet Kalashnikovs, and turn them loose to loot, pillage, and kill Dinka, without whose support the SPLA would be crippled. In one of the most fateful policy decisions of his administration Sadiq in February 1987 transformed the pasturelands of the Bahr al-Ghazal into killing fields.

Throughout the remainder of 1987 the SPLA expanded the war in the North. In July the "Volcano" Battalion under Yusif Kuwa, whose courage and military skill became legendary, occupied the eastern Nuba *jabals*, surrounded Talodi, and recruited significant numbers of Nuba into the SPLA. In Wau the SPLA enabled the beleaguered Dinka police to hold their own against the superior forces of the army garrison and the Fartit militia, the *jaysh al-salaam*, under the command of the ruthless Major-General 'Abu Qurun, known within the army as "Our Hitler," whose departure in November 1987 enabled the Dinka and Fartit to reach an uneasy peace. While fighting raged in the Bahr al-Ghazal, the SPLA captured Kurmuk and Qaissan just 450 miles southeast of Khartoum, creating war hysteria in the capital, and demonstrating that the government was incapable of operating a successful war or negotiating a viable peace (see p. 167 above). In January 1988 those Anya-Nya II who had accepted the DUP–SPLM/A peace accord in November joined the SPLA with their government-issued weapons, which momentarily sustained the SPLA offensive. Not all the Anya-Nya II, however, rushed to embrace the SPLA. Paulino Matiep commanding his Bul Nuer units in West Upper Nile had a long-standing grievance with the SPLA high command and refused to join, for his Bul Nuer were handsomely compensated to become a government militia and defend the Bentiu oil fields.

The success of the SPLA was, ironically, accompanied by growing internal dissent over the absolute authority wielded by John Garang. In order to weld together men of diverse and often hostile ethnicity into a disciplined force trained in insurgency with a smattering of military homogeneity he required firm control, particularly over the Nilotes who historically were deeply suspicious of authority. Garang tolerated no insubordination; he alone determined SPLA strategy and refused to include his field commanders in the decision-making process, which spawned a brooding resentment among his senior officers. Being forewarned by Mengistu in September 1987 that Kerubino was plotting against him, Garang had him arrested. Other arrests of prominent SPLA leaders followed in February 1988, including the respected veteran of the Anya-Nya, Arok Thon Arok, who had been in contact with the government offering to challenge Garang's leadership, and the old politician Joseph Oduho, an outspoken critic of Dinka domination. There were others charged with insubordination; some were executed, most were imprisoned in very harsh confinement. By summer 1988 Garang had crushed internal dissent and moved his headquarters from Bilpam in Ethiopia to the Boma Plateau in eastern Equatoria.

The capture of Kurmuk and defeat in the Blue Nile, southern Kordofan, and Bahr al-Ghazal had convinced Sadiq to retaliate with a major counter-offensive against the SPLA. He tried to push through the Constituent Assembly a bill that would legitimize the *razzias* of the *murahiliin* and other militias that the DUP and the Southern Bloc, even those southerners hostile to the SPLM/A, vehemently opposed. Some government officials admitted privately that arming the militia had been a "defensive" strategy that had gone badly wrong. The bill was temporarily shelved, but Sadiq was more determined than ever to seek a military solution in 1988. The army spring offensive was at first surprisingly successful, and the SPAF defeated several SPLA units, destroyed the largest SPLA camp in the Upper Nile in June, and recaptured Torit on 1 July 1988, a serious setback to SPLA operations in eastern Equatoria. In March 1988 Sadiq unilaterally unleashed the Missiriya *murahiliin* upon Dinka civilians, much to the disgust of professional officers in the army. Most *murahiliin* raids followed a similar pattern, one that was adopted by the *janjawiid* in Darfur fifteen years later. They would attack a Dinka village at dawn, kill all adult males who could not escape, rape the women, and enslave the children. The village would be burned, the wells stuffed with dead Dinka males, schools and clinics destroyed, and the huge herds of cattle rounded up as loot.

The four horsemen of the Apocalypse – Pestilence, War, Famine, and Death – now descended upon southern Sudan. Fatal disease was rampant, killing thousands of southerners; tens of thousands perished from malnutrition and starvation accompanied by an outbreak of rinderpest which killed over 1 million cattle in the Bahr al-Ghazal and the Upper Nile. When the rains arrived in August 1988 nearly 3 million southern Sudanese, one-third of the population of southern Sudan, had fled to refugee camps or the urban centers in the North, where some 2 million southerners hastily erected suburban shanty towns. The Ethiopian refugee camps – Itang, Dimma, and Asosa – were overflowing with 300,000 starving southerners preparing to die. Famine was also rampant in eastern Equatoria where the SPLA, using famine as a weapon of war, destroyed all bridges, mined the strategic Nimule–Juba road, and ambushed food convoys to prevent food relief reaching the starving garrison towns. By the end of 1988 over 250,000 southerners had died in southern Sudan alone, not to mention thousands more during the long march to Khartoum; for every ten Dinka fleeing from the Bahr al-Ghazal to Ethiopia only four arrived in the Ethiopian refugee camps, and of those who made it, one in four soon died from malnutrition or disease.

Suddenly and dramatically the rains returned to Sudan to break the great drought of the 1980s. They were brought by El Niño, which governs the northeast movement of the ITCZ from the South Atlantic. After dropping copious quantities of rainfall on southern Sudan, the ITZC unexpectedly moved north to Khartoum, where it collided with a violent line of squalls from the Indian Ocean. In 24 hours 9 inches of rain fell on a city with an average annual rainfall of 7 inches. Seventy people died, hundreds were injured, and over 100,000 homes were destroyed. Over $400 million would be needed for reconstruction, with assistance from the World Bank and Western donors conveniently diverting government famine relief funds previously allocated for the South. If the rains brought recovery for Sudan, they also restored the SPLA. Garang had improved his political position by the November 1988 peace agreement with Muhammad 'Uthman al-Mirghani, which made it easier for him to launch a military offensive after the New Year.

On 28 January 1989 the combined forces of William Nyuon Bany's SPLA and Gordon Kong's former Anya-Nya II captured the strategic Upper Nile town of Nasir after heavy fighting and losses on both sides. The capture of Nasir by the SPLA was a staggering blow to the government, precipitating a succession of SPLA military victories that changed the course of the civil war by mid-summer 1989. Torit was recaptured on 27 February 1989; Parajok, Nimule, Mongalla, and Gemmaiza were overrun in March. In April Akobo fell to the SPLA, followed by Waat in May. In the Nuba Mountains the SPLA had crushed a combined force of army and *murahiliin* at Korongo Abdallah in January 1989, to be followed by the entry of the New Kush Battalion led by Yusuf Kuwa in March. By mid-summer the SPLA controlled a large swath of territory from the northern Bahr al-Ghazal to eastern Equatoria that allowed them to besiege Juba. The irony of these defeats was the demise of the *murahiliin*. As the SPLA offensive gained momentum the fearful *murahiliin* were forced to request protection from the regular army, who despised them. By the end of 1989 *murahiliin* raids into the Bahr al-Ghazal were few, and in the Nuba Mountains the armed forces actually opened fire on the Missiriya *murahiliin* when they refused to end their raids on the Nuba. By spring 1989 morale within the army disintegrated as the SPLA displayed a disciplined unity of purpose under the iron fist of John Garang de Mabior, who parleyed his military victories into a successful visit to Washington and London to give the impression that he, not the dithering Sadiq, was in control of affairs.

ENIGMATIC FOREIGN AFFAIRS AND ECONOMIC DEGRADATION

Both the TMC and Sadiq actively sought to disassociate their administrations from Numayri's foreign policy. The first priority of the TMC was to restore relations with Mu'ammar Qadhafi of Libya with whom Numayri had been at logger-heads since his refusal to participate in the Tripoli Charter of 1969 and over Qadhafi's incessant clandestine efforts to bring Darfur into his orbit for a greater Libyan Sudanic empire (see Chapter 10). His hostility toward Numayri had led him to provide arms and money to the SPLA, but in July 1985 he signed an agreement to provide the TMC with light weapons, trucks, and air support and in September terminated all support for Garang. In return the TMC expelled a coterie of anti-Qadhafi Libyans who had been given sanctuary in Khartoum by Numayri and did not object when Qadhafi infiltrated 200 agents and money into Khartoum and Darfur which he ultimately hoped to detach from Sudan. Sadiq continued to cultivate closer relations with the man who had given him refuge in exile and the resources for his attempt to overthrow Numayri in July 1976, but he soon found himself on the horns of a dilemma in which his perennial indecisiveness immobilized his options. On the one hand, he was obligated to Qadhafi, but on the other, he was not prepared to have Darfur slip into the Libyan Sudanic empire. He resolved this conundrum by denying any reports of a Libyan military presence in Darfur while distancing himself from Qadhafi's appeals for Libyan–Sudanese unity when he had visited Khartoum in September 1986, particularly when a poll conducted by *al-Soudani* newspaper reported that only 12 percent of the Sudanese in April 1987 favored close ties with Libya. Most Sudanese regarded the eccentric Qadhafi as a buffoon.

Thereafter, the Libyan presence in Darfur grew rapidly. Qadhafi's Arab Legion opened a new road from Kufra to Kutum in northern Darfur for a convoy of 400 trucks carrying Libyan troops to Kutum and Tiné on the Chad border. Elsewhere the Islamic Legion openly recruited hundreds of Baqqara youth who swaggered around Darfur towns in Libyan dress; northern and central Darfur were soon awash with Libyan weapons, particularly the favored Kalashnikovs. Although this concentration of Libyan regulars and the Islamic Legion in Darfur was primarily to invade Chad, their defeat at Abu Suruj and Tendelti in Wadai by the Forces Armées Nationales Tchadiennes (FANT) forced a retreat back into Darfur, where they were joined by Acheikh ibn 'Umar's infamous Vulcan Force to dominate all of western and northern Darfur. Sudanese officials helplessly watched the Vulcan Force relocate to Geneina, and Libyan arms continued to flow into Darfur

from Ma'tan al-Sarra to Arab Gourane in central Darfur, the southern Rizayqat Baqqara, and as far south as Dar Fartit in the western Bahr al-Ghazal.
A more ominous development was the emergence from the shadows of
the mysterious Arab Gathering (*failaka al-islamiya*), an amorphous and
secretive collection of Arab supremacists in Darfur, whom Qadhafi eagerly
supplied with money, weapons, and military training at the Kufra Oasis.

In order to defend themselves from the Arab Libyan/Baqqara threat, the
Fur immediately established their own Federal Army of Darfur, consisting
of some 6,000 *jakab* Fur fighters armed by Chad with automatic weapons.
In response Musa Madibbu, Shaykh of the Rizayqat, appealed to Sadiq
for more arms to supplement those coming from Libya, which General
Burma Nasr swiftly provided. In autumn 1988 the conflict between Fur and
Rizayqat, known as the "War of the Tribes," erupted, reviving a long-
standing feud between them from the time of Sultan Tayrab in the eighteenth century. The Fur Federal Army was crushed, the survivors slaughtered in what *al-Ayam* newspaper described as "genocide." Governance
from Khartoum had all but vanished from Darfur.

The very visible military presence of Libyans in Darfur and the collapse
of the Fur, whom the government could not protect, or did not seek to,
caused considerable anguish in Khartoum that was compounded by the
government's repeated denials of any Libyan presence. When that transparent prevarication could no longer be sustained, Sadiq lamely requested
Qadhafi to withdraw his troops. He refused, calling in his markers accumulated during his support for Sadiq in the 1970s, knowing that Sadiq did
not have the resources to expel his Libyan troops, the Islamic Legion, or
the Vulcan Force. Throughout 1988–89 Darfur remained a battleground in
the forty years' war for control of the Chad Basin between Libya and Chad.
Khartoum no longer had any control throughout the northern, western,
and much of the central regions, which inspired a continuous stream of
delegations between Ndjamena and Khartoum that produced a good deal
of rhetoric and unworkable agreements. The Constituent Assembly repeatedly demanded that the borders with Libya and Chad be sealed, but the
government was helpless to close a frontier it did not control.

Relations with Egypt were equally complicated, but without the violence. Siwar al-Dhahab had visited Cairo in October 1985 and requested
the extradition of Numayri to stand trial in Khartoum. Mubarak was not
about to surrender his most loyal ally and friend in the Arab world, and
within the year extradition was no longer an issue. The election of Sadiq
al-Mahdi, however, did not immediately improve relations. Sadiq represented the historic Mahdist hostility toward Egypt and perceived fears of

Egyptian pretensions in Sudan rekindled during the Numayri years. After months of polite verbal sparring Sadiq realized he needed the support in his coalition government of the pro-Egyptian DUP and had neither the power nor the resources to prevent the presence of Egyptian influence in Sudan. Mubarak needed a friendly, stable, and united Sudan that could prevent another military coup d'état with unpredictable consequences for Egypt and contain the rising tide of Turabi and the NIF. In the South the Egyptians wanted peace within a united Sudan to finish the Jonglei Canal and complete the extensive plans for the conservation and canalization of the waters flowing from the Congo–Nile watershed. Consequently, the Egyptians scrupulously avoided taking sides in a futile attempt to satisfy both parties which satisfied neither. By 1989 the Egyptians had become exasperated with the indecision, crass manipulation, and prevarication of Sadiq, his government, and all the parties to exploit Egypt's historic relations with Sudan in order to promote their own interests at the Egyptians' expense. The limit of Egyptian patience appears to have been reached when Sadiq appointed as his foreign minister Hasan al-Turabi, the Islamist fundamentalist who was anathema to President Mubarak. Thereafter, Cairo would not be upset if Sadiq were overthrown and, to their later regret, welcomed the Bashir coup d'état of 30 June 1989.

Relations between Sudan and Ethiopia were of greater complexity than those with either Libya or Egypt. The Ethiopians were convinced that the TMC and the government of Sadiq al-Mahdi represented no change of policy in Khartoum. Skepticism was added to suspicion. During the passing years of the third parliamentary government a succession of delegations from the NASC, rival Sudanese parties, and the coalition government passed through the Ethiopian capital, leaving behind an impression of confusion, contradiction, and insincerity in their talk of peace. Sadiq frequently repeated that Ethiopia was using their puppet, John Garang, for their own communist self-interests in order to establish a Marxist government in Sudan or at least in the South. In November 1987 the hostile relations between Ethiopia and Sudan plunged to their nadir when the SPLA captured Kurmuk, but after Kurmuk was retaken in December cooler heads prevailed. Sadiq and Mengistu agreed to meet at the twenty-fifth anniversary conference of the OAU in Addis Ababa in May 1988. Their discussion, despite the vigorous efforts of Egypt and the OAU as intermediaries, failed to produce more than a disingenuous pledge to improve relations.

The military victories by the SPLA and the Eritreans and Tigreans, not OAU diplomacy, did more to bring about a temporary modus vivendi during the winter and spring of 1989. Superficially, Ethiopia and Sudan could cement friendly relations if each ceased to support the insurgents of the other, but major differences between the SPLM/A and the Eritreans and Tigreans limited each of them from abandoning their surrogates. The Eritreans were determined to secede from Ethiopia; the SPLA was seeking a united Sudan with a new, democratic, and secular government. Moreover, each government had a different relationship with the insurgents they were supporting. On the one hand, Sudan provided shelter for Eritrean and Tigrean refugees and political offices in Khartoum, and let the fighters of the Eritrean Liberation Front and the Tigray People's Liberation Front roam freely within Sudan and across the border, but it did not supply arms and military equipment to them. On the other hand, however, Ethiopia and Cuba had provided at first large amounts of arms, equipment, and training for the SPLA, and although the SPLA had become increasingly self-sufficient they still welcomed the Ethiopian connection.

If Sadiq's dealings with Libya, Egypt, and Ethiopia were ambiguous at best, his relations with Saudi Arabia and the Gulf states were positive and profitable. King Fahd had welcomed the downfall of Numayri and the restoration of the Sudanese northern elite, with whom the Saudis had long and cordial relations, and he pledged a huge $1 billion credit each year for three years and $700 million worth of goods, mostly badly needed oil, and another $300 million to help with Sudan's deplorable balance of payments. The Sudanese overwhelmingly approved of these dramatic improvements in Saudi–Sudan relations, to the credit of the prime minister. Sadiq's relations with the United States did not fare nearly so well. Washington was furious when the names of US embassy officials and CIA agents were exposed during the trial of General 'Umar Muhammad al-Tayib. Relations further deteriorated after a US communications officer in the embassy, William J. Cokals, was seriously wounded by a member of the Palestinian Black September Movement while driving in Khartoum. Ordinarily, the incident would have elicited only a firm admonition from the United States to apprehend the culprits, but Washington had not forgotten that thirteen years earlier Yasir Arafat's Black September Movement had assassinated the newly sworn-in Ambassador, Cleo A. Noel, and the Foreign Service Officer, George "Curt" Moore, on 2 March 1973 in the Saudi Embassy in Khartoum. The US Ambassador, Alexander Horan, was promptly recalled, the staff of the US embassy was reduced from 200 to 55 personnel, and normal relations were not renewed until December 1986, when Secretary of State George Schultz and Sadiq met in Washington, but the United States remained circumspect and suspicious.

After the "April Revolution" the TMC had studiously refused to make any significant decisions regarding the economy except to cancel Numayri's deals with Adnan Kashoggi and a West German industrialist, Henry J. Leir, to dump nuclear waste in the northwest desert. By the time Sadiq had formed his first coalition government the economy had slipped into a state of permanent crisis. The causes were many and varied: the decrease in crops for export, bargain-basement prices on the world market for cotton, continuing drought, a civil war costing $2 million a day, and foreign debt. Negotiations for financial assistance from the IMF were not promising. By 1986 Sudan was £S500 million in arrears for debt repayment to the IMF and could expect no further loans without strict conditions, including the removal of all subsidies on bread, oils, and basic commodities. After riots, precipitated by food shortages in October, the government refused to cancel food subsidies but agreed to devalue the Sudanese pound. Sadiq had high expectations from remittances of foreign exchange by Sudanese Nationals Working Abroad (SNWA) to help finance essential needs and reduce the foreign debt, but when he refused to remove all restrictions on currency transfers and reopen private houses of exchange, the means to transfer foreign exchange were few, resulting in an acute shortage of foreign currency to pay for critical commodities, machinery, and spare parts. Most soap factories were closed for several months in 1987, and the inability to import foreign wheat flour produced bread lines in Khartoum. By the summer of 1987 the accumulated chaos in the economy forced the government to declare a state of emergency.

Looming over and contributing to the deteriorating economy was the eternal foreign debt. In March 1987 Sudan's debt had reached $10.6 billion, over 32 percent of which was owed to other Arab countries and the Soviet Bloc, mostly for arms bought during the Numayri years. The Sudan government reached an agreement with the East Europeans in 1987 by which half the debt would be repaid in commodities and hard currency, which severely reduced, however, Sudan's ability to acquire desperately needed foreign exchange when its export commodities were shipped as repayment to Eastern Europe. In desperation Sadiq in April 1987 proposed an international conference to discuss the problems of foreign debt in the Third World and presented a ten-point program for discussion, but nothing of substance came of his initiative. In the Constituent Assembly the Minister of Finance, Dr. 'Umr Nur al-Da'im, attributed the debt crisis to mismanagement, lack of accountability, and unstable political institutions, but he could offer no ready solutions. By the end of the year Sudan had become the third most indebted nation and one of the four least developed countries in Africa.

Despite his numerous promises to streamline government bureaucracy, both in the central and regional governments, Sadiq did little except make sure that his extended family received preferred employment and the invaluable commercial licenses. By 1988 government employees represented 3 percent of the population but consumed 70 percent of the national budget. By September of that year the government had no other choice but to go hat-in-hand to the IMF in Washington, where an agreement was signed on 3 October 1988. The Sudanese pound was effectively devalued by almost 80 percent and all subsidies on sugar and gasoline were terminated, but not those on basic commodities – bread, oils, and kerosene – in return for a $4.8 billion aid package over a four-year period. When the terms of the deal were made public, angry students swarmed through the streets; the NIF and the SCP demanded that the government cancel the agreement.

The continuing economic crisis soon produced strikes and demonstrations protesting mandatory nine-hour power cuts and shortages of bread that infuriated the powerful bakers' union, which went on a three-day strike in June 1988. Frequent rallies continued in July against water shortages, and the accountants' union's five-day strike cost the Treasury $9.5 million in revenues. By mid-July the agricultural laborers joined the urban demonstrators to begin a ten-day strike over pay. Bank employees and at least twenty-two other unions staged protests against the privatization of some seventy-six state-owned enterprises, including four public-sector banks. Demonstrations diminished somewhat during the autumn after the government proposed its long-overdue Economic Recovery and Development Programme (ERDP) in November 1988 to achieve sustained economic growth, reduce inflation, ensure self-sufficiency in food production, and curb the crutch of foreign aid. The response to the ERDP from the Paris Club (an informal group of financial officials from nineteen of the world's richest countries providing financial services, particularly debt relief, restructuring and cancellation) and six Islamic, Arab, and African development funds was quite positive. They pledged substantial aid if the ERDP was successfully implemented along with a cease-fire in the civil war. This sudden wave of optimism, however, soon turned to gloomy skepticism in December 1988, when the government announced a raise in the minimum wage accompanied by major increases in the price of commodities: the price of sugar rose 500 percent. Mass demonstrations and riots erupted once more in all the major towns. Thousands of people stormed through the streets of Khartoum, Atbara, and Wad Medani demanding the resignation of the government in demonstrations that even hundreds of riot police could not fully contain. After three days of violent protests and strikes the government relented and revoked the increased price of sugar, but the riots continued into a fourth day, by which time two people had been killed and hundreds injured. Although the government was the principal villain, the demonstrators also shouted and stoned NIF "religious merchants" who were accused of making huge profits by monopolizing scarce goods. The government canceled the mission of the World Bank and IMF and suspended negotiations until spring 1989, as inflation spiraled out of control, running at a rate of 80 percent a year.

The doleful tragedy of three years of parliamentary government rendered all the more poignant the wave of hope and optimism that had swept over Sudan at the fall of Numayri. The "April Revolution" had overthrown the "May Revolution." The tyranny of military dictatorship had been cast aside and leadership bestowed on the heir to the Mahdiya, Sadiq al-Mahdi, who symbolized both the historic past and, with his Western education, an ebullient future. It was not to be. Sadiq al-Mahdi failed to rise to the challenge, and at the end he ironically resembled Numayri in his obsession to remain in power at any price, which led to political deals with the DUP, the NIF, and the army, but he lacked the skills of the "master manipulator," all of which undermined the parliamentary process. His vacillation and indecision over the September Laws exasperated the Islamic fundamentalists, alienated the secular Sudanese, and convinced the southerners he was not to be trusted. When he appeared willing in June 1989 to negotiate with the SPLM/A for an end to the civil war, many northern and southern Sudanese believed it was simply yet another maneuver to avoid a difficult situation and remain in power, but it was not to be.

CHAPTER 7

The Islamist revolution: the Turabi years, 1989–1996

On the night of 30 June 1989 a select group of middle-ranking army officers led by Brigadier 'Umar Hasan Ahmad al-Bashir overthrew the civilian coalition government of Sadiq al-Mahdi in a bloodless coup d'état. Like the Numayri coup in 1969, it was swiftly executed by Bashir's former comrades-in-arms in the elite paratroop brigade backed by the army engineers at the strategic Khartoum airport. In 1988 Bashir had been promoted to brigadier in command of the 8th Infantry Brigade fighting the SPLA insurgency in southern Sudan, but in spring 1989 he had been selected to attend a class at the G. A. Nasser Military Academy in Cairo. In early June he left his headquarters in southern Kordofan for Khartoum, ostensibly to prepare for his studies at the Academy. Here he met with 'Ali 'Uthman Muhammad Taha, head of the NIF Party in the Constituent Assembly, and spent the next three weeks planning to seize the government.

The officers, who called themselves the National Salvation Revolutionary Command Council (NSRCC) or Revolutionary Command Council (RCC) for short, were an unimpressive and politically naïve lot whom the Sudanese elite benignly regarded as just another effusive outburst by junior officers that would not last six months. During his early morning address over Radio Omdurman Bashir gave no indication of the goals of the coup, simply denouncing "al-Mahdi's democracy . . . [and] the failures of the democratic government to respect international human rights and to make good foreign relations with Central Africa," a most peculiar statement to justify the overthrow of a government. Indeed, most of the citizens in the Three Towns never envisioned that these guileless officers would install an Islamist regime.

Within hours of the coup 20 leading Sudanese politicians and some 100 military officers were arrested and incarcerated in Kobar prison, including Prime Minister Sadiq al-Mahdi, Muhammad 'Uthman al-Mirghani, leader of the DUP, and Muhammad Ibrahim Nugd of the SCP. To demonstrate their impartiality the RCC also arrested their ideological patron,

Map 9 Sudan

Hasan al-Turabi, who, however, was allowed to go home and pack a suitcase for his symbolic stay in a minimum-security cell. In Kobar, Turabi exuding his characteristic aplomb and patience, lectured his fellow prisoners on how a new chapter in Sudanese history was about to be written. *Shari'a* would remain the law of the land, and an Islamic state would be created despite the protestations of southern Sudanese and Muslim heretics, the *kafirin*.

The charade of his symbolic imprisonment became apparent upon his release in December 1989 when, in an extraordinary gesture of obeisance, all the members of the RCC, including 'Umar Hasan Ahmad al-Bashir, took the *bay'a* oath of allegiance to Hasan al-Turabi. This affirmation of obedience confirmed what everyone suspected: that Turabi was, indeed, the theological architect, patron, and *shaykh* of the Islamist revolution. Bashir was quite content, if not proud, to execute Turabi's instructions for the movement "without hesitation."

Outside Sudan 'Umar Hasan Ahmad al-Bashir was unknown and within the country an enigma. Born on 1 January 1945 to working-class parents in the small rural village of Hosh Bannaga, near Shendi, he graduated from the Ahlia Middle School in Shendi. His family moved to Khartoum at the end of the 1950s, where he received his secondary education while helping to supplement the family income by repairing automobiles. He was admitted to the Sudanese military academy as a cadet in the paratroopers and during the 1973 Arab–Israeli War distinguished himself fighting alongside the Egyptians, which won him rapid promotion and a transfer to an infantry brigade. While there he obtained a masters degrees in military science from the Sudan College of Commanders and from the Malaysian Military College. Although he had remained aloof from any demonstrable political affiliation, Bashir had no use for sectarian political parties (*taifiya*) and, the same as Numayri, had a particular dislike not only of the powerful Umma Party of Sadiq al-Mahdi and his Ansar but also of the DUP of the Mirghani family and their Khatmiyya supporters.

At first the 30 June coup appeared to be little different from the two previous military coups, but there was much more intellectual and political ideology behind the June Revolution than just another bunch of disgruntled junior officers seizing the government. When the RCC formally established a government in October 1989 they adopted the term "Islamist" preferred by Hasan al-Turabi to distinguish themselves and their followers from "other" Muslim fundamentalists and to differentiate their politics and theology from those of the secular political parties – the communists, Baathists, and democrats. Within a week the RCC had stifled all protest. All unions and political parties were banned and their property confiscated. Virtually all senior army and police officers not affiliated to the NIF were unceremoniously sacked. All newspapers except *al-Guwat al-Musalaha* (The Armed Forces) were closed down; radio and television, placed under government supervision, launched a massive campaign to assure the Sudanese that the members of the RCC were committed to orthodox Islam, Islamic law, and Islamic dress. Sudanese cultural identity was defined as the struggle between the sacred and profane, religious and secular, and Arab-Islam and Western Christianity, the former founded on the Qur'an and in which the true Muslim could become a part of a new pan-Islamic society.

Despite the apparent collegiality of the RCC, secular Sudanese professionals in Khartoum were convinced that its major decisions were not those of Bashir and the RCC but an enigmatic council (*majlis*) grandly called the Council of Defenders of the Revolution and popularly known as the Committee of Forty that included prominent members of the NIF, young Islamist army officers, and members of the RCC who met after curfew in a new mosque in downtown Khartoum and later at its headquarters in the Manshiya Extension (a suburb of the city). The chairman of the council was none other than 'Ali 'Uthman Muhammad Taha, president of the NIF. Within a few months the ubiquitous Committee of Forty were determined to impose their Arab, Islamist ideology upon unwilling Sudanese by means of a government that had no popular support in the rural areas and little in the towns. The enforcement of their political and theological correctness, however, they delegated to the officers of the RCC, who swiftly performed with a systematic ruthlessness hitherto unknown in Sudanese society that deeply disturbed many Sudanese, particularly the intelligentsia. There was a deep tradition of freedom of speech and tolerance in public affairs that was a source of great pride among the Sudanese. In the past when an unpopular government was overthrown, the deposed rulers were pensioned off or allowed to depart into exile. Bloodshed and revenge were not characteristic of political life in Sudan.

Officially, the Sudanese intelligence services were under the authority of the minister of the interior, and all security agencies were responsible to him, but in December 1989 the somnolent Sudan Security Bureau (SSB) of Sadiq al-Mahdi was entrusted to one of the original leaders of the 30 June coup d'état, Colonel (later Major-General) Bakri Hasan Salih, an efficient and sinister defender of the revolution. He reconstructed a completely new intelligence apparatus institutionalized by the National Security Act 1990, amended with more arbitrary powers in 1991 and 1992. Originally known as the Security of the Revolution-Revolutionary Intelligence Agency, its convoluted Arabic name was too much even for the RCC, who shortened it to "Internal Security" or "Islamic Security" (*al-amin al-dakhili*), which the Sudanese called the Internal Security Bureau, or IS-SOR. "External Security" (*al-amin al-khariji*) operated abroad especially to maintain surveillance of exiled Sudanese, and a third agency, "Sudan Security" (*al-mukhabarat al-'ammah*), was essentially concerned with military intelligence. Opponents of the new regime accused Salih of recruiting Islamist fanatics from the NIF for IS-SOR to intimidate the civilian populace. Others argued that IS-SOR was the creation of Bashir at the prodding of Turabi and Taha. Whoever made the decisions soon became irrelevant, for IS-SOR dramatically demonstrated its autonomy through its extreme brutality.

In an unprecedented effort to crush any real or potential dissent IS-SOR emasculated Khartoum's political life, sweeping through the Three Towns and the provincial urban centers and arresting human-rights activists, intellectuals, and university professors, as well as professionals, particularly doctors, lawyers, and journalists. Some were arbitrarily imprisoned; others were held in detention centers, the infamous "Ghost Houses" (*bayt al-ashbah*) operated by a special branch of IS-SOR that acquired a fearsome reputation for bestial interrogation, torture of every conceivable means, and mock executions, as well as the use of drugs, electric shock, and death. Many Sudanese simply "disappeared," their whereabouts unknown, their deaths unrecorded. Others were publicly flogged for the manufacture, possession, or consumption of alcoholic beverages; others were publicly executed for possession of heroin or undocumented foreign currency. Prominent scholars were singled out for arrest and torture, including the venerable scholar, then dying of cancer, Muhammad 'Umar Bashir, who was sacked from the university. Female employees were also singled out for dismissal, and those who remained were required to dress in the "Islamic style."

By the winter of 1989–90 there began a stream that soon became a flood of the best and the brightest Sudanese in a massive Diaspora to Egypt, Saudi Arabia, and the Gulf, but also to Europe, North America, Pakistan, and Malaysia, where they were welcomed for their skills and given refuge. For those who remained in Sudan, arbitrary arrest and detention without charge, solitary confinement, and torture had by spring 1990 become institutionalized and were routinely used in the infamous "Ghost Houses" in all the major cities and towns in Sudan. Despite official denials that torture was practiced in the "Ghost Houses" the evidence was overwhelming from the survivors of immersion head-first in cold water, hanging from the hands, cigarette burns, electric prods, mock executions, and rape, accompanied by beatings and humiliation in tiny cells. Many Sudanese suffered permanent disabilities after their release. Some detainees were simply tortured and released; others were charged and tried in special Islamist courts under summary procedures without due process of counsel. There was no right of appeal, and sentences, particularly public flogging, were carried out immediately.

As a means of intimidation many suspects were simply ordered to report to security, where they were detained for hours, then arbitrarily released and ordered to return the following day to repeat the process of intimidation. Relatives and friends of detainees were frequently harassed and ordered not to leave town without prior permission. Meetings more social than political were often arbitrarily dispersed by security officers, and the relatives of political exiles were singled out for repeated detention and torture. The leaders of the SCP and trade unions were a favorite target, for communists were godless unbelievers, while the massive arrests and the torture of union activists were followed by the Union Act 1992 that denied the right to organize or join a trade union for an extensive list of occupations, both skilled and professional. The RCC had wasted no time after 30 June 1989 in banning all non-governmental media, and despite a promise in 1993 to relax the prohibition on print, no independent newspapers were given permission to exist. Even a solid Islamist like Mahjub Muhammad al-Hasan Erwa, owner and editor of an Islamist daily, *al-Sudani al-Doulia*, had his offices closed, its presses seized.

Immediately upon seizing power, Bashir had appointed two vice-presidents, a cabinet, a council of ministers, and the supreme commander of Sudan's military forces. This was to be expected. His purge of Sudan's judiciary was not. The Sudan Bar Association, which had a long and distinguished tradition of independence, was prorogued, and the RCC effectively emasculated the judiciary by appointing as chief justice, a post formerly elected by sitting judges, Jalal 'Ali Lutfi, an Islamist and stalwart member of the NIF. Lutfi summarily imposed an Islamist judicial system on Sudan that embraced all civil and criminal courts, security courts for national security cases, and tribal courts that operated in isolated rural areas. It also had oversight responsibility for secretive military courts, where legal counsel was not permitted. Lutfi did not act on his own initiative, however. With his formal legal education and as dean of the Khartoum University Law School and attorney-general, Hasan al-Turabi, whose father had been a *qadi*, had a particular interest in the administration of justice. Turabi argued that jurists were necessary for the success of the political and economic process. They were to be active in Islamic banking and "informally monitor" banking practices to determine whether they were "in accordance with Islamic law, forbidden, desirable or not recommended." Jurists should review parliamentary laws to see they conformed to their Islamic content; *shari'a* must be the core of the legal system "to control government and guide it."[1] The Islamists dominated the military, the executive, and now the judiciary.

The RCC and NIF regarded the sectarian political parties as useless remnants of a pernicious Western secular presence. Many of their members fled the excessive tyranny of the regime to join the massive global Sudanese Diaspora. They were replaced by a Transitional National Council (TNC) appointed by the RCC and consisting of trusted, theologically correct individuals who benignly and routinely approved the government's domestic policies. The TNC would serve until the revolutionary government had time to build a political structure in the vast Sudan countryside through an evolutionary approach to government that Hasan al-Turabi had advocated for many years as the essential precondition for the establishment of an Islamist state based on *shura* and *ijma'a*. The concept of discussion arriving at consensus was not to be confused with Western democracy, for only morally qualified individuals would act on behalf of the Muslim community. Arabic would replace English in Turabi's Islamic Republic of Sudan and make Christians, not to mention Africans who adhered to their traditional religions, second-class citizens. A theocracy would determine gender roles, and protect the honor and *ird* of women. Prostitution, pornography, and the exhibition of the female form for commercial purposes would be proscribed. Sudanese women would have to wear their traditional garb (*tobe*), and the progress they had made in Sudan to achieve equality in the professions would be restrained, despite the well-known views of Turabi's feminist wife, Wisal al-Mahdi, sister of Sadiq.

The Islamist revolution dramatically terminated any expected compromise over the *shari'a* September Laws. After months of interminable dialogue, on 31 December 1990 the RCC announced more comprehensive and stringent *shari'a* laws than the 1983 September Laws of Ja'afar Numayri, to be enforced by the Popular Police Force, made up of special IS-SOR units of dedicated NIF members. The most important change in *shari'a* was Section 126 of the 1991 Sudan Penal Code, which expressly mandated the death penalty for any Muslim who advocated apostasy, although he could also save himself by swiftly recanting his failure to observe the faith. Among the Muslim Sudanese the heaviest burden of the fundamentalist interpretation of *shari'a* was the public discrimination aqainst women, which frequently violated internationally recognized standards of human rights. During the early purges thousands of women were arbitrarily dismissed from their jobs, for according to the NIF the ideal Sudanese woman was a devout Muslim who took care of her reputation, husband, children, and household, remaining aloof from a place in the market economy. After the passage of the Popular Police Force Act in December 1991 women appearing in public had to be appropriately dressed to cover the entire body and head, and were prohibited from wearing trousers; their public behavior was strictly defined. The number of arbitrary arrests without warrants of women charged with

"scandalous conduct" or "immodest dress" under the Popular Police Force
Act numbered in the hundreds, with severe penalties, flogging being the
preferred punishment.

The harsh imposition of *sharī'a* created a very serious dilemma for that
one-third of the Sudanese who were non-Muslims. Theoretically, non-
Muslims who supervised Muslims were excluded from every senior government office, but in practice this blatant discrimination was harsher against
those of traditional African religions, the *kafirin*, unbelievers, than against
the people of the book – Christians, Jews, and Zoroastrians. More than
2 million southern Sudanese IDPs surrounding Khartoum practiced their
traditional African religions or Christianity, not to mention the tens of thousands of Copts and Christians in the capital. In the Nuba Mountains there
were hundreds of thousands of Nuba practicing their traditional African
religions or Christianity, and several million more in southern Sudan, who
were all subject to the Islamic *hudud* punishments. Ministers, priests, and
their congregations were regularly harassed and their humanitarian relief
work consistently disrupted, in sharp distinction to the favoritism granted
to Islamic relief organizations. In 1992 a host of new religious laws were
promulgated and enforced. Punishment for stealing was now defined as
amputation of one hand for the first offense and the remaining hand for
the second. Adultery was punishable by death from stoning, prostitution by
public flogging. The distinctions between violation of *sharī'a* and human
rights were frequently fuzzy, particularly in the war zones. Numerous and
credible reports flowed steadily out of Sudan of forced labor, the conscription of children, and arbitrary Arabization, much of which was the work
of Arab militias armed by the government.

As part of its ideologically inspired indoctrination of Arabization and
Islamization, the new regime was determined to enlarge the size of the
armed forces to complete its domestic program and reverse the series of
defeats suffered by the army in its continuing civil war against the SPLA.
This ambitious program for military and internal security placed an enormous strain on the very limited resources of the Sudan economy, and was
made all the more difficult by a soaring rate of inflation ranging from 40
to 80 percent a year and a 1989–90 defense budget of some £S2.15 billion ($478.2 million), a sum which did not include another £S450 million
($105 million) for internal security. Consequently, by the end of 1990 there
were only sufficient resources to increase the army by 20 percent to 65,000
(instead of the goal of 78,000), easily achieved from the high numbers of
unemployed but insufficient to win the civil war and defend the revolution.
The size of the air force was doubled, but the number of combat aircraft

actually declined as a consequence of inadequate maintenance and a lack of spare parts caused by the scarcity of foreign currency. Unable to meet its goal of 78,000 men, and under growing pressure from the NIF to secure the revolution, the RCC fulfilled its promise upon coming to power of imposing conscription, for the first time in the history of Sudan.

In summer 1989 the RCC could not rely on the SPAF to turn the tide of the civil war or on the secular professional officer corps to defend the revolution. Consequently, and under great pressure from the NIF, the RCC reluctantly decided to create a more organized militia than the ragtag *murahiliin*, the People's Defense Force (PDF), to secure the regime and expand the faith when it could no longer rely on the army. Recruits for the paramilitary PDF were conscripted from a universal and very unpopular draft that numbered 150,000 by 1991 and from which numerous wealthy parents in Khartoum were able to purchase their sons' immunity. The draftees were introduced to weaponry by instructors from the Sudan army, but their indoctrination was more religious than military, with interminable lectures on Islam delivered by known members of the NIF and the Muslim Brotherhood. Hasan al-Turabi had long argued in private and public that it would be impossible to "Islamize" the Sudanese army because its professional officers had been "secularized." In order to achieve "consensus," Islamist Sudan needed to create "a small standing army and a large popular defense force" to combat the non-Muslim insurrection in the South and political or religious dissent in the North. The RCC was less than enthusiastic about the creation of a rival to its army by the NIF, but it could hardly object, given the past success of the *murahiliin*. Perhaps some discipline might be imposed on these unruly militia if they were integrated into the PDF.

The Islamist indoctrination of the PDF was entrusted to Ibrahim al-Sanussi, who in the Egyptian media was referred to as the leader of the NIF's "military wing." He frequently lectured at the camps of the PDF, and his speeches and Islamist propaganda were widely distributed among the recruits. The few weeks of military training for recruits in the PDF camps consisted of many lectures on Islamist teaching and very few on how to become soldiers. It was no secret in Sudan and the world intelligence community that the Sudanese PDF would become neither a revolutionary guard nor an efficient paramilitary organization. It was a rabble in arms, whose volunteers were used by the Sudan army in its southern civil war as cannon fodder and whose depleted ranks had to be regularly replenished by the forced and unpopular conscription. The newer PDF units experienced their first test in the Blue Nile Province, where they suffered heavy casualties at the hands of the SPLA, to the consternation of many families in Khartoum and Omdurman. Thereafter, the PDF was employed only after the army had suffered severe defeats. The most dependable units were eventually handed over to civilian control by members of the NIF to become "Public Order Police," an NIF Party militia called Youth of the Home Land, considered more reliable than the regular police, to suppress civilian or student demonstrations.

<h2 style="text-align:center">THE POPULAR ARAB AND ISLAMIC CONGRESS</h2>

Throughout the first year of the June Revolution Hasan al-Turabi was rarely mentioned in the government-controlled media. He spent most of his time either in jail or under house arrest, working with his wife to create the International Organization of Muslim Women, founded at Khartoum in November 1989. Upon his release from confinement he became a roving emissary for the Foreign Ministry and personal representative of President Bashir. This attracted little publicity, but following the rapid conclusion of the First Gulf War (1990–91), Turabi emerged from the shadows to leave no doubt as to who Sudan's most powerful civilian politician was. The ignominious defeat of Arab Iraqi troops by the US coalition and the latter's continuing presence on Muslim soil had aroused very hostile Islamist feelings throughout Saudi Arabia and Yemen, where it was felt that any attack on a brother Arab nation, no matter how justifiable, did not exculpate the overwhelming presence of Western, Christian troops in Saudi Arabia. Nor could the Islamists stomach the apparent subordination of Saudi policy to that of the West and the United Nations (UN). Turabi was now no longer content to play the role of éminence grise in the NIF and the Bashir regime now that the humiliation of an Arab nation by both Western and secular Arab states demanded a radical reassessment of the role Islamists were to play in the post-Gulf War period and throughout the Muslim world.

In March 1990 President Bashir announced at a meeting of the Arab and Foreign Investors' Symposium in Khartoum that henceforth all "Arab brothers" would be allowed to enter Sudan without a visa. The doors were now open for Afghan-Arab *mujahidiin* seeking a safe haven after the Soviet withdrawal from Afghanistan and the establishment of contacts with Islamist terrorist organizations. Hasan al-Turabi appeared in December 1990 at a poorly publicized Islamic Committee for Palestine (ICP) Conference, "Islam: The Road to Victory," in Chicago, where he personally met many prominent members of the Islamist movement. Returning

Figure 20 Sudan's opposition Islamist leader Hasan al-Turabi talks during an interview with Reuters in Sudan's capital, Khartoum, 11 July 2005.

to Khartoum by spring 1991 he had clearly established his dominant position in the NIF and the regime, which he sought to exploit by publicly announcing in April the creation of a Khartoum-based Popular Arab and Islamic Congress (PAIC), *al-mutamar al-arabi al-shabi al-islami*. The PAIC, or General Assembly as its delegates called it, was in fact the culmination of a quarter-century of Turabi's study, political activity, and international globe-trotting, for which the First Gulf War had been the catalyst for him to establish the PAIC for that convergence of Arab and Islamist beliefs that the Organization of the Islamic Conference (OIC) and Arab nationalists had failed to accomplish because of the personal greed of their leaders and their regional interests. His PAIC would become the forum for the worldwide Islamist revolution to coordinate the anti-imperialist movements in some fifty Muslim states. With consummate enthusiasm the Sudan government described the first meeting of the PAIC General Assembly as "the most significant event since the collapse of the Caliphate."

The first PAIC General Assembly was held in Khartoum for 3 days, from 25 to 28 April 1991, and was attended by 300 Sudanese and 200 other delegates from 45 states. Islamists from the Middle East were, of course, well represented, but there were delegates from North Africa, Great Britain, and the United States, as well as more exotic members, such as those from the Abu Sayyaf movement in the Philippines. The first PAIC General Assembly, oddly, did not receive much publicity even in the Khartoum press, but the delegates agreed to establish the "Armed Islamist Internationale" – an umbrella organization for Sunni Islamist international terrorism. At the close of the conference a permanent secretariat was created with Turabi its secretary-general, now the leader of an intellectual Islamic renaissance who would lead the PAIC as the instrument of revolutionary Islam. Turabi himself visited Pakistan and Afghanistan in September 1991 and by December appears to have consolidated arrangements for Islamist recruits from South Asia to train in Afghan-Arab *mujahidiin* camps near Peshawar, Pakistan. By 1992 Turabi's essays, tape recordings, videos, and radio broadcasts had made him a popular speaker throughout the Muslim world. Indeed, Sudan, perched on the frontier of Islam and culturally, politically, and theologically marginalized from the mainstream of the Arab and Islamic worlds, appeared a strange place from which to spawn a worldwide Islamist revolution. Nevertheless, the RCC/NIF government was the only Arab state willing to embrace the Islamist revolution as its own and spread their revolution throughout the Muslim world by any means necessary. Sudan soon became the center for training unemployed Afghan-Arab *mujahidiin* seeking to continue the Islamist *jihad* in Algeria, Bosnia, and Yemen. *Mujahidiin* from the jama'at al-islami of Pakistan and India, the hizb-i islami and jamiat-i islami of Afghanistan and the hizb-ul mujahiieiin of Kashmir joined the PAIC, as well as Islamists from Egypt, Hizbullah in Lebanon, the Islamic Salvation Front (FIS) in Algeria, and the NIF in Sudan. In December 1991 Turabi enthusiastically welcomed Usama bin Ladin to Khartoum.

Usama had already purchased a nondescript office on Mek Nimr Street in downtown Khartoum, opened accounts at the al-Shamal, Tadamun, and Faisal Islamic Banks, and moved into a sumptuous villa in the fashionable Riyadh suburb near the home of the NIF's leader, 'Ali 'Uthman Muhammad Taha. Turabi organized a lavish reception in his honor at which bin Ladin pledged $5 million for the PAIC. Their alliance was further cemented when Usama married Turabi's niece as his third wife, and in return Turabi arranged for bin Ladin to import expensive construction equipment and vehicles duty-free. Usama bin Ladin and his family settled into their villa, where they entertained Turabi, Taha, and other prominent members of the NIF, while the al-Qa'ida leadership made themselves at home in the spacious guest house and moved freely in and out of Sudan.

Customs formalities were facilitated by a "delegation office" for them and Afghan-Arab *mujahidiin* who were given Sudanese passports and met with Colonel 'Abd al-Bashir Hamza, the Sudanese intelligence liaison officer for al-Qa'ida. Special members of al-Qa'ida were given Sudanese diplomatic passports; others were made Sudanese citizens. In return, al-Qa'ida screened the credentials of incoming Afghan-Arabs for Sudan state security.

Thereafter, bin Ladin, the legitimate entrepreneur, established Taba Investments and also Ladin International, an umbrella organization that included Qudurat Transportation; a bakery; furniture, fruit, and vegetable export companies; and the al-Ikhlas Company, which imported sweets and honey. His al-Hijra Construction Company employed over 600 people to build the major arterial road from Khartoum to Port Sudan. On Thursday evenings the al-Qa'ida leadership met at his large farm near Soba, and it was common for members to attend lectures on Islamic issues delivered by bin Ladin. Construction equipment brought from Afghanistan was stored at the Soba farm with his beloved horses and used to build nineteen training camps for Afghan-Arab *mujahidiin* scattered in the semi-desert around Khartoum. Bin Ladin personally provided funds for three al-Qa'ida camps, but the others were mostly funded by more than a dozen, mostly Saudi, Islamic charities that had established offices on al-Jamahriya Street in Khartoum through which funds were channeled to support the camps and then laundered for weapons and operations abroad.

The RCC continued to give its tacit support to its Afghan-Arab "visitors" with customary Sudanese hospitality, raised no objections to the creation of terrorist training camps, and arranged for the security services to facilitate for the Afghan-Arabs the maze of paperwork for which Sudanese bureaucracy was infamous. The Sudanese by and large ignored the presence of the Afghan-Arabs, who kept themselves in their camps. Members of the NIF were extremely helpful in providing funds and opportunities for the visitors, and a symbiotic relationship soon developed between the PAIC and the al-Qa'ida Islamist revolutionaries from more than a dozen countries. In turn, al-Qa'ida supported Turabi's political objectives in Sudan and used the PAIC as a cover for its international operations. After bin Ladin was forced to leave Sudan in 1996, President Bashir blandly commented that he had never really had partisans or a "network" in Sudan, but failed to mention that his government had refused to pay Usama for his road construction.

After three years in power the RCC sought to improve its image as a tightly integrated military cabal. On 16 October 1993 the RCC dissolved itself on condition that 'Umar Hasan al-Bashir became president of the

Islamic Republic of Sudan. This cosmetic change, however, did not mean a retreat for the Islamist revolution. In Constitutional Decree No. 7, The Principles Guiding the Policy of the Government, Islam remained the source of government laws, regulations, and policies for a unified Sudan. Commitment to Islam was obligatory, and there would be no return "to hateful party fanaticism and moribund sectarian parties." The most important officials were now Turabi loyalists whose Islamist ideologies shaped official policy, but as the ideological patron of the Islamist revolution Turabi scorned any prominent position in the government, leaving the pedestrian details of every-day governance to the military and civil drones of administration. Between 1992 and 1996 'Umar Hasan al-Bashir appears to have reconciled himself to a subordinate relationship to Turabi in order to secure the revolution and enjoy the perquisites of power, but to most Sudanese and certainly to the *khawadja* the internal dynamics of the Islamist regime remained obscure at best and opaque at worst. Meanwhile, Turabi traveled widely to promote his Islamist ideology, his brilliance, and his fame. He imagined himself a theological mediator between Sunni and Shi'a, Christianity and Islam.

In late April 1992 Turabi had delivered his Muslim world view to the Royal Society for the Encouragement of Arts, Manufactures, and Commerce in London. He condemned the "introduction of the nation state" at the expense of the Muslim community, the *dar al-islam*. It was the "[First] Gulf War [that] did more than anything else to arouse the Muslim masses and give impetus to the international manifestation of pan-Islam" from which was emerging the faith by which the Muslim world's "ultimate ideal" would be achieved.[2] In May he arrived in the United States to attend a round table of American scholars of Islam sponsored by the World and Islam Studies Enterprise and the Middle East Committee at the University of South Florida to declare that the worldwide Islamist movement was "a populist phenomenon." From Florida Turabi flew to Washington, where, in an interview with the *Washington Post*, he emphasized that the Islamist movement would never accept the existence of Israel or the presence of the US military in the Persian Gulf, and lectured members of the House Subcommittee about "Islamic Fundamentalism," which he called an "Islamic Renaissance," who listened in disbelief to learn that all the Sudanese were Arabic-speaking and that their knowledge of Islam was superior to that of the *'ulama'* in Iran. Leaving Washington for Ottawa to meet with government officials, members of parliament, and Arakis, a Canadian Oil Company, he was attacked in the reception area of Ottawa airport by a disgruntled Sudanese expatriate and karate expert who left him near-dead.

He recovered in a Canadian hospital, recuperated in Switzerland, and in the spring of 1993 returned to Khartoum to lead the second PAIC later in the year.

The spread of Turabi's reputation, the assault in Canada, and his recovery coincided with the continued support of the Sudan government for what the US Department of State called "state-sponsored terrorism." In 1992 the RCC and PAIC openly began to assist radical Somali Islamists, particularly the Somali Islamic Unity Party, *al-ittihad al-islami al-somalia*. The RCC provided weapons and food; bin Ladin sent his trusted lieutenants, 'Abu Hafs and 'Abu Ubaydah al-Banshiri, and in November approved a *fatwa*, enabling faithful Somalis to oppose any intervention by US armed forces as part of the abortive UN "Operation Restore Hope" in November 1992. On 26 February 1993 a bomb exploded in the World Trade Center in New York, killing six Americans. The attack had been planned by the blind Egyptian Shaykh 'Umar 'Abd al-Rahman and was carried out by his Egyptian Islamic Group, *jama'at al-islamiyya*, with the assistance of Sudanese diplomats from its mission at the UN. On 18 August 1993 Sudan was accused of providing sanctuary for a variety of terrorist organizations, including such Palestinian groups as the Palestine Liberation Organization (PLO), Hamas, and Islamic Jihad, Lebanon's Hizbullah, the Algerian FIS, Tunisia's *al-nada*, the Yemeni *al-islah*, and the Egyptian *jama'at al-islamiyya*, and the Department of State promptly added Sudan to its list of countries accused of promoting state-sponsored terrorism. The Sudanese government reacted by launching a barrage of verbal abuse and assaults and orchestrating anti-American demonstrations in Khartoum, accusing the United States of a conspiracy against Islam.

The Second People's Arab and Islamic Congress was held from 2 to 4 December 1993 in Khartoum, which Hasan al-Turabi now envisaged as the center, if not the headquarters, of the new Islamist world. He deeply believed that an Islamic revolution was happening throughout the Muslim world and that Sudan was now the leader of the Islamists and the center of influence in the "New World Order" precipitated by the demise of the Soviet Union. Five hundred delegates swarmed into the capital, and Turabi had personally invited an all-star cast of Islamists that included the Ayatollah Mahdi Karrubi, head of the Society of Combatant Clergy from Tehran, and Husayn Fadl 'Allah of the Lebanese branch of Hizbullah. Gulbaddin Hekmatyar represented the Afghan Islamists. Rashid al-Ghannushi, Tunisian leader of *al-nada*, and from Algeria 'Abd Allah Jaballah and Rabih Kabir from the FIS were in attendance. The prominent Russian Islamist Geidar Jamal had come to discuss with Turabi the plight of Muslims in Russia, and General Mizra Aslam Beg, former Pakistan commander-in-chief, was an honored guest, for he had a long relationship with Usama bin Ladin and his support of Pakistan's Inter-Services Intelligence (ISI) for the Islamist Taliban in Afghanistan, *mujahidiin* in Kashmir, and the *markaz-dawat-al-arshad*, a Pakistani charity that openly boasted of financing international Islamic terrorism. Even the mastermind of the World Trade Center attack, Shaykh 'Umar 'Abd al-Rahman, eluded the authorities in Egypt to attend.

The delegates vigorously discussed the "New World Order"; the role of the PAIC in promoting Islamic hegemony in the Muslim world; the repression of Muslim minorities in Europe and the United States; and the challenge to Islam from the West. As during the first PAIC General Assembly in 1991, the media were strictly controlled, and the only television coverage to reach the West was provided by the Canadian Broadcasting Company (CBC) which included staged chants of "Down with the USA!" in English and "Death to the Jews!" in Arabic. At the conclusion of the PAIC Turabi could confidently declare "the future is ours," and at the sixth Student Union Conference at the University of Khartoum that followed he urged Muslim youths throughout the world to take up the challenge of uniting the Islamic *jihad*, "for Islamists will prevail where truth defeats falsehood and all Muslims will live in a united Islamic nation." By 1994 the Islamist ideologies of the PAIC had permeated every political and social development in Sudan and virtually every evolving Islamist movement in Africa, Asia, and Europe.

WAR AGAINST THE SOUTH AND CIVIL WARS WITHIN

After an unwieldy committee created by the RCC to seek peace with the SPLM/A had ignominiously failed and former US President Jimmy Carter in his eagerness for a settlement had proved an embarrassment to both the SPLM/A and the RCC in December 1989, each came to the erroneous conclusion that a military solution was in sight. Between January and May 1989 the SPLA had won a string of stunning victories in the South, southern Kordofan, and the Nuba Mountains, and in October once again briefly captured Kurmuk. As in November 1987, the SPLA seizure of Kurmuk provoked a massive outpouring of patriotic fervor in Khartoum. Army units were diverted from the southern front to retake Kurmuk and all the villages lost to the SPLA in the southern Blue Nile by the end of the year, which created an illusion among the members of the RCC that victory was near.

During the late winter, spring, and early summer of 1990 there was a general lull in the fighting as both sides agreed to a cease-fire that produced unexpected international sympathy and support for the SPLM/A, particularly from African states that hitherto had remained aloof from the southern insurgency. John Garang made a successful tour of Europe and the United States, followed by visits to Botswana, Mozambique, Zambia, and Zimbabwe, the so-called Front-Line States, as well as Tanzania and Zaire. Everywhere he went he emphasized that the peace program of the SPLM was for a democratic, secular, and united Sudan, which had great appeal for those African states increasingly suspicious of the racist, Arab, Islamic rhetoric of the RCC/NIF diarchy, whose credibility had dissolved on account of its use of intimidation, terror, and arbitrary violations of human rights. The relative peace of 1990 also gave the SPLM/A an opportunity to persuade suspicious and skeptical Equatorians to temper their long history of hostility toward the Dinka. Many Equatorians had been stalwart separatists since the days of the Anya-Nya and were deeply suspicious of John Garang's emphasis on a united Sudan. Although John Garang worked assiduously to conciliate the delegations of Equatorian politicians, the Islamist government's use of arbitrary imprisonment and terror, advocacy of *sharïa*, and rejection of the DUP–SPLM peace agreement, along with the misbehavior of the Sudanese army, and Garang's efforts to instill discipline into the SPLA did much more to appease Equatorian hostility toward the SPLM/A than his friendly palavers with their politicians.

During the early years of the SPLA insurgency Garang had become dependent for arms, logistical support, and training on Mengistu's Ethiopian army and on the site near Addis Ababa for the popular and very effective Radio SPLA. In return the SPLA had become increasingly involved in Mengistu's campaigns against the Gaajak Nuer militia in the Gambella region, the Anuak Gambella People's Liberation Front (GPLF), and the more formidable Muslim Oromo Liberation Front (OLF), all of whom received support from the Khartoum government. The more the SPLA was successful against the OLF, particularly after 1985, the more support it received from Addis Ababa. All of this suddenly came to an end after the collapse of the Mengistu government in May 1991. Throughout the 1980s every government in Khartoum had supported the Eritrean People's Liberation Front (EPLF) and the Tigray People's Liberation Front (TPLF), which in 1991 became the principal force of the Ethiopian People's Revolutionary Democratic Front (EPRDF) against the communist Derg government led by Mengistu. The EPRDF quickly repaid its debt to Khartoum by severing all ties with the SPLM/A, shut down Radio SPLA, closed

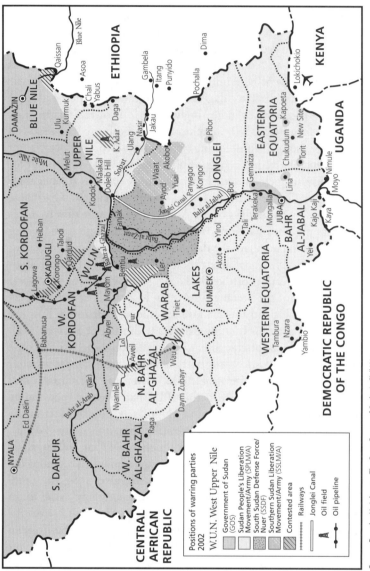

Map 10 The southern Sudan civil wars

Source: Douglas H. Johnson, The Root Causes of Sudan's Civil Wars.

all the SPLA training camps in Ethiopia, and ceased the steady flow of arms and supplies. Having lost its secure bases, the organizational structure of the SPLA became dislocated. Then the political headquarters of the SPLM in Addis Ababa was closed, and the former files of Ethiopian intelligence about the SPLM/A were handed to the Sudan government.

The greatest loss, however, was not to the SPLA but some 250,000 Sudanese refugees huddled in the Itang, Fungyido, and Dimma refugee camps. When it was certain in February 1991 that the Mengistu regime was doomed, the SPLA had organized a massive evacuation from all three camps. Some 132,00 passed through Nasir and another 100,000 appear to have settled in the greater Pochalla region along the Akobo and Pibor rivers, while an estimated 20,000 arrived around Pakok near the Boma Plateau. In the chaos precipitated by such a mass movement of people the international relief efforts were hopelessly inadequate and too ill-coordinated to respond to so many on the move with so little, and they were often obstructed by the USAID decision to use its considerable food aid to stabilize the new, pro-Western EPRDF government in its western provinces below the highlands. The poor harvests in the Sobat, Pibor, and Akobo rivers, combined with the failure of appropriate relief programs, provided the Khartoum government with infinite opportunities to manipulate relief aid to its advantage and intervene to divide those who hitherto had been sympathetic to the SPLM/A.

After eight years the militarization of the SPLM/A had become complete by 1991 and was characterized by the authoritarianism of a military hierarchy in which there was little interest in programs of rehabilitation in the liberated areas and even less in building social and economic development for the civilian population. The SPLA was basically a peasant army with little political consciousness. It was divorced from the concerns of ordinary southerners, concentrating solely on military force to achieve success without any popular participation. To the southern Sudanese the only way to participate in the liberation struggle was to join the SPLA as a military combatant. Not surprisingly, the movement created a military elite of senior officers who abused their authority for the sake of self-promotion and the arbitrary accumulation of wealth, usually in the form of livestock. They were devoid of any sense of accountability, responsibility, or criticism of the leadership. Surrounded by sycophants overflowing with flattery, John Garang had become increasingly intolerant and vindictive, which encouraged his officers seeking promotion to devote their energy more to the manipulation and vilification of their rival colleagues than to fighting the enemy. The evolution of a formidable military machine was not commensurate with political or ideological development, so that officers and men of the SPLA abused civilians for their own pleasure or gain, which often made them indistinguishable from the *murahiliin*, PDF, or SPAF.

On 28 August 1991 three senior commanders of the SPLM/A, Lam Akol Ajawin, Riek Machar Teny-Dhurgon, and Gordon Kong Cuol, publicly announced that John Garang had been dismissed as chairman of the movement. They justified their decision in a pamphlet entitled *Why John Garang Must Go Now* – because of his "dictatorial" leadership. They promised respect for human rights and an independent southern Sudan. Certainly, John Garang's leadership had been dictatorial, but his leadership had achieved a cohesion and coordination that had produced a succession of military victories and control of virtually all southern Sudan. Dissent was not tolerated, critics were ruthlessly removed or imprisoned, and in April 1993 Garang had two senior commanders executed for allegedly plotting against him. The Political-Military High Command (PMHC) had never formally met until mid-summer 1991, eight years after the founding of the movement, and decisions were made solely by John Garang and a few loyal aides. By disposition Garang remained aloof, always on the move between Addis Ababa, the Boma Plateau, and SPLA camps in Ethiopia and Sudan, as well as undertaking his international tours, so that as the years passed there was no central forum to raise questions of political, financial, or military strategy.

The initiative for the coup d'état appears to have come from Lam Akol, a Shilluk (Chollo), who had an infinite capacity for alienating his subordinates and even his most stalwart supporters. He was considered arrogant and insensitive, and his first SPLA command in Shillukland was a complete failure. He never bothered to build a political base among the Shilluk and, as a commoner, became embroiled in a bitter disagreement with the revered *Reth* of the Shilluk, Ayang Kur Nyidhok, over SPLA looting, raping women, and stealing cattle, which had alienated many of his subjects. Thereafter, Lam Akol was more successful as the director of external relations for the SPLA, in which post he won a good deal of sympathy and support for the movement. By 1990, however, his imperious and independent attitude forced Garang to reassign him as zonal commander to join Riek in the Upper Nile, which both of them regarded as a political demotion as the focus of SPLA operations shifted from the Upper Nile to eastern Equatoria under the personal command of Garang and his kinsman, Kuol Manyang Juk. Infuriated, Lam heaped verbal and written abuse upon Garang that effectively ruined their relationship in a spate of personal acrimony.

In preparation for the ousting of Garang, Riek had been in contact with the Khartoum governor of the Upper Nile in Malakal, who was delighted to provide military support for the rebels in Nasir. Despite this assistance, however, the conspiracy soon began to unravel. Shilluk officers, who might have followed Lam out of ethnic solidarity, strongly advised him to desist from this ill-advised adventure, and even those officers and men directly under the command of Lam in Maban refused to obey his orders. Moreover, SPLA commanders sympathetic to Lam and Riek now argued against any dramatic change of leadership until the SPLA had recovered and reorganized from its losses in Ethiopia. Many other SPLA commanders simply refused to respond, leaving Lam and Riek with only the Nuer commanders around Nasir and the former Nuer commander of Anya-Nya II, and that perennial secessionist, Gordon Kong Cuol. Having publicly announced that "John Garang Must Go," Lam, Riek, and Gordon had no other option but to form their own armed force called the "Nasir Faction" or "SPLA-Nasir," consisting only of Nuer units around Nasir, the Bul Nuer, and the Luo Nuer from Anya-Nya II, which drastically changed the controversy over leadership into an ethnic conflict between Nuer and Dinka.

Garang's initial response was to ignore the Nasir rebels. He told southern exiles he had no plans to attack them, but conflict between the Nasir Nuer and the SPLA Dinka was virtually inevitable during the autumn of 1991. Fighting first erupted around Ayod in late September. The SPLA was forced to retreat, leaving the Nuer to inflict heavy casualties on Dinka civilians, until SPLA reinforcements from Bor drove north to Kongor and destroyed large amounts of fuel and supplies for SPLA-Nasir flown into Ler by government cargo planes. Riek, against the advice of several of his officers, launched a major counter-offensive, hoping for a swift victory that would cause SPLA commanders sitting on the fence to join SPLA-Nasir and topple John Garang. The Nuer invasion of Dinkaland was composed of units from SPLA-Nasir, Anya-Nya II, and hundreds of Nuer civilians armed by the steady flow of weapons from Khartoum known as the *jiech mabor* (White Army). They swept southward through Kongor to Bor, slaughtering thousands of Dinka, including women, children, and the elderly. No Dinka was spared. Many were mutilated in a spate of atrocities, and Bor was methodically destroyed, its citizens massacred. When reports of what became known in southern folklore as the "Bor Massacre" reached Garang, he mobilized a large SPLA force from Torit, recaptured Bor, and dispersed the Nuer rabble to Ayod with heavy losses. Surrounded by a small circle proclaiming him the "Moses of south Sudan" and "Liberator" of the Nuer, Riek grandly created an Interim National Executive Committee (INEC) and an Interim National Liberation Committee (INLC), with himself as chairman of the INEC and Lam Akol as secretary for external relations, but neither the INEC nor the INLC remained much more than another of the pretentious abbreviations that have characterized political life in southern Sudan.

Instead of winning over wavering SPLA commanders, the indiscriminate slaughter of thousands of Dinka civilians precipitated outrage among the southern Sudanese and anger in the international community, and solidified Garang's control of the movement. The SPLA-Nasir pledges to respect human rights became a fiction and the promise of independence for the South a mere charade in an ill-disguised attempt to conceal the alliance with Khartoum in return for weapons, supplies, and large amounts of money. Lam Akol met with Bashir's representative, Al-Hajj Muhammad, in Nairobi and in Frankfurt, Germany, in January 1992 where they signed a joint statement granting the South "special political and constitutional status" that significantly made no mention of self-determination or independence. Riek appears to have seriously believed that accepting government support was but a tactical maneuver to defend him from the SPLA who had rallied to John Garang. Bashir and the NIF were not content simply to exploit the split by arming and financing SPLA-Nasir but seized this golden opportunity to launch an offensive in February 1992 in which the army was given free passage through SPLA-Nasir territory to recapture Pocahalla, Pibor, Bor, Kapoeta, and the strategic SPLA town of Torit, which forced Garang to transfer SPLA military headquarters to Chukundum in the deep forests of the Didinga Hills.

In an attempt to deflect the government's offensive Garang ordered a full-scale attack on Juba in June and July 1992 during which the SPLA was repulsed with heavy losses and the summary execution of southerner soldiers and civilians in the city. Moreover, during the chaos following the failure to take Juba, William Nyuon Bany and other Equatorian commanders defected to SPLA-Nasir, while Kerubino Kuanyin Bol and Arok Thon Arok escaped from harsh SPLA imprisonment to offer their services to SPLA-Nasir. On 26 March 1993 the leaders of all those opposed to the SPLM/A met at Kongor to transform SPLA-Nasir into SPLM/A-United and coordinate their military operations against the SPLA. Heavy fighting continued throughout 1993 between the SPLA, now sometimes referred to as "SPLA Mainstream," and SPLA-United around Kongor, Ayod, and Waat. In June the SPAF began its offensive in the Yei–Juba–Nimule triangle but were only able to reoccupy Morobo, while a heavily armed column from Wau failed to capture Rumbek despite continuous aerial bombardment.

The army had greater success in the Nuba Mountains. On 25 August 1993 the last town held by the SPLA, Um Durain, fell, and in October Bashir boasted that the SPAF would complete the conquest of the Nuba during the next dry season.

Over the winter months of 1994–95 the SPLM/A was able to recover from its serious losses in 1992 and successfully continued the conflict with SPLA-United through greater unity in the beleaguered movement, the unraveling of SPLA-United, and support from the international community. The Dinka commanders closed ranks to remain loyal to Garang, and SPLA-Nasir and later SPLA-United simply could not reconcile its demands for southern independence with its support for and its dependence on an NIF Islamist regime in Khartoum determined to prevent independence. This irreconcilable paradox destroyed the credibility of its leaders and in the end dismantled the movement. The international community, which hitherto had remained aloof from the civil war, now began active mediations. In May 1992 President Ibrahim Babangida, president of Nigeria and the new head of the OAU, convened a peace conference at Abuja, but the rival SPLA factions agreed on little else but self-determination, which the Sudan government summarily rejected. In May 1993 during a second round of talks the government failed to reach any substantive agreement with either faction. The failure of Abuja II resolved the heads of state from Ethiopia, Eritrea, Uganda, and Kenya in their capacities as members of the Intergovernmental Authority on Drought and Development (IGADD, subsequently IGAD) to replace the Nigerians as mediators, to which Bashir, Garang, and Riek responded positively in September. Under pressure from the US Congress, which had begun to take a special interest in Sudan's civil war, John Garang and Riek Machar met in Washington DC on 21–22 October 1993. This resulted in an innocuous joint "Washington Declaration" designed more to placate Congress than to be a serious effort at reconciliation.

Despite vehement objections by the Sudan government and even the Sudanese DUP leader-in-exile, the IGAD brought together the rival factions between 4 and 6 January and again in Nairobi between 17 and 22 May 1994, when they accepted an Ethiopian draft of a "Declaration of Principles" (DoP) in which the IGAD governments, the SPLA, and SPLA-United agreed to endorse self-determination and a democratic secular Sudan for the southern Sudanese. These principles were discussed at length in Nairobi between 18 and 19 July in the third round of IGAD peace talks but were again rejected by the government. Undeterred, the IGAD convened a fourth and subsequently final round of talks on 19 September 1994 at which the government again peremptorily rejected self-determination and a secular state, but the DoP was not forgotten and formed the basis of future negotiations fully supported by the West as "Friends of the IGAD."

Throughout 1993–94 SPLA-United commanders William Nyon Bany and Kerubino Kuanyin Bol, having been rearmed and supported by the SPAF and its militias, destabilized and wreaked havoc among the SPLA strongholds in eastern Equatoria and the Bahr al-Ghazal. At the same time SPLA-United was achieving military success, however, the split in the SPLA along ethnic lines – SPLA-Nasir Nuer against SPLA Dinka – ironically also created deep divisions within the Nuer nation that ultimately brought about the disintegration of SPLA-United. The failure of the 1991 harvest had precipitated raiding between the Gaawar and Luo Nuer in 1992, exacerbating inter-Nuer grievances that Riek should have resolved but simply ignored. Moreover, he had favored the Jikany Nuer, upon whom he was directly dependent, in disputes with their historic rivals, the Luo, over scarce pastures. Luo commanders sought and received arms from the government in Malakal, precipitating open warfare between Jikany and Luo and culminating in the destruction of Ulang and Nasir, with heavy civilian casualties. There followed an abortive Luo–Jikany peace conference from 6 to 15 September 1994. In an attempt to repair the damage, SPLA-United held its first National Convention at Akobo from 26 September to 16 October 1994 at which the movement was renamed the South Sudan Independence Movement/Army (SSIM/A), firmly committed to the independence of southern Sudan. Having dismissed those commanders who had collaborated with the government – Nyuon, Kerubino, and Lam Akol – Riek became the undisputed leader of the SSIM/A.

After Riek had summarily dismissed Lam from SPLA-United in February 1993, he retired to the government station at Kodok on the White Nile on 7 September 1994 where he announced that henceforth he had assumed the leadership of the rump SPLA-United. By the end of 1995 virtually all southern leaders had distanced themselves from Riek. The Nuer commanders in Equatoria were disgusted at his failed leadership. Some went home; others defected to the SPLA, as did Nyuon Bany. Arok Thon Arok accused Riek of "dictatorial behavior." More a freebooter than a guerilla warrior, Riek, in desperation, traveled to Addis Ababa in a futile gesture to join the Sudanese opposition, the National Democratic Alliance (NDA), in which Garang was a dominant partner. His appeals fell on deaf ears, and the Ethiopian government summarily ordered him to leave the country. Crossing the border at Jokau he made his way to his home near Ler, where he continued to lead his dwindling core of loyal followers and signed a cease-fire with

Sudan's First Vice-President, Major-General al-Zubayr Muhammad Salih, as a prelude to visiting Khartoum accompanied by Kerubino. There they surrendered by signing a Peace Charter with President Bashir on 4 April 1996.

By signing the Charter Riek had virtually agreed to abandon his previous insistence upon independence for the South and become a supporter for the unity of Sudan in a federal system of twenty-six states designed by the NIF in which *shari'a* was the source of all legislation. The concluding articles of the Peace Charter promised that there would be a referendum for the southerners "to determine their political aspirations" at some future time, but this was neither a promise nor a guarantee. Riek disingenuously interpreted this ambiguous clause to mean that the South would one day be given its independence, but no other southerners believed this fantasy except his loyal Nuer. Now in alliance with the government, the Riek rump SSIM/A continued to fight the SPLA, more to preserve the Nuer as a political force against the SPLA than to struggle for some opaque notion of independence to be gained from those who had no intention of delivering it. The isolation of Riek and his credibility among his loyal followers were further underlined and compromised respectively when Paulino Matip, now a major-general in the Sudan army and furious that the government had singled out Riek to lead the Nuer militia, refused to serve under him or redeploy his Bul Nuer from their well-paid task of protecting the Bentiu oil fields on behalf of the government.

While Riek Machar was becoming another failed Sudanese leader, John Garang had made a concerted effort to recover from the great "split" and criticism of his leadership to regain control of the SPLM/A he had nearly lost. In mid-February 1993 he decided, for a myriad reasons, to hold a "National Convention" (NC) of southern Sudanese. Since 1991 there had been increasing pressure on Garang for greater definition of the military chain of command, a more robust civilian administration, and more democratic dialogue within the SPLM/A at a time when the military fortunes of the SPLA were in decline after the fall of Mengistu and the defection of the Nasir group. Perhaps the most compelling reason was to demonstrate by a national gathering of southerners that the SPLA was not defeated and that, despite the fact that the NIF had launched its biggest offensive in eleven years, "the elephant was not yet dead." The NC of the Sudan People's Liberation Movement/Army convened at Chukudum in eastern Equatoria from 2 to 11 April 1994. Of the 825 southerners invited, an astonishing 516 arrived at Chukudum. The largest single group, by far, was appointed directly or indirectly by John Garang. Others represented their geographical regions, including the Nuba Mountains and the southern Blue Nile, and were largely appointed by regional SPLA military commanders; some were chiefs. Although civilians accounted for only 40 percent of the delegates, compared with 60 percent from the military commands, their presence was substantial and a sufficient number to provide legitimacy to Garang's claim that the movement was fighting on behalf of the civilians. Delegations from the Misiriyya and Rizayqat Baqqara, former enemies, were included to give the convention a "national" appearance. Given the dearth of SPLM "Chapters" abroad and the great expense of transportation, only thirteen delegates from the Diaspora arrived at Chukudum, but astonishingly only eighteen members from the General Field Staff Command Council attended out of the eighty invitations sent by the Convention Organizing Committee (COC). Perhaps they were more concerned about war than policy.

The NC convened for business on 2 April 1994, passed resolutions, elected officers, and closed on 11 April with speeches of pride and optimism. Garang laid down the purpose and agenda of the convention in his long opening address, but subsequent discussion ranged widely not only on the floor of the convention but also in a variety of committees and in critical separate meetings with John Garang. These important and intimate meetings were more than symbolic, for hitherto the SPLM/A leadership had hardly ever condescended to discuss or decide policy with large numbers of local or ordinary southerners. At the time, the NC was widely regarded as a great success that during the ensuing years has been enshrined as the founding symbol for some southerners of a "New Sudan" but that to others was a demonstration in favour of an independent southern Sudan because of the convention's overwhelming endorsement of self-determination. It represented a long-overdue political renewal of the SPLM/A through its intention to establish civilian administration in those areas of the South under its control. It confirmed to the leadership that they were indeed the legitimate representatives of the southern Sudanese people.

The optimism, renewal, and restoration of unity and morale in the movement created by the NC was soon demonstrated by the reversal in the military fortunes of the SPLA against SPLA-United, the SSIM/A, Nuer civil militias, and the Sudanese army. The collapse of Riek and his SSIM/A precipitated massive defections to the SPLA combined with increasing tension between the SPAF and units of the PDF, which now bore the burden of combat, with heavy casualties (including the brother of President Bashir), which contributed to the military recovery of the SPLA. It won a succession of victories in Equatoria in July and October 1994, the Bahr al-Ghazal in February 1995, and the Nuba Mountains in May.

In an effort to rebuild a battered army and increase the size of the security forces Bashir sought to rigorously enforce conscription throughout 1994–95 for all males between the ages of 16 and 26, using press-gangs to seize them in the streets for the PDF. Wealthy parents no longer were able to purchase deferments for their sons, who now avoided venturing outside the house in daylight to avoid forcible induction into the PDF to fight in the South. In the first four months of 1995 alone the armed forces had sustained 9,000 dead and over 15,000 wounded, most of whom were PDF conscripts. Desertions multiplied, and despite strict censorship rumors and reports of defeat and heavy losses in the swamps, forests, and elephant grass of the southern savanna swept through Khartoum and the towns of northern Sudan. At the beginning of 1996 two whole battalions of regular troops simply refused to move into the countryside from their garrisons, and even visits by Hasan al-Turabi and 'Ali 'Uthman Muhammad Taha failed to raise their morale. Bashir purged another 162 officers from the SPAF as retribution for defeat.

In October 1995 the SPLA recaptured Parajok and Owiny-ki-Bul, Joseph Lagu's old headquarters near Uganda, and successive victories followed swiftly. In November the SPLA retook Obbo, Panyikwara, Ame, Moli, Pageri, Loa, and Kit. The Mundari militia, which had long been hostile to the SPLA, now committed themselves to the movement, and the Hawazama Baqqara from Kadugli in the Nuba Mountains made peace with Yusuf Kuwa and his resurgent SPLA in the *jabals*. A futile government counter-offensive along the Kit river collapsed in mid-December. By the New Year 1996 the SPLA offensive appeared unstoppable. Aswa was recaptured on 8 January 1996, followed by Khor Yabus and Chali in southern Blue Nile and Pochalla in March, and the surrender of a whole Sudanese battalion at Yirol southeast of Rumbek. The reconstitution of the SPLM/A, now supported by a string of military victories in 1996, was accompanied by less dramatic, more subtle, but equally crucial changes in the NIF, the Islamists, and the Bashir government.

THE NDA, PAIC THREE, AND A FAILED ASSASSINATION

Within months of the coup d'état of 30 June 1989 an impotent opposition had coalesced into the National Democratic Alliance (NDA), a loose and omnibus political alliance committed to the overthrow of the Islamist regime of the NIF and composed of the prorogued thirteen political parties and some fifty-six trade unions, armed factions, and prominent Sudanese individuals. It ultimately established its headquarters at the former embassy of Sudan in Asmara, Eritrea. The NDA was formally founded on 21 October 1989 by Mubarak al-Fadl al-Mahdi, and on 31 October Mubarak signed a provisional charter of cooperation with the SPLA, a gratuitous gesture by John Garang symbolized by granting the NDA airtime on Radio SPLA. Undeterred, Mubarak al-Mahdi continued to pursue his tortuous negotiations with the SPLM/A, which culminated in March 1990 when a more substantive formal charter was signed in Cairo between the SPLM/A and the opposition political parties, trade unions, and professional organizations. Neither side, however, demonstrated any urgency to form a common program to topple the government, for in the past many of its members had been bitter rivals carrying their own political baggage into exile. They were divided on self-determination for the southerners and remained studiously silent over the inevitable but intransigent issue of *shari'a*. Although Garang and the SPLM/A were warmly welcomed into the NDA, the southerners remained deeply suspicious, cynically regarding the sudden embrace by northern parties after nearly fifty years of hostility as only motivated by the fact that the SPLA was the sole armed force that could topple the government on behalf of its northern partners in the NDA. Although presumably welded together by its omnibus charter, the NDA remained little more than an umbrella under which disgruntled politicians, trade unionists, insurgents, and Sudanese exiles gathered to condemn the regime and plot its demise, but do nothing to achieve it.

In 1991 the NDA was suddenly stunned by the split within the SPLM/A. Hitherto, its northern members had been satisfied with Garang's sincere pronouncements that a united Sudan was the only solution, to discover that he was now seriously challenged by secessionists from SPLA-Nasir and SPLA-United demanding independence. These initial concerns became more troublesome when the NDA could no longer equivocate on the question of *shari'a* as the source of legislation for a united Sudan despite the reluctance of the influential Umma and DUP members to commit themselves. By 1994 Hasan al-Turabi and the NIF had become the dominant partner in the diarchy government of 'Umar Hasan al-Bashir, for even his efforts to co-opt the Umma and DUP had been skillfully derailed by Turabi, who did not want the return of these powerful sectarian parties to challenge the singular authority of the NIF. Isolated, impotent, and without strong leadership, the members of the NDA uneasily had to accept the powerful arguments by Garang that self-determination was completely compatible with the NDA's commitment to democracy and human rights as endorsed by the members of the IGAD and the international community.

Although Muhammad 'Uthman al-Mirghani, leader of the DUP, had denounced self-determination and the secular state in May 1994, Sadiq and the Umma Party gradually accepted, in principle, self-determination for the South as the only viable alternative to outright secession, and in December 1994 signed an agreement with the SPLM/A at Chukudum accepting most of the IGAD DoP. Although Sadiq and the Umma Party at Chukudum were committed to self-determination for the South, it was not until a summit meeting chaired by John Garang was held at NDA headquarters in Asmara on 17 June 1995 that the SPLM, DUP, Umma, USAP, SCP, trade unions, the Lundin Mining Corporation (LMC), Sudanese Allied Forces (SAF), and the Beja Congress signed the "Declaration of Political Agreement" to continue the war until the NIF government was overthrown. The "Asmara Accords" provided for an interim government after the overthrow of the NIF regime, self-determination as a "basic, original, and democratic right of all peoples," and referendums for Abyei, the Nuba Mountains, and southern Blue Nile to decide whether or not to join the South. The declaration, however, remained vague about religion, simply affirming the "non-use of religion in politics" and remaining silent about the "secular" state. Ironically, the Chukudum agreement and the Asmara Accords were almost identical to the SPLM/A proposals at the Abuja meetings in 1992 and 1993 that the northern members in the NDA had scorned. The evolution within the NDA leading to the Asmara Accords was largely the work of its host government, Eritrea. The Eritreans had been adamant in rewording the Ethiopian draft of the DoP so that the language guaranteeing self-determination for the South and a secular state for the North was unequivocal, for they had broken diplomatic relations with Khartoum because of the NIF government's efforts to meddle in Eritrean internal affairs. Two months before Sadiq had accepted self-determination at Chukudum, Hasan al-Turabi opened and chaired the second Conference on Inter-Religious Dialogue in Khartoum in October 1994.

The purpose of this conference, like the first in April 1993, was "to define common ground between Islam and Christianity." Ignoring the devastating civil war in southern Sudan, which had killed 2 million non-Muslims, Turabi in his opening address exhorted the delegates to introduce a dialogue (*hiwar*) to close "the gap" between Western and Arab-Islamic civilizations. He received loud and long applause. After this personal triumph, he successfully called for the Third Popular Arab and Islamic Congress in Khartoum between 30 March and 2 April 1995, which was enthusiastically attended by 300 delegates from 80 countries, including the most active Islamists in the world. Four of the most influential and effective terrorist organizations – Hizbullah, Hamas, Islamic Jihad, and al-Qaʾida – were well represented, as were the Algerian FIS and its more extremist rival, the Algerian Armed Islamic Group (GIA), in addition to the radical Egyptian Islamic Jihad and its rival, the Egyptian Islamic Group, *jamaʿat al-islamiyya*, of the imprisoned Shaykh ʿUmar ʿAbd al-Rahman. Also present was Abu Sayyaf from the Philippines, and the lesser-known Gathering of Followers, *usbat al-ansar*, from Lebanon.

Unlike the previous two congresses the third PAIC General Assembly was fully covered by the international media, both East and West. Despite Turabi's charm, reason, and opening address to an enthusiastic audience, the third PAIC General Assembly soon degenerated into what Turabi feared – a divisive and dysfunctional debating society. On the second day Shaykh Muhammad Bashir Osmani from Benin demanded the word "Arab" be excised from the title of the Popular Arab and Islamic Congress, because it was discriminatory and racist. His motion was enthusiastically supported by the Muslim delegates from Eritrea, Kenya, Nigeria, Senegal, and South Africa, and even by the Afro-American organization of Louis Farrakan. The Palestinians, among whose factions Turabi had been a successful mediator, were furious, as were other North Africans, who objected to the change at a time when the Islamic world was confronted by a serious challenge from the West. The debate was raucous and uncontrolled. Several Arab delegations indignantly stormed out of the proceedings, and when Turabi sought to regain control with a promise to consider a name change in the future, the alienation of the non-Arab African Muslims was complete.

Despite these set-backs and divisive debates the General Assembly finally approved that "Islamists" throughout the world would begin in the summer of 1995 to destabilize moderate Arab regimes and train "larger and more professional terrorist cadres . . . in Pakistan, Sudan, and Iran pending deployment to Egypt and the inevitable escalation of the Islamist armed struggle."[3] Although he had crushed the Islamist opposition in Syria, Hafez Assad was thoroughly alarmed by the presence of Syrian Islamists at the PAIC General Assembly and began to improve relations between Damascus and Tehran in order to contain the Islamists in Syria and Khartoum. The Egyptian government, not surprisingly, was much more concerned than Assad, for delegations from the Egyptian Muslim Brothers and Labor Party were in attendance when Turabi brokered a truce between Egypt's radical Islamic Jihad and the Islamic Group, *jamaʿat al-islamiyya* – the first time since 1983 that the two banned Egyptian revolutionary movements had agreed to work together. As the delegates departed to prepare for the Islamist *jihad*, Khalid Duran, a Moroccan Muslim intellectual, reflected on the work of the PAIC General Assembly and the role of Hasan al-Turabi in the Islamist movement:

[Turabi] tells the western media what they want to hear, but in practice he implements a program for society that is one of the most obscurantist and one of the cruelest in regard to human rights . . . What, indeed, have the Islamists brought to Iran, Sudan, Afghanistan, Kashmir, Palestine, and Algeria if not hate?[4]

Husni Mubarak had been closely following the activities and travels of Hasan al-Turabi, his PAIC General Assemblies, and the endless stream of verbal support for the Islamists. In March 1992 he had used the querulous dispute between Egypt and Sudan over the contested sovereignty of the Halayib Triangle on the Red Sea coast to single out Turabi as the principal troublemaker. During his state visit to Washington in April 1993 Mubarak had angrily denounced Islamists from Sudan, the Maghrib, and the Middle East, and particularly Hasan al-Turabi, as a danger to Egypt. Thereafter, Mubarak unleashed his security and intelligence services, the *mukhabarat al-harbiya*, to crush the Islamists in Egypt. In January 1995 he began yet another crackdown on the Muslim Brotherhood and Egyptian relief agencies operating in Bosnia, Somalia, and the Yemen. Mubarak's onslaught in 1994–95 against the Islamists coincided with meetings in Khartoum between Turabi and Egyptian Islamists, the Peshawar commanders of *jama'at al-islamiyya*, and Dr. Ayman al-Zawahiri of Egyptian Islamic Jihad in March 1995 to plot the assassination of Mubarak. Later, after the PAIC General Assembly had adjourned, he met again with Zawahiri in Geneva, where he must surely have learned the details of the plot but appears to have made no effort to dissuade the conspirators.

In June 1995 President Mubarak arrived in Addis Ababa to attend the annual meeting of the OAU. Fortunately, the *mukhabarat* had taken the precaution of sending ahead his armored limousine, for on 26 June 1995 assassins from *jama'at al-islamiyya* opened fire on the vehicle. Two were killed in the fierce exchange of gunfire with Mubarak's bodyguards; three others escaped. Five days later Ethiopian security agents found them hiding in Addis Ababa and killed one, but another three escaped, including one of the gunmen. The Ethiopian government soon confirmed that the NIF government in Khartoum had supplied the assassins with Sudanese and Yemeni passports and weapons delivered by Sudan Airways. Radio Cairo immediately denounced Khartoum and specifically Hasan al-Turabi for "masterminding" the conspiracy. On that same evening of 26 June 1995 Turabi issued a bland statement over Radio Omdurman denying any connection with the attempted assassination and expressing his regrets.

He subsequently did little to conciliate Mubarak's fury, however, calling the assassins "messengers of the Islamic faith," and declaring that "Egypt is today experiencing a drought in faith and religion, but Allah wants to be revived from Sudan and flow along with the waters of the Nile to purge Egypt from obscenity."[5] He lectured foreign journalists at his home in Omdurman denying Sudan had anything to do with *jama'at al-islamiyya*, which had claimed responsibility for the attack on Mubarak, but he "saluted" the *mujahidiin* who had hunted down the "Egyptian Pharaoh" in Addis Ababa.

When an angry Mubarak learned that the safe-house used by the killers in Addis Ababa had been rented by a Sudanese, Muhammad Siraj, a special agent for NIF intelligence chief Nafi 'Ali Nafi, Radio Cairo unleashed a stream of vitriolic accusations against the NIF and the "pygmy despot," President Bashir. Massive organized demonstrations denouncing Sudan as a "fountain of terrorism" and a "hub of murderers and assassins" were organized and swept through the streets of Cairo. Despite threats to invade Sudan and strike at Sudanese terrorist training camps, influential Egyptians urged moderation, and after a bellicose confrontation over the Halayib Triangle, the fury and hostility began to subside, but it was not forgotten. In fact, the attempted assassination of President Mubarak proved to be a turning-point for the growing concern in the West about Islamist terrorism, an awakening among the Arab states of the internal threat posed by Islamist terrorism, and a change of direction within the government of President 'Umar Hasan al-Bashir.

Although the assassins had failed to kill Mubarak, they inadvertently killed the PAIC, initiated the subsequent decline of Turabi's influence in the Muslim world and Sudan, and inaugurated a movement within the NIF itself to end the isolation of Sudan as a pariah state. There now appeared a visible rift along that obscure fault line between NIF moderates and hard-liners who hitherto had presented an opaque façade of impenetrable unity. Quietly, and completely ignored by the Sudanese and international media, the Sudan government on 6 August 1995 abandoned its policy of permitting any Arab or Muslim to enter Sudan without a visa, which essentially staunched the flow of *mujahidiin* seeking a safe haven and further terrorist training in Sudan. There emerged within the NIF government a growing concern that Khartoum was surrounded by weak friends and determined enemies who formed a "circle of animosity" from Libya in the West to Eritrea and Ethiopia in the East.

More and more African leaders publicly denounced the NIF government of 'Umar Hasan al-Bashir and Hasan al-Turabi as racist, bigoted, and totalitarian. Egypt, Eritrea, Ethiopia, Kenya, and Uganda were all hostile. On the Congo–Nile watershed, the southwest frontier of Sudan, eastern Zaire had plunged into anarchy; the Central African Republic and Chad were impoverished and unstable. By the New Year 1996 Sudan had become encircled by hostile states. In the past Sudanese governments could count on allies in the Gulf and the West to overcome internal political problems and international tensions on its borders. Internally, the NIF now had to confront a reconstituted and revived SPLM/A and a strong vote of confidence in the leadership of John Garang, who in October 1995 had launched an SPLA offensive that swept to a series of victories in the winter of 1995–96. At the same time the Beja Congress, armed by the Eritreans, began their devastating raids throughout eastern Sudan, and Ethiopian President Meles Zenawi had become implacably hostile to the Khartoum regime, not only for its part in the attempted assassination of Mubarak, but also for its continuing support for the insurgent Somali Islamic Union Party, *al-Ittihad*, in northern Somalia.

The repercussions from the failed Mubarak assassination finally culminated in December 1995 when the UN Security Council demanded Sudan extradite the three missing gunmen. Its UN representative prevaricated, answering that the UN had no evidence they were in Sudan. This callous reaction galvanized the Security Council into action, and in January 1996 it passed Resolution 1044 imposing sanctions on Sudan for refusing to cooperate in the assassination investigation. The United States accused Sudan of complicity with and providing safe haven for terrorists. When Sudan continued to refuse to cooperate, the UN imposed more harsh sanctions against Sudan in Resolution 1054 of 26 April 1996, including the reduction of the Sudanese delegation at the UN and restricting travel in the United States for its diplomats. In 1996 Sudan was isolated, a pariah within the international community. This led to the growing rift within the NIF, the reorganization of the Sudan security services, the decline of Turabi's fortunes, the end of his beloved PAIC, and the decision to offer Usama bin Ladin as a sacrificial lamb to improve Sudan's relations with the Arabs, Africans, and the West.

CHAPTER 8

The Bashir years: beleaguered and defiant, 1996–2006

THE DOWNFALL OF HASAN AL-TURABI

By 1994 Colonel Bakri Hasan Salih, one of the original leaders of the 30 June coup d'état, had forged IS-SOR and the other security forces into an effective, feared, and pervasive presence in Sudan. He himself had established an unassailable position in the regime, displaying talents that were respected and intimidating even to his superiors. The security services he supervised presented to the Sudanese an impregnable façade of invincibility which, however, was suddenly shaken by two unrelated incidents that sharply split the intelligence community between those who favored and those who opposed the extradition of terrorists, a split that soon spread to divide the NIF membership in the government as well. Those incidents were the arrival in Sudan of "Carlos the Jackal" (Ilich Ramirez Sanchez) and the failed assassination of President Mubarak.

In 1993 Carlos the Jackal arrived in Khartoum and soon proved to be an embarrassment on account of his ill-disguised Marxism, drinking, and fornication. The French had been tracking Sanchez since his terrorist bombing of the Saint-Germaine drugstore in Paris in 1974, and Bashir, the NIF, and Turabi were quite prepared to permit the French Direction Générale de la Sécurité Extérieure (DGSE) to abduct the Jackal on the night of 13 August 1994. The regime hoped to dispel its image as a safe haven for global terrorism in return for French military equipment, training for the Sudanese police, financial assistance for Sudan Airways, and a desalinization plant for Port Sudan. On 16 August 1994 Charles Pasqua, French minister of the interior, announced after a meeting with Turabi that the Khartoum regime had broken with terrorism. Few believed him, but the "sale" of Carlos, ostensibly a trivial incident soon forgotten, exacerbated growing dissension within the hitherto unified ranks of the NIF. 'Ali 'Uthman Taha had vigorously denounced the kidnapping of the Jackal and began to distance himself from Turabi, preferring Bashir and his military colleagues in the

RCC. Although 'Ali 'Uthman Taha, at a meeting of the Arab League foreign ministers in September 1995, earnestly denied rumors of a widening rift between Bashir and Turabi, after the Mubarak affair (see below) Bashir and some of his military colleagues in the RCC began to discuss, evaluate, and question the cost to Khartoum of continuing to do business with bin Ladin and his al-Qa'ida colleagues.

The growing rift between the security services, NIF Islamists, and Bashir and the military had been further exacerbated by massive demonstrations against the regime in September 1994, when Khartoum University students led some 15,000 protestors through the streets of the capital over high prices and shortages of basic foodstuffs. IS-SOR had failed to anticipate or warn Bashir of the impending riots, which required assistance from NIF militia and Afghan-Arab Islamists to drive the students from the streets and suppress determined protestors, twenty of whom were killed as the violence spread from the capital to El Obeid, Wad Medani, Port Sudan, and the larger towns in northern Sudan. The NIF demanded a sweeping reorganization of the security services. This was confirmed in the General Security Act of January 1995 that delegated even greater powers to the security forces, now dominated by civilian members of the NIF. When the reorganization, however, did not end two days of demonstrations in Omdurman that April protesting severe shortages of electricity and water, the worst in memory, and Khartoum University students once again led huge anti-government demonstrators against high prices and food shortages, Bashir and the RCC once again reshuffled the heads of the intelligence and security apparatus to return the control held by NIF civilians to the military. Although the NIF dismissed the change in security agencies as a "cosmetic exercise," it was most certainly not an ornamental reorganization.

By 1996 the connivance of Sudan in the failed assassination of Husni Mubarak, the gatherings of Islamists and known terrorists at the PAIC General Assemblies, and the government's moral, financial, and material support for *mujahidiin* fighting in Bosnia, Albania, Somalia, and Chechnya had finally isolated Khartoum from nearly all Arab and African governments and many in the Western international community. Since 1994 the reports of the UN Human Rights Commission special rapporteur for Sudan, Gaspar Biró, had provided incontrovertible evidence that the NIF regime was guilty of summary executions, arbitrary detention, torture, and the forced displacement of large civilian populations in the Nuba Mountains and the South. Two years later, in February 1996, the Commission condemned Sudan in one of the strongest resolutions of censure ever passed at the UN which now included extra-judicial killings, slavery, and incarceration of political prisoners without cause. A host of international NGOs supplied their own reports of massive human-rights violations, all of which contributed to the image of Sudan as a pariah that should be quarantined by the global community of nations.

Isolated from without and fiercely unpopular within, Bashir's inner circle, comprised mostly of the military heads of security, had become convinced by 1996 that Usama bin Ladin and al-Qa'ida were an unnecessary liability, particularly after the failed attempt on Mubarak, when rumors began circulating in Khartoum that al-Qa'ida was planning to assassinate Sadiq al-Mahdi, which antagonized his large following of Ansar and Umma, who represented the most serious threat to the survival of an unpopular NIF government. Bashir first offered to extradite bin Ladin to Saudi Arabia, but when the Saudis refused for fear of domestic repercussions, he requested them to act as intermediaries to facilitate bin Ladin's delivery to the United States. Bashir's confidant, Al-Fathi 'Urwah, met with representatives of the Central Intelligence Agency (CIA) in Rosslyn, Virginia, across the Potomac river from Washington in February 1996, and offered to have Sudan security seize bin Ladin and extradite him to Jidda, where the Saudis would turn him over to the American authorities. By 1996 officials in the State Department deeply distrusted the RCC and NIF, and had little confidence they would uphold their end of the bargain, forgetting that the French displayed no such squeamishness over snatching Carlos the Jackal. Not wishing to become involved in an extra-judicial kidnapping, US officials from the National Security Council rejected the offer at the same time, ironically, that Ambassador Tim Carney was preparing, much against his will, to close the American embassy, for its diplomatic staff could no longer be protected from the *mujahidiin jihadists* in the terrorist training camps surrounding Khartoum.

While Bashir pursued one course of action to be rid of Usama bin Ladin, Turabi decided on another. To forestall a scandal that could damage his image, his political career, the PAIC, and his position as secretary-general of the NIF, Turabi contacted the Sudanese ambassador to Afghanistan, Atiya Badawi, a former Afghan-Arab who spoke Pustu, and urged him to facilitate bin Ladin's return. Yunis Khalis, a former *mujahidiin* commander operating out of Jalalabad, Afghanistan, agreed to provide a safe haven for bin Ladin and al-Qa'ida. On 18 May 1996 Usama bin Ladin quietly disappeared from Khartoum on a chartered plane bound for Peshawar and Jalalabad with his family, a few friends, and twenty al-Qa'ida bodyguards. Fleeting as his departure may have been, Usama bin Ladin had previously terminated all his business in Sudan, bitterly complaining that he had

Figure 21 President 'Umar al-Bashir (left) raises hands with his parliament speaker, Hasan al-Turabi (right), during a military parade in Khartoum.

lost over $160 million and describing the NIF government as a mixture of religion and organized crime. Through the mediation of Dr. Ayam al-Zawahiri, he relocated the headquarters of al-Qa'ida to Kandahar, but within days of the al-Qa'ida bombing of the Khobar Towers in Dhahran, in which nineteen US servicemen were killed and 250 others wounded, bin Ladin disappeared from Jalalabad to join the Taliban.

In an effort to improve the domestic authoritarian image of the government, President Bashir in 1995 had approved the Thirteenth Constitutional Decree of the RCC, known as "Decree 13," designed to replace the Transitional National Assembly (TNA) with one popularly elected. From its inception the RCC and NIF had given pious pronouncements about hold-ing elections after the proper *shura* conferences had been established at the local level. By 1995 over 16,000 local conferences had been convened to hold elections for provincial councils that, in turn, elected delegates for a national conference in Khartoum. After extended deliberations the TNA approved the "Charter of the Sudanese People" which authorized direct elections and defined the functions of the president and those of a national assembly. The president would be elected for five years by a majority vote, the TNA to be replaced by an elected 400-member National Assembly (*majlis watani*) frequently but erroneously called a parliament or *shura* as envisaged by Hasan al-Turabi.

Of the 400 seats in the National Assembly 125 were appointed in January 1996 and another 50 seats were reserved for loyal members and support-ers of the NIF; the remaining 225 seats of the National Assembly were to be chosen by the voters. Frustrated by having had no elections since the demise of the Sadiq government, over 1,000 candidates enthusiastically campaigned for those remaining 225 seats in elections held from 6 to 17 March 1996. Many candidates were "favored" by "popular committees" of NIF supporters in each voting district to ensure that the council would be securely dominated by the NIF. Indeed, electoral registers frequently went missing, and thousands complained they were unable to vote, especially where non-NIF members were running for office. Many NIF stalwarts and forty-seven other elected candidates ran unopposed, which also ensured an NIF majority. During the election Turabi continuously denied any interest in political office, but that did not prevent him from standing for elec-tion in the al-Sahafa District of south Khartoum, where he had suffered an embarrassing defeat in the elections of 1986. He was opposed by two Islamists who had impeccable credentials but who mysteriously withdrew, and Turabi returned triumphant to public life, overwhelmingly elected speaker of the National Assembly.

'Umar Hasan Ahmad al-Bashir was elected president with over 75 percent of the vote and securely controlled the military and his cabinet. Opening up the electoral process had changed little. It was Islamist politics as usual, with a government completely dominated by the NIF, and the most con-summate Islamist of the day, Hasan al-Turabi, now speaker of the National Assembly, was the acknowledged leader of an elite cadre of young men who had secured the most important positions in the civil service, military, and the government and who were divorced from and did not represent the rest of Sudanese society. Sadiq al-Mahdi described the elections as a farce and the new parliament absurd. Mustapha Mansur, the "General Guide" of the Muslim Brotherhood, dismissed it as an appointed body, not the *majlis al-shura*, the ideal Islamic model of Turabi, for it had been achieved through and remained dependent upon the military. Turabi's energies were now absorbed by his new position as speaker of the National Assembly, where he immersed himself in parliamentary politics, which subtly began to change his image from an Islamist theologian to a stolid parliamentarian. In August 1997 Usama bin Ladin appears to have returned briefly to Khartoum, where he met with Turabi, but there was no longer money or enthusiasm to reconstitute the PAIC General Assembly. Turabi carried on his long-standing feud with President Mubarak of Egypt, who emphatically declared he would have nothing to do with the Sudan government. Sudan was conspicuously absent at the meeting of fifteen interior ministers from Arab countries that adopted a strong resolution prohibiting terrorists from planning, organizing, or carrying out acts of terrorism from their countries through greater coordination among Arab security agencies.

The creation of a National Assembly hardly representative of Sudan, self-inflicted isolation from the Arab and international community, and the relentless decline of the economy did not inspire any confidence in Bashir and Turabi among the Sudanese. The lethargy of the Islamist state was only enlivened by the spectacular escape of Sadiq al-Mahdi from Khartoum while Hasan al-Turabi was attending a wedding ceremony in Sadiq's own garden, which enabled him to slip away from the large gathering unnoticed. In 1996 he was warmly welcomed in Asmara by the leaders of the NDA and SPLM/A, but particularly by members of his own Umma Party. In January he was in Cairo to meet with his historic political and sectarian rival, Muhammad 'Uthman al-Mirghani, the titular head of the NDA, and together they met with President Mubarak and the Egyptian Foreign Minister, Amr Musa, to discuss their opposition to the NIF government in Khartoum. Hasan al-Turabi, however, remained unimpressed by his brother-in-law's escape, and cynics in Khartoum believed that Bashir and Turabi had purposely let Sadiq slip away to Asmara knowing he would only create disarray within the NDA opposition, which is what Sadiq ultimately managed to accomplish.

NIF domination of the government became ever more visible in the early months of 1998 after an Antonov-26 military aircraft attempting to land at Nasir in turbulent weather overran the runway and plunged into the Sobat river on 12 February 1998, killing twenty-six passengers, among whom was First Vice-President, Major-General Zubayr Muhammad Salih. The other twenty-five were senior government officials, including the old southern warrior, Arok Thon Arok. Having lost Zubayr and so many NIF ministers,

Figure 22 President 'Umar al-Bashir declaring a state of emergency after dismissing Hasan
al-Turabi as speaker and dissolving the National Assembly.

Bashir announced on 8 March 1998 the replacement of some fifteen new
ministers and four presidential advisers. 'Ali 'Uthman Taha, president of the
NIF, was appointed first vice-president and, of the twenty-four ministers,
sixteen were NIF stalwarts, leaving only two former Umma members and
the usual three token southerners among whom, nonetheless, was Lam
Akol, head of the rump SPLA-United and now minister for transport.
This reconfiguration of the cabinet, however, was only the prelude to the
passage by the National Assembly three weeks later, on 28 March 1998, of
a draft constitution in which *shari'a* became the sole source of legislation
and which significantly increased the powers of the presidency, specifically
President Bashir. Six weeks later, on 8 May 1998, the Sudanese went to
the polls to vote for or against the draft constitution in a referendum that
passed it by an overwhelming 96 percent, and it was signed into law on 30
June 1998, the ninth anniversary of the 1989 coup. The new constitution
symbolized the legal completion of the revolution and presumably settled
once and for all the constitutional questions over *shari'a* that had plagued
every government since independence.

Encouraged by the considerable powers given him in the May 1998 referendum and the resolution of the intractable constitutional question, Bashir
now sought to continue his ambivalent campaign to improve Sudan's image

by widening democracy without sacrificing his authority or power. On 8 December 1998 he signed into law the Political Association Act that supposedly restored Sudan to multi-party politics, banned since July 1989. A political party (*hizb*) was now permitted to organize under the guise of a political alliance (*tawali al-sayast*), which appears to have been the inspiration of Turabi when in November 1998 he had urged many former Sudanese parties to become involved in the political process. The Umma Party of Sadiq al-Mahdi and the DUP of the Mirghani family were now able to emerge after a decade of hibernation. Sadiq, however, had exacerbated old wounds within the Ansar, and Wali al-Din al-Hadi al-Mahdi sought to challenge his political and religious authority by establishing a breakaway Islamic Umma Party. Other *tawali* immediately appeared in Sudanese politics, including the communists, the Sudanese Central Movement, the Muslim Brotherhood, the Socialist Popular Party, the Islamic Movement, and the Sudanese National Party, numerous petty parties of little significance, and a plethora of southern "alliance" parties. There was even a Sudan Green Party committed to environmental issues, and the old Sudanese tradition of generous treatment for fallen rulers was revived when Ja'afar Numayri was permitted to return to contest the presidency after fourteen years in exile. He was warmly welcomed by his old comrades, but his People's Toiling Forces Party was never taken seriously.

Determined to seize political control in this proliferation of parties, Turabi sought to reorganize the NIF into the National Congress Party (NCP) by consolidating his authority over the Sudanese National Council, a national consultative body of some 600 members, most of whom were loyal to him. He proposed to do this by obtaining the presidency of its executive committee, the *shura* general commission, composed of sixty members. Once that was achieved, he would then have the power to reorganize the NCP, including its Leadership Office of 30 members and its Leadership Council of 110 members, at that time firmly under the control of President Bashir, who ratified all nominations for vice-presidents, ministers, and senior officials before their names were submitted to the National Assembly for pro forma approval. Although Bashir defiantly opposed any constitutional changes that would limit his presidential authority, Turabi spent the summer and autumn of 1999 touring the country, lobbying old allies, and ensuring the personal loyalty of individual members from the NIF. Bashir's political base was limited to the military; Turabi proposed to abolish both the Leadership Office and the Leadership Council of the NCP, whose powers would be assumed by the speaker of the National Assembly. This set the stage for a major confrontation with Bashir.

Under Turabi's skillful management the general assembly of the NCP duly confirmed him as party leader and then, at his bidding and by a near-unanimous vote, dissolved the Leadership Office and Leadership Council. They were replaced with a single sixty-member Leadership Authority loyal to Turabi with power to approve the nominations for vice-presidents, ministers, and senior government officials before they were submitted to the National Assembly for ratification which he, as speaker, controlled. In a clever and dexterous political coup d'état Hasan al-Turabi now had the instrument to drastically reduce the powers of President Bashir, on the one hand, and ensure his control of the civil administration on the other. Although Bashir surprisingly agreed to serve as chairman of the NCP, an honorific position of no substance, real power now resided with Turabi as secretary-general and chairman of the Leadership Authority which created a committee of seven chaired by him to draft legislation shifting the constitutional powers of the presidency to the National Assembly controlled by the NCP of which he was chairman. As a sop to Bashir, he would be the NCP candidate for president in the next elections, scheduled for 2001, to inherit an emasculated and subservient presidency.

If Turabi expected Bashir to quietly submit, he had sorely misjudged 'Umar Hasan Ahmad al-Bashir. In an address to the PDF Defenders of the Faith Brigade (*liwa humat al-watan*), he pledged his determination to continue the path of the RCC to save the Sudanese people from "disintegration and disunity." Having generously returned all assets of the Umma and DUP leaders confiscated after 30 June 1989, he sought reconciliation in November 1999 with the NDA, which deeply disturbed Turabi, who in turn offered to meet with the NDA in Mecca, a proposal that Muhammad 'Uthman al-Mirghani contemptuously dismissed as a "devious and dubious scheme."

Upon his return to Khartoum, Bashir engaged Turabi in public and provocative exchanges over the constitutional amendments to limit the powers of the presidency, culminating in a four-hour meeting that resolved nothing. Reconciliation having failed, Bashir invited more than 100 members of the Assembly to a sumptuous dinner at his home in an attempt to persuade his guests of Turabi's folly in weakening the presidency that appears to have had little success. In December 1999 Turabi proposed legislation for direct elections of the powerful governors in each of the twenty-six state governments, which would have eliminated Bashir's authority to select them. Moreover, he sought to push through a constitutional amendment that would permit a two-thirds vote to depose a president. This proved to be the last straw for 'Umar Hasan Ahmad al-Bashir. Ideologically, Bashir and the military had been less committed to the Islamist ideal, its fuzzy economic policies, and Turabi's machinations to achieve power through the legislative process at the expense of their chief and president. On 12 December 1999, two days before the National Assembly was to vote on curbing the powers of the presidency, soldiers and tanks surrounded the legislative building; Bashir peremptorily dismissed Turabi as speaker and dissolved the Assembly.

Bashir declared a state of emergency and announced new elections to the National Assembly in December 2000. Despite the boycott of the Umma Party and the DUP, elections were duly held in northern Sudan in which President Bashir received 86 percent of the vote. During his ten years as ruler of Sudan he had assiduously cultivated his popularity with the military, particularly the officer corps, for he was one of them. He never lost this base for his power, and he never forgot he was a soldier first and a politician second. The senior officers never trusted Turabi or Taha and were determined not to permit the rabble of the PDF to supersede their authority in the armed forces. Moreover, the fall of Turabi was welcomed by the leaders of Sudan's neighboring states as the end of the Islamist experiment, and Saudi Arabia, Bahrain, the United Arab Emirates, and President Husni Mubarak of Egypt strongly supported Bashir, who assured him that Turabi would not stage a comeback. In January 2000 he replaced nine ministers close to Turabi but retained several of his former protégés, including 'Ali 'Uthman Muhammad Taha, who had made the transition from determined Islamist to pragmatic Islamic politician, to remain first vice-president. Bashir circumscribed Turabi's family business interests and terminated the flow of government funds to him that had subsidized the PAIC, whose buildings were seized on 10 February.

In May 2000, when Hasan al-Turabi made his seventy-third and last public appearance on the popular Arabic *al-Jazeera* television station, he exhorted the Sudanese to take to the streets, as they had done in 1964 and 1985, to defend the Islamist revolution and free Sudan from military dictatorship. He was henceforth banned from any political activity and removed as secretary-general of the NCP, and his loyalists in the security and the civil services were quietly removed. Turabi, however, was not about to be suppressed or marginalized. On 27 June he gathered his followers, left the NCP, and founded his own Popular National Congress (PNC); his party's newspaper, *Rai al-Shaab*, continued to publish political broadsides denouncing Bashir and his government. In a bizarre and quixotic moment in February 2001 he inexplicably signed in the name of the PNC a "memorandum of understanding" with the SPLM/A, his life-long enemies, to seek a final resolution to eighteen years of civil war. Despite all his high intelligence this was a very serious mistake: for the famed Islamist to suddenly become the ally of African *kafirin* insurgents was treason. He was arrested on 21 February 2001, jailed in Kober and later placed under house arrest, and threatened with criminal charges for communicating with the enemy. Thirty of his associates were imprisoned the following day, and the PNC was proscribed.

The time had come for the military to divest themselves of the "Islamist Pope." The PAIC General Assembly, the light that had burned so brightly in 1991, had been extinguished, and the Afghan-Arabs had largely left Sudan. The monopoly on power by the NIF, Turabi's own political creation, had eventually led to a schism within its ranks and no resolution to the debilitating civil war. His mission was to define the ideology and objectives that would inspire others to physically lead the Islamist *jihad* against Muslims and non-Muslims – apostates, heretics, and unbelievers. When confronted by supporters, critics, and skeptics his words were more a rhetorical call to arms without the marching orders to achieve the Islamists' ideal. His Islamist ideology may have been inspirational, but the contradictions and ambiguities of his thought and speech obscured the path to the utopian world of peace and fellowship governed by a beneficent but demanding Islam. His leadership may have been inspirational, but when his followers required instructions on the methods to build the Islamist society he had no practical answers except pious pronouncements and his association with a network of unsavory terrorists. The more he employed his oratorical skills, the more he exposed the contradictions of his thought and message. The more he held up the revolutionary government of Sudan as the model for the Islamic renaissance, the more he became the prisoner of his own hubris. The more dependent he became on the use of terrorism to overthrow secular Islamic states and then the West, the more he fell into denial. To his supporters, Hasan al-Turabi remains the charming salesman of a dysfunctional mission, exposed on 19 February 2001 by his signature on the memorandum of understanding with the SPLM/A. It appeared to all but the faithful a desperate, if not cynical, last hurrah from a disillusioned old man seeking a place in history.

OIL: CURSE AND BOOM

On 31 May 1999 President Bashir officially opened the new tanker terminal at Marsa Bashayir, south of Port Sudan, for the 1,000-mile pipeline from the Heglig and Unity oil fields built by a consortium from China, Canada, and Malaysia at a cost of $600 million. Initially planned for a capacity of 250,000 barrels of oil per day (bopd), the pipeline enabled Sudan to record in 1999–2000 its first trade surplus and a forecast of economic growth of 6 percent after the first tanker with 600,000 barrels of Sudan crude left Marsa Bashayir on 27 August.

After Anya-Nya II insurgents in February 1984, had attacked the Chevron camp at Rub Kona, killing four employees, COPI had terminated its successful drilling operations, withdrawn from Sudan and limited its activities to seismic work in order to keep its concession until June 1992, when it decided to invest no more in Sudan and sold its production and exploration rights to a Sudanese construction company, Concorp, for the bargain-basement price of $12 million. The first foreign company to express an interest in the Concorp purchase of the Chevron concession was the State Petroleum Corporation of Canada (SPCC), a small and insignificant oil company whose chairman and chief executive officer (CEO), Lutfur Rahman Khan, had founded the SPCC in November 1991. Despite the fact that the SPCC was not a major producer of petroleum, Turabi and his NIF friends gave the company their unqualified support, which was sufficient for the Ministry of Energy and Mining and the Ministry of Finance to negotiate an agreement whereby the SPCC would generously receive 70 percent of production revenues until its initial investment was recovered. Thereafter, revenue would be evenly divided between the SPCC and the government. The company acquired thirty-four wells but, more importantly, also Chevron's impressive seismic database that would allow the SPCC to build on an existing estimated 300 million barrels of recoverable reserves.

Instead of seeking collaboration with a substantial oil producer the SPCC in November 1992 approached the unknown Arakis Energy Corporation of Canada for help in financing the Sudan project. Arakis had little "upstream" exploration and producing experience and no "downstream" marketing or refining capability. Worse, it did not have a productive oil field and thus no serious cash flow from operations, but an agreement was concluded between the SPCC and the Arakis president, the smooth-talking J. Terry Alexander, by which Arakis would acquire the SPCC concession for the Heglig, Unity, and Kaikang fields. On 29 August 1993, a year after Khan and Alexander had completed their agreement, Arakis secured a production-sharing agreement with the government, and overnight a minor and unknown oil company, Arakis Energy, owned a 12.2 million-acre concession: an astonishing opportunity for Terry Alexander. The development of the oil fields appeared the only hope to revive the Sudan economy and restore

Source: USAID

Map 11 Concessions for oil exploration and pipeline to Marsa Bashayir

confidence in the world's international financial community, and Arakis Energy appeared to be the solution.

In May 1994 Arakis agreed to construct the 1,000-mile pipeline from Heglig to Port Sudan, purchased the remaining SPCC shares, and announced that $30 million would be spent on testing and exploratory drilling, including fourteen new wells. Arakis Energy stock surged upward after Terry Alexander had entered into a contract with the Arab Group International for Investment and Acquisitions Co. Ltd. (AGI) chaired by His Highness Prince Sultan bin Saud bin 'Abdullah of Saudi Arabia, who agreed to provide $750 million, manage the exploration, drilling, and development of oil fields within the concession, and undertake the construction of a 24-inch pipeline. The partnership soon began to unravel after the Saudi Arabian embassy in Washington informed the US State Department that "Prince Sultan" was a very distant relative indeed of the royal family whose creditability and cash were questionable. On 18 September 1995 the AGI abandoned its financing agreement with Arakis; Terry Alexander resigned as chairman in January 1996, and Arakis' new CEO, John McCloud, opened direct talks with the Chinese National Oil Development Corporation (CNODC) and Petronas Carigali Overseas Sdn Bhd, a subsidiary of the National Petroleum Company of Malaysia.

China has had a long and agreeable but ambivalent relationship with the Sudanese since the first Chinese arrived with programs for assistance in the 1970s. On the one hand, the Sudanese welcomed the Chinese, who established excellent health clinics and built hospitals, textile mills, hydro-electric dams, and the great Friendship Hall in Khartoum without appearing to ask for anything in return. At one time, Hasan al-Turabi had advocated the bizarre notion that the Chinese should emigrate to Sudan, intermarry, and produce a hard-working people. On the other hand, the Chinese were a puzzlement to the gregarious and social Sudanese, for they did not mingle or socialize but kept to themselves within walled compounds, sallying forth on their daily tasks only to retire into isolation at the end of the day when the Sudanese come alive in the cool of the evening. Militarily, China was Sudan's most dependable source of arms. Politically, it was considered one of the countries upon which Sudan could rely to defend its Islamist issues in international politics. Having been isolated from the West as an ally of Iraq's Saddam Hussein, Sudan needed a friend in the UN Security Council, and China served that purpose. China, however, was quietly seeking new sources of petroleum. A joint committee for commercial and technological cooperation led by the Minister of Industry and Commerce, Dr. Taj al-Sir Mustafa, visited Beijing in August 1995 seeking Chinese cooperation in the exploration and exploitation of Sudan oil. He was followed by President Bashir in October on a state visit to China, where he was warmly received.

On 2 December 1996 with great fanfare Lutfur Khan of the SPCC announced the founding of the Greater Nile Operating Petroleum Company (GNOPC) and its new partners – the SPCC holding 25 percent, the CNPC 40 percent, Malaysian Petronas Carigali 30 percent, and the Sudan National Petroleum Corporation (Sudapet) 5 percent – to guarantee that the interests of the Sudan government continued to be respected. The CNPC, Petronas, and Sudapet agreed to construct and operate an export pipeline to send 250,000 bopd to an oil export terminal on the Red Sea coast, Marsa Bashayir. The founding of the GNOPC opened the door for smaller oil companies to participate in the bonanza. In 1997 the Qatari Gulf Petroleum Corporation began drilling in the Adar Yal fields of northern Upper Nile and the Lundin Independent Petroleum Corporation in partnership with Petronas Carigali, the Austrian OMV Exploration GmbH, and Sudapet began operations in the Adok-Ler area. In August 1998 the SPCC sold its 25 percent share in the GNOPC to the Talisman Energy Corporation, the largest independent oil and gas company in Canada, for $175 million to become a partner with the Chinese and Malaysians in the GNOPC. Dr. Jim Buckee, Talisman president, assured Khartoum that his company would invest at least $780 million in order to complete the Sudan project by 2001.

The CNPC had scored a major success in the competitive world of international petroleum, and the signing ceremony in Khartoum was broadcast live on Radio Beijing and on television in March 1997. The immediate goal was to raise Sudanese crude oil production from 10,000 to 150,000 bopd by mid-1999 and make Sudan self-sufficient in oil with petrol from the new Khartoum Oil Refinery at al-Jaili 20 miles north of the capital built by the Chinese with a capacity of 50,000 bopd, equal to Sudan's daily consumption. On 28 February 1998 the CNPC began its largest undertaking overseas when it took over the greatest percentage of the 12.2 million-acre Arakis concession. After the completion of the pipeline and terminal at Marsa Bashayir in August 1999, the oil began to flow and with it desperately needed revenue into Sudan's impoverished treasury. The Ministry of Defense began to purchase arms, France promised support in the European Union (EU), and the United Kingdom restored its embassy to full operations, but there was widespread criticism aimed at Talisman of Canada when the Sudan government forced thousands of villagers to flee from their oil fields. Unfortunately, any prospects for peace now seemed buried by the black gold, estimated to be worth $1 billion a year when in full production. The political demise of Hasan al-Turabi and the emergence of Sudan as an oil producer and OPEC observer had gone a long way to mollify former enemies in the Arabian peninsula and the Persian Gulf. Sudan, however, still bore the burden of a crushing external debt, but for the first time in a decade Sudanese exports exceeded imports.

Despite their ethnic and internecine struggles the southerners were adamantly opposed to the exploitation of southern oil by foreigners for the benefit of northern Sudanese Arabs protected by southern militias, the PDF, and the army. When the Sudanese armed forces and the Baqqara *murahiliin* began the systematic depopulation of those parts of West Nile earmarked for drilling oil wells in 2001, they were assisted by armed Chinese workers and Afghan-Arab *mujahidiin*. They swept through the region burning villages, killing people, and capturing large herds of cattle before they became embroiled in firefights with the SPLA. Having cleared the land, the area was secured and patrolled by the Bul Nuer of Paulino Matip, a major-general in the army, and his autonomous militia paid by the government and later hired by the CNPC and Petronas Carigali as security guards. The oil companies built all-weather roads and landing strips which the Sudanese armed forces freely used to attack the civilian settlements and refugee camps in an ever-widening circle around the oil fields.

This planned destruction and death, however, disrupted the relief organizations of Operation Lifeline Sudan (OLS) and made a charade of government claims about working for "peace from within." Since 1999 independent human-rights organizations, particularly Amnesty International, Christian Aid, and Human Rights Watch, had issued full reports about the gross violations in the oil fields corroborated by condemnatory and explicit documentation from the UN Commission on Human Rights and the Harker Report for the Canadian government. A coalition of Canadian churches was particularly active in the withdrawal and sale of Arakis to Talisman who, with Lundin Petroleum, now had to bear the brunt of withering criticism. Lundin continued to dissimulate and deny there were any displacements of Sudanese surrounding their extremely profitable wells, disingenuously arguing that the socio-economic and humanitarian gains for the Sudanese produced by oil production would improve the prospects for peace. Even the Canadian government began to prevaricate over its threat of sanctions against Talisman after the publication of the Harker Report. Under pressure from the powerful Canadian oil lobby it settled for a vacuous "ethical code of conduct" from Talisman which did little to placate human-rights activists. Like Lundin, Talisman consistently denied that civilians had been displaced, despite the vast amount of incontrovertible evidence to the contrary.

Talisman was embarrassed and exasperated that they, as a private company vulnerable to demands for accountability from human-rights activists protected by freedom of speech and the press, had been singled out for censure while national oil companies, who were equally culpable, remained immune and untouchable. In response, a high-profile class-action lawsuit claiming that Talisman had collaborated with the Sudan government to deprive Sudanese of their human rights was filed in the Federal District Court of New York, which elicited from Jim Buckee a vehement denial that "constructive engagement" was a viable option in a war zone embracing the oil fields in West Nile. Although the class-action suit was to drag on for many years, it appears to have been the last straw for Buckee, who entered into negotiations to rid Talisman of its Sudanese albatross. At the end of 2002 he sold its 25 percent holdings in the GNOPC for $690 million to the Indian Oil and National Gas Corporation (ONGC) subsidiary, ONG Videsh Ltd (OVL), empowered by the government of India to manage all international exploration and production of petroleum, much to the dismay of the remaining partners in the GNOPC who had put great pressure on Talisman to sell its stake to them. Other companies followed Talisman's departure. The Russian-Belarus firm Slavneft closed its Sudan office in 2002 and in the summer of 2003 Lundin Petroleum sold its working interest in Block 5A of its concession to Petronas Carigal, but Total SA of France continued to hold its large concession that stretched along the east bank of the Bahr al-Jabal from Nuerland to Equatoria. It had never engaged in any exploration and production because of the war but was content to await the day when peace in the South would provide sufficient security to permit the development of its concession free of the insecurity that had forced Chevron, Talisman, Lundin, and Slavnet to withdraw, leaving oil exploration and production to the national oil companies of China, Malaysia, and India free from worries about accountability, the media, shareholders, or humanitarian watchdogs.

Every new government of independent Sudan had inherited the economic wreckage of its predecessor, and the revolutionary regime of 'Umar Hasan Ahmad al-Bashir was no exception. Although economic reporting from Sudan had been notoriously unreliable since the economic chaos of the Numayri years, the facts were now even more obscured by the secrecy surrounding the RCC and NIF. The demise of Turabi ensured even less transparency in the impenetrable internal operations of the tight cabal of a half-dozen, mostly security, officials surrounding Bashir. In the years following the 30 June coup Bashir outlined his economic priorities in numerous broadcasts over Radio Omdurman that were full of rhetorical platitudes about combating corruption and hoarding, and controlling foreign currency exchange, and pious but vague pronouncements about establishing committees of experts to sort out the dysfunctional Sudanese economy. None of these solutions, however, could resolve the intractable problem of the debt. In July 1989 Sudan had an estimated $13 billion debt, an annual deficit equal to 25 percent of its GDP, and hyper-inflation running between 80 and 100 percent. The shortage of hard currency resulted in a dearth of spare parts and reduced the capacity of ports, railways, and factories to less than 20 percent. On 14 September 1990 the IMF had issued a dire warning of "non-cooperation" to Sudan. In April 1993 the World Bank in exasperation suspended any further loans, and four months later Sudan was expelled from the IMF. When the United States added Sudan to its list of states sponsoring terrorism in 1994 another $190 million in aid was terminated. To the ordinary folk (*nas*) the national debt was of little interest or concern, but the periodic food shortages in basic commodities – bread, rice, cooking oil – and long lines to buy bad bread at hyper-inflated prices frequently erupted in demonstrations for which the World Bank and the government were to blame. Perhaps a more reliable indicator as to the state of the economy was the dramatic decline of the Sudanese pound from £S17 to £S300–S£500 to the dollar in the summer of 1994, despite a 75 percent devaluation in 1993 during which the currency was renamed the dinar, to make it ideologically correct. There were frequently four- to six-week periods during which the country had no foreign currency.

By 1995 the Sudan economy appeared to have managed a modest economic recovery for some 27 million Sudanese, and a real growth rate of 6 percent that enabled Sudan to try to implement an agreed program of repayment of its $1.7 billion debt to the IMF, despite the continuing suspension of its membership. Stringent controls on the price of basic commodities helped to bring down prices and inflation, and a widespread ban on the importation of a long list of foreign goods was revoked in January 1995. By 1996 favorable prices for cotton and gum arabic on the world market combined with exceptionally good weather, rains, government economic policies, and the patience of the IMF to allow the country to extricate itself from the economic malaise that had compromised the goals of the regime and dimmed the prospect of military success in the South. Agricultural development, which occupied the lives of 75 percent of the Sudanese, continued to improve during the next four years, despite the usual constraints of inadequate transport and the disruption caused by the civil war.

By January 1999 the *dura* crop had exceeded the record harvest of 1986 by more than 33 percent.

Although most of the rapidly increasing oil revenues were spent on weapons, the impact of the infusion of petrodollars became visible in 2003. The GDP continued above 6 percent, as did the per capita income of 32 million Sudanese to about $450, which complemented the government's program of macroeconomic stability, its eagerness to attract foreign capital, and privatization which spawned a small but growing number of Sudanese millionaires. Despite the IMF refusal to extend new loans, the government actually made a substantial payment of $1.5 billion in 2002, a meager contribution, however, to its extensive debt, which had grown to over $23 billion. The Bashir government was nonetheless determined not to spend its oil revenues on debt repayment and adamantly refused to pay more than $5 million a month, when the Sudanese treasury was accumulating several hundred million dollars.

Moreover, after years of diminishing exports Sudan after 1999 began to experience a steady increase in exports, most of which were derived from oil, but there was also sustained growth in the export of agricultural products – cotton, sugar, and gum arabic – to Japan and China, which together now provided over 20 percent of Sudanese imports. The balance of payments was also helped by the production of locally refined petroleum and the steady flow of remittances from over 1 million Sudanese in the Diaspora, but they were insufficient to eliminate the regular annual budget deficit of some $32 billion, which represented 14 percent of the GDP and did not include substantial funds for the military and security forces, which remained hidden from official accounting. The two most successful government policies were its program of privatization and the war against inflation, which began to show significant results after the turn of the century to stabilize the economy and promote steady economic growth propelled by rapidly increasing oil revenues. By 2005 the GDP had risen to 8 percent and to 12 percent in 2006, stoked by 512,000 bopd.

Economic stability and oil revenues attracted large amounts of capital from Saudi Arabia, the Gulf, and Asia. Between 2000 and 2006 direct foreign investment in Sudan exploded from $128 million to over $2.3 billion. In 2001 the Arab Fund for Economic Development and the Kuwait Fund for Arab Economic Development provided their first loans to Sudan in many years for the massive Merowe Dam, over 4 miles long and 200 feet high, and its hydroelectric power plant at Handab at the fourth cataract of the Nile to be completed by the Chinese in 2008, while the German electrical giant, Siemens, built the necessary grid to provide Khartoum for the first time with a reliable supply of electricity. Coca-Cola and Pepsi both opened new and expansive plants, and in 2004 a Turkish company opened a huge mall, anchored by a massive megastore, the Hypermarket, carrying thousands of items many of which hitherto had been unavailable or unaffordable. The long lines in Khartoum to buy a few loaves of inferior bread were now just a bad memory. The most explosive growth, however, was in telecommunications. By 2003 Sudan's own privatized phone company, SudaTel, had over 1 million lines in operation, and its cell-phone subsidiary, Mobitel, had nearly 200,000 subscribers. Much more dramatic was the $4-billion development of 1,500 acres of a sprawling complex for office towers, duplexes, and even a golf course at Alsunut south of Khartoum on the White Nile, the biggest commercial site in Africa, which the government expects will become a major commercial and financial center for Islamic northeast Africa, transforming Khartoum's skyline with its towers to house the headquarters for the GNPOC and Malaysia's Petronas.

Gradually, almost imperceptibly, a new and rapidly expanding class of wealthy Sudanese entrepreneurs rode to riches by exploiting government dismantling of unprofitable state corporations with their own money or by participating in joint ventures with foreign capital to establish very profitable enterprises with headquarters in Khartoum. The Sudanese Dal Group alone invested over $700 million in the infrastructure for Alsunut. Unlike the flamboyant nouveaux riches of the Numayri years and despite their penchant for substantial villas, they retained a low profile, remained aloof from opposition politics, and refrained from criticizing the government over implementation of the Comprehensive Peace Agreement (CPA) with the SPLM/A, Darfur, or its religious regulations (see Chapter 10). They were careful not to let their wealth compromise their piety, but these pragmatic businessmen kept their distance from the Islamist movement, which some regarded as a theologically inspired charade and which even some members of the NCP believed no longer possessed sufficient momentum to achieve its goals. Both sides greatly benefitted from this unholy alliance between the powerful, commercial entrepreneurs of Khartoum and the moribund religious revolutionaries of the Turabi era, an alliance that was facilitated by intimate networks of influential members from the old NIF, both hardliners and moderates, who had became inextricably intertwined with the commercial elite. By 2007 a "gentlemen's agreement" had quietly settled over Khartoum whereby the class of rich businessmen remained aloof from the impotent political opposition, leaving the task of governing to Bashir and his coterie of supporters from the security forces and the NCP. Bashir and his cronies would continue to enjoy the perquisites of political power to which they had grown accustomed, becoming more secure in office than at any time during the revolution. The price for the allegiance of their pragmatic commercial allies was freedom from interference by the state in their pursuit of profits: no political harassment, theological intimidation, or inhibiting bureaucratic regulations.

The new and expanding wealth of the Khartoum boom may have been a reality in the capital, but elsewhere in Sudan it was little more than a chimera. Very little of this new wealth "trickled down" into the country-side, and the vast majority of Sudanese did not participate in the prosperity of Khartoum. Sudan remained a country awash in wealth in the capital and sunk into poverty in the country. In 2005 Sudan's per capita income remained stagnant at $640, while the GDP grew by 12 percent. Ever since the founding of Khartoum in 1825 and the concentration of an expanding territorial Sudan during the nineteenth century, political power, administrative authority, and financial control have been concentrated in the center at Khartoum. Although the theme of the incompatible antagonism between the center and periphery can trace its beginnings to the nineteenth century, the consolidation of the state under the British and its evolution during the fifty years of independence made continuing conflict between center and periphery inevitable, made manifest by civil war in the South, disaster in Darfur, discontent in the east, and even smoldering resentment among the Nubians in the North. The gleaming towers soaring skyward and the luxury hotels of the new Khartoum were more an ominous symbol of the deep division between the "haves" at the center and the "have-nots" on the margins than the rising phoenix of a new nation.

ANATOMY OF A FOREIGN POLICY

Despite the departure of Usama bin Ladin relations between the governments of the United States and Sudan continued to deteriorate after 1996. During a brief stop-over in Khartoum at the end of March 1994, Secretary of State Madeleine K. Albright bluntly informed Bashir that if Khartoum wanted to improve relations with Washington, he must observe personal human rights, cease support for terrorism, and seek a peaceful solution with the SPLM/A, statements for which she was harshly condemned by leading members of the NIF. In fact, the United States possessed only limited diplomatic, commercial, and financial leverage against the Bashir regime surrounded by an array of terrorist organizations. In exasperation the United States finally decided in February 1996 to remove its diplomats, American staff, and their families, some of whom had experienced unnecessary harassment, but refrained from a formal dissolution of diplomatic relations. This perfunctory decision proved to be a serious miscalculation, for the absence of an active embassy in Khartoum deprived the United States of a vital listening post in the world of international terrorism, an omission that at the time Washington did not fully appreciate or understand.

Thereafter, US–Sudanese relations remained in suspended animosity. Despite repeated requests from Khartoum to reactivate the US embassy, President Clinton issued an executive order on 4 November 1997 that prohibited the importation of any goods or services of Sudanese origin, froze all Sudanese assets in the United States, and forbad a host of financial transactions. These sanctions were even more severe than those imposed in 1993, but even the cynics had to smile when the importation of Sudanese gum arabic, an essential ingredient in the manufacture of American soft drinks and adhesives, was made an exception. Three weeks after the destruction of the US embassies in Nairobi and Dar es-Salaam on 7 August 1998 by al-Qa'ida, President Clinton authorized the launch of thirteen Tomahawk cruise missiles from US naval vessels in the Red Sea that demolished the al-Shifa pharmaceutical factory in Khartoum North suspected of manufacturing the nerve gas Empta used in making the virulent VX nerve gas. The decision to strike the plant appears to have been more a petulant response by the White House than the result of a consensus of opinion among the US intelligence community: the evidence for the attack was later proved to be dubious and the production of Empta an invention. In May 1999 the assets of the owner of al-Shifa, Salih Idris, frozen after the attack, were released as a face-saving gesture. The Bashir regime's fears of US military intervention soon dissipated when there was no further aggressive action.

During the next several years relations remained much the same, with each side committed to its own agenda, which did little to improve a hostile relationship. The appointment of Florida Congressman Harry Johnston as President Clinton's special representative to investigate human-rights abuses in Sudan was regarded in Khartoum as an unfriendly gesture, particularly when the Clinton administration had been providing millions of dollars for "non-lethal" assistance to the SPLM/A that Khartoum believed concealed military hardware. Congress was now becoming increasingly involved in the cause of the SPLM/A led by that most unholy alliance in American history of the Black Caucus, the Neo-Christian Right, and the Jewish lobby. In June 1999 Kansas Senator Sam Brownback led a delegation to meet with John Garang and SPLM/A leaders in Nairobi, from where he slipped across the border into SPLA-held Yei and Lafone. Bashir was not amused. Brownback was followed by Secretary of State Madeleine Albright, who on a six-nation tour of Africa met with Garang in Nairobi on 23 October 1999 to discuss food aid for southerners, which cleared the way for President Clinton to sign a bill allowing such aid. This elicited an outcry from many humanitarian aid groups and some members of the administration who objected to the use of food as a weapon of war.

Although an embarrassed United States reactivated its embassy in April 2000, staffing it with rotating diplomats who proved more ineffectual than productive, this rather feeble effort to reopen communications between Washington and Khartoum was further compromised when Susan Rice, Assistant Secretary of State for African Affairs, and Harry Johnston slipped into SPLA-held territory without consulting Khartoum. The Sudanese were furious, declaring their visit an egregious breach of sovereignty. They retaliated by refusing visas to US envoys and declaring a US diplomat *persona non grata* for meeting with NDA opposition figures inside Sudan. The most powerful influence on relations between Sudan and the United States in the early years of the twenty-first century, however, were Christian Americans seeking beleaguered Christians in southern Sudan to witness their historic struggle on the frontier of Islam symbolized by periodic bombings of their churches and hospitals, and harassment of southern Sudanese Christians in areas controlled by the security forces. During the first fifteen years of the second civil war in the isolated southern Sudan the international media coverage had been superficial and oddly was never cultivated or exploited by the SPLM/A. By 2001, however, the colossal tragedy of the southern Sudanese had become very visible to members of the American Christian movements, both evangelical and orthodox, after the resettlement in the United States of almost 4,000 of the "Lost Boys" who had fled from the *murahiliin* raids in the 1980s to refugee camps in Ethiopia. They were displaced in 1991 after the fall of Mengistu and made their way hundreds of miles through treacherous terrain filled with predatory animals and reptiles to the Kakuma refugee camp in Kenya, where those who remained lived for another ten years before being resettled in the United States by the State Department. The stories of their tribulations were given extensive media coverage and made all the more inspiring by their own eloquent testimony, sponsored by innumerable church groups that focused public attention on US policy toward Sudan and reinforced the new mission of Christian Solidarity International.

President George W. Bush could not ignore the Christian movement that had contributed so much to his successful election. Secretary of State Colin

Powell declared in testimony before the House Subcommittee on Africa in March 2001 that the greatest tragedy on earth was unfolding in Sudan, and in May the president's speech singled out Sudan for its violations of religious freedom. Congressmen and Senators making the regular rounds of their constituents denounced Sudan for its record on human rights, terrorism, and the harassment of Christians. To placate the Christians and Congress, and to demonstrate his sincere concern about human rights, President Bush appointed Senator John C. Danforth his special envoy to Sudan on 6 September 2001. An ordained Episcopal minister, "Jack" Danforth had served twenty years in the Senate, had been the US ambassador to the UN, and was now to bring peace to Sudan. Five days later Islamist suicide terrorists hijacked four American airliners, crashing two of them into the World Trade Center and one into the Pentagon. Some 3,000 Americans died in the cataclysm, as well as the 19 terrorists, all of whom were affiliated to al-Qa'ida. This dramatically focussed US foreign policy on the "war on terror."

Although bin Ladin had been forced to flee Sudan, terrorist training camps had been closed, and the Islamist experiment was in disarray, the Islamic charities and terrorist organizations and their personnel remained in and around Khartoum, whose inhabitants vividly remembered the US cruise missile destruction of the al-Shifa plant. The Sudanese quickly realized that in order to relax the array of sanctions imposed by the United States their interests would best be served by expanding the nascent cooperation between US and Sudanese intelligence agencies investigating terrorism. Consequently, several weeks after the attack on the World Trade Center the United States lifted the UN travel ban on members of the Sudan government. Sudan reciprocated with the appointment of Salih 'Abdullah Gosh, major-general and head of the National Security Service (NSS), to expand and coordinate anti-terrorist intelligence with the Americans. Gosh was a Shayqi who began his career in the security services in the early 1980s and rose to senior positions in the mid-1990s as a loyal member of the NIF. Moreover, the momentary thaw in Sudan–US relations coincided with the arrival in Khartoum of Senator Danforth, who promptly made the most of the cordial atmosphere.

As special envoy he toured territory in the South held by the SPLA and successfully negotiated a cease-fire in the Nuba Mountains, implemented by an international team of monitors. Both sides also agreed to cease "targeting" civilians in the South, investigate the charges of slavery, and recognize zones of "tranquility" so that NGOs could carry out immunization for polio, Guinea worm, and rinderpest. In January 2002 the Sudan government and the SPLM/A formally signed the cease-fire and monitoring agreements in Switzerland, after which the United States sought to resume more normal diplomatic relations by appointing Jeff Millington chargé d'affaires at the end of May. In Khartoum these gestures were regarded with skepticism, however, for on 21 October 2002 President Bush signed Public Law 107–45, known as the "Sudan Peace Act." This piece of legislation was largely the work of the Christian movement and the Sudan lobby in Congress. It authorized $100 million each for 2003, 2004, and 2005 for relief and development in areas not under the control of the Sudan government – which, in effect, meant the SPLM/A. Moreover, the Act was explicit that if peace negotiations were not carried out in good faith, the law empowered the secretary of the treasury to use his influence and, more important, his vote to prohibit the IMF and World Bank from extending credits to Sudan. If negotiations broke down, the president was given the authority to seek an arms embargo against Sudan, prevent Sudan oil revenues being used to purchase weapons, and downgrade the diplomatic initiative made in the spring. Bashir and the NIF were not pleased.

The Sudanese government launched a lengthy diatribe denouncing the Sudan Peace Act, claiming that the SPLM/A was attempting to recast itself from the specter of a fanatical Marxist-Leninist organization, which it had never been, currying favor with the US Congress by aligning itself with Christian Solidarity International and Norwegian People's Aid, the NGO of the Norwegian churches. The State Department responded by singling out Sudan as one of the principal violators of religious freedom in its annual November 2002 report on religious freedom throughout the world. Although there appeared a window of opportunity to improve this sad saga of diplomatic and national antagonism when the CPA was signed on 9 January 2005 between the Sudan government and the SPLM/A, ending twenty-two years of civil war, that window was quickly shut by the devastating conflict in Darfur. Neither the administration nor Congress could wish to ignore, and indeed they did not ignore, the storm of protest against the atrocities perpetrated in Darfur, and the powerful Save Darfur Coalition and the American public would not accept the United States lifting sanctions and establishing normal diplomatic relations as a reward to the Sudan government for signing the CPA for peace and a new era in the South. During the long and tortuous negotiations leading to the CPA on 9 January the United States had applied enormous diplomatic and political pressure on NIF negotiators to compromise and grant the SPLM/A generous terms.

The moderates within the NIF now expected to receive their reward by the United States lifting its sanctions against Sudan. When the disaster in Darfur rendered it domestically impossible for the Bush administration to reward "genocide," the moderates and Bashir felt shamelessly betrayed and deeply embittered.

If Sudan's relations with the United States were dismal during the first fifteen years of the Bashir regime, they were even worse with its powerful and historic neighbor, Egypt. The early years had been embittered by the personal feud between Hasan al-Turabi and Husni Mubarak and the lengthy, tiresome dispute over the Halayib Triangle which Egypt had forcefully seized, occupied, and claimed sovereignty over in September 1992. Outgunned in Halayib and humiliated in Cairo ten years later on 17 August 2002, President Bashir lamely announced that the Halayib Triangle still belonged to Sudan, which no one believed. After the political demise of Hasan al-Turabi in 1999 both Egypt and Sudan sought to repair their tattered relations. President Mubarak welcomed Sudan's efforts to end its isolation in the Arab and international communities. During meetings of the OIC and the Arab League Egypt responded to Sudan's diplomatic efforts to restore its relations with the United Arab Emirates, Algeria, Syria, and Saudi Arabia. As always, the geography of the Nile waters dictated that the long-term interests of Egypt would not be served by unremitting hostility toward Khartoum, and consequently Mubarak organized a "reconciliation meeting" in Cairo on 22 May 1999 during which Sudan, as a gesture of goodwill, agreed to restore Egyptian properties confiscated in Khartoum, including twenty buildings belonging to the important Egyptian Ministry of Public Works primarily concerned with the Nile waters. The meeting was followed by a tripartite agreement between Sudan, Egypt, and Ethiopia in November for cooperation in the development of the Nile waters. On 24 December 1999 Sudan and Egypt decided, at long last, to restore full diplomatic relations with each other. In March 2000 the new Egyptian Ambassador, Muhammad Asim Ibrahim, arrived in Khartoum to reopen the Khartoum branch of Cairo University closed since 1993 after the Egyptians had seized Halayib.

Egypt, again with the Nile waters very much in mind, joined with Libya in playing an active role in the IGAD peace process. In May 2000 John Garang met with President Mubarak in Cairo and convinced him that the SPLM/A was not seeking the division of Sudan, which Egypt feared, but a new united, democratic, and secular Sudan, which held great appeal for Mubarak. Although Mubarak continued to remain deeply suspicious of the

Bashir regime, he was content to work through regular diplomatic channels while exerting Egyptian influence at Khartoum and with the IGAD to protect the Nile waters. Egypt had regained its position to shape the views of Arab and Western governments of Sudan, leaving the Sudanese free to continue their historic task of manipulating an arrogant and powerful northern neighbor.

CHAPTER 9

War and peace in southern Sudan

THE SPLA TAKES THE OFFENSIVE

By the beginning of 1996 John Garang had recovered from the great split in the SPLM/A. He had received a vote of confidence from his followers at Chukudum in 1994 and in October 1995 launched a very successful dry-season offensive (until the onset of the rains in April 1996 curtailed any further aggressive action by the victorious SPLA); a defeated SPAF and demoralized PDF retired to regroup. In January 1997 the SPLA 13th Division launched Operation Black Fox to open its dry-season offensive by once again capturing Kurmuk, Qaissan, and other posts in southern Blue Nile that provoked, as in 1989, hysterical demands in Khartoum to repulse the invaders. The government mobilized a mechanized column that forced the SPLA to withdraw from Kurmuk and recaptured Meban and Chali al-Fil in southern Blue Nile before being routed by the SPLA, which seized large quantities of equipment and weapons, and decimated a 2,000-man brigade. Another government force failed to retake Menza, and the SPLA Tana Brigade of the 13th Division repulsed a major counter-attack north of the Blue Nile at Khor Gana and Yakuru by five battalions of the SPAF and PDF.

Having repulsed the army counter-offensive in the Blue Nile by the end of February 1997, the SPLA launched Operation Thunderbolt in March. It swept through central Equatoria and inflicted very heavy casualties, reportedly killing some 8,000 government troops and taking another 1,700 prisoner. The SPLA also decimated the West Nile Bank Front (WNBF), a government militia, in fierce battles at Morobo and Yei, killing 800 and taking over 1,000 prisoners who were delivered to the Ugandan government. When the Juba garrison counter-attacked to secure the Juba–Yei road, they were driven back by the SPLA with heavy losses. The momentum gained by the SPLA during March soon swept them to further victories in April. The SPLA captured Amadi, Lui, and the remaining garrisons in central

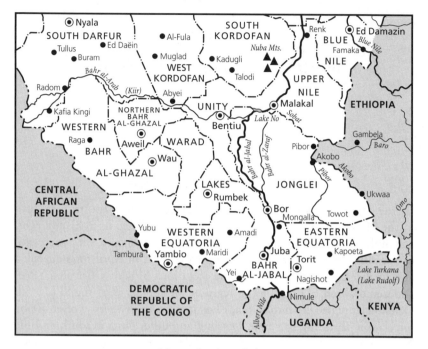

Map 12 Southern Sudan

Equatoria, followed by Rumbek and Wunrok on the Lol river in the Bahr al-Ghazal won from Kerubino's SPLA-Bahr al-Ghazal. In May, Tonj and Warrap fell to the SPLA before the beginning of the rains.

In a futile attempt to reverse the rising tide of SPLA victories Khartoum sought to unify the six southern factions opposed to the SPLA, provide them with additional weaponry, and coordinate an offensive. Although Riek Machar of the SSIM/A, Kerubino Kuanyin of the SPLA-Bahr al-Ghazal, Arok Thon Arok of the Independence of Bor Group, Dr. Theopholus Chang Loti of the Equatoria Defense Force, Kawac Makuei of the Independence Movement for Southern Sudan, and Muhammad Harun Kafi of the SPLA-Nuba all signed an agreement on 21 April 1997 to cooperate, their personal rivalries and incompetent leadership prevented any effective offensive against the SPLA. Their failure was made all the more visible when a New Joint Military Command of the NDA was established in July 1997 with John Garang as commander-in-chief and Lieutenant-General 'Abd al-Rahman Sa'id, the former deputy chief of staff of the Sudanese army who had defected, as his deputy.

Having failed to mobilize the fractious southern opposition, in October 1997 Bashir authorized a more complete conscription than the earlier draft of 1993 by which all male students between the ages of 18 and 32 would have to serve 12 to 18 months of compulsory military service. Six weeks later Bashir also ordered all government departments to implement a planned mobilization whereby employees were given lucrative bonuses to join PDF units. This mandatory draft of some 70,000 students was highly unpopular and provoked an outcry in Khartoum, particularly from parents. Special units were employed to hunt down draft-dodgers; young males were shang-haied on the streets and in the *suq*, and even dragged from private cars and public buses, to be sent to training camps. By April 1998 there were numerous incidents of desertion, and hundreds of recruits at the large Ailafun military camp south of Khartoum escaped, amid growing public outrage.

Bashir also sought to seize the administrative initiative in the South by instigating a twenty-three-member South Sudan Coordinating Council, often simply called the Council of the South. It was appointed in August 1997 with Riek Machar as president. Although on paper the council was to provide civilian rule for the South during the next four years, it possessed no credibility among the southern Sudanese, seldom met, and possessed no resources to enforce its decrees, which were simply ignored. After his failure to coordinate the southern factions Bashir tried to gain greater control over the southern militias by formally reinstating their commanders into the regular army. Kerubino Kuanyin was promoted to major-general, the others were made brigadiers. Kerubino's promotion, however, was insufficient to satisfy his inflated self-esteem, and he was insulted when appointed deputy to Riek Machar in the Council of the South. Angry and bitter, six months later in January 1998 he re-defected in a huff to the SPLM/A, taking with him the troops of the SPLA-Bahr al-Ghazal. Lam Akol, however, had made his peace with the government on 20 September 1997 when he signed the "Fashoda Accord," whereby he and his SPLA-United, which was predominately Shilluk, controlled the strategic area around Malakal and both banks of the White Nile to Malut on behalf of the government. Lam, however, was increasingly isolated from the South, for of all the southern peoples the Shilluk had a long history of cooperating with their Arab neighbors.

No sooner had Kerubino defected to the SPLA than he coordinated an attack on Wau, capital of the Bahr al-Ghazal. The SPLA provided him with some 2,000 men who, with their families, infiltrated the town to support from within the SPLA attack from without. The assault on 29 January 1998 was a stunning but brief success. The airport, railway station, and most of the town were seized, as well as the surrounding towns and agricultural fields, and held for two days before the government launched a counter-attack. Fierce fighting raged for another ten days until the army and militias gradually regained control of Wau, where they promptly butchered hundreds of Dinka residents and rounded up 150 students from Wau University who later "disappeared." Over 80,000 residents fled to safety in the countryside. It remains unclear who initiated the plan to capture Wau, but it was probably Kerubino's idea, for he was very well informed as to the strength of the government forces in the Bahr al-Ghazal and was sorely in need of a victory to vindicate his return to the SPLA. John Garang, despite his personal differences with Kerubino, apparently wanted to keep him within the fold of the SPLM/A. Although the assault on Wau was an audacious gamble undertaken by a highly motivated and well-armed SPLA, its failure demonstrated the vulnerability of the SPLA when pitted against an entrenched garrison with artillery and air support, and it was not to be repeated.

At the beginning of the 1998 rainy season the Bahr al-Ghazal settled into a sterile stalemate that was resolved by simply declaring a three-month mutual cease-fire, while western Upper Nile dissolved into bloody fighting between Riek Machar's rump SSIM/A, renamed the South Sudan Defense Force (SSDF), and Paulino Matip's South Sudan Unity Movement/Army (SSUM/A). Paulino Matip was the quintessential freebooter, willing to ally himself with god or the devil, depending on which would supply him with the resources to sustain his panache and his private army. Matip had long held a grudge against Riek over the Peace Charter of April 1996, which he had refused to sign. To add insult to injury, Bashir had then appointed Riek president of the Council of the South with the rank of a national vice-president, which precipitated Paulino Matip's withdrawal from the SSIM/A and his subsequent, petulant founding of the SSUM/A as a rival to Riek's SSDF. The rivalry between Paulino and Riek became increasingly hostile after a shoot-out at Paulino's residence on the outskirts of Khartoum between their respective bodyguards in June 1998 and following a second incident at a wedding in Omdurman in August that sparked a spiral of violence between Matip's SSUM/A and Riek's SSDF in Unity State in West Upper Nile. Late in August the SSUM/A sacked Ler, Riek's home town, and over 400 were killed in factional fighting around Bentiu before the government intervened to negotiate a cease-fire.

During this personal vendetta Riek had alienated other militia leaders in the Upper Nile and Bahr al-Ghazal. Lawrence Lual Lual and his SPLA-Bahr al-Ghazal forces withdrew from the SSDF in October 1998. The following month an SSDF battalion in the Upper Nile broke with Riek and defected to the SPLA. Riek further compromised himself in January 1999 when he organized a United Democratic Salvation Front and registered it as a political party for the new elections announced by Bashir. This futile gesture further antagonized many southerners, for all registered political associations were bound to defend the unity of Sudan and accept *shari'a* as the foundation for all laws. Having declared himself fighting for an independent south Sudan in the great "split" with Garang in 1991 and having reaffirmed this commitment at the founding of the SSIM/A, he had then sold out to Khartoum in the Peace Charter and peace agreement of 1996 and now done so again with his new political party in 1999, which effectively destroyed his credibility. The Nuer militia leader, Gatwic Gatkuoth, immediately broke with Riek to organize the SSDF-2. By April 1999 even Bashir had had enough of Riek's duplicity and shifted the government's support to Paulino Matip, which precipitated fierce fighting in May between Riek's SSDF and Matip's SSUM/A around the Thar Jiath oil wells.

Disaffections within the SSDF were now rampant, and on 31 December 1999 Riek officially resigned as minister for southern affairs and president of the dysfunctional Council of the South to declare he had returned to his roots to fight for an independent southern Sudan. Isolated and with only a dwindling cadre of loyal followers, Riek Machar could no longer play in the game. Elaborate and Byzantine negotiations continued throughout 2001 in Nairobi between representatives of the SPLM/A and those of his Sudan People's Democratic Front (SPDF), the SSDF having been dissolved. A tentative agreement was reached in May 2001 and culminated in the "Nairobi Declaration" of 6 January 2002, an affirmation of unity between John Garang and Riek Machar. He, with Lam Akol and Gordon Kong, had nearly brought down John Garang, had succeeded in precipitating violent civil war among the Nuer, and had made possible the government's control of the oil fields in West Upper Nile – he was another in the long list of Sudan's failed leaders. Garang was gracious: he appointed Riek vice-president of the SPLM/A, and although he remained quietly suspicious of his old comrade-in-arms, there was in fact little he had to fear from Riek Machar.

Kerubino Kuanyin Bol was another matter. He had a long-standing feud with Garang and bitter memories of six years in his SPLA prison. Despite his later defection to the SPLA in January 1998, his failure to capture Wau appears to have exacerbated the long-smoldering personal hostility between them. Kerubino now believed that Garang had purposely failed to support him sufficiently at the battle of Wau, while Garang probably regretted his agreeing to let Kerubino attempt to take Wau, which had resulted in military failure and massive loss of Dinka lives. In November 1998 Kerubino made his way to Nairobi, where he had a verbal confrontation with Garang, who ordered his security agents to raid Kerubino's residence. Five days later, on 15 November 1998, a group of Kerubino loyalists assaulted the Garang residence in the Kileleshwa section of Nairobi and staged a shoot-out with his bodyguards before the police intervened. A month later Kerubino clandestinely flew to join Paulino Matip at Mankien, where he was killed by the SPLA on 10 September 1998 in heavy fighting. Although the rumor that Garang ordered Kerubino Kuanyin Bol assassinated still lingers, Kerubino remained to the end a quintessential warlord whose frequent defections were motivated more by self-interest than ideology. Tens of thousands of Dinka civilians in the Bahr al-Ghazal were either killed or displaced because of him, and some 60,000 died in the famine of 1998 that his raiders had helped produce. Few mourned his passing.

John Garang had many concerns other than Riek, Kerubino, or Lam Akol in order to maintain the military momentum of the SPLA. During the 1999 dry season the government had launched its offensive earlier than usual in the Nuba Mountains, attacking on four fronts in November with some 2,000 SPAF regulars, who captured eight SPLA airstrips that were not retaken until March 1999. The army returned the following dry season in March 2000 in greater force with eight regular army divisions from Kadugli that displaced some 14,000 Nuba and destroyed many villages until the SPLA counter-attacked in mid-April. During the dry-season offensive in January 2001 the impact of the oil revenues' bolstering the armed forces first became apparent in the Nuba Mountains when the SPLA began to lose ground. Although they were able to stabilize their battle line by the beginning of the rains, it was the timely arrival in November of President Bush's Special Envoy, Jack Danforth, that ensured a continuous SPLA presence in the Nuba Mountains.

Senator Danforth had been sent to Sudan not to mediate peace but to gauge whether the SPLM/A and the government were willing to do so. He devised four humanitarian "tests" of their sincerity: a cease-fire, "zones of tranquility" in the Nuba Mountains, a cessation of air raids on civilians, and a demonstrable commitment by the government to end slavery. Although his "tests" were severely criticized as timorous and without innovation, emphasizing humanitarian issues and not the root causes of the conflict, he successfully negotiated one of the "tests," a cease-fire between the SPLA and SPAF in the Nuba Mountains, signed in Geneva on 19 January 2002. The following month government forces flagrantly violated the Geneva agreement: a Hind D helicopter gunship attacked the important UN relief center at Bieh on 22 February, killing women and children waiting for food. The SPAF overran the Nhialdiu airstrip, and UN-World Food Program flights carrying food and medicines to some forty-five locations throughout the South were banned, producing an international outcry. In late March 2002 the government agreed to abide by the remaining three Danforth proposals, as had the SPLM/A.

In order to ensure that both sides honored their commitments, Danforth had established the important principle of "outside intermediaries," teams of international monitors to validate each of the "tests," which led to the deployment of the Joint Monitoring Mission (JMM), the Joint Military Commission (JMC), and ultimately the Civilian Protection Monitoring Team (CPMT). Moreover, the Nuba, who traditionally demonstrated rugged individualism in their political affairs, had established a unified coordinating council for the future of the Nuba Mountains consisting of three hitherto rival groups, the Nuba Mountain General Union, the Sudan National Party, and the Sudan National Free Party, who signed the Charter for Coalition in Khartoum in September 2001. Largely through the work of the devoted international monitors, the Nuba Mountains were no longer in the front line of the struggle for control of southern Sudan.

While the SPLA was able to hold its own in the Nuba Mountains its forces in the southern Blue Nile and eastern Sudan were more successful, thanks to help from the NDA and the Beja Congress. The Beja consist of the Hadendowa, Amarar, Bishariyin, and Bani Amer, who are non-Arab Muslims with a long nomadic tradition as breeders of fine camels and livestock, 80 percent of which were destroyed in the great drought of the 1980s, reducing them to impoverished agricultural workers and stevedores in Port Sudan. With the return of the rains at the end of the 1980s their dry pastures were soon filled by immigrant farmers from West Africa and Nubians resettled after the loss of their beloved date palms as a result of inundation from Lake Nasser, but the most entrepreneurial group to prosper from Beja impoverishment were the Rashaida Arab pastoralists on the Eritrean–Sudan border, who jumped at the opportunity to seize Beja lands. Other large parcels, including 1 million acres granted to Usama bin Ladin, were leased at minimal rates to the new class of "gentlemen farmers" – wealthy merchants, well-connected civil servants, and military officers – who transformed the fragile topsoil of grassland into large, profitable mechanized farms for cotton, *dura*, and sesame. After the collapse of the

Mengistu regime in 1991 additional Beja lands were confiscated for terrorist training camps and surrounding farms to feed recruits from the Afghan-Arab *mujahidiin*, Eritrean Islamic Jihad, Hizbullah, Hamas, and the Oromo Islamic Jihad.

Harassed by NIF Islamist agents who sought to impose an Arab, Islamist culture on the non-Arab Beja, conscripted into the PDF, and embittered by the loss of their lands, they revived the Beja Congress in 1994. Thereafter, fighters of the Beja Congress, who numbered only some 500 men, carried out raids against military installations along the Eritrean frontier, the strategic Khartoum–Port Sudan Road, and mechanized farms in their fight for recognition by Khartoum of their long-standing grievances, but the brunt of the insurgency in eastern Sudan was left to the Umma Liberation Army and the SPLA New Sudan Brigade, numbering some 2,000 guerillas. The Umma Liberation Army of 400 men had begun its operations in eastern Sudan with little success until joined by the 1st NDA Unified Brigade and by the SPLA New Sudan Brigade, which overwhelmed the army garrison at Dar al-'Umda Hamid, captured Umbireiga near Kassala in April 1999, and in May repulsed the SPAF offensive to retake the border towns of Kurmuk, Ulu, and Meban.

In January 2000, however, the NDA received a serious setback when Sudan restored diplomatic relations with Eritrea and Ethiopia. The headquarters of the NDA in the former Sudanese embassy in Asmara was returned to Sudan, and Ethiopia's refusal to continue support for the NDA facilitated Khartoum's offensive along the border in March, which displaced another 160,000 Sudanese. The Sudan government lost no time in exploiting its diplomatic success with a military victory. In November 2000 the SPAF launched an assault against NDA forces at Hamesh Koraib, northeast of Kassala. The bulk of the garrison, which consisted mainly of the SPLA's New Sudan Brigade, was driven from the town with very heavy losses, but during the remainder of the year and in 2001 fighting in eastern Sudan became bogged down in stalemate, each side suffering defeats and victories as the war began to enter a new phase. On the one hand, the SPAF and the PDF began to receive new weapons, equipment, and recruits, bringing the SPAF up to 104,000 active soldiers, 20,000 of whom were conscripts, and the PDF up to 15,000 supported by another 85,000 reservists. On the other hand, the IGAD and the international community, including some of Sudan's neighbors, were increasingly determined to mediate a lasting peace.

The revitalization of Sudanese armed forces coincided with the first barrel of oil to be exported from Marsa Bashayir in May 1999. Thereafter, the greatest percentage of oil revenues was used to modernize the army. By 2000 the Sudan defense budget accounted for nearly half the national budget, costing over half a billion dollars. On the same day that Sudan loaded its first tanker of oil, a shipment of tanks arrived from Poland. In March 2000 Sudan and Bulgaria signed a secret arms agreement, followed by yet another more generous accord for closer military cooperation with China, by now the major source of arms for the SPAF. A bevy of military delegations arrived in Khartoum from Iraq, Iran, and Kazakhstan. By 2002 the defense budget had increased to $665 million to provide for the purchase of new weaponry amounting to more than half the annual budget and some 5 percent of the GDP, but ironically Sudan was still spending much less on its armed forces than most African countries, including big spenders like Nigeria, the Democratic Republic of the Congo, South Africa, and Angola. Oil revenues were not, however, the panacea to revive the once-proud "fighting Sudanese." The officer corps had long ago ceased to be a professional, secular elite unit and under the Islamists had been purged of those theologically incorrect. Theological orthodoxy now was a requirement to enter the military academy and thereafter earn promotion. Once Sudan had become completely isolated in the early 1990s the opportunities for advanced officer training closed not only in the West but in the Arab world as well until the exploitation of oil by the Chinese enabled Sudanese officers to receive their further training in China and Malaysia, but these programs were no longer so required for advancement as they had been in the Numayri years. The officer corps still remained dominated by the riverine *awlad al-bahr*, among whom the historical nepotism of the Shayqiyya prevailed.

If the officer corps could no longer be depended upon to plan and execute successful campaigns, the regular army, its 20,000 conscripts, and the PDF were equally incapable of fighting an insurgency. There was little training in guerilla warfare and even less incentive to engage in it. The SPAF was essentially a garrison army content to remain behind its fortifications in the main towns protected by extensive minefields where the boredom and frustrations of garrison duty undermined discipline and eroded morale. In the seclusion of their forts fear of the dark and dense bush beyond spread like a cancer that sapped their effectiveness. Historically the ranks had been filled largely by southerners, Nuba, and Darfuris, who had a long and honorable military tradition as warriors but whose loyalty had become highly suspect, for their kinsmen were the insurgents fighting to secure equality, justice, and respect for their people. The position of the marginalized rankers in the SPAF became all the more compromised by the success of the monitored cease-fire in the Nuba Mountains, the prospects for a satisfactory settlement for the southern Sudanese, and the eruption of insurgency in Darfur. Moreover, the decline in the effectiveness of the regular army could not be offset by conscripts, most of whom came from the riverine towns, possessed no military tradition, and despised the regulars from the periphery. Despite continuing appeals to *jihad* they were very unwilling soldiers, and when pitted against SPLA veterans on their own turf, it was an unequal contest.

Although the new oil revenues were used to purchase more modern military equipment, weapons, and airplanes, they could not transform the past inadequacies or provide competent officers and well-trained troops. The army possessed some 280 main battle tanks, which were mostly old Soviet T-55s and of little use in the swamps and bush of southern Sudan where roads, except in the oil fields, were impassible during the rains and mere tracks in the dry season, and along which ambush and elusive guerillas awaited. Moreover, the armored vehicles were a hodgepodge of Soviet, Chinese, British, and other foreign makes, each with different parts, which complicated replacement, repair, and maintenance by those with few qualifications and little training to carry it out. Historically the Sudanese have never displayed much interest in, talent for, or appreciation of proper maintenance, which had long been a common complaint among exasperated foreign military advisers. Highly trained technicians to keep vehicles operational were scarce and continually frustrated by a lack of spare parts, comprehensible manuals, and (until Sudan became self-sufficient in oil) the perpetual problem of adequate supplies of petrol.

Like its tanks and armored vehicles, the Sudan military's air force consisted of planes from different countries with different capabilities and different needs. The air force had only some 3,000 men and consisted of Soviet Antonov An-24 bombers, Soviet and Chinese tactical fighters, and the feared Soviet Hind D helicopter gunships purchased from Belarus in 2002, which had proved in Afghanistan to be the most effective aircraft against a guerilla insurgency. The half-dozen Antonov bombers were originally transport aircraft with no capability for precision bombing, so that its bombs were simply pushed out from the rear of the plane, indiscriminately spreading terror among civilians but few losses among the SPLA. The Soviet and Chinese jet fighters were often flown by foreign mercenaries seeking targets for which they were not designed. Moreover, these jets required very specialized maintenance, much of which was done by Iranian, Iraqi, or Chinese technicians. The international conglomerate of aircraft was most pronounced in the transport wings upon which the SPAF garrisons were dependent for supplies and military equipment. There were British, French, German, and Canadian transports, and three US Lockheed C-130 Hercules capable of carrying heavy loads. During the rains virtually all SPAF garrisons in the South were supplied by air at great expense and risk of attack from SPLA SAM (surface-to-air) 7 missiles. During the dry season truck convoys were able to pass in the South, but they were very vulnerable to ambush, at which the SPLA became extremely proficient with their intelligence networks and command of the roadsides.

During its insurgency the SPLA had been confronted by numerous government-supported militias, particularly after the great Nilotic "split" in 1991, but each of these southern militias – Mundari, Taposa, Anuak, Nuer – had been largely contained, if not incorporated into the SPLA. In 1994, however, the SPLA was suddenly confronted by a government-supported non-southern militia in its own backyard of eastern Equatoria, the Lord's Resistance Army (LRA), an Acholi insurgency. Although some Acholi live in southern Sudan, their heartland lies in northern Uganda, and they are regarded by Equatorians as predominantly Ugandan, and so the LRA therefore was seen as a "foreign" militia. After the overthrow in January 1986 of Uganda's President Tito Okello, an Acholi, by the National Resistance Army (NRA) of Yoweri Museveni, the Acholi feared the NRA would replace the dominant role of the Acholi in the Ugandan army and inflict retribution for the brutal Acholi counter-insurgency campaign waged in the Lowero Triangle, home of Museveni's people. By August the Acholi had staged a major insurgency in northern Uganda, and from the chaos emerged the Holy Spirit Movement led by Alice (Aruma) Lakwena, inspired by visions that those who responded to her divine millennarian message would be immune from bullets. Her movement was organized as a regular army whose invincibility, however, disappeared before real bullets in its futile and failed offensive to take Kampala in August 1987. Alice fled to safety in Kenya, and although both her immediate family and her cousin, Joseph Kony, denied he was her successor, each employed divine revelation and mystical charisma to mobilize their followers. Kony combined the sanctity of the Ten Commandments with Acholi tradition to impose his authority through a mixture of coercion, secretiveness, and isolation enforced by extreme discipline that transformed Alice's millennarian movement into a unique guerilla army.

For the next twenty years Kony and his LRA eluded all attempts by the Ugandan People's Democratic Army to capture him, terrorized the Acholi people (some of whom quietly supported him), and forced them into sprawling refugee camps throughout northern Uganda. During its regular and brutal raids for supplies, the LRA seized the children, who were carried into the thick bush and forests of Acholiland. Here they were viciously indoctrinated to kill their friends, fellow child-soldiers, and parents by mutilation and emasculation if so ordered by Kony and his subordinates. After the Ugandan army utterly failed to capture Kony, prevent his raids, or end the abduction and indoctrination of children, there were sporadic and unsuccessful negotiations, culminating in an ultimatum by President Museveni for him to surrender in February 1994. Kony refused.

Thereafter, Kony and his LRA units slipped across the border into southern Sudan, seeking sanctuary in the heavily forested mountains and ravines of the frontier where, desperate for supplies, weapons, and ammunition, Kony readily agreed to ally his forces with the SPAF as a militia in its campaigns in Equatoria against the SPLA. Although the LRA continued its main field of operations in Acholiland in Uganda, it established a network of fortified camps in the borderlands of southern Sudan, the largest of which was at Jabalain, 25 miles south of Juba, which the SPLA captured on 14 September 1998, wounding Kony, who managed to escape. Kony and his LRA crossed over the border into the Democratic Republic of Congo, regrouped, and returned to southern Sudan, where their depredations depopulated many Madi and Kuku villages, among which the LRA was known as *tonga-tonga* (chop-chop). The SPLA has largely contained and weakened the LRA, and in 2006 Riek Machar, vice-president of the Government of south Sudan, inaugurated mediation between the LRA and Uganda, but a peaceful settlement remains elusive.

When the SPLA in May 2000 began to shift its forces in the Bahr al-Ghazal to the Nuba Mountains, the southern Blue Nile, and along the Kassala border, the government seized the opportunity to send the strong SPAF garrison at Babanusa to regain control of the railway to Wau and rebuild the rail bridges over the Kiir and Lol rivers. To exploit this success the government launched its dry-season offensive in January 2001, sweeping through Aweil West with units from the SPAF, PDF, and Misiriyya and Rizayqat *murahiliin* that defeated the SPLA, destroyed scores of villages, captured large herds of cattle, and drove large numbers of Dinka civilians from their land. This offensive was accompanied by Baqqara herdsmen whom the government sought (with little success) to settle on Dinka land depopulated by the armed forces. Rather than attempt to regain their losses in the northern Bahr al-Ghazal the SPLA opened, for the first time, a new front in the western Bahr al-Ghazal in May and June 2001. This was a curious decision. Perhaps the Dinka-dominated SPLA regarded this offensive as another exercise in the historical expansion of

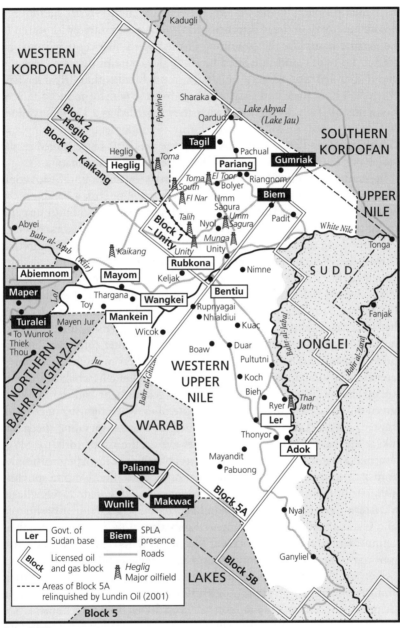

Source: USAID

Map 13 Conflict for control of the oil fields between GOS and the SPLA, 2002

the Dinka people, but the western Bahr al-Ghazal, *dar fartit*, had been a remote sanctuary in the nineteenth-century slave trade largely forgotten in the twentieth, and by the beginning of the twenty-first century it was an isolated no-man's-land inhabited by a conglomerate of displaced peoples who had rallied around petty chieftains, more bandits than tribal leaders. The SPLA took Raga and Daym Zubayr in June which produced tens of thousands of IDPs fleeing from what they regarded as a Dinka invasion. By October 2001 the SPLA, unable to supply its units over the long and hazardous "Raga Road," withdrew, for there was little to be gained in the wastelands of the western Bahr al-Ghazal from its hostile inhabitants.

In August 2001 intense fighting resumed in the oil fields. Elite SPLA commandoes briefly captured oil installations in Heglig, sank a barge on the White Nile carrying petroleum equipment, and forced Lundin to suspend its drilling operations in Block 5A of their concession. The fiercest fighting occurred along the new all-weather Bentiu–Ler road built by Lundin that allowed the SPAF to move deep into SPLA territory with armored vehicles and tanks. Here the SPLA, led by Peter Gatdet, had been fighting Paulino Matip, whose Bul Nuer guarded the oil fields, and as the fighting raged throughout February 2002 the government rushed reinforcements from the Nuba Mountains and Kassala up the road to its garrison at Pultuni near the Lundin oil wells and contained Gatdet's counter-offensive. Further south in eastern Equatoria the government launched an intensive bombing campaign in June 2002 just before the signing of the Machakos protocol (see pp. 263–4 below) by which the Sudan government and the SPLM/A agreed on a cease-fire that held until September, when fighting once again erupted. The SPLA recaptured the strategic town, suspending the peace talks at Machakos, Kenya. Determined to avenge the loss of Torit, the SPAF launched a major offensive in October, recapturing the town before the government and the SPLM/A signed yet another cease-fire. Despite sporadic outbursts of fighting precipitated by Baqqara *murahiliin* attacking villages in western Upper Nile in January and February 2003, President Bashir and John Garang met for the first time at Kampala in July 2003 to pledge their commitment to the peace process at Machakos. This signified a major shift from war to peace after twenty years of implacable conflict.

Southern Sudanese civilians had paid a very heavy price to prevent their domination by the northern Arab Muslim Sudanese. More than 2 million had perished; another 4 to 6 million had been driven from their homes either as IDPs or refugees in the sprawling camps across the border in Ethiopia, Uganda, Zaire, and the Central African Republic. For twenty years southern Sudan had been laid waste, its fragile infrastructure destroyed, its resources

Figure 23 Chairman of the Sudan People's Liberation Movement/Army (SPLM/A)
Dr. John Garang speaking to his troops in eastern Equatoria, 2002.

ravaged. Warfare in the South had been characterized by weeks, if not
months, of ominous quiet suddenly punctuated by fierce firefights before
each side paused to regroup and fight again. Although the government
had the advantage of more men, more armor, and more firepower, the
SPAF and the PDF were at a distinct disadvantage, having to conduct their
campaigns in swamps, grasslands, bush, and deep forests, terrain alien to
them. They were confined to their fortified posts, and "seek-and-destroy"
missions were unknown. Southern Sudan was a fearful, foreign place for
the ill-trained regular officers and men, conscripts, and northern Arabs of
the PDF fighting an unwinnable war for which they had little enthusiasm
or reasons to prevail. Like so many conscripted by an unpopular draft into
a conflict they did not understand, they were unconvinced of the cause for
which they had been sent to fight and counted the days until their term of
service expired, when they could go home to the arid plains and riverine
towns. Northern Sudanese conscripts were not the only ones confused as
to why they were fighting, for most of the insurgents in the SPLA had
little interest in Garang's new, united Sudan. They were men and boys of
little sophistication who were determined to defend their homeland from
the historic depredations of the Arabs for their land, resources, and slaves,

rather than to build a new Sudan in an unholy union with their historic and hated enemies.

SLOUCHING TOWARD A SETTLEMENT

Throughout the first fifteen years of the SPLM/A insurgency there had been regular overtures from both sides for peace that had proved an exercise in futility, for neither the government nor the SPLM/A displayed much willingness to make the necessary concessions and compromise to achieve it. The agenda and presentations at their sterile meetings were often convoluted and abusively critical of each other, or a forum to entice support from neighboring states or appeal to the sympathies of the international community. Each side had its hard-liners convinced that a military solution was imminent, and when that did not happen, the more moderate members of the NIF and SPLM simply were not prepared to make the political, religious, or territorial sacrifices for a sustained peace. Thus, the war dragged on from one year to the next, with little hope of a settlement, further exacerbated in the late 1990s by the exploitation of the oil fields. The principal mediators seeking a resolution to the conflict were the patient and persevering members of the IGAD whose unstinting efforts appeared to have come to an end in September 1994 when the Sudanese spokesman at the Nairobi talks, Ghazi Salahuddin Atabani, had absolutely refused to consider the IGAD Declaration of Principles (DoP). Despite this blunt rebuff, the IGAD continued to press for acceptance by the Sudan government of the DoP as a viable basis for negotiations. John Garang had readily agreed, but Hasan al-Turabi was adamantly opposed and sought to use his charm to persuade President Moi of Kenya to disassociate himself from the IGAD. Moi politely refused and sent Turabi back to Khartoum empty-handed. During the next three years the IGAD continued without success to break the deadlock between the two sides, a process enlivened only by the well-meaning but embarrassing intervention of former US President Jimmy Carter seeking to mediate a cease-fire.

Suddenly, and not without a little drama, at the meeting of the IGAD from 8 to 9 July 1997 Khartoum accepted the DoP as a non-binding starting-point to end the civil war but reserved the right to reject any one of its principles. The reasons for Khartoum's volte-face remain obscure. Was it recognition that John Garang had recovered from the great "split" of 1991 to be in a stronger position, with the solid endorsement of the National Conference at Chukudum in 1994? Was it an acknowledgement that the SPAF and the PDF could not impose a military solution after the string of victories by the SPLA in 1996? Perhaps it reflected a subtle sea-change within the NIF in which those who were willing to compromise began to prevail over the intransigent members, something that coincided with the decline in the influence of Hasan al-Turabi, the pragmatism of Bashir, and the end of Usama bin Ladin and support for *jihadist* terrorism, or was it an attempt to end the isolation of Sudan as a pariah state?

The document that both the Sudan government and the SPLM had now accepted was really nothing more than a set of principles in which the difficulties are always in the details. Between 27 October and 11 November 1997, under the watchful eye of the IGAD, the two sides sparred over the intractable questions of unity or separation. The Sudan government proposed the perennial federal solution; the SPLM/A insisted on the right to self-determination after a two-year confederation between North and South, a jerry-built structure invented by John Garang in 1992 to reconcile his own vision of unity with the separatist passions of his followers. Khartoum countered by accepting the principle of self-determination but only within a united, federated Sudan of North and South. The negotiations were suspended, but the adversaries met again from 4 to 6 May 1998 in Nairobi to disagree on religion, the state, and even the boundaries of southern Sudan. Nevertheless, neither party wanted to appear obstructionist, which enabled the IGAD to persuade them to sign a rather vague, non-committal document acknowledging the South's right to self-determination by means of a referendum supervised by a team of international monitors, but exactly when that referendum would be held, if ever, remained obscure.

Encouraged by this dialogue, the IGAD sponsored another meeting on 4 August 1998 that dissolved in bitter denunciation two days later over which territories constituted southern Sudan. The SPLM/A made an expedient but important concession that the Nuba Mountains, the southern Blue Nile, and Abyei would hold separate referendums to determine whether they wished to belong to the North or South. In effect, the SPLM/A was willing to abandon their front-line allies in the civil war to ensure their referendum in the home provinces of Equatoria, Bahr al-Ghazal, and the Upper Nile. All other issues, particularly *shari'a*, appeared hopelessly irreconcilable. After prodding by the IGAD, both sides agreed to meet again, when desultory discussions continued without the slightest indication of progress. Exhausted and frustrated, the IGAD mediators convened a final meeting at Lake Bogoria, Kenya, in October 2000, but to no avail. The IGAD initiative appeared spent, until it was revived by the personal intervention of President Moi of Kenya. After rather fumbling efforts by Egypt and Libya to rejuvenate the peace process in summer 2001, President Moi appointed the able, energetic, and persevering Lieutenant-General Lazarus Sumbeiywo as Kenya's special envoy for the IGAD peace process. General Sumbeiywo convened a first "technical meeting" at Karen, Nairobi, from 2 to 5 May 2002, at which the Sudan government and SPLM/A were invited to agree on an agenda and at which were present observers from the United States, the United Kingdom, and Norway who had bonded in a "troika" that had emerged from a London lunch in 2000 as a core group to provide strong leadership for the rambling discussions of the Friends of the IGAD.

By 2002 both the government of Sudan and the SPLM/A had more reason to be conciliatory and willing to compromise than at any time in the previous twenty years. The 9/11 hijackings that had destroyed the World Trade Center may have transformed US foreign policy, but they also had a major impact on Khartoum. After 9/11 Sudan hoped to normalize relations with the United States by offering cooperation against international terrorism and peace in the South. Despite the doubling of the military budget for modern weaponry, the SPAF and the PDF had yet to claim a significant victory over the SPLA. Moreover, their conduct of the war had produced an increasing volume of international condemnation for targeting relief centers, and women and children desperately seeking humanitarian food aid banned by the government. Instead of victories, the number of body bags from southern Sudan had escalated, and at the same time the number of eager recruits had drastically declined. Finally, the diversion of oil revenues into military expenditure simply exacerbated the perennial economic problems that had bedeviled Sudan since the Numayri years. Although the specter of past food shortages had all but disappeared, prices were high and discontent was running deep. Unemployment among university graduates who had completed their military service was nearly 70 percent, small business firms were unable to secure loans, medical services were expensive and only for the rich, civil servants were still not regularly paid, pensions had disappeared, and schools closed when unpaid teachers took other jobs. Budgets were never balanced, and so the debt relentlessly expanded to $21 billion in 2002. Many members in the NCP now began to accept peace as the best possible solution to resolve or at least ameliorate Sudan's socio-economic problems.

John Garang had his own equally compelling reasons for consummating that elusive peace. His reconciliation with Riek Machar in January 2002 and with Lam Akol in 2003 effectively ended ten years of internal civil war and fratricidal strife between Dinka and Nuer, which greatly strengthened the

SPLM at the bargaining table. Moreover, by 2002 the SPLA had evolved into an effective fighting force that consistently inflicted severe defeats on the SPAF and the PDF. He also understood that oil revenues would not immediately turn the tide of war in favor of the North, but in the long run they would make the SPLA increasingly vulnerable and revive the discarded notion that a military solution could be achieved. Finally, Garang was acutely aware that his people were weary of war; the southern Sudanese longed for peace. If he could deliver an acceptable solution it would guarantee his authority in the South, solidify his image as a national leader in the North, and ensure his memorial as the founder of the new, secular, democratic and united Sudan.

General Sumbeiywo convened a second conference at Machakos on 18 June 2002 at which he insisted that discussion must now be sustained within a discrete timeline, unlike previous IGAD meetings, which had been characterized by endless discursive dialogue. Moreover, Sumbeiywo was now strongly supported by envoys from Eritrea, Ethiopia, and Uganda, and by international observers from the troika and Italy. After a month of intense negotiations the Machakos Conference ended on 20 July 2002 with a protocol signed by Ghazi Salahuddin Atabani, who had conveyed Khartoum's rejection of the DoP in 1994, and by Salva Kiir on behalf of the SPLM/A, and witnessed by Sumbeiywo. It was a landmark agreement, a dramatic breakthrough in what many had regarded as an intractable and irreconcilable confrontation of radically different views. Essentially, the protocol was a grand compromise by which the North agreed to self-determination for the South in return for acceptance that *shari'a* would be the source of legislation in the North. The right to self-determination would be settled by a referendum after a six-year transition period, by which the Islamist government committed itself to the possibility of an independent southern Sudan. Critics argued that there was nothing new in this concession. The government had acknowledged the right to self-determination of the South in 1994, 1997, and 1998, but on each of those occasions Khartoum had unilaterally conceded that principle only after pressure from the military and not because of direct negotiations in which the two belligerent parties agreed on a protocol with very precise language witnessed by international observers. The protocol alluded to *shari'a* as the source of legislation in the North but was very clear that the source of legislation in the South would be by "popular consensus." The real significance of this difference was that the North had abandoned its historical Islamization of the South by *shari'a*, while the South renounced its commitment to a secular Sudan.

The Machakos protocol dramatically reinvigorated the IGAD peace process and established a momentum for peace that had hitherto been absent from negotiations. Despite the exuberance at the signing the more somber members realized that the hard core in the NCP, religious scholars, and Islamist army officers were strongly opposed to the protocol. The southern response was much more positive. Many regarded the right to self-determination as just another logical step toward independence. Some of the SPLA field commanders were concerned that Abyei, the Nuba Mountains, and the southern Blue Nile had been relegated to the periphery of SPLM priorities. Others were critical that there were many ethnic and political groups, including the NDA, that had been excluded from the Machakos negotiations but that demanded the right and continued their agitation to be present and represented in any future negotiations for a comprehensive peace agreement at Naivasha, Kenya (see pp. 267–8). Their continued agitation only hardened the resolution of both the government and the SPLM to exclude their northern and southern rivals from the tortuous negotiations and was undoubtedly a major reason for their success.

At the time few realized that another long, agonizing thirty months would pass before the Machakos protocol was transformed into the CPA signed on 9 January 2005. What had transpired to prolong the negotiations? The international observers used their diplomatic skills to keep the Sudanese negotiators at the bargaining table, but they had little influence on the pace of the deliberations and even less on the terms. Moreover, the dirty details were complex, contentious, and emotional for some of the negotiators, which clouded their judgement. Finally, there was the eruption of the impending disaster in Darfur in February 2003, which created confusion among the international community and compromised the government just as the international monitors were organizing their teams in the Nuba Mountains and the US Congress was passing the Sudan Peace Act (see pp. 241–3).

The JMM and JMC in the Nuba Mountains began operations in March 2002 under the command of Norwegian Brigadier-General Jan Erik Wilhelmsen. Their mission was regarded as a great success, for there were no violations of the cease-fire, which enabled 150,000 Nuba IDPs to return and humanitarian NGOs to resume their assistance programs. The CPMT, monitoring assaults on southern civilians by the SPAF, PDF, and their militias, however, was another matter. The CPMT began operations in September 2002 but was staffed by former members of US special forces employed by private security firms with little knowledge of Sudan and less of the southern Sudanese, who regarded their mission strictly as military monitoring with little concern for establishing local contacts, gathering information, or mapping. Its members successfully identified government abuse of human rights and the continuation of government efforts to destabilize the South, but it simply did not have sufficient personnel or experience to do little more than write reports.

After the SPLA captured the strategic town of Torit in October 2002, the IGAD brokered a cease-fire and a Memorandum of Understanding (MoU) on the Danforth model in December 2002 for a brief "period of tranquility" that collapsed in February 2003 when fierce firefights between government militias and the SPLA erupted again in the West Nile oil fields. The IGAD intervened this time, however, to enforce the MoU by the establishment of a Verification and Monitoring Team (VMT), the effectiveness of which was compromised by an ill-defined relationship with the CPMT, producing a host of internal, often petty, controversies over accountability that compromised cooperation. Moreover, the VMT was under the personal command of General Sumbeiywo, who was completely absorbed in the peace process, and the IGAD secretariat had no experience, equipment, or personnel to oversee a mission in the field. The ensuing confusion inhibited contributions from donors, keeping the VMT strapped for funds, personnel, and logistical support. The limitations of the VMT became embarrassingly visible when Lam Akol defected to the SPLM/A in October 2003, which precipitated fierce fighting between Lam's SPLM/A and a pro-government rump SPLM/A-United in a civil war during which scores of villages were destroyed and tens of thousands of Shilluk displaced. It was not until April 2004 that the VMT was finally cleared to conduct its own investigations, but this was too little too late, for the damage and loss of lives had been done.

If the deployment of foreign monitors had mixed results, the impact of the Sudan Peace Act was more symbolic than substantial. Signed by President Bush on 21 October 2002, the law had no provisions for specific sanctions against foreign oil companies or other foreign companies that were operating in Sudan and raising funds in US capital markets. The president was obliged to render a report every six months to Congress as to whether *both* parties were negotiating in good faith in an "internationally sanctioned peace process," but he was more concerned that Congress was using the Sudan Peace Act as a constraint on his presidential authority in foreign affairs. Moreover, the types of sanctions the administration could use were of little threat to the Islamist government of Sudan. Loans from the IMF and World Bank had been blocked by the US Treasury for many years, and to use the Sudan Peace Act to impose sanctions appeared quite incompatible with the eagerness of the administration to enlist Sudan in the war on terror.

After the heady atmosphere at Machakos had dissipated, a cloud of reality settled over the participants: the protocol had not addressed the three critical issues of power-sharing, wealth-sharing, and security. Relations between the Sudan government and the autonomous Regional Southern Sudan in the 1970s had been littered with agreements dishonored by Khartoum, which the southerners bitterly remembered and the SPLM/A were determined not to repeat by insisting on precise wording and unalterable safeguards in any agreement. Such specific wording was not in the northern Sudanese political tradition, according to which agreements should be designed so that the language allows for flexibility and subtle change for room to maneuver. Moreover, negotiations after Machakos were conducted by 'Ali 'Uthman Muhammad Taha, the first vice-president, Mustafa Isma'il, the foreign minister, and his deputy, Mutrif Sadiq, none of whom had been consulted before the Machakos protocol was signed. Meanwhile, John Garang was surrounded by his legislative council, many of whom were closet separatists, and most of his field commanders were certainly not fighting for a unified Sudan.

The first post-Machakos negotiations opened under the firm hand of General Sumbeiywo on 14 October 2002 and were adjourned a month later, on 18 November, having reached agreement on the general principles for power-sharing in government and on elections during the interim period. Negotiations resumed after Ramadan on 23 January 2003, and for the first time negotiators met face to face for discussions, having hitherto relied on the clumsy process of passing proposals to the other side via mediators. This now enabled the delegations to subdivide into mixed working groups. When the negotiators adjourned once again in early February 2003 two additional documents on power and wealth-sharing had been signed. The next round of talks began on 8 April 2003 at which General Sumbeiywo introduced a new format to accelerate the pace of negotiations by involving the top leadership to break deadlocks at the bargaining table and by introducing a "compromise plan" as a basis for discussion at the opening of the sixth round of talks on 6 July 2003 at Nakuru. The SPLM/A readily accepted Sumbeiywo's "compromise plan," but the government delegation appeared astonished and vehemently rejected his draft. They denounced Sumbeiywo's "plan" as hopelessly flawed in favor of the SPLM/A; Bashir swore the IGAD mediators could "go to hell" and bitterly complained that the concessions to the southerners were all aimed at dissolving the unity of Sudan. He was most upset about the provisions regarding the national capital and the power-sharing document that strengthened the authority of the regional southern government at the expense of the powers of the president. Nothing was more sensitive to Bashir than any attempt to circumscribe his presidential powers, as Hasan al-Turabi had learned to his regret in 1999, and he was able to stall the negotiations until the Nakuru document was quietly set aside.

Where, indeed, was the road map to unity? This was as much an imponderable conundrum for Garang as for Bashir. Garang had sought to resolve his search for unity in diversity by his scheme for co-federation that he introduced in 1992 to placate the separatists while retaining a veneer of unity. This convoluted proposal had never found many supporters. It required the SPLM/A to argue that unity would be sustained not by some complicated wizardry of political science but by the resolution of southern grievances, which was a price the Islamist government was unwilling to pay. Many members of the NCP of every persuasion strangely and unnecessarily feared that too many concessions would lose their constituency to Turabi's rump PNC or the impotent opposition parties in the NDA. The Islamist government had dismissed Sambeiywo's Nakuru document as simply a charter for separation, and Bashir hoped to terminate negotiations, only to discover he could not. The SPAF was on the defensive in Darfur, there was little enthusiasm among the people and politicians in Khartoum to end the peace process, and even Egypt and the Arab League were loathe to abandon the IGAD, which had the overwhelming support of the international community.

The talks resumed in mid-August 2003 in Nanyuki but were immediately deadlocked on the SPLM/A insistence that the Nakuru document be the basis for negotiations; the government refused. In order to break the impasse Kalonzo Musyoka, foreign minister of Kenya, suggested face-to-face discussions between the principals, to which 'Ali 'Uthman Muhammad Taha and John Garang readily agreed, to take place at the Simba Lodge on the shores of Lake Naivasha in early September 2003 free from any interference from mediators, extremists, or meddlesome foreigners. As their intimate discussions progressed, as so often happens in these situations, the two adversaries began to build a bond of trust that transcended hitherto intractable demands and improbable propositions. Without consulting their advisers or mediators, they fixed the schedule for their own uninterrupted meetings. Western observers no longer attended the talks, but they remained in constant contact and monitored proposals, gossip, and rumor as to the progress of the discussions. In October 2003 Secretary of State Colin Powell visited the Simba Lodge to encourage both Taha and

Garang to finalize a settlement, but the role of the international community, including the "troika," has often been exaggerated by an ebullient Western press.

As the talks progressed the dark shadow of Darfur fell over Lake Naivasha. In February 2003 the long-smoldering discontent in the west erupted when the Sudan Liberation Movement (SLM) and the Justice and Equality Movement (JEM) declared their insurgency and overran police stations, army posts, and El Fasher airport in April, destroying military aircraft and capturing a Sudanese air force major-general. At the time there were probably no more than some 4,000 government troops in Darfur, for the overwhelming number of SPAF and PDF units were still concentrated on the southern and eastern fronts, which proved an incentive for the government to conclude a deal with the southerners in order to shift its armed forces to the west and frustrate any anticipated demands by both rebel movements in the east and now in the west to be included in the peace process. By mutual agreement the Naivasha peace process was quietly adjourned until January 2004. As the vision of a quick victory in Darfur evaporated, the insurgency became internationalized, heaping opprobrium and reprobation on Khartoum, which made it all the more essential to conclude a settlement with the SPLM/A at Naivasha before the Sudan government lost its remaining credibility with the international community as peacemakers. At the end of May 2004 the protocols were signed regarding power-sharing and the future arrangements for the Nuba Mountains, Abyei, and the southern Blue Nile, which had been the last remaining political stumbling-blocks, but in July 2004 the government baulked. Its delegation at Naivasha rejected IGAD efforts to conclude the implementation modalities to accompany the six signed protocols, for there were unwarranted concerns in Khartoum, more rumor than fact, that international sanctions imposed for atrocities in Darfur could precipitate the collapse of the Islamist regime.

When the UN Security Council at an unusual special session in Nairobi on 18–19 November 2004 conspicuously failed to condemn the Sudan government for non-compliance with its earlier demands concerning Darfur, its members emphasized the need for the Sudan government to finalize the IGAD negotiations. This intervention was crucial. Both the SPLM/A and the government committed themselves to peace by the New Year, and by then all the protocols and memoranda of understanding for implementation had been signed. The CPA was a complex document dealing with security, wealth-sharing, and power-sharing, with annexes and modalities that included the Machakos Protocol signed on 20 July 2002, the Agreement on

Security Arrangements of 25 September 2003, the Agreement on Wealth-Sharing of 7 January 2004, and the Protocols on the Resolution of the Conflict in Southern Kordofan, the Blue Nile, and Abyei, and the Protocol on Power-Sharing, all of which were signed on 26 May 2004. In addition there were two annexes signed on 31 December 2004 that included detailed modalities for implementation by which the two combatants declared a permanent cease-fire.

Security was the most important issue and the first to be settled: both the North and South were to maintain separate armed forces, the 91,000 northern troops in the South were to be withdrawn within two and a half years, and the SPLA was to retire its forces from the North within the next eight months. The protocol also included integrated units composed of 21,000 men, half of whom would be SPAF, the other half SPLA, to be established during the six-year interim period after which, if the South decided not to secede, both sides were to unify into a 39,000-strong force. John Garang and the SPLM/A had been acutely aware that the great flaw in the Addis Ababa Agreement of 1972 had been the concession by Joseph Lagu and the SSLM over integrated units without keeping a separate southern armed force to defend the Addis Ababa Agreement when it was unilaterally abrogated, which forced John Garang to start from scratch to forge a new effective fighting force in 1983.

The thorny question of wealth-sharing, principally oil, was resolved by evenly dividing its revenues between the Khartoum government and the interim government in southern Sudan. Power-sharing was much more complicated. During a six-year interim period southern Sudan would be governed by the autonomous Government of South Sudan (GoSS), at the end of which time a referendum would be held, in 2011, supervised by international monitors. In it the southern Sudanese would decide either to remain an autonomous province in a unified Sudan or to become an independent republic. Until that time the central transitional government was divided 70 to 30 percent between the Sudan government and the GoSS, while the personnel for administration and governance in the contentious areas of the Nuba Mountains, Abyei, and the Blue Nile was split 55 to 45 percent. The position of 'Umar Hasan Ahmad al-Bashir as head of state was confirmed, but John Garang would serve as first vice-president, while 'Ali 'Uthman Muhammad Taha was relegated to second vice-president in a transitional government of national unity. The intractable question of *shari'a*, the rock upon which so many earlier ships of peace had foundered, would be applicable in the North, but the constitution would be amended so that non-Muslims throughout Sudan would not be adjudicated by *shari'a*

Figure 24 Sudan's First Vice-President 'Ali 'Uthman Muhammad Taha (left) and Sudan People's Liberation Movement/Army (SPLM/A) Chairman Dr. John Garang (right) share a joke before the signing of the Comprehensive Peace Agreement in Nairobi, 9 January 2005.

laws. The status of *shari'a* in the capital had long been a contentious issue, which had doomed the Nakuru document, for if the central government was composed of 30 percent southerner officials many of them would presumably be liable to *shari'a*, not to mention nearly 4 million southern Sudanese IDPs surrounding the city. In order for this seemingly petty and peripheral issue not to disrupt the possibility of a settlement, it was simply postponed and left to the elected national assembly.

There were numerous other articles in the CPA that were as much symbolic as substantive. A dual banking system was created, the GoSS having its own bank and currency, the GoSS pound, the North retaining its dinar. The implementation of this dual system was one of the most vague in the CPA, for it was never made clear whether the Bank of the GoSS was to be separate or be a branch of the Central Bank of Sudan, which would undoubtedly lead to future difficulties. There were other symbolic gestures, however, that meant a lot to the southerners. The GoSS would fly its own flag, sing its own anthem, and have its own insignias and seals.

On 9 January 2005 at a grand celebration in Nairobi the Comprehensive Peace Agreement was signed by John Garang de Mabior for the SPLM/A and 'Ali 'Uthman Muhammad Taha for the government of Sudan, and witnessed by the president of Kenya and US Secretary of State Colin Powell, among other distinguished guests. Precisely five months later, on 8 July, John Garang, accompanied by his wife, Rebecca de Mabior, and his ministers, made a triumphal return to Khartoum to be sworn in as Sudan's first vice-president of its new transitional government of national unity. He was greeted at the airport and through the streets of the capital by over 1 million northern and southern Sudanese there to welcome Dr. John as leader and visionary, and the symbolic beginning of a new and glorious era. Three weeks later John Garang was killed, on 30 July 2005. He was returning from a meeting at Rwakitura with his old friend, President Yoweri Museveni, in the presidential Mi-172 helicopter from Entebbe, when it crashed just after dark in the rugged Didinga Mountains fifteen minutes from Garang's headquarters at Chukudum. He was buried on a small hill outside Juba four days later amid the greatest outpouring of grief ever witnessed in modern Sudan. His sudden and mysterious death at the pinnacle of his greatest triumph instantly spawned a host of conspiracy theories, and thousands took to the streets in anger, frustration, and grief in all the major towns. Forty-five people died in the riots that swept through Omdurman and Khartoum. John Garang had many enemies, but an international team of experts found no evidence of sabotage and ample room for pilot error in the dark mountains and deep ravines of the Didinga Mountains. He will be remembered not for his intolerance of dissent, his imperious and aloof manner, his micro-management of affairs, and his incapacity to delegate authority, all of which will soon be forgiven or forgotten, blown away by the wind, for he was the only Sudanese leader in the history of modern Sudan who for twenty-five years consistently advocated, plotted, and fought for a democratic, secular, and unified Sudan. Whether he would have accomplished that objective will never be known, but he will be remembered for that vision as a national leader for all Sudanese.

CHAPTER 10

Disaster in Darfur

DARFUR IN HISTORICAL PERSPECTIVE

Although the crisis in Darfur has generated more commentary, reports, and media coverage in recent years than the twenty violent years of the second Sudan civil war in the South, few have understood that the disaster is not some spontaneous eruption against neglect, misgovernment, and racism, but the latest episode in the forty-year tragic conflict for control of the great basin of Lake Chad. Geographically, Darfur is the eastern region of that basin and not, as many have assumed, a part of the Nile valley. Although the watershed between the two basins is almost indiscernible, meandering northward from the Congo–Nile Divide along the administrative boundary between Darfur and Kordofan, the Sudanic plain of Darfur tilts gently to the west, broken by the Jabal Marra massif, an extinct volcano rising nearly 10,000 feet above the plain. This westward geographical orientation has shaped the pre-colonial history of Darfur, the "Land of the Fur," and Turra in northern Jabal Marra is still venerated as their ancestral home.

Some time in the mid-seventeenth century Sulayman Solong founded the Keira dynasty and transformed the Fur tribal kingdom into a multi-ethnic sultanate. In the traditions, he was a mighty warrior who carved out an empire by conquering the Masalit, Mararit, Zaghawa, Birgid, and Tunjur, leaving behind the ruins of his spacious palace at Turra. His expansion westward provoked the sultan of Wadai who, like Sulayman, had forged a plethora of petty chieftaincies into a powerful state until his expansion eastward was checked by Sulayman and his Fur army. Sulayman's victory, however, was only the first of numerous wars between Darfur and Wadai in the eighteenth century for control of the borderlands. When the Keira sultans were strong, they conquered Wadai; when weak, they retired into the defensive fortress of Jabal Marra. Sulayman's successors ruled as divine kings over a Fur state administered by Fur officials that embraced an increasing number of different ethnic groups administered in turn through

Map 14 Darfur

their traditional authorities. During the eighteenth century the Fur sultans extended the kingdom to the west and north, where the Zaghawa, after stiff resistance, submitted.

After a dynastic succession struggle in the late 1750s Muhammad Tayrab ibn Ahmad Bukr (1752–87) emerged as the new sultan. He subdued the powerful nobility, centralized the state, and made peace with Wadai which lasted, except for the usual border skirmishes, for another century. Sultan Tayrab, the greatest of the Keira sultans, inherited a multi-ethnic state in which the Fur played a less dominant role, having to share the powerful offices of state with non-Fur. He also moved his *fashirs* down onto the plains east of the mountain massif, which reoriented the center of government eastward toward Kordofan. Here the Fur sultans were continuously threatened by the Musabba'at who had been driven from Jabal Marra into

Kordofan by Sulayman and thereafter had worked assiduously to over-throw the Keira dynasty. When the Musabba'at ruler, Hashim ibn 'Isawi, assembled a large mercenary army in 1782 to invade Darfur, Tayrab and the Fur host crushed Hashim and his army and occupied Kordofan, placing it under Keira rule for another forty years.

Another succession struggle followed the death of Sultan Tayrab in which 'Abd al-Rahman was accepted as their sultan by the Keira nobility and the army about 1792. He died ten years later, but not before centralizing the kingdom, with a permanent capital at El Fasher northeast of Jabal Marra in which the warrior sultans were succeeded by seventy-five years of weak sultans, palace intrigue, and the growth of Islam. The stable Fur occupation of Kordofan during the early nineteenth century provided security for wandering Muslim holy men, *fakis*, from the Nile valley to reach Darfur, hitherto regarded as a remote and barbarous land. They were a diverse group composed of a few learned *'ulama'* from al-Azhar, but many were simple, semi-literate *fakis* who were more rainmakers and spiritualists than holy men. They would settle, intermarry, and become integrated members of the village community. The sultans encouraged *faki* immigration by issuing charters of land grants, granting exemption from customary taxes (*jah*) and military service, and building mosques, particularly around El Fasher. In return, the *fakis* were expected to use their writing and diplomatic skills, learned in the larger world, for the sultan, which created over time a new cadre of loyal bureaucrats free from clan and tribal obligations.

The spread of Islam and Arabic in Darfur was slow, sporadic, and differed significantly from that which evolved in the Nile valley. The acceptance of Islam and Arabic at court made little impression on the rural Fur. More-over, the Islam practiced by the Fur and Masalit had adopted many African syncretic rituals in their observance that distinguished the indigenous Islam of western Darfur from the more orthodox Islam of the Darfuris east of Jabal Marra practiced by the Birgid, Mima, and Berti which has tradition-ally marked the divide between Islamization and Arabization in Darfur. By the end of the twentieth century the Nilo-Saharan languages of those Darfuris living on the eastern plains have yet to be replaced by Arabic. This process of acculturation was slow but steady until it was accelerated by the military conquests of Muhammad 'Ali in 1821 and again fifty years later by the Ja'ali slave trader and freebooter, al-Zubayr Rahma Mansur, whose mercenaries, equipped with Remington repeating rifles, decimated the Fur army, killing the sultan; he incorporated the independent sultanate, which had been ruled by ten Fur sultans over 200 years, into the Turco-Egyptian empire on the Nile, until it in turn was swept away by the religious rebellion of Muhammad Ahmad al-Mahdi in 1885. In the full flush of his great victory, however, the Mahdi had unexpectedly died on 22 June 1885. He was succeeded by his Khalifa 'Abdallahi Muhammad Turshain, a Ta'a'ishi Baqqara from southern Darfur. Between 1885 and 1892 the Khalifa had to combat plots from within and rebellions from without intended to overthrow him, all of which he ruthlessly suppressed. By 1892 the Khalifa still ruled at Omdurman, surrounded by his kinsmen, the Ta'a'isha, who were secure in their autocracy and quite able and prepared to prevent any Sudanese challenge to his authority. What the Khalifa had not foreseen, and perhaps could not have done, was the invasion by a powerful Anglo-Egyptian army determined to destory the Mahdist State and secure the waters of the Nile for Britain and Egypt. Their victory was won on the plains of Karari outside Omdurman on 2 September 1898 through the triumphant technology of British military firepower (see pp. 30–1). The Mahdist State collapsed, and the titular Fur sultan of Darfur, 'Ali Dinar Zakariya Muhammad al-Fadl, who had been confined and watched by the Khalifa's agents, gathered together a few followers and headed west to regain his throne (see pp. 35–6). He captured El Fasher from its Mahdist garrison, defeated a rival claimant to the sultanate, and seized the throne. In 1900 the Anglo-Egyptian Sudan government, which was effectively British, officially recognized him as the sovereign of the independent Fur sultanate of Darfur in return for a nominal symbolic tribute. 'Ali Dinar organized his satrapy in an efficient, if barbarous, manner and crushed all opposition, except the Rizayqat Baqqara. When the Rizayqat refused to pay him tribute in 1901, 'Ali Dinar sent Tirab Sulayman, commander of his personal bodyguard, to punish them, but his campaign was indecisive. Thereafter the sultan was preoccupied with incursions by the French on his western frontier, and it was not until 1913 that 'Ali Dinar was able to return to his old feud with Shaykh Musa Maddibu, the able leader of the southern Rizayqat, demanding tribute, acknowledgement of himself as suzerain, and the surrender of Darfuri dissenters who had taken refuge in Dar Rizayqat. When Musa refused in October 1913, the Fur army of some 6,000 men, half of whom were cavalry, advanced into Dar Rizayqat burning and looting until confronted by the Rizayqat forces at Tumburko. Here the two armies fought for five days with, for African warfare, very heavy losses, but on 1 November the Fur retreated, pursued by their enemy, a victory vividly remembered in the folklore of the Rizayqat. Under implacable pressure from Sir Slatin Pasha, the former Governor of Darfur in the Turkiya, prisoner of the Khalifa during the Mahdiya, and now the powerful inspector-general of the Condominium government in Sudan, Musa Madibbu, *shaykh* of the Rizayqat, submitted to the authority of 'Ali Dinar as sultan of all Darfur. Musa Madibbu had little choice. Dar Rizayqat had been ravaged and only saved from total extinction by the unexpected victory at Tumburko, and he needed a friendly and powerful ally in Khartoum to ensure his authority as *shaykh* and the integrity of the Rizayqat Baqqara.

After the outbreak of the First World War in 1914 the British rulers in Khartoum began to have second thoughts about 'Ali Dinar. The Sudan government had been no help in 'Ali Dinar's efforts to stem the French advance into his tributary states on his western frontier, and he had become increasingly truculent toward the Sudan government, whose British rulers were now the allies of his French enemies. When the Caliph of Islam and his Ottoman empire joined the war on the side of Germany and the Christian British in Egypt deposed the Turkish Khedive, his ill-temper turned to open belligerence. He joined the *jihad* against the European *kafirin* and in 1916 sent large reinforcements to his border posts on the Kordofan frontier, which provided the British with the necessary pretext for a campaign against him. An Anglo-Egyptian flying column of 2,500 men defeated the Fur army, captured El Fasher, and occupied the sultan's sumptuous palace of shady gardens, fish ponds, and colonnaded arcades on 23 May 1916. Five months later "Huddleston's Horse," a hundred-strong, surprised and killed 'Ali Dinar in his camp at Giubu. A boundary agreement was concluded with the French in 1919 whereby Dar Masalit remained part of Darfur, but the border sultanates of Dar Tama, Dar Sila, and Dar Qimr, which had previously acknowledged 'Ali Dinar as their sovereign, became part of French Equatorial Africa.

Having conquered this vast unwanted addition to Anglo-Egyptian Sudan, British administrative policy throughout the Condominium was to keep the peace in Darfur at minimal cost. This policy was studiously executed by only a handful of British political officers, who governed Darfur by Native Administration, or Indirect Rule, whereby the authority of the traditional *shaykh, nazir, 'umda,* and *shartais* was recognized so long as they behaved themselves, settled intertribal disputes, and maintained a semblance of law and order. The British refrained from any obtrusive taxation, exacting only a symbolic tribute. Egyptian administrative officials, whom the British regarded as troublemakers, were purposely excluded, and those left behind from the Turkiya were eliminated from the administration. Inspired by the preaching of the Mahdi, the Baqqara of Darfur, following their defeat in 1898, returned to fertilize a blossoming Mahdism that became deeply rooted among the Darfuris. At first, outbursts of Islamic extremism by exuberant Ansar were few, isolated, and easily contained, until the uprising at Nyala in September 1921, when some 6,000 Ansar led by a Masalit *faki* nearly captured Nyala post, killing two British officers and forty-one Sudanese soldiers before being forced to retreat, leaving behind some 600 dead. Peace in southern Darfur was not fully restored until the end of the year by a powerful government patrol that inflicted heavy losses on the Baqqara and circumscribed the spread of Mahdism.

The greatest problem for Native Administration in Darfur was its failure to accommodate any form of modernization. By 1935 Darfur had one elementary school and two sub-grade "literary schools," and the total budget for education was only £E1,200 a year for a school-age population of 500,000. The director of education's request for £E55 to introduce "some education" was rejected. Among many British officials there was great fear of the "half-educated man," those with a smattering of education who became a detribalized, discontented class of semi-literate troublemakers. Consequently, in Darfur the government-sponsored *kuttabs*, for teaching literacy, were gradually replaced by *khalwas*, where the curriculum consisted mostly of rote-learning the Qur'an under the instruction of a semi-literate *faki*. All the few available places in the remaining government *kuttabs* were reserved for the sons of a *shaykh, nazir*, or *shartai* who would inherit the tribal administration of their fathers. In June 1938 the British Governor of Darfur could boast: "We . . . have been able to limit education to the sons of Chiefs and native administration personnel and can confidently look forward to keeping the ruling classes at the top of the elementary tree for many years to come." Public health, like education, was also contained by benign neglect. Darfur was the only province in Sudan without the popular maternity clinics. Epidemics were endemic, disease often being carried by the pilgrims from West Africa; smallpox, cerebrospinal meningitis, relapsing fever, and kala-azar (leishmaniasis) were common.

When the British departed from Sudan at independence in 1956 they left behind in Darfur a record of a conspicuous lack of interest and studied indifference. Not one new boys' school had been opened since 1932. Until 1947 there were no provincial judges or education officers, and never a provincial agriculturist, who were common elsewhere throughout Sudan. Native Administration was gradually being strangled by aging, incompetent, and often drunk traditional leaders concerned more with their own personal self-interest than their subjects'. During the forty years of British rule in Darfur there were never more than a dozen British political officers in any year to oversee the administration of the traditional leaders in a region the size of France. During the last 200 years no government, Turk,

Mahdist, British, and most certainly Sudanese, has ever made any pretense of governing Darfur, the administration of which was either ephemeral or an illusion in the hands of the traditional *shaykh, nazir, shartai,* or *'umda*.

On 1 September 1969, three months after Colonel Ja'afar Numayri had seized the government of Sudan, Colonel Mu'ammar Qadhafi engineered a military coup d'état to depose King Idris of Libya. Qadhafi proclaimed himself a reformer for "Libya, Arabism, and Islam" in the progressive path of the "Freedom, Socialism, and Unity" preached by the Free Officer Movement of Gamal 'Abd al-Nasser. He was obsessed by geopolitics and dreamed of a Greater Arab Libyan "Islamic State of the Sahara," following in the footsteps of the Muslim merchants and *fakis* to continue their historic mission on the frontiers of Islam. He first sought, however, to unify Libya, Egypt, and Sudan into a single state with his Tripoli Charter but was rebuffed by both Presidents Sadat and Numayri, despite the fact he had rushed to Numayri's assistance when he had been threatened by a communist coup in July 1971. He never forgave Ja'afar Numaryi for this humiliating rejection, and thereafter directed his energies and great wealth toward building an Arab Libyan Sudanic empire in which Darfur was to play a strategic role.

Qadhafi became the patron of the Front de Libération Nationale du Tchad (FROLINAT) and the host of Sadiq al-Mahdi. He supplied arms and training camps at al-Judda'im and Ma'ra in southern Libya to train over 2,000 of Sadiq's Baqqara Ansar from Darfur and units from Qadhafi's mercenary Islamic Legion (*failaka al-islamabad*) in preparation for Sadiq's attempt to overthrow Numayri in July 1976. After Sadiq's coup had been suppressed at considerable cost, Qadhafi concentrated his energies on building his presence in Darfur. The Forces Armées du Nord (FAN) of Hissène Habré controlled most of western Darfur where he and some 10,000 Zaghawa and Bedeiyat had sought safe haven after their defeat in 1980 by the Chad National Army. Northern and central Darfur were now awash with automatic weapons, the favored Kalashnikovs, passed out to Sadiq's followers, which precipitated a plethora of raids and counter-raids between African Fur farmers and Arab Rizayqat herdsmen in which the Sudan government forces were powerless to intervene. During 1981 the United States continued its weapons shipments to Numayri in the naïve expectation that he would somehow contain the 5,000-man Islamic Legion backed by the Libyan army which now controlled all of Darfur north of Kutum, the administrative center of northern Darfur.

After the overthrow of Numayri in April 1985 the TMC restored friendly relations with Qadhafi in return for oil, and a Libyan–Sudanese commission was promptly established to explore closer ties between Khartoum and

Tripoli. The TMC, however, refused Qadhafi's demands to give his Islamic Legion a free hand in Darfur, although it did not object when some 200 Libyan agents established a very active and visible presence in the capital. After the elections in April 1986 Sadiq sought to transform his former warm relationship with his patron into something more tangible but with little success, leaving Hissène Habré, now president of Chad, to mobilize his old FAN to be re-equipped by the French and renamed the Forces Armées Nationales Tchadiennes (FANT) to drive the Islamic Legionnaires back through northern Darfur to Kutum, before advancing another 100 miles to the Wadi Huwar, when their ammunition and supplies were exhausted and they withdrew to Chad. During the ensuing months the Islamic Legion, now joined by Acheikh ibn Umar's Vulcan Force, were resupplied and re-equipped by Qadhafi to counter-attack across the border north of Arde in November 1987 with the blessing of Sadiq al-Mahdi. It was during these same months that Hasan al-Turabi, whose NIF had won 51 seats in the 1986 elections, began to organize the Baqqara Arabs into a "Human Belt" of Arab Islamists across southern Kordofan and Darfur to complement the emergence of the Arab Gathering (*failaka al-islamiyya*).

On 5 October 1987 the Arab Gathering came out of the closet by publishing an open letter to Sadiq al-Mahdi in *al-Ayam* signed by twenty-three prominent Darfuri Arabs asserting the claims of the Arab supremacists and threatening a "catastrophe" if "the neglect of the Arab race continues." In their later publications they were less circumspect, bluntly asserting that they intended "to kill all *zurqa*. Darfur is now Dar al-Arab."

Three months later, on 1 January 1988, President Hissène Habré of Chad devoted most of his New Year message to denouncing Qadhafi's control of northern and western Darfur. Acheikh's Vulcan Force had relocated to al-Geneina, and a steady flow of Libyan weapons from Ma'tan al-Sarra in the Aozou Strip in southern Libya poured into central Darfur for the Arab Gourane and the southern Rizayqat Baqqara, and as far south as Dar Fartit in the western Bahr al-Ghazal. This influx of arms was the most unsavory act by Qadhafi in his thirty years of war to control Chad and his efforts to destabilize Darfur. In order to defend themselves from the Arab–Libyan/Baqqara threat, the Fur immediately established their own Federal Army of Darfur, consisting of some 6,000 *jakab* Fur fighters armed by Chad with automatic weapons. In response Musa Madibbu, shaykh of the Rizayqat, appealed to Sadiq for more arms to supplement those coming from Libya, which General Burma Nasr swiftly provided. In autumn 1988 the conflict between Fur and Rizayqat, known as the "War of the Tribes," erupted, reviving a long-standing feud between them from the time of

Sultan Tayrab in the eighteenth century. The Fur Federal Army was crushed, the survivors slaughtered in what *al-Ayam* described as "genocide," none of which was reported in the international media.

The very visible military presence of Libyans in Darfur and the collapse of the Fur, whom the government could not protect, or did not wish to, caused considerable embarrassment in Khartoum that was compounded by the government's continuous denial of any Libyan presence. When that transparent prevarication could no longer be sustained, Sadiq lamely requested Qadhafi to withdraw his troops. He refused, and Sadiq's authority in Darfur virtually disappeared throughout the northern, western, and much of the central regions. The Constituent Assembly repeatedly demanded that the borders with Libya and Chad be sealed, but the government was powerless to close a frontier it did not control. Libyan delegations continued to arrive in Khartoum always pressing for a Libya–Sudan union, but Sadiq had become a bundle of indecision, using the excuse of Egyptian, Saudi, and US opposition to divert Qadhafi's insistence on an Arab alliance.

On 1 April 1989 Idriss Déby Itno, commander-in-chief of the FANT, attempted to overthrow President Hissène Habré. In the subsequent shoot-out at the presidential palace Déby and his Zaghawa guards were forced to flee, seeking safety in Darfur, where they were joined by other FANT units defecting from the Niger frontier and central Chad, and by 2,000 soldiers who had been guarding the capital. Sadiq personally flew to El Fasher to meet Déby and fly him to Tripoli. Qadhafi seized this opportunity to advance his influence in Darfur and ordered Déby to reorganize his troops, the Islamic Legion, and a host of unsavory mercenaries from Chad, mostly Zaghawa and the Abbala Arabs in Darfur, who flocked to Déby, bought by the generosity of Qadhafi's paymaster, Hassan Fadl. Déby settled in western Darfur and rebuilt his insurgency, known as the "1 April Movement" or more pretentiously the Movement Patriotique du Salut (Patriotic Salvation Movement, MPS). During the subsequent and most dismal months of Sadiq's stewardship the opposition in the Constituent Assembly vehemently criticized him for the failure of his government to defend Darfur, sarcastically announcing that he had created an "Independent Republic of Darfur."

In spring 1989 civil war erupted to fill the vacuum left by Sadiq's government. In May 3,000 Fur were "murdered" (i.e. exterminated) near Nyala; another 1,500 Fur were killed by the Bani Halba and Salamat Arab militias around Jabal Marra. Fur and Baqqara supported by Islamic Legionnaires fought a two-day battle in which the Fur suffered heavy losses from the superior firepower of the Baqqara Libyan weapons. In April Qadhafi had sent Sadiq another $4 million "to prepare for the invasion of Chad," and rebuilt the strategic Sudan army base at Saq al-Na'am in the Kabkabiya district of northern Darfur for the Islamic Legion. By May the fighting had spread from Jabal Marra into the southwest border region with Chad, where Libyan arms were distributed to hundreds of Bedeiyat and Zaghawa Chadian refugees to settle old scores with the Fur. After a week of fighting with losses on both sides the exhausted combatants reverted to the historic institution called *ajawiid muatamarat al-suhl*, the traditional conference by which disputes had been resolved in the past and whose decisions were immutable. The Baqqara chiefs boycotted the conference. No other gesture could have been a greater insult. No other symbol could convey the arrogance of those convinced of their superiority, on account of the firepower of their weaponry, over the Fur, whom they regarded as defeated. They believed negotiations unnecessary, for the dispute had been settled by force of arms in their favor. It was not, however, settled. Fighting between Baqqara and Fur immediately resumed with uncontrolled ferocity, and several hundred on either side were killed in a fierce firefight on 22 June 1989. Over 50,000 Fur sought refuge in Nyala. Sudanese officials were powerless to halt the fighting. The Governor defiantly declared he would consider an invasion from Chad a "hostile act" but remained helpless in El Fasher in late June 1989 when Habrè's FANT crossed the border once again to cut a 100-mile swath of destruction through western Darfur before retiring to Wadai.

On 30 June 1989 Brigadier 'Umar Hasan Ahmad al-Bashir overthrew Sadiq's impotent government and established the Islamist Revolutionary Command Council (RCC) to fulfill the pan-Arab Islamist Agenda of the NIF. He immediately turned to Qadhafi who, at last, hoped to see his vision of a pan-Arab union of Libya and Sudan. A Libyan–Sudan Joint Ministerial Committee was formed to negotiate the terms, and members of the RCC subsequently shuttled back and forth from Khartoum to Tripoli returning with arms, oil, and their official acceptance of a Libyan presence in Darfur. Brigadier al-Tijani al-Tahir, a devout Muslim, born near Kutum, and a regular guest at the Libyan embassy in Khartoum, was appointed "political supervisor" for Darfur. Although a Fur, he was not inclined to prefer his kinfolk in favor of his own personal interests. A regular commuter to Tripoli, he signed a treaty, originally proposed by Sadiq al-Mahdi in 1988, that gave Qadhafi and his Islamic Legion a preferred status in Darfur. Neither Tahir, who passionately hated Habrè's Toubou, nor his colleagues on the RCC had any intention of reducing their support for Qadhafi in Darfur and prepared to re-establish the historic Islamic Arab traditions of those who had ruled the *bilad al-sudan* for centuries.

On 16 October 1990 Hissène Habré launched another massive offensive to drive Qadhafi and his Islamic Legion once and for all from Darfur. "Operation Rezzou" cut another swath of destruction 120 miles to Kutum and a final confrontation with Déby's MPS and Qadhafi's Islamic Legion. Very heavy fighting swirled around Kutum for a week destroying hundreds of villages with many civilian casualties and very heavy losses for both the FANT and MPS, but especially the Islamic Legion, which was forced to retreat with their wounded to Libyan bases at Aponu and Maarten Bishalla. Having exhausted their ammunition and supplies the FANT retired once more into Wadai, but the defeat of Déby's MPS and the Islamic Legion had brought Qadhafi and the RCC closer together. In November he offered to pave the old caravan route from Kufra to El Fasher for an all-weather road to bind Darfur more closely to Tripoli than Khartoum, a project for which Brigadier Tahir proved an accommodating and enthusiastic advocate. In return, Bashir promised an "integrated region" consisting of Darfur in Sudan and Kufra in Libya and blandly signed the Libya–Sudan Integration Charter of April 1990. On paper at least Mu'ammar Qadhafi had achieved his twenty-year dream of a Libya–Sudan union first envisaged in his 1969 Tripoli Charter. Bashir needed Libyan cash, resources, and arms to bring the civil war in the South to a successful conclusion. There remained the ancient and troublesome Ansar in Darfur loyal to Sadiq al-Mahdi who needed to be contained. The recognition of Libyan influence in Darfur was the price Bashir was prepared to pay so long as the pact of unity produced Libyan oil to fuel the Sudanese economy and Libyan arms to resurrect an army that had degenerated under Numaryi into a "rabble in arms."

On the very same day in April 1990 that the Libya–Sudan Integration Charter was published in the Khartoum newspapers, Idriss Déby launched his reorganized and rearmed MPS across the frontier into Chad shielded by a huge *habub*. They overwhelmed the FANT border posts, inflicting heavy casualties and taking 1,000 prisoners. On 7 April Habré ordered a counter-attack on a 100-mile front, but Déby, given advance warning by Bashir, withdrew for safety deep into the interior, and the FANT once again occupied most of western Darfur, burning villages and displacing hundreds who fled seeking refuge. Qadhafi rushed reinforcements from Kufra accompanied by SU fighter-bombers. Arabs from Zalengei took advantage of the FANT invasion to resume their "long-standing feud" with the Fur in which several Arabs were killed, providing Bashir in turn with a pretext to have non-Arab dissidents – Fur, Masalit, and Meidob, and including over 100

Fur leaders – arrested and imprisoned in the execrable Shalla Prison south of El Fasher. In June another thirty "prominent" Fur were arrested, and there were reports of Sudanese government troops intervening to assist the Baqqara militia. In Darfur 'Ali Shimal, a prominent member of the NIF and a committed Muslim Brother with ties to the Arab Gathering, founded a People's Defense Force from which the Fur were purposely excluded. The Chadians and the French, however, had now lost all confidence in Hissène Habré, who had become notorious for his flagrant violation of human rights. His army was weary of war and short of ammunition, and when the French refused any further military assistance, Habré was doomed. In early November 2,000 of Déby's MPS crossed the border into Chad on a broad front; after a week of fierce fighting the FANT collapsed, and the MPS swept through Chad in their "technicals." On 2 December 1990 Idriss Déby entered N'Djamena as Habré fled into exile.

After the departure of Déby and his MPS from Darfur the Islamist junta in Khartoum, like Numayri in 1983–84, failed to respond to the famine of 1990–91. By 1991 shortages in western Darfur had driven thousands of refugees into Wadai seeking food. Many who remained quietly perished, but the RCC expressed little interest in the suffering of the westerners, and Islamist Arab officials from Khartoum, who were slowly returning to fill the vacuum left by the MPS, simply ignored the plight of the Darfuri Arab and non-Arab alike as the death toll mounted. Moreover, in N'Djamena and Khartoum Mu'ammar Qadhafi was regarded with growing disdain as a middle-aged Nasserite who represented a threadbare political ideology unredeemed by a Muslim theology acceptable to either Sunni or *sufi*. He had never been a *talib* of the nineteenth-century Islamic reformers or the Grand Sanussi of Libya, whose followers Qadhafi had ruthlessly suppressed. Unlike Hasan al-Turabi, the patron of the Islamist revolution in Sudan, he was unprepared to play, or incapable of playing, any significant intellectual or political role in shaping the destiny of Islam at the end of the twentieth century. When he warned Bashir in January 1991 that his Islamist advisers led by Turabi were taking Sudan down a dark and dangerous path in Darfur, he was politely ignored. Qadhafi was tired of war and increasingly alarmed by the return of radical Afghan-Arab *mujahidiin* seeking sanctuary in Sudan and slipping into Libya. The Afghan-Arabs, including Usama bin Ladin, had been warmly welcomed by the Islamists and Hasan al-Turabi, and the RCC and NIF were energetically building an Islamic theocratic state to prepare for the destabilization of secular Arab governments, particularly Qadhafi's neighbors, Tunisia and Algeria. Qadhafi responded by launching a ruthless persecution of Islamic fundamentalists in Libya, and his presence in Darfur was no longer welcomed by the RCC and NIF.

While Idriss Déby and Mu'ammar Qadhafi were preoccupied with the long-standing dispute over the Aozou Strip, the Islamist government of 'Umar Hasan al-Bashir relentlessly sought to reassert its control in Darfur. In August 1991 he appointed as Governor of Darfur the sinister Colonel al-Tayib Ibrahim Muhammad Khair, chief of Islamic security and known as *al-sjikka* (the iron bar), which he used to quell anti-Islamist street riots in Khartoum. *Al-sjikka* began the methodical suppression of the Fur but also of the Zaghawa, who were forcibly disarmed, and some 12,000 of them repatriated to their kinfolk in Chad by February 1992. In February 1994 the Minister for Federal Affairs and dedicated NIF Islamist, 'Ali al-Hajj, arbitrarily redrew the administrative district boundaries of Darfur into separate states. This seemingly innocuous administrative reshuffle to conform to the new program of federalism was deliberately designed, however, to promote the Arabization of Darfur by gerrymandering the hitherto ethnically homogeneous districts, so that the Fur would henceforth be a marginalized minority in each. The administrative officials of these new states, which now constituted the whole of Darfur, had been appointed without consultation, which was bitterly resented by Arab and non-Arab Darfuris alike. In their eagerness to promote Arabization these new officials were contemptuous of local customs, including the indigenous mechanisms for conflict resolution, the *ajawiid muatamarat al-suhl*, that were now replaced by the arbitrary judgments of riverine NIF Islamists from Khartoum with little knowledge of local customs and traditional institutions.

Having effectively immobilized any concerted Fur opposition, the Islamists next turned to the compact hierarchical Masalit in 1997. All the traditional Masalit chiefs, who wielded great influence in Dar Masalit, were stripped of their authority; some were imprisoned, others tortured. The fiercely independent Masalit prepared to retaliate by means of guerilla war, which erupted the following year, 1998, when the Arab Bani Husayn from Kabkabiya in North Darfur State began to move south much earlier than usual with their herds and flocks, which frequently trampled the crops of Masalit farmers. During the subsequent clashes several hundred Masalit were killed, over 100 villages were destroyed, and some 5,000 Masalit fled to Geneina as IDPs or to Chad as refugees. Despite a fragile agreement, in which £S9 million was levied on both sides as blood-money compensation, the fighting resumed in January 1999, when the Bani Husyan again arrived in Dar Masalit. The conflict, now fueled by revenge for the depredations of the previous year, turned into fierce firefights with significant casualties. Khartoum called the Masalit insurgents a "fifth column of the SPLA," sealed Dar Masalit, and unleashed the Arab militias. In 1999 these militias had yet to win the infamous sobriquet *janjawiid* that hitherto had long been a common term in Dar Masalit for bandits of any ethnicity operating from Chad. The Masalit were thoroughly crushed. Over 2,000 were killed, nearly 3,000 *tukls* burned, and large numbers of livestock looted. Fourteen Masalit leaders were sentenced to death by hastily contrived special courts; some 40,000 Masalit fled to refugee camps in Chad, where more than 100 were killed when Arab militias attacked the camps in a cross-border raid. The Masalit sulked in the ruins of their *dar*, swearing vengeance.

Throughout Darfur an ominous silence settled over the land as General 'Abdallah al-Safi al-Nur, an Abbala, influential in the Arab Gathering and an outspoken advocate of Arab supremacy, was appointed Governor of North Darfur State in 2000. His first orders were to collect all arms from the non-Arab police, the *zurqa*, who historically had composed nearly 80 percent of the police force in Darfur during and since the days of British rule. Having methodically neutralized the only legally armed force who could oppose Arabization, he handed over the weapons to Musa Hilal of the Um Jalul Abbala, the "Shaykh of the Swift and Fearsome Forces," actively recruiting 2,000 Chadian Arab and Baqqara for the nucleus of the *janjawiid* or *peshmerga*, as they were known in western Darfur. In that same year, the *Black Book* (*al-kitab al-aswad*) was published clandestinely in Khartoum by Darfuri militants in the capital. Ironically, there was little in the *Black Book* that had not already become common knowledge, but its publication shocked Sudanese society. The *Black Book* dared to expose that 80 percent of all government jobs from ministers to ministerial drivers during the fifty years of independent Sudan had been occupied by members of the *awlad al-bahr*, specifically the Danaqla, Shayqiyya, and Ja'aliyyin, from which the westerners from Kordofan and Darfur, the *awlad al-gharib*, had been systematically excluded in a long history of discrimination and marginalization by those Sudanese who sought to pretend they were pure "Arabs." To be sure, the *awlad al-gharib* were Muslims, but they were Muslims whose religious practices had been deeply influenced by *sufi* and African traditional rituals and most certainly were not of the same religious purity as the *salafist* Islamists in Khartoum. Their heresy was further complicated by the fact that some 40 percent of the troops in the Sudan army were westerners whose riverine officers persuaded them that as good Muslims they should wage war against the southern Sudanese *kafirin* "in the name of 'progressive' Arabism versus 'reactionary' Africanism."

The following year, on 21 July 2001 a group of Fur and Zaghawa activists met at Abu Gamra in Jabal Marra and swore an oath on the Qur'an to co-operate in their opposition to the Arabization of Darfur. The Fur were represented by 'Abd al-Wahid al-Nur, a communist lawyer, Ahmad 'Abd al-Shafi, a student in education, and Abdu 'Abdallah Isma'il, a graduate in modern languages; the Zaghawa by Khatir Tur al-Kalla, 'Abdallah Abakir, and Juma'a Muhammad Hagar, all of the Tier branch of the Sudanese Zaghawa who had accompanied Idriss Déby during his victorious march to N'Djamena in November 1990. They were all inexperienced in insurgency and politically naïve, but Wahid al-Nur had organized Fur armed units in Jabal Marra as early as 1998. 'Abd al-Shafi returned to Khartoum, where he was able to raise considerable funds from Fur "cultural groups" at the 'Ali Dinar Centre for Education and Culture of the Fur and the Darfur Students' Union to support the military training camps in the wilds of Jabal Marra. They set out to forge an alliance of the non-Arab peoples of Darfur and met with Masalit activists in November 2001 to seek logistical and political support for the movement and begin training Fur and Zaghawa guerillas in camps hidden in the Jabal Marra massif. On 25 February 2002 they staged their first joint operation, an assault against an isolated garrison in the southern mountains between Nyala and Tur that marked the beginning of the disaster in Darfur.

In an effort to bring a more unified leadership to this collection of embittered Fur, Masalit, and Zaghawa, most of whom had their own weapons and were principally concerned with defending their own turf and interests, a meeting of the principals was convened in western Jabal Marra in October 2002 during which a triumvirate was elected, with 'Abd al-Wahid al-Nur as chairman. The post of deputy chairman was reserved for a Masalit, 'Abdallah Abakir, and a Zaghawa was elected chief of staff, an arrangement haunted by old ethnic animosities that made a mockery of a unified movement. These deep ethnic divisions soon eroded the fragile façade of a united front in its strained relationships with the international humanitarian community and any future negotiations with the government. Moreover, these new leaders were young and inexperienced in societies that venerated the wisdom of older leaders, many of whom regarded them as a cabal that spent more of its time abroad as "hotel guerillas" than at home building the political and military cadres, as John Garang had done, at considerable personal cost, for the SPLM/A in southern Sudan.

INSURRECTION IN DARFUR

On 26 February 2003 some 300 rebels calling themselves the Darfur Liberation Front (DLF) and led by 'Abd al-Wahid Muhammad Ahmad al-Nur seized the town of Gulu, capital of Jabal Marra Province in western Darfur and raided scattered police and army posts before retiring to their training camps in Jabal Marra. Two weeks later the DLF, now called the Sudan Liberation Movement/Army (SLM/A), briefly recaptured Gulu in a fierce firefight, killing 195 government soldiers and forcing the garrison to flee. Secretary-General of the SLM, the political arm of the movement, Minni Arku Minnawi, released its Political Declaration to the press in which the SLM/A opposed the policies of Arabization, political and economic marginalization, and "the brutal oppression, ethnic cleansing, and genocide sponsored by the Khartoum Government."

The second insurgency organization in Darfur, the JEM, was very different from the secular SLM/A and more of a rival than an ally in the struggle against the Sudan government in Darfur. Unlike the indigenous African Fur origins of the SLM/A, the JEM's beginnings were among the "riverized" Darfuris, a patronizing term used by traditionalists to describe those from Darfur living in Khartoum who had adopted many of the customs and characteristics of the riverine Arabs. Like their country cousins, however, many had become increasingly embittered by marginalized treatment and discrimination toward them, despite their partial integration into the urban life of the capital. In the early 1990s they had embraced with considerable enthusiasm the Islamist revolution engineered by Hasan al-Turabi and were, paradoxically, stalwart members of the NIF. Led by Dr. Khalil Ibrahim Muhammad, a physician who had been minister for education in the old Darfur Province and a fervent Islamist, secret cells were established in El Fasher as early as 1993, Kordofan in 1994, and Khartoum in 1997, the latter consisting of Darfuri university graduates, most of whom were Islamists increasingly disenchanted with the monopoly and abuse of power by the *awlad al-bahr* in all levels of government. Unlike the members of the SLM, they were not about to abandon their Arab Islamist beliefs, but instead they sought to reform the NIF from within to give the *awlad al-gharib* the proper recognition in the central and now regional government that had been denied to them ever since the British left Sudan in 1956.

Khartoum University students have always been compulsive organizers, and the Darfuri graduates were no exception. They formed a committee of twenty-five in 1997 who began to collect the appalling statistics of their economic and political marginalization, culminating in the publication of the *Black Book* in May 2000 which convinced its members that reform from within had to be replaced by a more active program of reform from without. It remains unclear how many were willing to abandon their Islamist principles, but they no longer believed they were the answer to the Darfur Problem, which only an armed insurrection, appropriately called *the Justice and Equality Movement*, could resolve. In August 2001 Dr. Ibrahim grandly announced the founding of the JEM at a press conference in the Netherlands and called for "a comprehensive congress to redress injustices perpetuated by 'a small group of autocratic rulers'." The JEM sought a utopian solution in Sudan whereby all Sudanese, not just Darfuris, would have equal rights, basic services, and economic development in every region, from which social injustice and political tyranny would be extirpated. Unlike the SLM/A, who demanded the separation of church and state, the leaders of the JEM could not entirely discard their Islamist roots and somewhat ambiguously agreed that *shariʿa* should not be imposed upon non-Muslims, but that "believers in other faiths must not oppose Muslim attempts to apply the laws of religion for themselves."

Within a few days of the SLA victory at Gulu the government security committee for western Darfur swiftly opened negotiations with the SLM and arranged a fragile cease-fire. It soon collapsed. On 18 March 2003 an Arab militia assassinated a respected Masalit leader, Shaykh Salih Dakoro, near Geneina. This was followed by Sudanese air force Hind helicopter gunships destroying the town of Karnoi. The SLA retaliated on 25 March, seizing the strategic Masalit town of Tiné on the Chad frontier and capturing large stocks of arms and equipment from its garrison. Thereafter, fighting raged throughout West Darfur State during which the easy victories of the SLA dramatically revealed that the several thousand government troops stationed in Darfur were ill-prepared and inadequate to contain a major insurgency. Consequently, on Friday 25 April 2003, a combined SLA/JEM force, sometimes speciously called the "Opposition Forces," with thirty-three "technicals" staged a hit-and-run attack on the airport outside El Fasher during which they destroyed helicopters and Antonov bombers, occupied army headquarters, and captured air force Major-General Ibrahim Bushra, while another SLA unit seized four tanks in clashes outside Kutum and captured Colonel Mubarak Muhammad al-Saraj, chief of intelligence for public security in Aynshiro, north of Jabal Marra. In late May the SLA destroyed a Sudanese battalion, killing 500 and taking 300 prisoners north of Kutum. In mid-July they attacked Tiné again, inflicting heavy losses, and on 1 August 2003 took Kutum and seized large quantities of arms and ammunition before retiring.

Since the army could not suppress the insurgency, Khartoum hastily rearmed and unleashed the Darfuri Arab militias, the *janjawiid*, to rescue the army, just as Sadiq al-Mahdi and Burma Nasr had unleashed the *murahiliin* Baqqara on the Bahr al-Ghazal Dinka in 1986, with similarly devastating results. The *janjawiid* had begun their ethnic cleansing as early as October 2002 from their camps in Jabal Kargu, Boni, and Idalghanam in southern Darfur, with some 5,000 *janjawiid* each equipped and trained by the Sudanese army. The Fur, whom Salah 'Ali Alghali, the Governor of southern Darfur, had openly vowed to exterminate, were the primary targets for the mounted *janjawiid* commandoes, usually comprised of 100 raiders who would sweep down on a village just before dawn. The pattern of destruction was the same. The men were killed, often mutilated, the women raped, and the children sometimes abducted or killed. The village was burnt, livestock seized, fields torched, and the infrastructure – wells, irrigation works, schools, clinics – methodically destroyed in a systematic scheme to drive the African population from their ancestral lands – ethnic cleansing for Arab colonization. By January 2003 hundreds of Fur had been killed, thousands wounded, and tens of thousands had fled from the wasteland left behind by the *janjawiid*, more units of which were now being trained in camps in North Darfur State.

Supported by helicopter gunships and Antonov bombers, the *janjawiid*'s killing and displacement of Fur, Masalit, and Zaghawa escalated throughout the summer and autumn of 2003, while the Sudan army defeated the SLA north of Kutum in late August with heavy losses, including two of its leading commanders. In order to regroup and regain the initiative the SLM/A signed a cease-fire in September, but it was short-lived. Throughout the remainder of 2003 fighting raged on, particularly in western Darfur, with rhetorical claims of victory by both sides and occasionally a reliable report. On 27 December the JEM ambushed a *janjawiid* column moving against the rebel-held town of Tiné on the Chad border, inflicting very heavy losses, and in January 2004 the JEM repulsed another attempt to take Tiné once more inflicting heavy losses. Increasingly, *janjawiid* columns would pursue and kill those they had evicted, even crossing into Chad to hunt down fleeing refugees. By February 2004 the army had lost all hope of suppressing the insurgency after some 25,000 Darfuri officers and soldiers in the regular army, whose loyalty was highly suspect, were purged and replaced by units from the ineffectual PDF, leaving the *janjawiid* free to plunder. Unrestrained, the *janjawiid* pursued their ethnic cleansing and displacement of African *zurqa*, which conservatively claimed 30,000 lives and forced 1 million people from their lands as IDPs and another 200,000 as refugees to camps in Chad. Another 350,000 Darfuris were expected to die within the following nine months from famine and disease before the rains arrived in late spring. James Morris observed, "In all my travels as the head of the World Food Program, I have never seen people who are as frightened as those displaced in Darfur."

When the international humanitarian agencies became fully aware of the magnitude of the destruction and displacement in Darfur, they were met with manipulative obstruction in Khartoum, so that by the New Year 2004 "humanitarian operations had practically come to a standstill." All the international humanitarian agencies, including the International Crisis Group (ICG), Amnesty International, the Red Cross, Médecins Sans Frontières (MSF), and the various UN agencies were reporting the enormity of the disaster, the violation of human rights, and the need for relief assistance. Meanwhile the term "ethnic cleansing" to describe the devastation in Darfur became commonplace among diplomats, aid workers, and the media. The title of Amnesty International's report released on 3 February 2004 expressed the emotions of the international community: "Too Many People Killed for No Reason." Six days later President Bashir announced that the Sudan army and militias had crushed the rebellion. On 12 February 2004 the rebel forces, now numbering some 27,000 men, shot down two army helicopters. In the succeeding weeks they launched hit-and-run attacks near El Fasher and cut the road from Khartoum to Nyala, the capital of South Darfur State.

In late March, President Idriss Déby of Chad, who was deeply concerned about the influx of Sudan refugees and the violence in Darfur spilling into Chad, offered to mediate in N'Djamena, and on 8 April 2004 a forty-five-day cease-fire was signed, to be followed on 25 April by a political agreement to seek a comprehensive and final solution, which the SLM and JEM promptly disavowed, claiming their delegations had exceeded instructions. This revealed internal schisms within each movement – tensions between Zaghawa and Fur/Masalit in the SLM, and disagreements between the political wing of the JEM led by Dr. Khalil Ibrahim and his military commander, Jibril 'Abd al-Karim, whom he accused of being in the pay of Sudan Military Intelligence. Both the SLM and JEM would have nothing to do with an all-inclusive conference of Darfuris, insisting on direct political talks with the government to reach "a comprehensive settlement." The government announced it would continue its preparations for convening the forum at some future date.

Despite the international public outcry, declarations from the EU, and unanimous Congressional resolutions demanding "unconditional and immediate access to Darfur to humanitarian aid organizations," the Sudan government continued to frustrate the Western humanitarian efforts in Darfur with its wall of Byzantine bureaucratic procedures. The SLM/A had also not proven particularly helpful by emphatically rejecting humanitarian assistance coming from government-held territory that would give the *janjawiid* an excuse to attack the SLA and loot relief goods destined for the IDP camps. Having successfully lobbied the UNHCR not to appoint another Special Rapporteur for Human Rights and being convinced that the UN Security Council would not place ethnic cleansing on its agenda, the NIF government brazenly mobilized support in the UNHCR to refuse to consider the report on the humanitarian situation in Darfur by its own Acting High Commissioner for Human Rights, Bertrand Ramcharan, who described the "reign of terror . . . by the government of the Sudan and government-sponsored" *janjawiid*. On 14 May 2004 Sudan's Foreign Minister, Mustafa Isma'il, responded by contemptuously refusing to "disarm the militia as long as weapons remained in the hands of rebel forces." Five days later President 'Umar Hassan Ahmad al-Bashir arrived with no fanfare in Nyala to demonstrate his solidarity with the *janjawiid*, whom he reviewed as they paraded past him astride their fierce horses, shouting and brandishing their automatic weapons.

Throughout a long, hot summer of terror, flight, and struggle for survival the Western media – newspapers, magazines, journals, television, and the internet – relentlessly featured the plight of the beleaguered civilians of Darfur accompanied by demonstrations in Europe and the United States, countless public meetings, and speeches, both provocative and practical, exhorting governments to do something to protect the Africans of Darfur. The Arab media, even the usually strident *al-Jazeera*, were more subdued, embarrassed by a conflict that was between Arabs and Africans, not just among Africans as in Rwanda, and by the rhetorical appeals for Arab solidarity with Sudanese Islamists. Despite its humanitarian rhetoric, the political response from the West was ambivalent. With its armed forces ensnared in Afghanistan and Iraq, the United States was unwilling to commit its few remaining troops to a difficult military mission in yet another Muslim country. Although both Britain and France had regularly been involved in peacekeeping missions in Africa, neither was inclined to plunge into isolated Darfur to challenge an Arab Islamist government.

Both the United States and the EU sought to resolve this dilemma by urging the African Union (AU) and the UN to intervene. By August

2004 the AU Ceasefire Commission of 125 monitors under the Nigerian Brigadier General Okonkwo was in Darfur supported by 305 troops from Rwanda and Nigeria, which constituted the African Union Mission to Sudan (AMIS). They were limited to protecting only the UN monitors and providing security so that IDPs could avail themselves of humanitarian assistance; the AMIS was not a peacekeeping force. By mid-July the UN had established the Joint Implementation Mechanism (JIM) to monitor events in Darfur. The JIM's reports to the Security Council, combined with pressure from the United States, resulted in Security Council Resolution 1556 demanding that the Sudan government immediately cease all offensive military operations, disarm the *janjawiid*, arrest their leaders, and report back to the Security Council, but on 30 August UN Secretary-General Kofi Annan dutifully reported that Sudan had "not met its obligation" to stop "attacks against civilians and ensur[e] their protection." Even Olusegun Obasanjo, president of Nigeria and the AU, failed to convince the Sudan government and the SLM and JEM to reach an agreement at a meeting he convened in Abuja, Nigeria.

By February 2005 the ethnic devastation caused by the *janjawiid razzias* was so widespread and consistent that the humanitarian agencies began to declare a genocide in Darfur. In July the US Congress passed a unanimous resolution declaring the carnage in Darfur "genocide," but officials in the Bush administration, the UN, EU, and AU were more restrained. After their visit to Darfur at the end of June 2004, both Colin Powell and Kofi Annan had been reluctant to declare the situation in Darfur "genocide." In July the heads of the AU concluded there was no genocide in Darfur, as did the Arab League and the influential Organization of the Islamic Conference. The personal representative of Kofi Annan in Sudan, Jan Egeland, used the more sanitary "ethnic cleansing," which soon became fashionable. The reaction of the NIF Islamist government was complete denial. On 9 September 2004, however, Colin Powell, in testimony before the Senate Foreign Affairs Committee, concluded that "genocide has been committed in Darfur, and that the government of Sudan and the Janjawiid bear responsibility – and genocide may still be occurring." He was careful in his declaration, however, to invoke Article VIII of the Genocide Convention, which enabled its signatories to refer the matter to the UN to take whatever action it considers appropriate "to prevent genocide." By doing so the United States had legally fulfilled its obligations "to prevent genocide" without having to commit its armed forces. A new US resolution was consequently sent to the Security Council, but in fact "no new action [by the United States] is dictated by this determination [of genocide]."

Subsequently, on 18 September 2004 the Security Council adopted Resolution 1564 on Darfur, in which it "declared its [UN] grave concern that the Government of the Sudan had not fully met its obligations noted in Resolution 1556" (Article 1), the first Darfur resolution of 31 July, and endorsed "the African Union to enhance and augment its monitoring mission" (Article 2), but remained silent about any "peacekeepers" in Darfur, which the Sudan government had adamantly opposed. Finally, Article 12 of the resolution requested the secretary-general to "rapidly establish an international commission of inquiry . . . to determine also whether or not acts of genocide have occurred and to identify the perpetrators." In the event that Sudan does not comply with Resolution 1556 [31 July] "or this resolution," the Security Council "shall consider taking additional measures . . . such as to affect Sudan's petroleum sector" (Article 14). The resolution scrupulously avoided any mention of sanctions. Without peacekeepers, only monitors and vague demands for accountability, and without any provisions for enforcement, the Sudan government had satisfied its critics at home and abroad by means of the customary rhetoric of obfuscation and the token easing of restrictions on humanitarian agencies. The declaration by the United States of genocide in Darfur intensified the debate of this terrible tragedy, but the Sudan government remained inviolate behind its denials, assured that the threat of international intervention would dissipate, leaving them to practice their own diplomacy of "splendid isolation."

ABUJA AND AFTER

The declaration by Colin Powell in September 2004 that the Sudan government and the *janjawiid* had committed genocide reinvigorated the campaign for Darfur in the United States and Europe, characterized by public demonstrations, extensive media coverage, and Darfur "teach-ins" among university students, as well as the formation of the influential and well-financed Save Darfur Coalition. The public outcry could not be ignored by the European Parliament, which cast an extraordinary vote of 566 to 6 that the conflict in Darfur was "tantamount to genocide," a proposition few could vote against. The euphoria of this clarion call for humanity was, however, soon tempered by the reality of geopolitics. Neither the United States nor the EU had any intention of military intervention in Darfur, and there was no serious intention to commit North Atlantic Treaty Organization (NATO) troops, as had been done in the Balkans. The personal rift in the SPM/A between Minni Arku Minnawi and 'Abd al-Wahid al-Nur had now become very visible after the failure of the first Abuja talks and did not inspire the international community to proceed with an interventionist agenda.

As frustrating and fruitless negotiations recessed and resumed at Abuja the situation in western Darfur throughout 2005 continued to deteriorate: both the JEM and SLM/A began to lose control of their well-armed followers, some of whom resorted to *harab*, singling out the vulnerable humanitarian convoys carrying food and supplies. By September 2005 the UN had withdrawn most of its personnel from Darfur in response to the growing insecurity, and the flow of humanitarian assistance upon which hundreds of thousands of Darfuris depended drastically diminished. The rising violence clearly exposed the limitations of the 7,000-man force of AU monitors, which everyone had long known about. Now it had had to be admitted that the monitors were too few and that they had been sent with an inadequate, if not an impossible, mandate. In the meantime, the much-recessed talks continued at Abuja, but with little progress. Throughout 2005 the internal rivalries in and disagreements between the SLM/A and JEM over leadership, negotiation strategies, and policy were continually exploited by the representatives of the Sudan government, to the frustration and exasperation of the AU mediators and international observers at Abuja. In November, under intense pressure from the international community and after a positive intervention by Chad, the two SLM/A factions ostensibly reconciled and petulantly agreed to put aside their differences to cooperate with the JEM in a unified front that was as fragile as most marriages of convenience. Unfortunately, the factions within the JEM of Dr. Ibrahim were as contentious as those within the SLM/A, and in January 2006 there was an unseemly incident when rival JEM representatives came to blows over their petty quarrels.

By February 2006 the situation in the borderlands had continued to deteriorate as an increasing number of deserters from the Chadian army and rebels crossed into western Darfur, where they operated as bandits preying on the international NGOs, virtually suspending humanitarian aid. This produced a more strident outcry from the international community for immediate action to curb the spreading violence in Darfur. Throughout the autumn of 2005 and winter of 2006 the energies of the United States and its allies were directed toward transforming the AMIS from monitors to a robust UN peacekeeping force, which was strongly advocated by Secretary-General Kofi Annan. In April the extensive humanitarian efforts by the UN and international community had all but collapsed owing to continuing harassment by *janjawiid* and an alarming increase in well-armed bandit gangs. Over 200,000 inhabitants of Darfur had died in this unnecessary conflict; another 2.5 million had become IDPs or refugees in Chad. Those affected by the violence were estimated at almost 4 million, 700,000 of whom were now beyond the reach of humanitarian assistance. These were staggering numbers, and the only hope of disrupting this spiral of violence, slender as it might be, now focused on obtaining an agreement between the Sudan government and the fractious insurgent groups who continued to play charades.

Because one or another of the parties would refuse to continue discussions or because dissent arose within their own ranks, the Abuja talks were regularly disrupted, only to have the AU mediators, their host, the Nigerian President Olusegun Obasanjo, and international observers patiently restart the negotiations for yet another round. Slowly and painfully, amid President Bush's declaration that "Genocide in Darfur must be stopped" and dire warnings from frustrated aid workers who feared a disaster of "Biblical proportions," the AU and the international community persuaded the Sudan government, the SLM/A, and the JEM that the time had come to fix a final date, 30 April 2006, by which to reach a peace agreement. As the end of April drew near, a final draft had been completed to which the government readily agreed, which surprised many at Abuja, for the standard practice of the Islamist government in Khartoum during its many years as negotiators had been to raise objections at the last minute in order to extract more concessions. Some speculated that the speed and spirit of the cooperation shown by the government might have spooked the SLM/A and the JEM into fearing they had overlooked or neglected a specific issue, particularly in those articles about which they had grave reservations. As midnight on Sunday 30 April approached, the insurgents refused to sign the draft agreement.

The reaction to this abrupt rejection was outrage on the part of the envoys of the AU, the United States, Britain, the EU, and even the Arab League, which had consistently supported the Sudan government in its many confrontations with the West over Darfur. With the exception of the Arab League, each of these constituencies, but particularly the United States, was under enormous domestic pressure to end the genocide in Darfur. In the United States the very active Save Darfur Coalition had mobilized large demonstrations in Washington DC and across the country with the overwhelming support of Congress. There were also public demonstrations in Great Britain and Europe in which the demonstrators demanded their governments force some sort of an agreement, bring peace to Darfur, and end the carnage. On instructions from Washington, the US envoy in Abuja pressed for a forty-eight-hour extension until midnight Tuesday, to which everyone agreed, the SLM/A and JEM reluctantly.

Having bought time, high-level delegations descended upon Abuja to extract more concessions from the government while applying diplomatic pressure on the rebels to accept compromise and peace and to sign the agreement. US Deputy Secretary of State Robert Zoellick, accompanied by Assistant Secretary of State for Africa Jendayi Fraser, flew into Abuja from Washington. Secretary for International Development Hilary Benn arrived from London, and the Chairman of the AU and President of the Republic of the Congo, Denis Sassou N'Guesso, landed from Kinshasa. On Thursday 5 May the negotiators worked through the night and, after a new round of talks on Friday morning, 6 May, Minni Arku Minnawi, leader of the largest faction in the SPM/A, agreed to sign the latest amended version, known as the Darfur Peace Agreement (DPA), despite his concerns over power-sharing and security. Majub al-Khalifa signed for the government. Dr. Khalil Ibrahim of the JEM refused to sign, as did 'Abd al-Wahid al-Nur, leader of the larger, rival faction in the SLM/A. The JEM regarded the agreement as only a partial, not a national, solution. The refusal of 'Abd al-Wahid al-Nur to sign was more complicated. Although he had fewer fighters than the Minnawi faction of the SLM/A, he controlled more territory and represented the Fur who, more than any other ethnic group, had borne the brunt of the devastation from the government forces and the *janjawiid*. 'Abd al-Wahid al-Nur, however, did not have control over his own delegation, a number of whom thought he had made a serious mistake not to sign and emotionally embraced Minnawi after he affixed his signature to the agreement. Robert Zoellick made the best of his limited achievement by naïvely concluding that the two inflexible rebel factions could still be persuaded to sign or be ignored as the Abuja Agreement was implemented. His optimism appears to have been wishful thinking on the part of an experienced and skillful negotiator ignorant of the Sudanese and anxious to return to Washington, for the challenge ahead lay not in the signing but in the implementation of the Abuja Agreement.

The immediate reaction to the Abuja Agreement was mixed. Some believed that the agreement, however limited, at least committed the government and the SLM/A to end the slaughter and displacement of Darfuris. Others were pessimistic that this fragile peace agreement could hold against the historic violence that had been so destructive in the central Sahara, Sahel, and savanna for the past four decades without the concurrence of all factions to the agreement and a serious commitment to implement it. The Abuja Agreement was a complex, eighty-five-page document. The SLM/A finally agreed to integrate its fighters into the national security organizations and abandoned its insistence on a third vice-president, reluctantly settling for a post with similar powers, but without the pretentious titles. There was considerable concern that the Abuja negotiations would disrupt the implementation of the Comprehensive Peace Agreement (CPA), which placed a major constraint on the government negotiators, the international community, and the AU representatives. The *janjawiid* would be disarmed, but the authority of the Sudan armed forces over the *janjawiid* was precarious. Although President Bush claimed a "diplomatic victory," during the previous fifteen years the Sudan government had become infamous for never fully honoring many of its signed agreements.

Everyone seemed to agree that intense diplomatic pressure had secured an agreement and that it must now be sustained in order to persuade 'Abd al-Wahid al-Nur to sign. Indeed, the importance of a speedy implementation of the Abuja Agreement was made ever more emphatic by the ominous warnings from Jan Egeland, who reported that the massive displacements, violence, and killing of civilians in southern Darfur, which had forced the withdrawal of some AMIS personnel, were continuing without interruption. Few were under the illusion that diplomacy alone could consummate the implementation of Abuja, but the prospect of intervention by the United States or EU had long been forgotten. Consequently, in the weeks that followed, all expectations were now focused on the transformation of the AMIS from harried monitors into a large, robust, UN peacekeeping force, and on Tuesday 16 May Security Council Resolution 1679 was officially approved for the AMIS to become vigorous UN peacekeepers. Although it would be at least six months before any peacekeepers could be in Darfur, the UN had first to reach an agreement with the government of Sudan over a realistic mandate. When the AU had organized the AMIS in August 2004, Khartoum had been adamant that it was *not* a peacekeeping force and continued to vehemently object throughout the summer and autumn of 2006 to any UN intervention in Sudan, which was warmly supported by the Arab League. The new Sudanese foreign minister, a southerner, Dr. Lam Akol, blandly pointed out that there had been no mention of any transformation of the AMIS into UN peacekeepers in the Abuja Agreement.

No sooner was the ink dry on the Abuja Agreement of 6 May 2006 than it began to unravel. On 30 June the three Darfur insurgent groups who had refused to sign the agreement – the JEM of Dr. Khalil Ibrahim, the SLM/A faction opposed to Minni Minnawi and now led by Khamis 'Abdallah Abakr, and the new Sudan Federal Democratic Alliance (SFDA) of Ahmad Ibrahim Diraig – founded the National Redemption Front (NRF) in Asmara. The former able and respected Fur governor, Diraig had repeatedly warned Khartoum and Numayri personally as far back as 1983 that a catastrophe was inevitable in Darfur if humanitarian food aid was not forthcoming. Numayri had retreated into a state of denial; Diraig resigned in protest in 1984 and went into exile in Europe to establish a successful career in business, only to return at the outbreak of the insurgency to establish his SFDA and lead the NRF.

After the collapse of Abuja the crisis in Darfur was dominated by three catastrophic legacies. The first entailed the endless and frustrating negotiations over a UN peacekeeping force between the UN, supported by the West, and the Bashir government in Khartoum. The second was the rapid escalation in the scale of violence by the army and *janjawiid*, particularly those under Musa Hilal on the one hand and the NRF on the other, made all the more complicated and extreme by clashes between the supporters of the SLA/Minni Minnawi and those of 'Abdallah Bakr of the old SLM/A, now called SLA/ Group 19, in addition to the ever-increasing numbers of independent roving bandit gangs of former Chadian and Darfuri insurgents. The third was not unexpected, for once the last vestiges of security disintegrated in Darfur, the humanitarian agencies upon which hundreds of thousands Darfuris depended for survival began to withdraw their employees from the war zone, and all humanitarian assistance began to "melt down."

Throughout the autumn of 2006 President Bashir remained unmoved in the face of intense international pressure from Kofi Annan, the Security Council, and delegations from the United States, including abortive visits to Khartoum by Jendayi Fraser and Andrew Natsios, former Special Humanitarian Coordinator for Sudan in USAID and now the Special Envoy of President Bush, to allow a 20,000-man UN peacekeeping force into Darfur. Bashir was not without some reluctant allies for his intransigent opposition to a UN peacekeeping force, which he called an excuse for neo-colonialism. The Arab League chose to remain aloof from any commitment in Sudan, this being a conflict in which its members had no immediate self-interest. On 16 November 2006 a high-level [AU] consultation on the situation in Darfur at Addis Ababa insisted that the AU's mission in Darfur should continue and that the size of its force should be determined by the AU and the UN. This was subsequently ratified by the AU Peace and Security Council in Abuja on 30 November. A flurry of negotiations throughout

December culminated in a letter from President Bashir to Kofi Annan of 23 December, seven days before the UN deadline of 1 January 2007 for imposing more severe sanctions, stating that he would support a joint or "hybrid" AU–UN force for Darfur for which the UN would provide advisers, communications, transport, and logistical support, but stating also that the size of the AU contribution would only be determined by negotiations between the AU, UN, and Sudan in which the stonewalling diplomacy long used by Sudan left ample room for prevarication.

While the diplomats dithered throughout the autumn of 2006 the fighting (as noted above) escalated. The Sudanese armed forces, including *janjawiid*, suffered two severe defeats in November at the hands of the forces of the NRF. Banditry was rife throughout much of Darfur, and in early December *janjawiid* had looted El Fasher for three days before surrounding the city in a stand-off at the end of that month between the combined forces of the NRF and SLA/Group 19. By the New Year virtually all humanitarian operations in Darfur and eastern Chad were on the verge of complete collapse, the culmination of months of increasing harassment, looting, and killing of aid workers during the autumn and up until December, when senior officials representing a range of humanitarian organizations began to plan the wholesale evacuation of their people. On 18 December 2006 after the humanitarian agencies at Gereida, holding the largest concentration of IDPs (130,000) in Darfur, were attacked and its workers killed, virtually all humanitarian personnel were evacuated.

Few have any illusions about the future for Darfur. Little can be expected to change for the better, as the international community remains impotent to intervene and the Sudan government incapable of asserting its authority over the region. This is the latest and most tragic episode in the forty-year conflict for control of the Chad basin in which neither Chad, Libya, nor Sudan possess the human and material resources to dominate Darfur. The subsequent violence has precipitated an agrarian revolution by which subsistence farmers and herdsmen have been transformed into a society of urban poor living in permanent settlements as the impoverished, displaced wards of the international humanitarian community. Their camps have become shanty towns in which farmers and herdsmen are now poverty-stricken townsmen eking out a living from handouts and petty trade. Here they will remain, for even if peace descended upon Darfur there is no longer any incentive to return home, for nothing remains but a desolate and devastated land. The Darfuris will become African Palestinians.

Epilogue

Historians are neither fortune-tellers nor soothsayers with powers to predict the outcome of future events in Sudan. The three great issues that confront Sudan at present and in the future – implementation of the CPA, disaster in Darfur, and secession of southern Sudan – will remain unresolved for years to come. Without the prescience to predict, the historian can and should elucidate those four perennial themes that, since the time of Muhammad 'Ali in the first half of the nineteenth century, have woven themselves into the historical fabric of modern Sudan.

The first intractable theme has been the relentless contest between the center and periphery, between Khartoum and the distant provinces east, south, and west, that has haunted every government at Khartoum. There are many reasons for this perennial estrangement which have varied in time and place – ethnic, cultural, and religious differences, and the pursuit by the central government of the elusive goal of imposing political and religious homogeneity when there was none by exploitation and discrimination mixed with indifference and neglect on the part of the prosperous center for the poverty-stricken Sudanese in the periphery. All of these antagonisms run very deep, and whether the technological revolution in communications and transportation will enable the center to bind its discontented, marginalized, and rebellious citizens together remains part of the inscrutable future for Sudan.

The hostility between center and periphery was perpetuated by the inability of Khartoum at any time in the past 200 years to govern its remote provinces. The imposition by force of a façade of authority should not be construed as acceptable governance or administration willing to accommodate local customs, cultures, and jurisprudence. There was more to governance than simply flying the flag over some remote outpost in Darfur, the Bahr al-Ghazal, or the Red Sea Hills. This failure was exacerbated by the intellectual, cultural, and economic power of the *awlad al-bahr*, the people of the river, whose increasing economic prosperity contrasted dramatically with the poverty of marginalized Sudanese. This disparity was introduced in the years of Muhammad 'Ali but has relentlessly increased during the last 200 years until the present, when the affluence exuding from contemporary Khartoum continues to compromise the efforts to assert control by the center, control that, as in the past, declines in direct proportion to the distance from Khartoum.

Both of these themes are inextricably intertwined with those cultural, economic, military, and religious forces over which the individual has little control. The remaining two themes of the Sudanese past, however, are more individual, having to do with the strength and weakness of individual Sudanese leaders. First, politics in Sudan has always been an intensely personal matter in which dominant personalities, whatever their talents, have frequently been avaricious and arrogant, which has inhibited the development of party discipline, promoted political and personal manipulation, and encouraged personal defection into impotent political splinter groups, all of which has made a mockery of parliamentary government and corrupted military rule. To be sure, the leaders of the two great sectarian parties, the DUP and Umma, could rely on religious loyalty to maintain their political power, but that same loyalty was often incompatible with national interests. Consequently, in northern political life strong personalities, shaped either by talent or heredity, like Isma'il al-Azhari, Sadiq al-Mahdi, or Hasan al-Turabi, had their own set of priorities that had little to do with the interests of all the Sudanese people. Ja'afar Numayri certainly had his own personal agenda, which even the most charitable observers regarded as ill-conceived, of promoting an improvement in the lives of all Sudanese. The power of personalities was particularly prevalent in the political life of the South, but even after John Garang had imposed his iron-clad military discipline his movement nearly collapsed in 1991–94 over the great "split in the SPLM/A," which was motivated more by personal animosity, jealousy, and self-interest than the reform that each of the rival leaders languidly proclaimed and disingenuously defended. Personalities will always play a dominant role in politics, but in Sudan they have consistently triumphed over the national interest, which has led some to argue that the Sudanese have got the government they deserved. Those Sudanese who got what they deserved, however, were essentially the intellectual elite of greater Khartoum, while the millions of *al-nas*, the ordinary folk, most certainly deserved better leadership than the failed, avaricious politicians, military dictators, or religious mandarins who believed themselves destined to lead them.

Finally, the elusive search for a Sudanese identity continues to the present day and will do so into the future. This quest for identity only began to evolve with the rise of Sudanese nationalism after the First World War, becoming an obsession among educated Sudanese in the latter half of the twentieth century. Who are the Sudanese? Arab, African, Muslim, Christian, or Traditionalist? Belonging to two worlds, Arab and African, but not identified solely with either, the individuality of many ethnicities has been melted and forged into a new, unique, and distinct identity called "Sudanese." At the time when the evolution of this idea had gained its greatest momentum, it was suddenly and dramatically challenged in 1989 by the Islamist revolution, which sought to end the search for identity by the homogenization of Sudanese society in which all Sudanese would identify with being Arab and with practicing fundamental Islam. Despite the use of terror, torture, intimidation, and fear, the Islamist revolution failed to impose its own definition of being Arab and Muslim. Many Sudanese on the periphery were unwilling to adopt an alien identity that they hated and were prepared to fight and die to prevent its imposition. Others, particularly those from the professions and intellectual elite in the capital, simply disappeared into the outer world during the great Sudanese Diaspora of the 1990s in flight from Arab Islamists. After nearly twenty years in power the Islamist revolution appears to have lost its momentum. The signing of the CPA in the South, the peace agreement with the Beja Congress in the east, and the abortive DPA in the west have clearly indicated that the Islamist revolution has lost its fanaticism and objectives as its loyal supporters in the capital have abandoned their zeal to promote their mission at any cost in return for the more congenial prospect of becoming rich through globalization, which has transmuted the Islamist revolution in Sudan into an anachronism. Thus, in 2007 the elusive search for the Sudanese has revived, a search in which appeals to the race and religion of the Arab world continue to be challenged by those of the African and in which the old fears have reappeared that the Sudanese will be the despondent recipients of the worst of both worlds rather than the beneficiaries of the best of both, which in the past made the Sudanese unique among men.

Notes

1 THE MAKING OF MODERN SUDAN: THE NINETEENTH CENTURY

1. H. H. Calvert, HBM Acting Consul, Jidda, to Consul-General, Egypt, 29 March 1865 (PRO,FO 141/54), quoted in Richard Hill, *Egypt in the Sudan*, London: Oxford University Press, 1959, p. 102.

2 THE ANGLO-EGYPTIAN CONDOMINIUM

1. Lord Hailey, "Some Problems dealt with in *An African Survey*," *International Affairs*, March/April, 1939, p. 202.
2. C. A. Willis to H. MacMichael, February 18, 1929, CIVSEC I/3/7A; Robert O. Collins, *Shadows in the Grass: Britain in the Southern Sudan, 1918–1956*, New Haven: Yale University Press, 1983, pp. 141–47.
3. Isma'il al-Azhari to CS [Civil Secretary], 2 May 1938 in J. M. A. Bakheit (Bakhit), "British Administration and Sudanese Nationalism, 1919–1939," Cambridge PhD Dissertation, 1964, pp. 305–06. See also M. W. Daly, *Imperial Sudan: The Anglo-Egyptian Condominium, 1934–1956*, Cambridge: Cambridge University Press, 1991, pp. 82–83.
4. Quoted in Daly, *Imperial Sudan*, pp. 157–58.
5. "Note on the graduates' General Congress," quoted in Daly, *Imperial Sudan*, pp. 158–59.
6. Abu Hasabu and Afaf Abdel Majid, *Factual Conflict in the Sudanese Nationalist Movement, 1918–1948*, Khartoum: Khartoum University Press, 1985, p. 118; also quoted in Daly, *Imperial Sudan*, p. 167.
7. Robertson to B. V. Marwood, Governor Equatoria, December 16, 1946, BaG I/1/2; Collins, *Shadows in the Grass*, pp. 285–86.
8. "Proceedings of the Juba Conference on the Political Development of the Southern Sudan, June 1947," BaG I/1/1; Collins, *Shadows in the Grass*, p. 290.
9. Interview with M. F. A. Keen, 10 December 1962; Collins, *Shadows in the Grass*, p. 291.
10. "Upper Nile Province Monthly Diaries," August 1954, Equat.57/C/3; Collins, *Shadows in the Grass*, pp. 453–56.

4 THE GOVERNMENT OF JA'AFAR NUMAYRI: THE HEROIC YEARS, 1969–1976

1. Abel Alier, "Statement to the Peoples' Regional Assembly on the Proposed Jonglei Canal," National Council for the Development of the Jonglei Canal Area, Khartoum, 1974.
2. Environmental Liaison Center Press Conference, Nairobi, September 1977.

5 THE GOVERNMENT OF JA'AFAR NUMAYRI: THE YEARS OF DISMAY AND DISINTEGRATION, 1976–1985

1. *Africa Confidential*, 27 June 1983.
2. John Garang de Mabior, "Identifying, Selecting, and Implementing Rural Development Strategies for Socio-Economic Development in the Jonglei Projects Area, Southern Region, Sudan," PhD dissertation, Iowa State University, Ames, IA, 1981, p. 227.
3. *al-Sahafa*, 25 May 1984, quoted in Mansur Khalid, *Nimeiri and the Revolution of Dis-May*, London: KPI, 1985, p. 264.

6 THE TRANSITIONAL MILITARY COUNCIL AND THIRD PARLIAMENTARY GOVERNMENT

1. Quoted in Douglas H. Johnson, *The Root Causes of Sudan's Civil Wars*, Oxford: James Currey, and Bloomington: Indiana University Press, and Kampala: Fountain Publishers, respectively, 2003, p. 71.
2. *Sudan Times*, 20 October 1986.
3. *Sudan Times*, 27 December 1987.

7 THE ISLAMIST REVOLUTION: THE TURABI YEARS, 1989–1996

1. "al-Qa'ida estaria buscando armas de destruccion masiva," *N.C.O.*, Argentina, 20 November 2001, p. 14, from AP dateline Manama, Bahrein.
2. Hasan al-Turabi, "Islam as a Pan-National Movement and Nation-States: An Islamic Doctrine of Human Association," Royal Society for the Encouragement of Arts, Manufactures, and Commerce, London 27 April 1992, published by the Sudan Foundation, London, 1997.
3. Yossef Bodansky, "Peres and the New Middle East," *The Maccabean Online*, Houston: The Freeman Institute, December 1954.
4. Aicha Lemsine, "Muslim Scholars Face Down Fanaticism," *Washington Report on Middle East Affairs*, June 1995, pp. 17–92.
5. *Al-Sharq al-Awsat*, 6 July 1995.

Select bibliography

The history of Sudan has been the subject of greater inquiry than almost any other country of Sub-Saharan Africa. The scope and depth of the literature are overwhelming and cannot, and should not, be repeated here, for there are several excellent bibliographies that the general reader, student, or scholar can consult to investigate specific subjects. I have, therefore, been forced to limit the bibliography of this general history to selected books.

Abdin, Hasan, *Early Sudanese Nationalism, 1919–1925*, Khartoum: Khartoum University Press, 1985.

Abidin, 'Abd al-Majid, *Tarikh al-thaqafa al-'arabiyya fi al-Sudan, mundhu nash'atiha ila al'-asr al-hadith: al-din, al-itijima', al-adab*, 2nd edn., Beirut: dar al-thaqafa, 1967.

Abu Hassabu and Afaf Abdel Majid, *Factional Conflict in the Sudanese Nationalist Movement, 1918–1948*, Khartoum: Khartoum University Press, 1985.

Abu Salim, Muhammad Ibrahim, *al-ard fi a'l-Mahdiyya*, Khartoum: dar jami'at al-khartum li'l-nashr, 1970.

  Mudhakkirat 'Uthman Diqna, Khartoum: dar jami'at al-khartum li'l-nashr, 1974.

  Manshurat al-Mahdiya, Beirut: dar al-jil, 1979.

  al-haraka al-fikriyya fi al-Mahdiya, 3rd edn., Khartoum: dar jami'at al-khartum li'l-nashr, 1989.

  al-athar al-kamila li 'l-Imam al-Mahdi, 7 vols., Khartoum: dar jami'at al-khartum li'l-nashr, 1990–94.

  Tarikh al-Khartum, 3rd edn., Beirut: dar al-jil, 1991.

  Udaba' wa-'ulama' wa-mu'arrikhun fi tarikh al-Sudan, Beirut: dar al-jil, 1991.

  al-Khusumah fi Mahdiyat al-Sudan kitab fi tarikh fikrat al-Mahdiyah islamiyan wa-Sudaniyan, Khartoum: markaz abu salim li'l-dirasat, 2004.

Abu Sinn, 'Ali 'Abd Allah, *Mudhakkriat Abi Sinn an mudiriyyat Dar Fur*, Khartoum: dar al-watha'iq, 1968.

Abushouk, Ahmed I. and Anders Bjørkelo, eds., *The Principles of Native Administration in the Anglo-Egyptian Sudan, 1898–1956*, Omdurman: Abdel Karim Mirghani Cultural Centre, and Bergen: Centre for Middle Eastern and Islamic Studies, University of Bergen, 2004.

Affendi, Abdelwahab El-, *Turabi's Revolution: Islam and Power in Sudan*, London: Grey Seal, 1991.

Ahmad, Hassan M. M., *Muslim Brotherhood in Sudan, 1944–1969*, Washington D.C.: Joint Publications Research Service, 1985.

Ahmad, Su'ad 'Abd al-Aziz, *Qadaya al-ta 'lim al-ahli fi al-Sudan*, Khartoum: Khartoum University Press, 1991.

Ahmed, Abdel Gaffir M. and Leif Manger, eds., *Understanding the Crisis in Darfur: Listening to Sudanese Voices*, Bergen: Centre for Development Studies, University of Bergen, 2006.

Akol, Dr. Lam, *SPLM/SPLA: Inside an African Revolution*, Khartoum: Khartoum University Press, 2001.

SPLM/SPLA: The Nasir Declaration, New York: Inoverse, Inc., 2003.

Albino, Oliver, *The Sudan: A Southern Viewpoint*, London: Oxford University Press, 1970.

'Ali, Haydar Ibrahim, ed., *al-Tanawwu' al-thaqafi wa-bina' al-sawla al-wataniyya fi al-Sudan*, Cairo: markaz al-dirasat al-sudaniyya, 1995.

'Ali, Mussaddag A. El Haj, *The Redivision of the Southern Sudan: Decentralization in Sudan*, Khartoum: Khartoum University Press, 1987.

'Ali Taha, Faysal Abd al-Rahman, *'Am 'ala tatbiq al-shari'a al-islamiyya fi al-Sudan*, Khartoum: majlis al-sha'ab, 1984.

al-haraka al-siyassiyya al-Sudaniyya wa'l-sira' al-misri al-baritani bi-sha'n al-Sudan, 1936–1953, Cairo: dar al-amin, 1998.

Alier, Abel, *Peace and Development in the Southern Sudan: A Statement*, Khartoum: Ministry of Culture and Information, 1977.

Southern Sudan: Too Many Agreements Dishonoured, Exeter: Ithaca Press, 1990.

Al-Rahim, Muddathir, *Imperialism and Nationalism in the Sudan*, Oxford: Clarendon Press, 1969.

Al-Tayeb, Salah al-Din al Zein, *KUSU: The Students' Movement in the Sudan, 1940–1970*, Khartoum: Khartoum University Press, 1971.

An-Na'im, Abdullahi Ahmed, *Toward an Islamic Reformation: Civil Liberties, Human Rights, and International Law*, Syracuse, NY: Syracuse University Press, 1990.

and Peter Kok, *Fundamentalism and Militarism: A Report on the Root Causes of Human Rights Violations in the Sudan*, New York: Fund for Peace, 1991.

Anon (Speakers of Truth and Justice), *al-kitab al-aswad (Black Book of Sudan: Imbalance of Power and Wealth in Sudan)*, n.p., 2000.

Aspek, Joyce, ed., *Darfur Genocide before Our Eyes*, New York: Institute for Genocide, 2005.

'Ata, 'Awad 'Abd al-Hadi al-, *Ta'abdrikh Kurdufan al-siyasi fi l-Mahdiyya, 1881–1899*, Khartoum: Khartoum University Press, 1973.

Badal, Raphael K., Adlan Hardallo, Muddathir Abd al-Rahim and Peter Woodward, *Sudan since Independence: Studies of the Political Development since 1956*, London: Gower, 1986.

Bakheit (Bakhit), Ja'afar Muhammad 'Ali, "British Administration and Sudanese Nationalism, 1919–1939," Cambridge PhD Dissertation, 1964.

al-Idara al-britaniyya wa'l-haraka al-wataniyya fi al-Sudan, 1919–1939, trans. Hinri Royad, 3rd edn. Khartoum: al-matbu'at al-arabiyya lilpta'lif wa'l-tarjama, 1987.

Barnett, T. *Gezira: An Illusion of Development*, London: Frank Cass, 1971.

Bashiri, Mahjub 'Umar, *Ruwwad al-fikr al-Sudani*, Beirut: dar al-jil, 1991.

   Haqibat al-fann: shu'ara' wa-fannaun, Khartoum: mu'assasat ishraqa li'l-nashr wa'l-tawzi' wa'l-i'lam, 1994.

Bechtold, Peter, *Politics in the Sudan*, New York: Praeger, 1976.

Bedri, Babikr, *Ta'rikh hayati*, 3 vols., Omdurman: matba'at misr [Sudan], 1959–61.

   The Memoirs of Babikr Bedri, vol. I, London: Oxford University Press, 1969; vol. II, London: Ithaca Press, 1980 (translations of the *Ta'rikh*).

Bell, Sir Gwain, *Shadows on the Sand: Memoirs of Sir Gwain Bell*, London: Hurst, 1983.

   B. Dee et al., *Sudan Political Service, 1899–1956*, intro. by Harold MacMichael, Oxford: Oxonian Press, n.d.

   and A. H. M. Kirk-Greene, *The Sudan Political Service, 1902–1952: A Preliminary Register of Second Careers*, Oxford: St. Antony's College, 1989.

Beshir, Mohamed Omer, *The Southern Sudan: Background to Conflict*, London: Hurst, 1968.

   Educational Development in the Sudan, 1898–1956, London: Oxford University Press, 1969.

   Revolution and Nationalism in Sudan, London: Rex Collings, 1974.

   The Southern Sudan from Conflict to Peace, London: Hurst, 1975.

   ed., *The Nile Valley Countries: Continuity and Change*, Khartoum: Institute of African and Asian Studies, University of Khartoum, 1981.

   Terramedia, London: Ithaca, 1982.

   ed., *Sudan: Aid and External Relations*, Graduate College Publications No. 9, Khartoum: Khartoum University Press, and London: Ithaca Press, 1984.

   ed., *Regionalism and Religion*, Graduate College Publications No. 10, Khartoum: Khartoum University Press, and London: Ithaca Press, 1984.

Bestwick, Stephanie, *Sudan's Blood Memory: The Legacy of War, Ethnicity, and Slavery in South Sudan*, Rochester, NY: University of Rochester Press, 2004.

   and Jay Spaulding, eds., *White Nile Black Blood*, Lawrenceville, NJ: Red Sea Press, 1999.

Bjørkelo, Anders, *From King to Kashif: Shendi in the Nineteenth Century*, Bergen: s.n., 1983.

   Prelude to the Mahdiyya: Peasants and Traders in the Shendi Region, 1821–1885, Cambridge: Cambridge University Press, 1989.

   and Ahmad Ibrahim abu Shouk, *The Public Treasury of the Muslims*, Leiden: Brill, 1996.

Brown, Richard, *Public Debt and Private Wealth: Debt, Capital Flight, and the IMF in Sudan*, New York: St. Martin's Press, 1992.

   Sudan's Other Economy: Migrants' Remittances, Capital Flight, and Their Policy Implications, The Hague: Publications Office Institute of Social Studies, 1990.

Burr, J. Millard, *Quantifying Genocide in the Southern Sudan, 1988–1998*, Washington D.C.: US Committee on Refugees, 1998.

Cater, N., *Sudan: The Roots of Famine*, London: Oxfam, 1986.

Chevalerais, Alain, *Hassan al-Tourabi: Islam avenir du monde, entretiens avec Alain Chevalerais/Hassan al Tourabi*, Paris: J. C. Lattes, 1997.

Collins, Robert O., *The Southern Sudan, 1883–1898: A Struggle for Control*, New Haven: Yale University Press, 1962.

King Leopold, England, and the Upper Nile, New Haven: Yale University Press, 1968.

Land beyond the Rivers: The Southern Sudan, 1898–1918, New Haven: Yale University Press, 1971.

The Southern Sudan in Historical Perspective, Tel Aviv: Shiloah Center, 1975, and New Brunswick, NJ: Transaction Publishers, 2006.

Shadows in the Grass: Britain in the Southern Sudan, 1918–1956, New Haven: Yale University Press, 1983.

The Waters of the Nile: Hydropolitics and the Jonglei Canal, 1900–1988, Oxford: Clarendon Press, 1990, and Princeton: Markus Wiener, 1994.

Requiem for the Sudan: War, Drought, and Disaster Relief, 1983–1993 (with J. Millard Burr), Boulder, CO: Westview Press, 1994.

Africa's Thirty Years' War: Chad, Libya, and the Sudan, 1963–1993 (with J. Millard Burr), Boulder, CO: Westview, 1999.

Revolutionary Sudan: Hasan al-Turabi and the Islamist State 1989–2000 (with J. Millard Burr), Leiden: Brill, 2003.

Civil Wars and Revolution in the Sudan: Essays on the Sudan, Southern Sudan, and Darfur, 1962–2004 (with a complete bibliography of the Sudan writings of Robert O. Collins), Hollywood: Tsehai Publishers, 2005.

Darfur: The Long Road to Disaster (with J. Millard Burr), Princeton: Markus Wiener, 2nd ed., 2008.

Collins, Robert O. and Francis M. Deng, eds., *The British in the Sudan, 1898–1956*, London: Macmillan Press, 1984.

Cunnison, Ian, *The Baqqara Arabs*, Oxford: Clarendon Press, 1966.

Daly, M. W., *British Administration and the Northern Sudan, 1898–1924*, Leiden: Nederlands Institut voor het Nabije Oosten, 1979.

The Road to Shaykhan: Letters of Hicks Pasha . . . 1883, Durham: Durham Centre for Middle Eastern and Islamic Studies, 1983.

ed., *Modernization in the Sudan: Essays in Honour of Richard Hill*, New York: Lillian Barber Press, 1985.

ed., *al-Majdhubiyya and al-Makashfiyya: Two Sufi Tariqas in the Sudan*, Khartoum: Graduate College, University of Khartoum, 1985.

Empire on the Nile: The Anglo-Egyptian Sudan, 1898–1934, Cambridge: Cambridge University Press, 1986.

Imperial Sudan: The Anglo-Egyptian Condominium, 1934–1956, Cambridge: Cambridge University Press, 1991.

The Sirdar: Sir Reginald Wingate and the British Empire in the Middle East, Philadelphia: American Philosophical Society, 1997.

and Francis M. Deng, *Bonds of Silk: The Human Factor in British Administration in the Middle East*, East Lansing, MI: Michigan State University Press, 1990.

and Ahmad A. Sikainga, eds., *Civil Wars in the Sudan*, London: British Academic Press, 1993.

and Jane R. Hogan, *Images of Empire: Photographic Sources of the British in the Sudan*, Boston: Brill, 2005.

Darir, 'Abd 'Abd al-Rahman al-Amin, *Kitab al-'arabiyya fi al-Sudan*, Beirut: dar al-kitab al-lubnani, 1967.

Deng, Francis M., *Dynamics of Identification: A Basis for National Integration in the Sudan*, Khartoum: Khartoum University Press, 1973.

Africans of Two Worlds: The Dinka in Afro-Arab Sudan, New Haven: Yale University Press, 1978.

Recollections of Babo Nimr, London: Ithaca Press, 1982.

The Man Called Deng Majok: A Biography of Power, Polygyny, and Change, New Haven: Yale University Press, 1986.

Protecting the Dispossessed, Washington D.C.: Brookings Institution, 1993.

War of Visions: Conflict of Identities in the Sudan, Washington D.C.: Brookings Institution, 1995.

and Larry Minear, *The Challenge of Famine Relief: Emergency Operations in the Sudan*, Washington D.C.: Brookings Institution, 1992.

de Waal, Alex, *Famine Crimes: Politics and the Disaster Relief Industry in Africa*, Oxford: James Curry, and Bloomington: Indiana University Press, 1997.

Famine that Kills: Darfur, Sudan, rev. edn., New York: Oxford University Press, 2005.

Douin, Georges, *Histoire du règne du Khedive Ismaïl*, Rome: Stampata, 1933–41.

Histoire du Soudan égyptien, Cairo: Institut français d'archéologie orientale du Cairo, 1944.

Duffield, Mark, *Maiurno: Capitalism and Rural Life in the Sudan*, London: Ithaca Press, 1981.

Duncan, J. S. R., *The Sudan: A Record of Achievement*, Edinburgh: William Blackwood & Sons, 1952.

The Sudan's Path to Independence, Edinburgh: Willaim Blackwood & Sons, 1957.

Eltigani, Eltigani E., ed., *War and Drought in Sudan: Essays on Population Displacement*, Gainesville: University Press of Florida, 1995.

Eprile, Cecil, *War and Peace in the Sudan, 1955–1972*, Newton Abbot: David & Charles, 1974.

Evans-Pritchard, E. E. The anthropological writings on the peoples of southern Sudan (Anuak, Nuer, Zande, and others) are to be found in his many books and articles. Although mostly concerned with social anthropology, there is much of great interest to the historian in a land where the fine line between anthropology and history virtually disappears. There is much to be gained from his corpus of writing when used with discretion and discrimination. The reader is best advised to consult: E. E. Evans-Pritchard, *A Bibliography of the Writings of E. E. Evans-Pritchard*, compiled by E. E. Evans-Pritchard and T. O. Beidalman, London: Tavistock, 1974.

Ewald, Janet, *Soldiers, Traders, and Slaves: State Formation and Economic Transformation in the Greater Nile Valley, 1700–1885*, Madison: University of Wisconsin Press, 1989.

Fabumni, L. A., *The Sudan in Anglo-Egyptian Relations, 1800–1956*, London: Longman, 1960.

Fadwa, 'Abd al-Rahman 'Ali Taha, ed., *al-Sudan li 'l-Sudaniyya*, Khartoum: Khartoum University Press, 1992.

Fawzi, S. E. D., *The Labour Movement in the Sudan, 1946–1955*, Oxford: Clarendon Press, 1957.

Flint, Julie and Alex de Waal, *Darfur: A Short History of a Long War*, London: Zed Books, 2005.

Fluehr-Lobban, Carolyn, *Islamic Law and Society*, London: Frank Cass, 1987.
  and Kharyssa Rhodes, eds., *Race and Identity in the Nile Valley: Ancient and Modern Perspectives*, Lawrenceville, NJ: Red Sea Press, 2005.

Fouad, N. Ibrahim, *Desertification in North Darfur*, Hamburg: Institut für Geographie und Wirtschaftsgeographie der Universität Hamburg, 1980.

Gaddal, Mohammad Said al-, *al-siyasa al-iqtisadiyya li 'l dawla al-Mahdiyya*, Khartoum: Khartoum University Press, 1986.

Gaitskell, Arthur, *Gezira: A Story of Development*, London: Faber & Faber, 1959.

Ga'le, Severino F. B. T., *Shaping a Free Southern Sudan: Memoirs of Our Struggle*, Loa, Sudan: Loa Catholic Council, 2002.

Garang, de Mabior, John, *Revolution in Action*, Khartoum: Public Relations Bureau, Ministry of Southern Affairs, 1970.

Gray, Richard, *A History of the Southern Sudan, 1839–1889*, London: Oxford University Press, 1961.

Gurdon, Charles, *Sudan at the Crossroads*, London: Menas, 1984.
  Sudan in Transition: A Political Risk Analysis, London: Economist Intelligence Unit, 1986.

Hale, Sondra, *Gender Politics in Sudan: Islamism, Socialism, and the State*, Boulder, CO: Westview Press, 1996.

Hamid, Mohammed Beshir, *The Politics of National Reconciliation in the Sudan: The Numayri Regime and the National Front Opposition*, Georgetown: Center for Contemporary Arab Studies, 1984.

Hamid, Mohammed Elhachmi, *The Making of an Islamic Political Leader: Conversations with Hasan al-Turabi*, Boulder, CO: Westview Press, 1984.

Hamid, Musá A. A., *Tarikh al-nizam al-qada'i fi al-Sudan 1504 M–2004 M al-malamih wa-al-tatawwur*, Khartoum: manshurat al-khartum 'asimat al-thaqafah al-'arabiyah, 2005.

Harir, S. and T. Tvedt, eds., *Short-Cut to Decay*, Uppsala: Nordiska Afrikainstitutet, 1994.

Hasan, Musa al-Mubarak al-, *Ta'rikh Dar Fur al-siyai*, Khartoum, 1971.

Hasan, Yusuf Fadl, ed., *Sudan in Africa*, Khartoum: Khartoum University Press, 1971.
  al-Shillukh: Asluha wa-wazifatuha fi Sudan al-haraka al-wataniyya, n.p., n.d.

and Awad al-Sid al-Karsani, eds., *The Sudanese–British Relations*, Khartoum: Khartoum University Press, 2002.

Hassan, Ahmed Ibrahim, *al-imam 'Abd al-Rahman al-Mahdi*, Omdurman: jami'at al-ahfad li'l-banat, 1998.

Hassan, Dr. Idris El-, *Religion in Society: Nemeiri and the Turuq, 1972–1980*, Khartoum: Khartoum University Press, 1993.

Haydar, Ibrahim Ali, *Azmat al-Islam al-siyasi, al-jabha al-islamiyya al-qawmiyya fi al-Sudan namudhajan*, Rabat: markaz al-dirasat al-sudaniyya, 1991.

al-ustadh Mahmud Muhammad Tana, ra'id al-tajdid al-dini fi al-Sudan, al-Dar al-Bayda: markaz al-dirasat al-sudaniyya, 1992.

al-ikhwan wa'l-sulta fi al-Sudan, Cairo: markaz al-hadara al-'arabiyya li'l-i'lam wa'l-nashr, 1993.

al-Tanawwu'al-thaqafi wa bina'al-dawla al-wataniyya fi al-Sudan, Cairo: markaz al-dirasat al-sudaniyya, 1995.

Henderson, K. D. D., *The Making of the Modern Sudan*, London: Faber, 1952.

Sudan Republic, London: Benn, 1965.

Set under Authority, Somerset: Castle Cary Press, 1987.

and T. R. H. Owend, eds., *Sudan Verse*, London: Chancery Books, 1963.

Hill, Richard, *A Bibliography of the Anglo-Egyptian Sudan*, London: Oxford University Press, 1939.

Egypt in the Sudan, London: Oxford University Press, 1959.

Slatin Pasha, London: Oxford University Press, 1965.

Sudan Transport: A History of Railway, Marine, and River Services in the Republic of the Sudan, London: Oxford University Press, 1965.

A Biographical Dictionary of the Sudan, 2nd edn., London: Frank Cass, 1967.

On the Frontiers of Islam: The Sudan under Turco-Egyptian Rule, 1822–1845, Oxford: Clarendon Press, 1970.

and Peter C. Hogg, *A Black Corps d'Elite: An Egyptian-Sudanese Conscript Battalion with the French Army in Mexico, 1863–1867, and its Survivors in Subsequent African History*, East Lansing, MI: Michigan State University Press, 1995.

ed., *The Sudan Memoirs of Carl Christian Giegler Pasha, 1873–1883*, London: Oxford University Press, 1984.

Holt, P. M., *Holy Families and Islam in the Sudan*, Princeton: Princeton Near East Paper, No. 4, 1967.

The Mahdist State in the Sudan, 1881–1898, 2nd edn., London: Oxford University Press, 1970.

Studies in the History of the Near East, London: Frank Cass, 1973.

and M. W. Daly, *A History of the Sudan: From the Coming of Islam to the Present Day*, 5th edn., London: Longman, 2000.

Human Rights Watch/Africa (formerly Africa Watch), *Civilian Devastation: Abuses by All Parties in the War in Southern Sudan*, New York: Human Rights Watch, New York, 1994.

Behind the Red Line: Political Repression in Sudan, New York: Human Rights Watch, 1996.

Darfur in Flames: Atrocities in Western Sudan, Washington, D.C.: April 2004.

Darfur Destroyed: Ethnic Cleasing by Government and Militia Forces in Western Sudan, Washington D.C.: May 2004.

Empty Promises? Continuing Abuses in Darfur, Sudan, Washington, D.C.: August 2004.

"If we return, we will be killed": Consolidation of Ethnic Cleansing in Darfur, Washington D.C.: November 2004.

Sudan, Oil, and Human Rights Abuses, New York: Human Rights Watch, 2004.

Hurreiz, Sayyid H. and Elfatih A. Abdel Salam, eds., *Ethnicity, Conflict, and National Integration in the Sudan*, Khartoum: Khartoum University Press, 1989.

Hutchinson, Sharon, *Nuer Dilemmas: Coping with Money, War, and the State*, Berkeley: University of California Press, 1996.

Ibrahim, H., *The Shaqiyya: The Cultural and Social Change of a Northern Sudanese Riverain People*, Wiesbaden: Franz Steinger Verlag GMBH, 1979.

Ibrahim, Hassan Ahmad, *The 1936 Anglo-Egyptian Treaty*, Khartoum: Khartoum University Press, 1976.

Sayyid 'Abd al-Rahman al-Mahdi: A Study in neo-Mahdism in the Sudan, Leiden: Brill, 2004.

'Isá, 'Abd A.-R., *al-Fariq Ibrahim 'Abbud wa-ʾasruhu al-dhahabi*, Khartoum: 'abd al-rahman ahmad 'isá, 2005.

Islamic Banking, *Towards an Understanding of Islamic Banking in Sudan: The Case of Faisal Islamic Bank*, Monograph Series No. 21, Khartoum: Khartoum University Press, 1985.

Jackson, H. C., *Black Ivory and White: or the Story of El Zubeir Pasha, Slaver, and Sultan as Told by Himself*, Oxford: Blackwell, 1913.

Osman Digna, London: Methuen, 1926.

Sudan Days and Ways, London: Macmillan, 1954.

The Fighting Sudanese, London: Macmillan, 1954.

Behind the Modern Sudan, London: Macmillan, 1955.

Pastor on the Nile, London: SPCK, 1960.

Jendia, Catherine, *The Sudanese Civil Conflict, 1969–1985*, New York: Peter Lane, 2002.

Johnson, D. H., *Nuer Prophets: A History of Prophecy from the Upper Nile in the Nineteenth and Twentieth Centuries*, Oxford: Clarendon Press, 1994.

The Root Causes of Sudan's Civil Wars, Oxford: James Currey, and Bloomington: Indiana University Press, and Kampala: Fountain Publishers, 2003.

An Analysis of the Factionalism of Southerners' Dissidence: The Root Causes of Sudan's Civil Wars, 2nd edn., Oxford: James Currey, and Bloomington: Indiana University Press, 2004.

Jok, Jok Madut, *War and Slavery in the Sudan*, Philadelphia: University of Pennsylvania Press, 2001.

Kabbashi, al-Mikashfi Taha al-, *Tatbiq al-shariʾa al-islamiyya fi al-Sudan bayn al-haqiqa waʾl-ithara*, Cairo: al-zahara' liʾl-iʾlam al-ʾarabi, 1986.

Kapteijns, L., *Mahdist Faith and Sudanic Tradition: The History of the Masalit Sultanate, 1870–1930*, London: KPI, 1985.

Karrar, Ali Salih, *The Sufi Brotherhoods in the Sudan*, London: Hurst, 1992.

Keen, David, *The Benefits of Famine: A Political Economy of Famine and Relief in Southwestern Sudan, 1983–1989*, Princeton: Princeton University Press, 1994.

Kelly, Raymond C., *The Nuer Conquest*, Ann Arbor, MI: University of Michigan Press, 1985.

Kevane, M. and E. Stiansen, *Kordofan Invaded: Peripheral Incorporation and Social Transformation in Islamic Africa*, Leiden: Brill, 1998.

Khalid, Mansur, *Nimeiri and the Revolution of Dis-May*, London: KPI, 1985.

ed., *John Garang Speaks*, London: KPI, 1987.

The Government They Deserve: The Role of the Elite in Sudan's Political Evolution, London: KPI, 1990.

ed., *The Call for Democracy*, New York: KPI, 1992.

an-nukhba as-Sudaniyyawa Idman al-Fashel, 2 vols., Cairo: dar al-amin li'l-nasr wa'l-tanziya, 1993.

War and Peace in the Sudan: A Tale of Two Countries, London: KPI, 2003.

Khayr al-Muhami, Ahmad, *Kifah jil: tarikh harakat al-kirrijin wa-tatawwuriha fi al-Sudan*, 3rd edn., Khartoum: Khartoum University Press, 1991.

Khayr, al-Tayyib I. M., *Saf al-arajuz fi 'amaliyat tahrir Raja wa-Daym Zubayr*, Khartoum: mu'assasat al-abrar li'l-tiba'ah wa-al-nashir, 2004.

Kok, Peter Nyok, *Governance and Conflict in the Sudan, 1985–1995, Analysis, Evaluation, and Documentation*, Hamburg: Deutsches Orient-Institut, Mitteilungen 53, 1996.

Kulusika, Simon E., *South Sudan Right of Self-Determination and Establishment of New Sovereign State: A Legal Analysis*, Lusaka: University of Zambia Press, 2004.

Kurdufani, Isma'il 'Abd al-Qadir al-, *Sa'adat al-mustahdi bi-sirat al-Imam al-Mahdi*, Khartoum and Beirut, 1972.

Muhammad Ibrahim abu Salim and Muhammad Sa'id al Qaddal, eds., *al-tiraz al-manqush bi-bushra qatl yuhanna malik al-hubush (al-harb al-habashiyya al-Sudaniyya)*, Khartoum: dar jami'at al-Khartum li'l-nashr, 1972.

Kurita, Yoshiko, *'Ali 'Abd al-Latif wa thawra*, trans. Majdi al-Ma'im, Cairo: markaz al-dirasat al-sudaniyya, 1997.

Lagu, Joseph Major General, *Anya-Nya: What We Fight for*, Anya-Nya Armed Forces: Southern Sudan Liberation Movement, 1972.

Sudan: Odyssey through a State: From Ruin to Hope, Omdurman: MOB Center for Sudanese Studies, Omdurman Ahlia University, 2006.

Layish, Aharon and Gabriel Warburg, *The Reinstatement of Islamic Law in Sudan under Numayri: An Evaluation of a Legal Experiment in the Light of its Historical Context, Methodology, and Repercussions*, Leiden: Brill, 2002.

Lesch, Ann, *The Sudan: Contested National Identities*, Bloomington: Indiana University Press, 1998.

Lobban, Richard, *Historical Dictionary of Ancient and Modern Nubia*, Lanham, MD: Scarecrow Press, 2004.

Robert S. Kramer, and Carolyn Fluerher-Lobban, *Historical Dictionary of the Sudan*, 3rd edn., Lanham, MD: Scarecrow Press, 2002.

Lowrie, A. L., ed., *Islam, Democracy, the State, and the West: A Round Table with Dr. Hasan al-Turabi*, Tampa, FL: The World and Islam Studies Enterprise, 1993.

MacMichael, Sir H., *The Anglo-Egyptian Sudan*, London: Faber, 1934.

Mahjoub, Muhammed Ahmed, *Democracy on Trial*, London: Michael Joseph, 1973.

Mahmoud, Fatima Babiker, *The Sudanese Bourgeoisie*, London: Zed Books, 1984.

Majok, Damazo, *British Religious and Educational Policy, Southern Sudan: Regionalism and Religion*, Khartoum: University of Khartoum, Graduate College Publications No. 10, 1984.

Malwal, Bona, *People and Power in Sudan: The Struggle for National Stability*, London: Ithaca Press, 1981.

  The Sudan: A Second Challenge to Nationhood, New York: Thornton, 1985.

Martin, Percy F., *The Sudan in Evolution: A Study of the Economic, Financial, and Administrative Conditions of the Anglo-Egyptian Sudan*, London: Constable & Co., 1921.

Mawut, Lazarus Leek, *Dinka Resistance to Condominium Rule, 1902–1932*, Oxford: Clarendon Press, 1983.

  The Southern Sudan: Why Back to Arms, Khartoum: St. George Printing Press, 1986.

McHugh, Neil, *Holymen of the Blue Nile: The Making of an Arab-Islamic Community in the Nilotic Sudan*, Evanston, IL: Northwestern University Press, 1994.

Miller, Catherine, ed., *Land, Ethnicity, and Political Legitimacy in Eastern Sudan (Kassala and Gedaref States)*, Cairo: CEDEJ, and Khartoum: DSRC, 2005.

Minear, Larry, et al., *Humanitarianism under Siege: A Critical Review of Operation Lifeline Sudan*, Trenton, NJ: Red Sea Press, 1991.

Mubarak, Khalid al-, *Turabi's Islamist Venture: Failure and Implications*, Beirut: al-dar al-thaqafia, 2001.

Muddathir, 'Abd al-Rahim, *Imperialism and Nationalism in the Sudan, 1899–1956*, London: Oxford University Press, 1969.

  Raphael Badal, Adlan Hardallo and Peter Woodward, eds., *Sudan since Independence: Studies of the Political Development since 1956*, Aldershot: Gower, 1986.

  and al-Tayyib Zein al-Abdin, eds., *al-islam fi al-Sudan, buhuth mukhtara min al-mu'tamar al-awwal li-Jama'at al-fikr wa'l-thaqafa al-islamiyya*, Khartoum: dar al-asala li'l-sahafa wa'l-nashr wa'l-intaj al-i'lami, 1987.

Muhammad, Muhammad S., *Darfur harb al-mawarid wa-al-hawiyah*, London: dar kimbridj li'l-nashir, 2004.

Mustafa, Mustafa Mubarak, *Diwan al-shi'r al-sudani, 1880–1980*, vol. I, Doha, Qatar: al-mu'assasa al-'alamiyya li'l-yaba wa'l-nashr, 1992.

Nadel, S. F., *The Nuba: An Anthropological Study of the Hill Tribes in Kordofan*, London: Oxford University Press, 1947.

  Dhikrayati fi al-badiya, Beirut: dar maktabat al-hayat, 1964.

Najila, Hasan, *Malamoh min al-mujtama' al-sudani*, 3rd edn., Beirut: dar maktabat al-hayat, 1964.

Nasr, Ahmad 'Abd al-Rahim, *al-idara al-baritaniyya wa'l-mashi fi al-Sudan: Dirasa awaliyya*, Khartoum: wizarat al-tarbiya wa'l-tawjih, al-shu'un al-diniyya wa'l-awqaf, 1979.

Newbold, Douglas, *The Making of the Modern Sudan: Life and Letters of Sir Douglas Newbold*, Westport, NY: Greenwood Press, 1974.

Niblock, Tim, *Class and Power in the Sudan: The Dynamics of Sudanese Politics, 1898–1985*, London: Macmillan, 1987.

Numayri, Ja'afar Muhammad, *al-nahj al-islami li-madh? (The Islamic Way, Why?)*, Cairo: al-maktab al-misri al-hadith, 1980.

  al-nahj al-islami kayfa? (The Islamic Way, How?), Cairo: al-maktab al-misri al-hadith, 1985.

Nyaba, Peter A., *The Politics of Liberation in South Sudan: An Insider's View*, 2nd edn., Kampala: Fountain Publishers, 2000,

O'Balance, Edgar, *The Secret War in the Sudan, 1955–1972*, Hamden, CT: Archon Books, 1977.

  Sudan Civil War and Terrorism, 1956–1999, New York: Palgrave Macmillan, 2000.

Oduho J. and W. Deng, *The Problem of the Southern Sudan*, Oxford: Oxford University Press, 1963.

O'Fahey, Rex Sean, *State and Society in Dar Fur*, London: Hurst, 1980.

  and Abu Salim, *Land in Dar Fur: Charters and Related Documents from the Dar Fur Sultanate*, Cambridge: Cambridge University Press, 1983.

  Enigmatic Saint: Ahmad Ibn Idris and the Idrisi Tradition, London: Hurst, 1990.

  and Jay L. Spaulding, *Kingdoms of the Sudan*, London: Methuen, 1974.

Pons, V., ed., *Urbanization and Urban Life in the Sudan*, Hull: Department of Sociology and Social Anthropology, University of Hull, 1980.

Prendergast, John, *Diplomacy, Aid, and Governance in the Sudan*, Washington D.C.: Center of Concern, 1995.

  Dare to Hope: Children of War in Southern Sudan, Washington D.C.: Center of Concern, 1996.

  Frontline Diplomacy: Humanitarian Aid and Conflict in Africa, Boulder, CO: Lynne Rienner Publishers, 1996.

  Crisis Response: Humanitarian Band-Aids in Sudan and Somalia, London: Pluto Press, 1997.

  God, Oil, and Country: Changing the Logic of War in Sudan, Brussels: International Crisis Group, 2002.

Prunier, Gérard, *From Peace to War: The Southern Sudan 1972–1984*, Occasional Paper, Department of Sociology and Social Anthropology, 3, University of Hull, 1986.

  Darfur: The Ambiguous Genocide, London: Hurst, 2005.

Qaddal, Dr. Muhammad Sa'id al-, *al-Mahdiyya wa'l-Habasha*, Khartoum: dar jami'at al-khartum li'l-nashr, 1973.

  al-Imam al-Mahdi, Muhammad Ahmad bin 'Abdullah, 1844–1885, Lawha li tha'r Sudani, Khartoum: Khartoum University Press, 1985.

  al-Siyasa al-Iqtisadiyya li'l-dawlah al-Mahdiyya, Khartoum: Khartoum University Press, 1986.

Reining, Conrad C., *The Zande Scheme: An Anthropological Case Study of Economic Development in Africa*, Evanston, IL: Northwestern University Press, 1966.

Report of the Commission into the Disturbances in the Southern Sudan during August 1955 (The Cotran Report), Khartoum: McCorquedale, 1956.

Robertson, Sir James, *Transition in Africa: From Direct Rule to Independence*, London: Hurst, 1974.

The Last of the Proconsuls: The Letters of Sir James Robertson, ed. by Graham F. Thomas, London: Radcliffe Press, 1994.

Rolandsen, ystein H., *Guerilla Government: Political Changes in the Southern Sudan during the 1990s*, Uppsala: Nordiska Afrikainstitutet, 2005.

Rone, Jemera, *Famine in Sudan, 1998: The Human Rights Causes*, New York: Human Rights Watch, 1999.

Ruay, Deny D. Akol, *The Politics of the Two Sudans: The South and North, 1821–1969*, Uppsala: Nordiska Afrikainstitutet, 1994.

Sadiq, al-Mahdi al-, ed., *Jihad fi sabil al-istiqlal* (*The Struggle for Independence*), Khartoum: al-matba'a al-hukumiyya, 1965.

Yas'alunaka 'an al-Mahdiyya, Beirut: dar al-qadaya, 1975.

al-Islam wa-ma'alat janub al-Sudan, Omdurman: matba'at al-tamaddun, 1985.

al-dumuqqratiyya fi al-Sudan, Omdurman: private printing, 1989.

Safi, Mahasin Abdel Gadir Hag al-, ed., *The Nationalist Movement in the Sudan*, Khartoum: Khartoum University Press, 1989.

al-haraka al-wataniyya fi al-Sudan: thawrat, 1924, Khartoum: Khartoum University Press, 1992.

Saghayroun, A. A., ed., *Population and Democracy in the Sudan: The Quest for a National Policy*, Khartoum: Khartoum University Press, 1987.

Sa'id, Bashir Muhammad, *al-Sudan min al-hukm al-thuna'i ila intifadat rajab,* vol. I, pt. 3, Khartoum: sharokat al-ayyam li'l-adawat al-maktabiyya al-mahduda, 1982.

al-za'im al-azhari wa-'assuhu, Cairo: al-qahira al-haditha li'-tiba'a, 1990.

Salih, Mahjub Muhammad, *al-sohafa al-sudaniyya fi nisf qarn, 1903–1953*, Khartoum: Khartoum University Press, 1971.

Sanderson, G. N., *England, Europe and the Upper Nile, 1882–1899*, Edinburgh: Edinburgh University Press, 1965.

Sanderson, Lillian Passmore and G. N. Sanderson, *Education, Religion, and Politics in Southern Sudan, 1899–1964*, London: Ithaca Press, 1981.

Santandrea, Stefano, *A Tribal History of the Western Bahr el-Ghazal*, Bologna: Editrice Missionaria Italiana, 1964.

Luci e ombre dell'amministrazione britannica nel Bahr el-Ghazal, Bologna: Editrice Nigrizia, 1967.

The Luo of the Bahr al-Ghazal, Bologna: Editrice Nigrizia, 1968.

Ethno-Geography of the Bahr al-Ghazal, Bologna: Editrice Missionaria Italiana, 1981.

Savage, Elizabeth, ed., *The Human Commodity: Perspectives on the Trans-Saharan Slave Trade*, London: Frank Cass, 1992.

Sawi, abdul-Aziz Hussein al-, *The Sudanese Dialogue on Identity and National Unity: A New Perspective*, Cairo: The Sudanese Studies Center, 1996.

Scroggins, Deborah, *Emma's War*, New York: Pantheon Books, 2002.

Shaked, Haim, *The Life of the Sudanese Mahdi: A Historical Study of Kitab sa'adat al-muthadi bi sirat al-Imam al-Mahdi by Isma'il 'Abd al-Qadir*, New Brunswick, NJ: Transaction Books, 1978.

Sharkey, Heather J., *Living with Colonialism: Nationalism and Culture in the Anglo-Egyptian Sudan*, Berkeley: University of California Press, 2003.

Shibeika, Mekki, *British Policy in the Sudan, 1882–1902*, London: Oxford University Press, 1952.

The Independent Sudan, New York: Robert Speller, 1959.

Shukry, Muhammad Fu'ad, *The Khedive Ismail and Slavery in the Sudan. 1863–1879*, Cairo: dar al-fikr al-'arabi, 1938.

Al-hukm al-Misri fi al-Sudan, 1820–1885, Cairo: dar al-fikr al-'arabi, 1947.

Misr wa'l Südän, Cairo: dar al-fikr al-'arabi, 1963.

Shuqayr, Na'un, *Ta'rikh al-Sudan al-qadim wa'l-hadith wa-jughrafiyatuhu*, Cairo: 1903.

Jurjafiyyat wa-ta'rokh al-Sudan, 2nd edn., Beirut: dar al-thaqafa, 1967.

Sidahmed, Abdel Salam, *Politics and Islam in Contemporary Sudan*, Richmond: Curzon Press, 1997.

Sikainga, Ahmad Alawad, *The Sudan Defence Force: Origin and Role, 1925–1955*, Khartoum: Institute of African and Asian Studies, 1983.

The Western Bahr al-Ghazal under British Rule, 1898–1956, Athens, OH: The Ohio University Center for International Studies, 1991.

Slaves into Workers: Emancipation and Labor in Colonial Sudan, Austin: University of Texas Press, 1996.

City of Steel and Fire: A Social History of Atbara, Sudan's Railway Town, 1906–1984, Portsmouth, NH: Heinemann, 2002.

Siyufi, Ahmad, *Darfur wa-mu'amarat taqsim al-Sudan dirash maydaniyah wa-watha'iqiyah wa-tarikhiyah*, Ahmad al-Siyuf, S. 1: s.n., 2004.

Smith, Ian, *The Emin Pasha Relief Expedition, 1886–1890*, London: Oxford University Press, 1972.

Spaulding, Jay L., *The Heroic Age in Sinnar*, East Lansing, MI: Michigan State University Press, 1985.

and Lidwien Kapteijins, *After the Millennium: Diplomatic Correspondence from Wadai and Dar Fur on the Eve of Colonial Conquest, 1885–1916*, East Lansing, MI: Michigan State University Press, 1988.

An Islamic Alliance: 'Ali Dinar and the Sanusiyya, 1906–1916, Evanston, IL: Northwestern University Press, 1994.

Stiansen, Endre and Michael Kevane, *Kordofan Invaded: Peripheral Incorporation and Social Transformation in Islamic Africa*, Leiden: Brill, 1998.

Tayeb, Salah El Din El Zein El-, *The Students' Movement in the Sudan*, Khartoum: Khartoum University Press, 1971.

Tayyib, Abd Allah al-, *Muhadarat fi al-ittijjahat al-haditha fi al-nathr al-arabi*, Cairo: matba'at nahdat misr, 1959.

Theobald, A. B., *The Mahdiya*, London: Longman, 1955.

'Ali Dinar, Last Sultan of Darfur, 1898–1916, London: Longman, 1965.

Toniolo, E. and Richard Hill, *The Opening of the Nile Basin*, London: Hurst, 1974.

Tothill, J. D., ed., *Agriculture in the Sudan*, London: Oxford University Press, 1948.

Totten, Samuel and Eric Markusen, eds., *Genocide in Darfur: Investigating the Atrocities in the Sudan*, London: Routledge, 2006.

Trimingham, J. Spencer, *Islam in the Sudan*, London: Oxford University Press, 1949.

Turabi, Hasan al-, *Hiwar al-Din wa al-Fau*, Khartoum: The Islamic Culture Group, 1983.

Tajdid al-fikr al-islami, Jiddah: dar al-sa'udiyya, 1987.

al-Harakah al-islamiyyah fi al-Sudan: al-Tatwar wa-al-Kash wa-al-Manhaj, Khartoum: 1991.

Tvedt, Terje, *Angels of Mercy or Development Diplomats? NGOs and Foreign Aid*, Oxford: Africa World Press, 1998.

et al., *An Annotated Bibliography on the Southern Sudan, 1850–2000*, Bergen: University of Bergen Press, 2000.

The River Nile in the Age of the British: Political Ecology and the Quest for Economic Power, London: I. B. Taurus, 2004.

'Ulaysh, 'Abd A.-M., *Hadatha fi al-Sudan – yawmiyat al-dawla al-islamiyah*, Khartoum: dar 'azzah li'l-nashir wa-al-tawzi, 2005.

Ushari, Ahmad Mahmud and Suleyman Ali Baldo, *The Dien Massacre: Slavery in Sudan*, Khartoum: Private Printing, 1987.

Verney, Peter, *Slavery in Sudan*, London: Sudan Update and Anti-Slavery International, 1997.

Raising the Stakes: Oil and Conflict in Sudan, Hebden Bridge: Sudan Update, 2000.

Voll, John O., *A History of the Khatmiyya Tariqa in the Sudan*, Ann Arbor: University Microfilms, 1971.

Islam: Continuity and Change in the Modern World, Boulder, CO: Westview Press, 1982.

ed., *Sudan: State and Society in Crisis*, Bloomington: Indiana University Press, 1991.

and Sarah P. Voll, *The Sudan: Unity and Diversity in a Multicultural State*, London: Croom Helm, 1985.

Wai, Dunstan M., *The Southern Sudan: The Problem of National Integration*, London: Frank Cass, 1971.

The African–Arab Conflict in the Sudan, New York: Africana Publishing Co., 1981.

Walz, Terence, *The Trade between Egypt and the Bilad As-Sudan, 1700–1820*, Cairo: Institut Français d'Archéologie Orientale du Caire, 1974.

Warburg, Gabriel R., *The Sudan under Wingate*, London: Frank Cass, 1981.

Islam, Nationalism, and Communism in a Traditional Society: The Case of Sudan, London: Frank Cass, 1978.

and U. Kupferschmidt, eds., *Islam, Nationalism, and Radicalism in Egypt and the Sudan*, New York: Praeger, 1983.

Historical Discord in the Nile Valley, London: Hurst, and Evanston, IL: Northwestern University Press, 1992.

Islam, Sectarianism, and Politics in Sudan since the Mahdiyya, London: Hurst, 2003.

Wawa, Yosa H., *The Southern Sudanese Pursuits of Self-Determination: Documents in Political History*, Kampala: Marianum Press, 2005.

Wingate, F. R., *Mahdiism and the Egyptian Sudan*, London: Frank Cass, 1968.

Wöndu, Steven and Ann Lesch, *Battle for Peace in the Sudan: An Analysis of the Abuja Conference, 1992–1993*, Lanham, MD: University Press of America, 2000.

Woodward, Peter, *Condominium and Sudanese Nationalism*, London: Rex Collings, 1979.

Sudan since Nimeriri, London: SOAS, 1986.

Sudan, 1898–1989, The Unstable State, Boulder, CO: Lynne Riener, 1990.

Sudan after Nimeiri, London: Routledge, 1991.

Yongo-Bure, Benaiah, *Economic Development of Southern Sudan*, Lanham, MD: University Press of America, 2007.

Zaghi, C., *Gordon, Gessi e la riconquista del Sudan*, Florence: 1947.

Zintani, 'Abd A.-W. M., *Azamat al-Sudan bayna al-dimuqratiyah wa-al-diktaturiyah*, Cairo: dar gharib li'l-tiba'ah wa-al-nashr wa-al-tawzi', 2004.

Zulfo, I. H., *Karari: The Sudanese Account of the Battle of Omdurman*, trans. Peter Clark, London: Frederick Warne, 1980.

Index